To Ray,
With many thanks
for your support &
encouragement.
Best Wishes,
Michael

Law, City, and King

Changing Perspectives on Early Modern Europe

James B. Collins, Professor of History, Georgetown University
Mack P. Holt, Professor of History, George Mason University

(ISSN 1542-3905)

Changing Perspectives on Early Modern Europe brings forward the latest research on Europe during the transformation from the medieval to the modern world. The series publishes innovative scholarship on the full range of topical and geographic fields and includes works on cultural, economic, intellectual, political, religious, and social history.

Private Ambition and Political Alliances: The Phélypeaux de Pontchartrain Family and Louis XIV's Government, 1650–1715
Sara E. Chapman

The Politics of Piety: Franciscan Preachers During the Wars of Religion, 1560–1600
Megan C. Armstrong

"By My Absolute Royal Authority": Justice and the Castilian Commonwealth at the Beginning of the First Global Age
J. B. Owens

Meat Matters: Butchers, Politics, and Market Culture in Eighteenth-Century Paris
Sydney Watts

Civic Christianity in Renaissance Italy: The Hospital of Treviso, 1400–1530
David M. D'Andrea

Law, City, and King: Legal Culture, Municipal Politics, and State Formation in Early Modern Dijon
Michael P. Breen

Law, City, and King

Legal Culture, Municpal Politics, and State Formation in Early Modern Dijon

Michael P. Breen

University of Rochester Press

First published 2007

University of Rochester Press
668 Mt. Hope Avenue, Rochester, NY 14620, USA
www.urpress.com
and Boydell & Brewer Limited
PO Box 9, Woodbridge, Suffolk IP12 3DF, UK
www.boydellandbrewer.com

ISBN-13: 978-1-58046-236-5
ISBN-10: 1-58046-236-7
ISSN: 1542–3905

Library of Congress Cataloging-in-Publication Data

Breen, Michael P., 1967–
Law, city, and king : legal culture, municipal politics, and state formation in early modern Dijon / Michael P. Breen.
p. cm. – (Changing perspectives on early modern Europe, ISSN 1542–3905 ; v. 6)
Includes bibliographical references and index.
ISBN-13: 978-1-58046-236-5 (hardcover : alk. paper)
ISBN-10: 1-58046-236-7 (alk. paper)
1. Dijon (France)–Politics and government–17th century. 2. Municipal government–France–Dijon–History–17th century. 3. Justice, Administration of–France–Dijon–History–17th century. 4. Political participation–France–Dijon–History–17th century. I. Title.
JS5015.D53B74 2007
944'.426033–dc22

2007010416

A catalogue record for this title is available from the British Library.
This publication is printed on acid-free paper.
Printed in the United States of America.

For my mother
and in memory of my father

Contents

Illustrations

Maps

Figures

Tables

Acknowledgments

In researching and writing this book, I have accumulated more debts than I could ever hope to acknowledge properly. This project started as a doctoral dissertation under the direction of Philip Benedict at Brown University, and it has been my good fortune to work closely with Phil these many years. I have benefited tremendously from his encyclopedic knowledge, sharp intellect, and exhaustive commentary. Beyond graduate school, Phil has remained a generous colleague, a tireless supporter, and a valued mentor. Most important, he and his wife Judy have remained good friends, even though a continent, an ocean, and nine times zones now separate us. I would also like to thank the other members of my dissertation committee, Anthony Molho and R. Burr Litchfield, for all of their advice and assistance. Amy Remensnyder and Joan Richards also have my gratitude for their support and encouragement during my time at Brown.

Mack Holt and James Collins deserve particular thanks, both as editors of the *Changing Perspectives on Early Modern Europe* series and for their guidance over the years. The ideas we have exchanged via e-mail, at conferences, and in some of Burgundy's many fine restaurants contributed greatly to this book. Mack and Jim also kindly invited me to participate in an informal seminar with four other young early modern French historians: Sara Chapman, Greg Brown, Hilary Bernstein, and Megan Armstrong. Over the course of a weekend in July 2000, we read each other's work and discussed our book manuscripts in progress. Mine is the last book to emerge from this gathering; I hope it measures up to those that have preceded it. More important, I would like to thank Megan, Hilary, Greg, and Sara not only for their comments on my work, but also for their friendship, support, and encouragement over the years.

At various stages in researching and writing this book, I have also benefited from the assistance of many fellow historians, only some of whom I can acknowledge here. Julie Hardwick, David Bell, Sharon Kettering, and Sarah Hanley all read portions of the manuscript and have been unstinting with their advice, constructive criticisms, and support. I am also grateful to William Beik, Robert Descimon, and Al Hamscher for their generous advice and encouragement. James Farr and Robert Schwartz helped me find my bearings in Dijon and its fertile archives, while Jean Bart and Michel Petitjean generously answered my questions about Burgundian legal history and always provided a warm welcome during my visits to Dijon. Finally, I would like to thank Sara Beam, Mark Potter, and Jeffrey Houghtby for their support and friendship over the years.

At Reed, David Harris Sacks has been a tireless mentor, exemplary colleague, and valued friend. Much of this book's evolution owes a great deal to our many discussions and his astute advice. I am extremely fortunate to have had the opportunity to work with David and to have benefited from his insights and his generosity, not to mention his appreciation for good Priorat and Pinot Noir. I am also thankful for the advice of my predecessor, Raymond Kierstead, and the support and encouragement of the rest of my colleagues in the Reed History Department and the Division of History and Social Sciences. Lois Hobbs has been an invaluable help and an inspiration in every sense of the word. Fred Lifton also deserves thanks for his help in preparing the digitized versions of the images in this book.

This book could not have been completed without the generous support of research fellowships from the American Council of Learned Societies, the Fulbright Program, and the Brown University Graduate School. The Mellon Foundation funded a semester's paid leave from my teaching duties at Reed College, while Reed College's Michael E. Levine, Stillman Drake, and Dean's Funds provided crucial support in the final stages of writing and revision. All have my most heartfelt gratitude and appreciation. In a very different way, the archivists, librarians, and other personnel of the many repositories where I conducted my research also made this book possible. These include the Archives Départementales de la Côte d'Or, the Archives Condé, the Archives Nationales, the Bibliothèque Nationale (site Mazarin), and the Bibliothèque de l'Arsenal. The majority of the research for this book was conducted at Dijon's Archives Municipales and Bibliothèque Municipale, and I would like to thank the staffs of these two institutions for welcoming me over the years and making my visits as pleasant and productive as possible. Special thanks are due to André-Pierre Syren and Danielle Ducout for helping me obtain some of the images used in this book. In the United States, the librarians and staff at the Harvard Law School Library, the Houghton Library, the John Hay Library, the Brown University Library, the Gettysburg College Library, and above all the Reed College Library all helped facilitate my research. Finally, Suzanne Guiod, my editor at University of Rochester Press, has patiently answered my many queries and has been extremely helpful in shepherding this book through the publication process. For this she has my most sincere gratitude.

Portions of this book were previously presented to Emory University's Vann Seminar in Pre-Modern European History, the Baltimore/DC–area Old Regime Group, the Reed College Mellon Seminar on "Institutions," and the Reed Faculty Research Roundtable. I am grateful to Jim Stewart for organizing the Institutions seminar and Paul Silverstein for overseeing the

Faculty Research Roundtable. I would also like to thank the participants in these seminars for their many helpful comments and insights.

While completing this book, I have also accrued many personal debts. Although it would be impossible to acknowledge them all, I would like to thank Joanna Drell, Emily O'Brien, Raymond Douglas, Martin Götz, Kim and David Lewis, Kevin Cloud, John Richards, and Jeff and Gianna Durso-Finley for helping make graduate school more hospitable than it might have been. Susie Castellanos deserves special thanks for her support and friendship. In France, Pierre and Pascale Walgenwitz welcomed me into their home and helped me get established in Dijon. Michelle Mollard and Anne Leflot have been good friends over the years, while my teammates at the Cercle Sportif Laïque Dijonnais taught me about much more than basketball and introduced me to a side of life in France that I might not have experienced otherwise. Special thanks are due as well to Liberty and Lawrence Agbenowdouga. Although Liberty tragically departed this world much too soon, his courage, determination, and faith in the future have always been a source of great inspiration to me. More recently, Claude Patriat and his family have welcomed me into their home during several research trips to Dijon, while Vincent and Chantal Berthat have been extraordinarily kind hosts–always ready with good food, fine wine, and lively conversation.

Much closer to home, I would like to express my deepest gratitude to my family. Through the inevitable ups and downs of life, as well as those that come with completing a project such as this, I have always been able to count on the unconditional love and unwavering support of Maria, Sean, Chris, Meghan, and their families. Even if they did not always understand my odd fascination with history, let alone an obscure group of early modern French lawyers, they understood that it mattered to me. That was all that mattered to them, and that is all that matters to me. My godparents, John and Lily Perrotti, have also been a great source of support. Above all, I would like to thank my parents, Rick and Camille. It was they who instilled in me a passion for learning and a love for writing, as well as the self-discipline and persistence needed to undertake such a large project. Their love, encouragement, and support (both emotional and financial) made the completion of this book possible. I only regret that my father did not live to see its publication.

Finally, I would like to express my deepest love, most profound gratitude, and greatest admiration for my wife, Betsy Duquette. Without her companionship, warmth, humor, and love, this book would never have seen its way to completion. After writing so many words about men who lived in the past, I find that there are few that do justice to this woman in the present. Her remarkable intellect and indefatigable spirit inspire me every moment of every day; they are, I hope, reflected in many ways both large and small throughout the pages of this book.

Abbreviations

A.C.	Archives Condé, Chantilly
A.D.C.O.	Archives Départementales de la Côte-d'Or, Dijon
A.M.D.	Archives Municipales de Dijon
A.N.	Archives Nationales, Paris
B.M.D.	Bibliothèque Municipale de Dijon
B.N.	Bibliothèque Nationale, Paris
Garnier	Joseph Garnier, ed., *Correspondance de la mairie de Dijon, extraits des archives de cette ville,* 3 vols. (Dijon: J.-E. Rabutot, 1870), vol III
Muteau I	"Extraits des registres des délibérations de la Chambre de ville de Dijon," in Charles Muteau, ed., *Mémoires de Marc-Antoine Millotet des choses qui se sont passées en Bourgogne depuis 1650 jusqu'à 1668* (Dijon: J.-E. Rabutot, 1866): 305–455
Muteau II	"Extraits des registres des délibérations de la Chambre de ville de Dijon," in Charles Muteau, ed., *Anecdotes du Parlement de Bourgogne, ou histoire secrète de cette compagnie depuis 1650, par Claude Malteste* (Dijon: J.-E. Rabutot, 1864): 363–590

Introduction

Lawyers, Politics, and the State in Early Modern France

The summer of 1627 was a tense time in Dijon. The region's two main royal courts, the Parlement of Burgundy and the Chamber of Accounts, were locked in a bitter conflict that had spilled into the streets of the Burgundian capital. At issue was the Masters of Accounts' decision to purchase the offices of the newly created Cour des Aides et Finances, which conferred sovereign jurisdiction over several direct and indirect royal taxes, in spite of Parlement's pointed refusal to register the royal edicts creating the new tribunal. In early August, a president of the Accounts, whose arrest Parlement had recently ordered, accompanied by several other Masters of Accounts, drew a pistol on a parlementaire outside the Palais de Justice and threatened to kill him. Caught in the middle, the city's municipal government, the Mairie de Dijon, worked feverishly to calm the situation. Guards from the civic militia were posted in front of the Parlement building and at major public squares across the city. The mairie also prohibited all individuals, regardless of their status or social condition, from assembling, carrying weapons, or traveling through the city in groups without permission from the municipality's chief magistrate, the vicomte-mayeur.[1]

Two months later, the royal council intervened in an attempt to defuse the tension between the two courts, ordering the Chamber of Accounts transferred to the town of Autun, roughly fifty miles southwest of Dijon. At the Hôtel de Ville, Dijon's mayor and *échevins* (aldermen) debated the mairie's response to the monarchy's order. Guillaume de Berbisey, one of the city's legal counselors, or *conseils de la ville,* argued that the mairie should oppose it, "not by force, but by very humble remonstrances and supplications which will be made to the king and our lords of his council, based on the privileges of our city and on the articles given by the late king [Henri IV], at the city's surrender" to his forces in 1595. Berbisey also offered a procedural justification for the city's opposition, pointing out that the council had not heard from the mairie before rendering its order (or *arrêt*). He noted that the municipality would certainly have the support of Burgundy's governor, the Duke of Bellegarde, "who will willingly employ himself out of the particular affection he has always had for this capital city of his region." Observing that the removal of the Accounts would cause "irreparable damage" to the city's interests, Berbisey urged the mairie to convoke a general assembly of inhabitants as soon as possible.

At this point, Mayor Etienne Humbert intervened, throwing his considerable prestige and authority behind the Accounts' exile. "Having received the king's commands," he said, "he could not go against them, nor could he suffer any proposition on the subject contrary to the service of His Majesty." Humbert, a royal fiscal officer, then tried to move the council's discussions to another topic when Bénigne Pérard, an *avocat* (barrister) serving his third term on the échevinage, raised his voice in defense of both Berbisey's proposal and his vision of the mairie's larger obligations to the urban community. "Neither he nor the other échevins hold their charges to oversee the cleaning of the streets or that which has to do with the markets," he proclaimed. Rather, "they were elected for the consideration of the city's privileges, on which they have sworn an oath." According to Pérard, Humbert was the only member of the city council opposed to Berbisey's plan. "Removing the Chamber of Accounts from the city would be against the privileges accorded by King Henry the Great of happy memory," Pérard argued, noting that "the city has done nothing against His Majesty to be treated in this way." Perhaps angered by the échevin's recalcitrance, Humbert rose from his chair, accusing Pérard of "speaking against the service of the king." The avocat, in return, protested that he "had as much zeal and affection for the service of His Majesty as the sieur vicomte-mayeur." Humbert then objected that not enough échevins were in attendance to decide the question, nor to "make a good resolution on such an important matter," and forbade Pérard to speak further on the topic. Pérard, however, was not finished. "Does not every inhabitant have the right to make proposals to the *chambre de ville* for the public good?" he asked. Prevented from speaking as an échevin, Pérard withdrew to the gallery. When the assembled échevins decided to hear the rest of Pérard's speech, Humbert, in turn, left the council chamber, declaring that "he could not listen to any proposals contrary to the king's service." In the mayor's absence, Pérard described the economic hardships the city would suffer if the Accounts were transferred, as well as the damage that would be done to the city's prestige.[2]

The following day, the mairie summoned an assembly of notables to discuss the matter. Shortly thereafter, it named four deputies–Pérard, the respected avocat Etienne Bréchillet, and two others–to present the city's remonstrances to the royal council. In its petition, the mairie depicted the issue not as one of keeping order and calming the dispute, but rather, as one of preserving the city's privileges. It also asked Bellegarde to use his influence on the mairie's behalf and wrote to the Keeper of the Seals, Burgundy's intendant, and one of the secretaries of state, seeking their support.

In spite of its repeated protestations of respect for the Parlement, the mairie quickly incurred the wrath of Burgundy's highest court, whose first president threatened personal retaliation against the four deputies if they carried out their mission. While Bréchillet assured the first president that the mairie was "completely submissive and respectful" to Parlement and "in no way wanted to encroach on its authority," the four deputies nonetheless headed for the royal council over Parlement's objections.[3] As the city's deputies pursued their efforts with Bellegarde's support, the Marquis de Mirebeau, Burgundy's *lieutenant-général,* arrived in Dijon to oversee the transfer of the Accounts' archives to Autun, prompting an uprising by a small group of artisans and *vignerons* (wine growers), which resulted in the destruction of several carts loaded with the Accounts' papers. Although Bellegarde reproached the city magistrates for failing to prevent the riot, he also recognized that the "better inhabitants" had not taken part and pledged to continue his efforts to keep the Chamber of Accounts in Dijon.[4] Ultimately, however, Bellegarde's and the city's efforts came to naught. In January 1628, the Accounts left Dijon for Autun. The following year, in direct response to the mairie's behavior in the Chamber of Accounts affair, Parlement prohibited avocats and *procureurs* (solicitors) from practicing before it while serving as échevins.[5]

The mairie's actions in the dispute between the Parlement and the Accounts, though ultimately unsuccessful, nevertheless reveal a great deal about urban politics and the local operations of the early modern French state. In particular, they highlight the importance of university-educated legal professionals, known as avocats, as local *hommes politiques.* Avocats were, as David A. Bell has aptly described them, the "institutional technicians" of the *ancien régime* state.[6] They were the recognized experts of France's complex and multifaceted body of law, masters of arcane legal precedents and principles. They were highly knowledgeable about the workings of the various judicial institutions and privileged corporate bodies that made up the state's governing apparatus. At the same time, avocats, who saw themselves as the heirs of Cicero, Demosthenes, and the other great orators of the ancient world, emphasized the value of rhetoric and the importance of persuasion. They were thus well prepared to influence debates within bodies such as Dijon's mairie, to articulate the legal and other principles that justified their actions, and to seek the support of powerful patrons whose protection and influence were indispensable in the political environment of early modern France. It was not a coincidence that the avocat Bénigne Pérard rallied his fellow échevins in opposition to the monarchy's order exiling the Chamber of Accounts despite the mayor's strong objections. Nor was it a surprise that Pérard and the *conseil* Berbisey formulated the procedural and legal arguments–that the royal council had not heard the city and that the exile violated its privileges–that justified the mairie's opposition to the king's orders. Nor was it an accident that two of the city's four deputies, including its leading spokesmen, were avocats, or that these individuals were willing to risk professional repercussions to defend what they believed were the mairie's interests.

As this book will demonstrate, the avocats who dominated Dijon's city council during the first seven decades of the seventeenth century repeatedly performed these and other similar functions on the mairie's behalf. Indeed, I will argue, there was a kind of symbiosis between the mairie and members of Dijon's bar for much of the century. Avocats believed that their legal and rhetorical expertise, along with the personal virtues required by their profession, made them "hommes politiques" who were entitled (along with their fellow urban notables) to participate in the governance of their communities. Excluded from most sovereign royal courts by the spiraling price of offices, Dijon's avocats, like their counterparts in a number of other French cities, turned to the municipality to fulfill the public roles to which they believed they were entitled. The avocats' presence at the hôtel de ville, meanwhile, enabled the mairie to utilize the various channels of power and influence–the law courts and informal patronage networks–that made up the ancien régime state to defend the mairie's powers and privileges from other local governing bodies, including Parlement and the *Bailliage* of Dijon. For nearly seven decades, the avocats successfully defended the municipality's considerable powers from external "encroachments" and ensured that it (and they) participated actively at the local level of the early modern French state. All of this changed in the summer of 1668, however, when Louis XIV ordered a sweeping reorganization of the hôtel de ville. Divided by the bitter political conflicts of the previous generation and overly reliant on the authority and protection of Burgundy's governors, the Princes of Condé, the mairie and the avocats who played a leading role there proved unable to defend their political privileges as they had in the past. The smaller, more circumscribed mairie that remained quickly became absorbed into the increasingly impersonal and bureaucratic structure of the "administrative monarchy" that emerged during the late seventeenth century. Those who staffed the hôtel de ville found themselves transformed from governors of their city into administrative agents marginalized from the centers of power and decision making. Although a handful of avocats continued to serve on the city council, most found themselves excluded from public life, a change of affairs that prompted many to reexamine their beliefs about the nature of the French state, their own place within it, and the legitimate uses and limits of royal power. This book will examine how Dijon's avocats experienced local politics in seventeenth- and early eighteenth-century France, how they reacted to the various threats to the mairie's and their own places in local governance, and how they conceived of the state and their place within it over a span of more than a century. In so doing, this book will explore both the social and cultural consequences of political change at the local level during this period, changes that are all too often overlooked in current studies of French absolutism and processes of state formation in early modern Europe.

Cities and the State in Early Modern France

Early modern France's urban centers, though accounting for at most 10 to 20 percent of the kingdom's population, occupied a crucial nexus between the royal state and local society.[7] They were "important institutionally as the bottom level of various hierarchies, socially as an environment affecting politics, and physically as the geographical battlefield for conflicts of authority."[8] Municipalities fulfilled many of the fundamental functions of local governance and helped to keep order on a day-to-day basis. They were also home to the various law courts, administrative bodies, and their personnel, who collectively made up the state's institutional and human apparatus in provincial France. Cities were the sites where individuals most frequently came into contact with state authorities, and it was from the kingdom's urban centers that governmental authority radiated, however weakly and haphazardly, into the countryside where the vast majority of France's population lived.

Although urban centers played a crucial role in structuring the relationship between center and periphery in early modern France, the nature of political change and the ways it was experienced by urban notables remains poorly understood. Not surprisingly, historians interested in state formation and political change during this period have focused primarily on developments that took place closer to the centers of power. They have analyzed changes in royal finances and administration, the court, and the army.[9] Painstaking and careful scholarship has reconstructed the relationship among the crown and France's aristocracy and powerful provincial elites.[10] And the complicated interactions between the monarchy and major national and regional bodies such as the church, parlements and provincial estates have also attracted considerable interest.[11]

By contrast, provincial urban centers have received relatively meager attention. One reason for this seeming neglect, as Hilary Bernstein has noted recently, may be that as a distinct form of political community, cities did not fit neatly into early modern France's political imagination.[12] The overwhelming perception that the last two centuries of the ancien régime were a period of profound political decline for France's once wealthy and powerful *bonnes villes* undoubtedly also explains historians' relative lack of interest in municipal politics and the notables who dominated France's cities. As Alexis de Tocqueville famously argued more than one hundred fifty years ago, urban political life under the Bourbons witnessed the degeneration of vibrant "small democratic republics" where city officials "were freely elected by all the people and were responsible to them, where municipal life was public and active, where the city was still proud of its rights and very jealous of its independence," into "small oligarch[ies]" where "a few families ran everything to their own interest, far from the public eye and without being responsible to it."[13] Tocqueville's view has held considerable influence among modern historians. According to Bernard Chevalier, the desire of robe officers and legal men to elevate themselves socially by distancing themselves from the urban community and aligning themselves with the crown and its interests (the so-called "trahison des bourgeois"), combined with the territorial state's inexorable centralizing tendencies, undermined the civic culture of France's once-proud and fiercely autonomous *bonnes villes,* enabling the monarchy to domesticate them by the end of the sixteenth century. Nora Temple, for her part, located the crucial shift later, in the second half of the seventeenth century, when "the centralized absolutism created by the Bourbons transformed municipal officials into the petty agents of the bureaucracy." Notables who once defended their city's rights and privileges, she argues, became increasingly subservient to the crown. Hôtels de ville across France "fell under the control of a close circle of local notables." Similarly, Roland Mousnier concluded that "cities and communities were increasingly administered from Paris, then Versailles, by a multitude of *arrêts du conseil* rendered on the basis of intendants' reports."[14]

In recent years, however, a number of studies have suggested that cities and the notables who dominated them continued to play an important role in the early modern French state for much of the ancien régime. Although the power and autonomy of France's municipalities were clearly on the wane, cities nonetheless remained vital centers of governance and political activity. Indeed, it now appears that early modern French cities underwent an evolutionary process of political change during the seventeenth century. In contrast with the dynamic sketched out by Tocqueville and others, the relationship between the French crown and its cities was not always a zero-sum game. On the contrary, municipal regimes adapted to the new political realities of the Bourbon monarchy and altered their governing activities and ideologies in response to them. Bernstein's study of Poitiers has shown how municipal governments in the late sixteenth century could still serve as spaces for political negotiation and consensus building among a wider urban community through the persistence of a distinct, civic-oriented political culture. Moreover, she has demonstrated the advantages that "accrued to both civic elites and the monarch in conceiving of and representing their relationship in terms of cooperation rather than antagonism." Yann Lignereux, meanwhile, argues that the Lyon's transition from "bonne ville" to "absolutisme municipale" during the first half of the seventeenth century did not entail the political subjugation of the civic elite. Rather, he argues, Lyon's notables reconfigured local political culture to create a new identity that affirmed their status as guardians of the town's moral and spiritual well-being.[15] The crown, for its part, did not have a consistent policy of curtailing urban privileges, though it certainly did not hesitate to do so in order to maintain order and obedience. Rather, as Annette Finley-Croswhite has shown, Henri IV relied on a combination of patronage ties, generous concessions of privileges, and swift reaction to rebellion and disobedience to ensure the loyalty of the kingdom's cities. Robert Descimon has similarly highlighted Henri's efforts to ensure the election of obedient échevins while maintaining the traditional structure and delicate internal balances of Paris's hôtel de ville. Many municipalities, such as Toulouse and Nantes, retained active and powerful local governments by leveraging their position as counterweights to local parlements or other royal courts until the latter half of the seventeenth century. Only then, as Robert Schneider, Louis Trénard, and Guy Saupin have shown, did municipal elites abandon civic-oriented cultural values and behaviors in favor of those emanating from Paris and Versailles. "Royal absolutism ushered in a profound change in the political ethos of the men who served in municipal office," Peter Wallace observed in his study of Colmar. "They continued to administer day-to-day civic affairs," not out of a sense of pride in their local institutions and traditions, "but now as bureaucratic agents of the crown."[16]

Many of France's cities, then, were far from moribund as political and governmental centers during the seventeenth century. Although some urban centers were undoubtedly under close royal control, notables in many others maintained a strong sense of civic identity and attachment to their local political privileges and institutions, at least through the first half of the seventeenth century. Virtually all of these notables, it is true, were undoubtedly drawn into closer patronage relationships with the king, the high nobility, and other national and regional elites. This development, however, did not necessarily signal a declining commitment to the defense of local political culture and practices. On the contrary, as we will see below, such ties could often be part of an effective strategy to defend urban privileges against rivals, most notably royal courts. A strong monarchy could thus be a guarantor of local political rights and participation, not necessarily a threat to them. In this regard, as in so many others, Louis XIV's consolidation of power in the hands of both the crown, and the national and regional elites that cooperated with it, appears to have transformed decisively both the workings and the political cultures of many of France's municipal regimes. "In terms of power," William Beik observed for Languedoc, "the consulates were at the bottom of the provincial pecking order, and everyone else's gain was their loss." The few notables who governed France's cities under Louis XIV by associating themselves with his grandeur "enjoyed unprecedented security in the name of the king" but only at the cost of a substantial amount of their municipalities' power and independence.[17]

Understanding the political life of France's cities and those who dominated municipal governments thus provides us with a useful window into understanding the larger processes of state formation and their consequences for political participation during the early modern period. Scholars such as

J. Russell Major and Roland Mousnier have shown that a significant portion of France's upper and middle classes–ranging from the high nobility to urban notables–had a long history of participating in governance and politics, especially at the local level. At the outset of the seventeenth century, Mousnier argued, "subjects' rights were guaranteed by their participation in legislation, in *la police* or administration, or, to a lesser extent, in government, through orders and corporations of different sorts." As an increasingly assertive monarchy expanded its hold over provincial government over the course of the seventeenth century, however, the nature of political participation changed dramatically. As a result, the range of those who were entitled to a share in public life declined markedly.[18]

Historians of early modern France inevitably find themselves confronting the complex and tangled question of whether or not the political changes that occurred during this period amounted to the development of royal "absolutism." Put simply, was the French monarchy "absolute"? Indeed, what does the term itself mean? Was the era one of fundamental and sweeping transformations that witnessed the development of something resembling the modern state, or was it marked primarily by continuity and a revitalization of traditional authorities and elites? I will address these questions in greater detail below. For the moment, however, it is enough to note that at the local level, at least, the seventeenth century was a period of profound change in the processes and mechanisms of governance. These changes might best be understood in terms of what Michel Antoine and others have described as the transition from a "judicial monarchy" to an "administrative monarchy." The Renaissance "judicial monarchy" governed primarily through France's extensive network of law courts and legal officials. The king's most important function was to ensure the provision of justice and the maintenance of the proper distribution of authority among the many officers and institutions who governed their localities in his name. The "administrative monarchy" that emerged over the course of the seventeenth century did not do away with the older *état de justice,* but rather superimposed itself on top of it. The "administrative monarchy" sought as its principal goals to ensure the effective collection of taxes, the maintenance of order, and the adequate provision of the kingdom's rapidly growing military machine. The "administrative monarchy" exercised power primarily through the royal council, the king's ministers, and their agents in the provinces–most notably the royal *intendants.* Changes in the early modern French state, according to this model, took place largely within existing social, institutional, and personal frameworks. At the same time, however, they greatly altered the substance, if not always the form, of the state's operations and its relationship with those the monarchy governed.[19]

As the crown focused its energies on collecting revenues, supplying its armies, and ensuring the obedience of local populations, it became a more significant and constant presence in the daily lives of its subjects. Its agents adopted increasingly routinized and predictable procedures. They embraced new values of efficiency and professional application in service to the king. Intendancies gradually took on an institutional life and permanence of their own.[20] Unlike during the early seventeenth century, when the fall of a powerful member of the royal council could have a significant impact on the monarchy's ability to act in the provinces, the system of ministerial secretaries and officials that emerged under Louis XIV ensured continuity in the monarchy's administration of the provinces, even as changes at the top occurred with increasing frequency. With the current state of the scholarship, it is now possible to see the monarchy as increasingly bureaucratic and state power as increasingly abstract without falling into the teleological trap of seeing it as engaged in a process of "modernization" that would make it a forerunner of the modern nation-state. Although elements of the "judicial monarchy" persisted throughout this period, the emergence of the "administrative monarchy" had an important impact on the local realities of politics and governance in early modern France.[21]

The early modern French state, then, was characterized less by a royal monopoly on political authority than by a progressive alteration of the state's internal balances and reciprocal flows of power. Although the Bourbon monarchs and their ministers never had full control over the workings of the state, especially at the local level, their use of the considerable ideological, fiscal, and coercive powers at their disposal progressively changed the way the political game was played while simultaneously restricting the field of those who could legitimately participate. The result of this shift from a "judicial" to an "administrative" monarchy, as Denis Richet noted, was the creation of "un monde des exclus." Between those who were excluded and those who were not was a group that inhabited a newly created netherworld of political marginality, "these divided notables, these atomized elites and these *participants écartés*."[22] This book argues that by examining the careers and experiences of these *participants écartés* (removed participants), we can better understand the social and cultural consequences of state formation in early modern France and Europe. We can see how political changes, especially at the local level, helped set the stage in the seventeenth century for the transformation of French political culture in the eighteenth century. In particular, it enables us to see how the Habermasian "bourgeois public sphere" of the eighteenth century emerged out of what might be termed the "legal public sphere" of the preceding century.

What impact did these alterations in the balances and flows of power have on the political experiences of those who had long taken part in the workings of the French state at the local level? How did the monarchy's increased power and its imposition of new channels of power and authority change the character of the state, participation in urban governance, and the relationship between ruler and ruled during this period? How were the terms that defined who could participate in public life affected? How did these changes alter the ways those who belonged to the "political nation" understood the state and its functions? At the local level, how did the emergence of the "administrative monarchy" affect the relationships among different political actors and the interplay between local agents and central authorities? How did those who participated in the state attempt to justify and defend their claims to power and authority? What factors determined their success and failure? And finally, what were the social, political, and cultural consequences for those who found themselves *écartés* from the state by the growing power of the "administrative monarchy"?

Notables, Avocats, and the "Middling Sort"

An examination of the experiences of intermediate social and political groups such as urban notables, who at first glance seem to be of marginal social and political significance, can reveal a great deal about the nature and consequences of French state formation in the early modern period. As a number of studies of early modern revolts and popular culture have demonstrated, premodern states could govern effectively only when their actions enjoyed the tacit acceptance of the governed. Ironically, however, although a great deal of research has been done into those at the upper and lower levels of state and society, we still know relatively little about those who occupied the ranks in the middle. In many ways, historians have tended to overlook France's urban notables for many of the same reasons that they have until recently shied away from studying the political lives of the kingdom's cities. Unlike the nobility, clergy, or peasantry, notables were a relatively loosely defined group, characterized primarily by their intermediate and indeterminate sociocultural status. Overall, they lacked the wealth, titles, and prestige enjoyed by the kingdom's nobles, royal officers, and high clergy. At the same time, however, they enjoyed considerably more wealth and economic security than the vast majority of the population, both urban and rural, and often possessed at least some of the fiscal and personal privileges that marked a key dividing point in ancien régime society. Notables also shared much of the same cultural background–education, values, and social ties–as their social superiors. Unlike the latter, however, notables' claims to participate in public life rested not on their birth, family status, or ownership of offices. Rather, these claims were based on the notables' education and political skills, which provided them with access to political opportunities afforded by privileged corporations, most notably municipalities, where offices were generally obtained through election, cooptation, or appointment rather than by purchase and were usually temporary rather than permanent in nature.

Intermediate social groups have drawn considerable interest among scholars working on the early modern period elsewhere, most notably England. Their research into what is commonly termed the "middling sort" can be useful in gaining a perspective on the experiences of France's urban notables.[23] Although it would be wrong to draw simple parallels between England and France, it would be equally misguided to overlook some of the underlying similarities. As in England, local governance in France at the outset of the seventeenth century relied heavily on the activities and aspirations of respectable local inhabitants, those often referred to as *gens de bien*. In both England and France, these individuals were often modest figures when compared with the aristocracy, high-ranking royal magistrates, and the high clergy. By virtue of their property, respectable status, and local reputation, however, members of these intermediate social groups enjoyed preeminence over the vast majority of the local population and were therefore frequently entrusted with the often mundane but nonetheless essential duties of local governance. On the whole, the English "middling sort" and French notables shared a deep-rooted interest in preserving local order and promoting public morality, whether Puritan or Counter-Reform in nature. And although neither group may have wielded what Eric Wolf has termed "structural power," or the ability "to structure the possible field of action of others," they both enjoyed access to "tactical power"–the ability to utilize effectively and manipulate successfully existing power networks to pursue their interests.[24] In short, both groups were alike in their intermediateness; neither could dictate the rules of the game as monarchs or great aristocrats and officers could. Unlike the general populace, however, these "middling sorts" could wield a share of public authority and exploit the institutional, personal, and cultural apparatuses of the state to influence the distribution of power and resources, and to help define the proper social order in their communities.

Urban notables were also important intermediaries between the urban populace on the one hand and the upper levels of society and the state on the other. As a group, they were extremely self-conscious of their status and proud of their role in local governance. Their position, however, was a fragile one, based not on birth, wealth, and ownership of royal office but rather on longstanding urban traditions, corporate privileges that granted many cities considerable powers, and their ability as gens de bien to command respect from both the populace and their social and political superiors. The authority these notables exercised, then, depended largely on their ability to defend the legitimacy of their role as stewards of the local community. This, in turn, made them extremely sensitive to changes in the local political order and acutely aware of threats to their authority from both above and below.

Among the different social and professional groups that made up the notables of early modern France, one particular set of individuals stands out for both the extent and the quality of their political activity–the avocats who could be found in any city that housed a significant royal tribunal. During the sixteenth and seventeenth centuries, municipal governments throughout much of France came to be dominated by minor royal officials and members of the legal professions. Avocats, and to a lesser extent procureurs, appear to have enjoyed a particularly prominent role in local governance.[25] Avocats, especially, were well versed in the concepts, language, and procedures through which the state both functioned and legitimated its operations. Thus, rather than examining urban notables as whole, this study concentrates on the activities and experiences of a group of seventeenth-century avocats. In many ways, legal professionals in general and avocats in particular represented a leading element whose experiences and ideas largely encapsulated those of the broader urban notability in early modern France.

Law and the State in Early Modern France

The importance of legal institutions and legal professionals to early modern state formation has been widely acknowledged. For the most part, however, historians have focused on the role of university-trained jurists in articulating and elaborating the principles, procedures, and practices that underwrote the growth of state authority.[26] The diverse sources that comprised early modern law–Roman law, diverse regional customs, authoritative commentaries, royal edicts, previous court decisions, and vaguely defined principles of equity–could only be interpreted and used by those with the requisite training and professionally recognized expertise, usually signified by a university law degree. Described by contemporaries as “the priests of the law,” lawyers thus became experts in the state’s technical and intellectual workings. It was they who determined competing authorities’ jurisdictions, resolved the constant stream of procedural and conceptual conflicts that resulted from the haphazard expansion of state institutions and activities, and provided a powerful degree of symbolic and intellectual consistency that enhanced rulers’ authority.[27] Thanks to these jurists’ work, the law gained increasing importance, rivaling and even supplanting religion as a basis for political legitimacy. Not surprisingly, then, law courts were among the earliest and most highly developed governmental institutions throughout early modern France and Europe.[28]

Legal language and procedures were fundamental to early modern French politics and governance. Ancien régime France, Bell has observed, was above all a “judicial society” where “the experiences of the law courts were central to the way in which political action was conceptualized.”[29] Theorists distinguished the king’s “absolute power” from tyranny and despotism by emphasizing that the monarch governed in accordance with the law and the public interest, and not according to his personal will.[30] "The best kind of Commonweal," Jean Bodin wrote in his epochal *Six Books of a Commonweale* (1576), "is that wherein the sovereign holdeth what concerneth his majesty, the Senate maintaineth the authority thereof, the magistrates execute their power, and justice hath her ordinary course."[31] From local courts to the royal council, law provided the principal linguistic, cultural, and procedural framework through which individuals and corporations articulated, contested, and resolved disputes over the allocation of resources, status, authority, and power, even at the height of the "administrative monarchy." If we accept Keith Michael Baker's definition of political culture as "the set of discourses or symbolic practices" through which individuals and groups "articulate, negotiate, implement, and enforce the competing claims they make upon one another and upon the whole," then law was clearly a central element of early modern French political culture. It was the law that "constitut[ed] the meanings of the terms in which these claims [were] framed, the nature of the contexts to which they pertain[ed], and the authority of the principles according to which they [were] made binding. It shap[ed] the constitutions and powers of the agencies and procedures by which contestations [were] resolved, competing claims authoritatively adjudicated, and binding decisions enforced."[32]

Law under the ancien régime, it should be emphasized, was neither unitary nor fixed. In fact, the absence of an authoritative legal code or an established constitution in the modern sense was in many ways a source of its strength. Avocats and other early modern jurists, it is true, often delineated a hierarchy of authorities. One Burgundian jurist, for example, noted that whereas "French law is composed of the ordinances of our kings, the dispositions of custom, Roman law, canon law, the Pragmatic Sanction, the Concordat, the decisions of the superior courts of the realm, and the opinions of the most celebrated authors, which form our jurisprudence," the only true laws of France were royal ordinances, customs, *arrêts,* and the opinions of French jurists.[33] The reality, however, was usually far more ambiguous and complicated, as jurists routinely employed multiple, often conflicting, sources, as their needs dictated. In practice, law in early modern France resembled Roberto Bizzocci's description for Italy, consisting of "endless sources to interpret . . . both elegant and arbitrary, creative and inconclusive."[34]

The law–its contents, its procedures, and its institutional settings–was thus first and foremost a cultural system. Legal professionals were "experts at managing social and legal constructs" and at creating meaning and establishing at least a degree of certainty in the face of conflicting constructions of social reality.[35] Both Thomas Kuehn and Pierre Bourdieu have highlighted the fact that law is primarily a symbolic means for managing disputes. For Bourdieu, the "judicial field" acts by channeling conflicts into an environment where experts with recognized technical competence mobilize (often with unequal degrees of success) appropriate texts, arguments, and tactics in an effort to secure a peaceful resolution that favors their party.[36] "Law is multi-faceted in relation to society," J. A. Crook observed in his study of advocacy in ancient Rome. It consists on the one hand of "a set of rules to be obeyed, made by legislators and refined, interpreted, codified, and disputed about by jurisprudents." At the same time, however, "it is also a mechanism for allowing people to quarrel without blows, and so for argument (perhaps with skilled assistance) between people; at any particular moment the life of the law is contained in its litigation."[37] This is a useful way to understand how the law functioned in practice in early modern France. French law under the ancien régime did not provide clear-cut rules and principles; rather it provided a set of concepts, languages, and procedures "by which culture and community [were] established, maintained, and transformed."[38] Indeed, it was the law's very flexibility and adaptability–the fact that it could be (and frequently was) used by social actors from great noble families to individual peasants–and its capacity for justifying all sorts of actions, including outright opposition to state authorities, that ensured its widespread adoption and influence. Little wonder then, that Tocqueville would later describe the legal system as the last rampart of French liberty under the ancien régime.[39]

Despite its importance, the legal system of early modern France was far from autonomous in the modern, Weberian sense.[40] On the contrary, it was continuously subjected to the tremendous pressure and influence wielded by high-ranking nobles, ministers, and their kinship and clientage networks, as well as other external forces. This fact, however, does not diminish the law's importance in the workings of the early modern French state. As a set of principles and procedures for contesting and resolving disputes, the law worked in tandem with the clientage networks and other informal channels of influence that have drawn so much attention from scholars. Beik's description of the interdependence of the legal system and clientage networks is particularly apt.

> Despite the role of personal interventions by patrons in the process of getting one's way in political matters, it was still necessary to pursue a problem through institutional channels, using "legal-procedural" tactics and style. In a society where most rights were traditional and where the many levels of the judicial apparatus were far more highly developed than the institutions which created or enforced legislation, it is not surprising that the essence of local government was the pursuit of large numbers of cases in the courts.[41]

For the most part, historians have devoted more attention to the first part of this statement, focusing on "the role of personal interventions by patrons in the process of getting one's way in political matters" than on the second part. Reducing litigation to a mere façade for the operation of clientage networks, however, downplays the "all-pervasive legalism" of ancien régime society[42] and minimizes the importance that contemporaries placed on compelling legal arguments and effective procedural strategies. Even if courts rarely adjudicated political disputes outright, they played an important role in their resolution. Early modern law courts were only one part of a much larger system of dispute resolution that incorporated mediators, arbitrators, and other third parties who brokered, negotiated, or otherwise fostered informal settlements. Litigation, moreover, did not represent an abandonment of less formal means of dispute resolution; rather, it was inextricably bound up with them. It is well known, for instance, that the vast majority of lawsuits were abandoned before trial. Parties usually went to court not to win definitive judgments (which were often difficult to obtain and costly to execute), but rather to force their adversaries to negotiate or settle.[43] Nonetheless, the very fact of going to court or even the mere desire to avoid litigation, Thomas Kuehn has shown, compelled parties to articulate their grievances and define their claims using concepts and norms derived from the formal world of the law. According to Kuehn, "law's brooding presence, as an institutional mechanism and a body of rules" helped shape disputes even when formal litigation was only "something to be avoided."[44] The possibility that a dispute could escalate into litigation forced parties to distill their claims into a set of abstract claims of rights and principles supported by reference to appropriate texts and authorities. These norms, in turn, "provided ranges of discourse within which a comprehensible picture might be constructed, either by two parties directly negotiating or by a third party."[45] Far from being a mere façade for the "real" exercise of power "behind the scenes," then, the law was central to the mundane business of ancien régime governance–the resolution of the endemic jurisdictional and political conflicts that were the inevitable product of the overlapping authorities and poorly defined jurisdictions that composed the early modern French state.

By the very nature of their profession, avocats occupied an important but ambiguous place in the French legal system, the state, and society as a whole. In theory, all those who had obtained a *licence en loix* from a French university and had sworn the appropriate oath before Parlement or another royal court following an examination of their character could take the title "avocat." For the purposes of this study, however, the term avocat refers only those who practiced at the bar or in another legal capacity, and not those who simply took the title as an honorific, as many did.[46] Unlike judges, procureurs, and other legal officials, avocats did not own an office and did not belong to a professional corporation. Instead, they were free to consult and plead for individuals as they saw fit. Although there was a society of avocats in Dijon, it was considered to be a free association of individuals with limited ability to represent the bar as a whole or even to discipline its members.

Being an avocat, in short, meant more than exercising a *métier,* it was to have a certain *qualité,* or state of being.[47]

Because the avocat's profession emphasized education and individual ability over birth and inherited status, it was one of the ancien régime's preeminent avenues of social mobility. The bar of Dijon attracted not only the sons of avocats, *parlementaires,* and other robe families, but also the ambitious progeny of merchants, artisans, and lesser legal officials, for whom the bar was a step in their families' slow climb from obscurity to an ennobling office. In social terms, Dijon's avocats ran the gamut from the upper echelons of local society to modest, humble situations on a par with the city's artisans. Most, however, enjoyed a respectable status that placed them at the upper reach of the city's notables, ranking beneath the robe nobility of Dijon's sovereign courts but above other legal professionals, doctors, apothecaries, and other liberal professionals, as well as merchants, master artisans, and other nonnobles.[48]

Those who have written about French avocats prior to the eighteenth century have tended to describe the profession as being in a state of decline and its members as politically marginalized, especially during the seventeenth century.[49] Such characterizations, however, greatly underestimate the extent to which avocats permeated the French state. Although avocats were by no means a dominant force, they fulfilled multiple roles in the processes of governance, especially at the local level. In addition to their institutional expertise, avocats were also "members of an articulate as well as a learned profession in which success required some discipline of mind and was likely to bring the wealth and leisure to support general reflection."[50] Finally, the avocat's skills in framing issues, marshalling historical and legal precedents, and developing compelling (or at least plausible) arguments were also significant in obtaining the support of powerful patrons and effectively using the networks of informal influence that paralleled formal judicial and governmental institutions.

Avocats not only permeated the early modern French state by virtue of their technical and rhetorical skills, they also believed that the personal qualities required by their profession entitled them to do so. Members of the bar professed a commitment to the ideals of civic humanism, or at least to what Donald Kelley has described as "civil humanism," the belief that a commitment to justice and the study of the law "was the very foundation of public life and the education of the 'political man.'" The ideal, Kelley observed, was not a society ruled by a Platonic "philosopher-king," but rather one governed by "philosopher-jurists."[51] Indeed, the qualities avocats highlighted as particular to those of their profession–the cultivation of reason, disinterestedness, and self-sacrifice in defense of the public good–closely resembled those that royal apologists attributed to the king in his capacity as the sole "public person."[52] Unlike others who bought their offices or owed their position to the hazards of birth or royal favor, the avocat believed that he was a *homo politicus* because his mastery of law and eloquence enabled him to identify the public good and to persuade others to pursue it. Thanks to their training, professional activity, and self-conception, avocats were active in the formal and informal power networks of the early modern French state despite their relatively modest financial and social standing. By examining the political careers, experiences, and beliefs of a group of provincial avocats over the course of the seventeenth century, this book seeks to contribute to our understanding of three key aspects of political culture and practice during this period: the nature (and even the existence) of French absolutism, the processes and consequences of European state formation, and the relationship between the world of the law and the emergence of the so-called public sphere in seventeenth- and eighteenth-century France and Europe.

Local Government and the Problem of French Absolutism

The avocats and other notables who helped govern many of France's provincial urban centers were a long way–geographically, socially, and politically–from the centers of political power at Paris and later Versailles. Nonetheless, this book argues, a careful examination of their political experiences can contribute to the current scholarly debate over the nature and indeed the very existence of "absolutism" in early modern France. Until about twenty-five years ago, most historians believed that the following factors coalesced in the formation of an "absolute" monarchy: the crown's increasing claims to legislative sovereignty, its growing oversight of provincial government, and its use of legally trained, middle-class commissioners known as intendants to circumvent the kingdom's great noble families and established local authorities. According to this view, "absolutism" represented a dramatic break with the past, the replacement of a feudal regime characterized by personal loyalties and divided sovereignty with a rational, bureaucratic, and centralized forerunner of the modern state.[53]

In recent years, however, a wave of revisionist scholarship building on both Marxist and non-Marxist foundations has demonstrated how the early Bourbons enhanced their power by colluding with and co-opting leading noble families, officers, and provincial landholders. The result has been a new scholarly orthodoxy that has been aptly summarized by William Beik in a recent article: "The king ruled by collaborating with socially powerful elites–at court, in Paris and in the provinces. Government was characterized by compromise, negotiation and sharing of resources in a manner which maintained and supported hierarchical differences."[54] Revisionist scholars have highlighted the ways the early Bourbons revived traditional aristocratic values, restored feudal social structures, and supported the authority of existing institutions. Far from revolutionizing royal government, they contend, France's "absolute" monarchs used personal ties to ensure loyalty and asserted their control over the distribution of patronage to ensure obedience. According to the revisionist view, the seventeenth century was a time of continuity and even conservatism rather than an era of profound social, institutional, and structural change. Indeed, as Beik has noted, the monarchy's social-collaborationist approach to governance meant that "old practices became deeply entrenched and the well-being of the state became increasingly tied to defending them," thereby ossifying state and society and preventing them from adapting to changing circumstances in the eighteenth century.[55]

One of the main revisionist schools has drawn heavily on the class-based Marxist analysis first put forth by Perry Anderson.[56] Absolutism, according to Beik, one of the most influential revisionists, "must be seen . . . not as a modern state grafted onto a premodern society, but as the political aspect of the final, highest phase of a venerable, though modified, feudal society." King and nobility cooperated in extracting surplus wealth from the lower social orders and reinforced each other's authority and status within ancien régime society.[57] "Absolutism," notes David Parker, another influential Marxist, "looked backwards rather than forwards. Patrimonial mechanisms of rule remained more important than bureaucratic ones, whilst the ideas which legitimated the regime were profoundly traditional." It enabled a ruling class "much shaken and divided" by the crises of the late sixteenth and early seventeenth centuries to "renew" itself.[58]

Eschewing the Marxist framework of Beik, Parker, and others, James B. Collins also argues that a considerable degree of social collaboration underwrote the monarchy's expanding power in the seventeenth century. Crown and nobility often found themselves at odds when their interests clashed, Collins argues, especially when it came to fiscal matters. Status concerns, political interests, and other noneconomic concerns figure more prominently in Collins's analysis than those of his Marxist colleagues. Ultimately, he argues, the threat of chronic social instability and the tensions between traditional feudal elites and new commercial and fiscal elites worked as much as class and economic interests to draw the king and France's dominant classes together in defense of order and property.[59]

Louis XIV's success in expanding the monarchy's power, according to many revisionists, stemmed from his ability to work within the constraints of the aristocratically dominated society of early modern France. Perhaps the most extreme proponent of this view is Roger Mettam, who argued in rather overstated terms that Louis understood "that calm could be restored only by respecting privileges and returning to traditional and uncontroversial methods of administration." Louis, according to Mettam, increased his power by manipulating factional rivalries while developing a reputation as an impartial patron and mediator. More compelling is Sharon Kettering's view that Louis' success rested on his ability to monopolize the distribution of patronage and to co-opt the extensive clientele networks that had been the source of the great nobility's power and independence. Jay Smith has taken these observations a step further, arguing that Louis' "royal gaze" infused the entire French state, thereby extending the personal bonds of loyalty and reward that linked the king with his nobility throughout the entire kingdom.[60] Indeed, the most recurring image of the Sun King in the current scholarship is that of a patron in chief, using traditional idioms of personal political loyalty and long-standing webs of favor and reward to radiate authority "to all the lesser planets revolving in his solar system."[61]

Absolute monarchy thus appears to have ushered in a period of stability and magnificence. Nonetheless, in the eyes of Parker and many other revisionists, it lacked the powers to transform "the socioeconomic order on which it depended and in whose image it was created."[62] The Sun King's attention to hierarchy and status distinctions affirmed and enhanced the dominant social and political roles of the great nobility, large property owners, and powerful royal officers. Louis curtailed the jurisdictions of many traditional institutions but also protected their authority. For instance, he relied on traditional methods of favor and negotiation to keep the Parlement of Paris, one of the prime instigators of the Fronde (1648–53), in line. Although he took away the court's right to block the registration of royal legislation by issuing remonstrances, Louis also strengthened its legal jurisdictions and greatly curtailed the practice of transferring cases to the royal council, which had so infuriated the magistrates under Richelieu and Mazarin. In a similar vein, although Louis and his ministers used patronage, bribery, and the occasional act of intimidation to control the surviving provincial estates, they made no effort to abolish them. Estates that remained useful to the king as a source of ready credit, and to regional elites for their ability to shift tax burdens away from their wealth, thus endured.[63]

Despite their emphasis on the conservative nature of the Bourbon monarchy, many historians would agree that the seventeenth century witnessed a substantial increase in royal power and its level of efficacy in the provinces. Though rejecting the notion that the royal intendants supplanted aristocratic governors consigned to lives of courtly idleness at Versailles, revisionist scholarship has shown how the intendants helped to improve the coordination of local authorities acting in the king's name and to minimize the kinds of political conflicts that could lead to a larger breakdown of order. They also increased the flow of information between periphery and center, thus helping to reinforce, rather than undermine, the authority of governors and the regional elites who dominated parlements, estates, and other institutions that supervised provincial governance.[64] As Parker, himself a leading revisionist, put it, "there is no reason to doubt that these developments involved a concentration of power at the centre and apex of the regime. This point is worth emphasising given the tendency in some quarters to carry the revisionist critique of the concept of monarchical absolutism to the point at which it is simply seen as a particular type of 'limited' monarchy." The seventeenth century, he continues, witnessed "a visible diminution of the institutional restraints on the exercise of royal authority."[65] Nonetheless, many revisionists tend to emphasize the persistence of traditional mechanisms of government and stress the mutually beneficial relationship between the crown and entrenched provincial elites. In their view, the "absolute monarchy" was content to leave many of the details, and benefits, of governance to traditional institutions and the families who dominated them as long as they maintained order and provided the king with the resources he needed to pursue his military ambitions and enhance his glory at home and abroad.[66]

Revisiting the Revisionist Interpretation

Despite its successes, the revisionist interpretation of absolutism has faced mounting challenges in recent years. In a recent synthesis, for example, Fanny Cosandey and Robert Descimon note "we have arrived at the contradiction of an absolutism that we know incomparably in detail without a clear understanding of it as a coherent totality."[67] Although some historians have declared absolutism to be a "myth," others question whether the revisionists have overstated the cooperation between the crown and French elites.[68] Recent work has challenged some principal revisionist conclusions, arguing that the French state was indeed transformed in fundamental and lasting ways during this period. Where revisionists emphasize the monarchy's reliance on and cooperation with social elites, their critics have suggested that the increasingly powerful crown asserted its independence from and dominance over both elites and the institutions of government. In his recent study of the parlements under Louis XIV, for instance, John Hurt concluded "absolute government came at the expense of once influential institutions and subjects and weakened them for a long time, perhaps permanently." According to Hurt, the apparent cooperation between the king and the sovereign courts that revisionist studies highlight actually masked the reality of an authoritarian regime that suppressed parlementaires' political ambitions, financially exploited them and their families, and routinely acted contrary to the magistrates' interests.

Other recent studies have highlighted some of the monarchy's increasingly "modern" and "bureaucratic" tendencies. Louis XIV's reign, Michael Kwass has suggested, was "the beginning of a new and ultimately revolutionary stage of state formation" during which the crown "grafted a fragile yet strikingly modern branch of fiscal administration onto the still dominant regime of corporate privilege."[69] Recent studies of the French army, while disagreeing over the particulars, concur that Louis increased central supervision of the army and provincial governments and that he established the monarchy's ability to act independently of, and even in opposition to, the interests of the nobility and other elites.[70] In the words of Cosandey and Descimon, "the construction of the state apparatus gave the absolute monarchy the means of its doctrine," thereby creating an "unprecedented relationship between the king and his power."[71]

This study contributes to the debate over the historical reality and character of "absolutism" by focusing on the mundane workings of the French state and the ordinary nature of political experience at the local level. By looking from the periphery toward the center and from the lower rungs of the state upward, I believe we can gain a new perspective on the nature and consequences of political change in early modern France. The political experiences of Dijon's avocats, this book argues, neither fully supports nor entirely undermines the now dominant social collaborationist interpretation of absolutism. Rather, it demonstrates the limits of the revisionist view and adds support to those who maintain that the seventeenth century witnessed a fundamental and lasting transformation of both the state and political culture in France. Recent historians of absolutism are correct to point out the degree to which the expansion of royal power rested on mutually beneficial cooperation between the monarchy and entrenched national and regional elites. Similarly, there does appear to have been considerable continuity in institutional structures and methods of government at the state's upper levels. If the experiences of Dijon's avocats are any guide, however, this social collaboration at the summit of state and society was the product of a sharp and progressive narrowing of the ranks of those eligible to wield public power and participate in governance. The monarchy may have struck a bargain with those whose cooperation was necessary, but it did not hesitate to ride roughshod over the rest. In the process, it transformed not only the way the state operated at the local level, but also the social and cultural foundations of the relationship between ruler and subject in early modern France.

Local Governance and State Formation in Early Modern Europe

Analyzing the interplay between legal culture and municipal politics in Dijon also contributes to a growing body of recent scholarship that has reshaped our understanding of both the early modern state and the processes and consequences of European state formation. Scholars generally agree that the early modern period saw development of more elaborate institutional apparatuses and social networks that enabled central authorities to expand their control over the territories and populations they ruled. Driven by extreme military, fiscal, and social pressures, rulers recast old institutions and created new ones as they sought to extract ever-greater amounts of revenue and to mobilize ever-increasing amounts of resources from their populations. Although most scholars reject claims that the early modern state was the outcome of a deliberate drive to create bureaucratic, centralized regimes, they generally agree that gradual, ad hoc innovations in finance, administration, and political theory profoundly altered the relationship between states and the populations they ruled. In much of Europe, reciprocal bonds among princes, nobles, and other privileged groups were transformed into hierarchical relationships of command and obedience. The central state's institutions and personnel came to exercise greater supervision over local affairs as officials trained in law and finance, and dedicated to the sovereign's interests, supplanted traditional local elites and authorities.[72] Memories of brutal sectarian conflict and the near total collapse of social and political order in some regions prompted Europe's elites to support strong central rulers. Inspired by Neostoic philosophy and the moral and political example of imperial Rome, these rulers and their allies undertook a far-reaching "disciplining" of European society that "countered the conservative principle of feudal liberties by introducing a new rigour into all activities in public and private life." The result, according to Gerhard Oestreich, was an "absolutist society" increasingly regulated by a growing and better-organized state apparatus that fostered rational behavior, strict self-control, and obedience to one's social and political superiors.[73] Although elements of the old feudal system survived in the form of clientage relationships and other informal networks, political power became less personal and privatized as it was increasingly located in the growing institutions associated with central authorities and placed in the hands of officials dedicated to the interests of the ruler and the increasingly abstract "state" he headed. Intricate webs of privileges and corporate particularities that had shielded large portions of the population from heavy taxation, military service, and other burdens were undermined by the growing "necessity" of the sovereign and the state. Increasingly, the state took on a life of its own, becoming the machinelike Leviathan described by Thomas Hobbes, autonomous from and superior to not only the society it governed, but also the person or persons of the ruler. Governmental authority, which had been dispersed among multiple authorities and limited in scope, came to be concentrated in one person or body, a change that Oestreich characterized as "the most important development of the early modern period."[74]

Recent studies of European state formation have persuasively demonstrated that we should regard states during this period less in terms of their rulers, institutions, and personnel than as "network[s] of power relations which become institutionalized to a greater or lesser extent over time." The early modern state is best understood, Michael Braddick has argued, as a "coordinated and territorially bounded network of agents exercising political power."[75] Growing central institutions and authorities did not supplant local governing bodies and agents as much as they coordinated and streamlined them.[76] Government, in Steve Hindle's apt formulation, was less an institution or an object than a process, "a series of multilateral initiatives to be negotiated across space and through the social order."[77] The state, in turn, was the product of ongoing negotiations, contests, and exchanges among a web of individuals and groups who could claim a share of the legitimate exercise of political power. In the words of Pierre Bourdieu, it was an "autonomous field" with its own kind of capital that various actors sought to deploy and manipulate according to their unequal skills and capacities.[78]

As a result of these insights, historians have increasingly recognized that we can best understand the premodern state, in Giorgio Chittolini's words, as "a system of institutions, of powers and practices, that had as one of its defining features a sort of programmatic permeability to extraneous (or, if one prefers, private) powers and purposes while retaining an overall unity of political organization." In other words, the early modern state was hardly autonomous from the larger society from which it emerged. Rather, it was a composite of both formal institutions and informal networks of kinship, personal allegiances, clientage ties, and other relationships based on social status and individual influence. The state is thus best seen as "an arena for the mediation and political organization of various forces, or different actors and interests–as an 'enduringly ordered collective life in a political association'–without necessarily implying that its powers and its sovereignty conferred any special quality or efficacy." The understanding that early modern governing institutions "reflect shifting political force fields, changes in the classes and groupings that express interests, the variable character of the interests themselves . . . and the various organizational forms that those interests assume," has been one of the most important developments in the history of state formation in recent decades.[79]

In addition to these institutional and social components, the early modern state, as Denis Richet once observed, was also a cultural phenomenon. In recent years, historians have devoted more attention to ways that shared beliefs about the legitimate sources, uses, and boundaries of political authority constrained the operations of formal and informal power networks. "One of the first and principal functions of the state," Pierangelo Schiera reminds us, "consists precisely in providing a structure and apparatus capable of building and maintaining the consensus and participation of the citizen-subjects." Despite the existence of larger and more disciplined armies, rudimentary police forces, and more developed criminal justice systems, state institutions and officials still had limited *power* (understood as coercive force) at their disposal. Successful governance depended primarily on their *authority*–their ability to draw on accepted moral principles and assumptions about the proper order of things, to manipulate symbolic markers of status and deference, and to employ personal qualities or the attributes of office to secure the tacit consent and obedience of the governed.[80]

The tripartite character of the early modern state–institutional, social, and cultural–took on its greatest significance and found its fullest meaning in the thoughts and actions of those who composed what some have called the "political nation." Members of the "political nation," broadly speaking, were those whom state officials had to take into consideration when formulating policies and carrying out their duties. In many ways, they constituted a sort of early modern "public" whose support was essential to the effective operation of the state and its officials in a period when coercive power was often quite limited. They were, on the whole, stakeholders in the current system–"insiders" who were usually supportive of state authority and viewed it as a resource for maintaining order and as a bulwark against the constant threat of disorder and immorality emanating from the unruly and undisciplined lower classes. This support, however, was not absolute. Instead, it rested on widely shared cultural assumptions about the proper order of things and entailed considerable respect for the exercise of power through established institutions and procedures. Deviations from these cultural and procedural norms ran the risk of crossing the crucial boundary that distinguished the legitimize exercise of political power from the ever-lurking threat of tyranny. When this happened, those with the necessary social status, cultural background, and recognized claim on the legitimate use of public authority could, and often did, contest and frustrate the actions of state officials.[81] They could do so because, as Braddick and others have shown, the common cultural framework and sense of legitimacy that fostered the consent of the governed also provided the conceptual and procedural means for contesting the actions of state officials when they surpassed widely recognized limits. Officials and institutions that did not conform to these standards of legitimate behavior risked serious challenges to their authority from those who might otherwise be inclined to support it.[82]

In recent years, then, early modern state formation has come to appear "more like a dynamic process of communication between centre and localities rather than a one-sided drive towards ever greater penetration and acculturation."[83] Through these dialogues and confrontations "in which 'certain sorts of jurisdictional claims and legal practices, certain senses of the public good and public authority' were contrived and contested," Hindle argues, "state authority was created, negotiated, and deployed." Far from developing in opposition to society and asserting control over it, the early modern state was embedded in society and evolved in response to the needs of different social groups throughout its territory.[84] As "the bundle of ways in which the exercise of political power was routinely made legitimate," it was always in flux, open to redefinition, contestation, and change, "in one moment . . . more stable and in another more conflictual, in shifting combinations that spawn redistributions of power and gradually changing political orders and machineries." The state's form and function, Braddick concludes, "were shaped by the collective interests of those who could define political issues and administrative responses to them . . . but also by the political languages available to justify and lend credibility to their actions."[85] To be part of the state, especially at the local level, was to be caught up a process of constantly defining and contesting the identity of legitimate participants; the range of actions different individuals, officers, and institutions could take; and the meaning of the principles that governed and justified the behavior of all political actors.[86]

At the level of cities such as Dijon, then, the early modern state was "a process in which subjects were intimately involved, one which they learned to manipulate, to criticise, and even to change." This book will trace how one such group of subjects attempted to appropriate, manage and, when necessary, resist the forces driving state formation and political change at the local level. It will undertake a detailed examination of the actions, words, and ideas that shaped the political interplay between center and periphery during a period historians have described as one of intensifying contact and dialogue between both.[87] It will analyze the relationship between formal and informal power networks and the interactions between competing and overlapping authorities, ranging from the local level all the way up to the crown itself. In so doing, it will provide us with a better understanding of the experiences of those who found themselves caught in the profound processes of political change during this period and the consequences of these changes on political culture, practice, and participation at the local level in early modern France.

Lawyers and the Early Modern "Public Sphere"

Studying changes in the workings of the state and the experiences of notables at the local level can also help us better understand the history of a crucial phenomenon in early modern political culture–the development of the "public sphere." According to the highly influential model put forward by the German sociologist Jürgen Habermas, the "bourgeois public sphere" was the product of a confluence of cultural, economic, and political forces during the eighteenth century. The power of kings and state officials, which had previously been "represented" before an audience of passive, private individuals, was in the eighteenth century subjected to critical analysis and informed discussion by a "public" that claimed the authority to judge and even to oppose government actions and policies. This "public," Habermas argues, was composed of private individuals who came together through the use of print to use their collective reason to debate public affairs. The new "bourgeois public" developed as a result of the state's growth and its increasingly continuous activity in the lives of its subjects. Mounting fiscal pressures and the need to supply, maintain, and discipline ever-larger armies led, in turn, to larger and more active bureaucracies. The increasing depersonalization of the state, Habermas argues, fostered the creation of civil society, a development that coincided with the expansion of finance and trade capitalism. The need for continuous information about events at home and abroad among merchants and investors led to the commodification of news and the creation of a press that helped to feed individuals' interest in the workings of the state that increasingly impinged on their lives. By the mid-eighteenth century, the "public," which originally came into existence in the depoliticized realm of artistic and literary criticism, had become politicized, and "public opinion" had established itself as an alternative and even a superior source of authority and legitimacy to the state.[88]

Whereas Habermas argued that the bourgeois "public sphere" developed outside the state, emerging from the opposition between state and society, several historians have made persuasive arguments that in the case of France, at least, the "public sphere" developed from within the state. It emerged, they argued, from the world of the law, thanks in large part to the activities and writings of Parisian avocats, whose responses to the controversies over Jansenism and mounting concerns over royal "despotism" led them to cast themselves as representatives of the "public" and spokespersons for nascent "public opinion." Lucien Karpik, for instance, has described avocats as promoting a liberal politics of individual liberty and limited government. Bell has characterized them as "a sort of absolutely independent little republic at the center of the state," who used their ability to publish uncensored *factums* to appeal to public opinion against the monarchy's persecution of the Jansenists, Maupeou's coup against the parlements, and a number of other legal and political matters. Sarah Maza, meanwhile, has explored the theatrical and literary qualities of avocats' factums, showing how their adoption of Enlightenment (especially Rousseauian) language transformed what were technically internal court briefs into widely disseminated commentaries on late-eighteenth-century government and society as well as calls for political reform and moral regeneration.[89]

Although historians have long been aware that men of the law, especially avocats, dominated the municipal governments of many French provincial cities from the sixteenth century onward, the contributions of these pre-eighteenth century provincial avocats to the development of the "public sphere" remains virtually unexplored territory.[90] "Even those scholars whose interest in Habermas has sent them scurrying after the origins of the 'public sphere,'" Hindle has rightly noted, "have tended to overlook sixteenth- and early seventeenth-century legal developments."[91] This is at least partly due to the unfortunate disconnect between the scholars working on the state in seventeenth-century France and those working on political culture in the following century.[92] A profound tension has arisen between the revisionist emphasis on political stability and cooperation between king and elites during the seventeenth century on the one hand, and studies arguing that French politics "broke out of the absolutist mold" in the decades leading up to 1789 on the other.[93] As Kwass has so perceptively asked, "why would elites challenge a monarchy that was reinforcing their social position?"[94] The unfortunate result has been the obscuring of the connections between the processes of seventeenth-century state formation and the development of the "public sphere" in the eighteenth century. This study aims to highlight and explain these overlooked links and, in so doing, suggest ways in which divergent trends in the historiographies of seventeenth- and eighteenth-century France can be reconciled.

Indeed, historians are now beginning to recognize that the discontinuities posited by those who claim that the "politics of public opinion" emerged in the late eighteenth century are overstated. Several studies have pointed to the existence of "public opinion" and its impact on the workings of the state well before the second half of the eighteenth century. The "tribunal of public opinion," Peter Campbell argues in his study of early eighteenth-century politics, "existed in the eyes of ministers and courtiers long before the mid-eighteenth century." Even in the late seventeenth century, ministers recognized the force of public opinion.[95] "Whether the capitation is good or bad," Controller-General Pontchartrain wrote to the first president of the Parlement of Paris in 1695, "must ultimately be put to the public judgment."[96] In a similar vein, Colin Jones has noted that the "public" and "public opinion" had long been invoked in political arguments. Since the late sixteenth century, according to J. A. W. Gunn, "public opinion" scrutinized the reputations and actions of kings and ministers and passed judgment on the legitimacy of their actions in accordance with widely accepted moral and legal norms. "Changes in behaviour and in language of the mid-eighteenth century," Gunn concludes, "were less dramatic departures from past practices than they appeared to be–even to contemporaries who lived through them."[97] A number of other studies, meanwhile, suggest that Habermas's definitions of the "public" and the "public sphere" are too narrow to capture the historical reality of early modern France.[98]

Whatever the nature of the pre-eighteenth-century "public sphere," avocats certainly played an important role in it. A series of articles by Sarah Hanley, for instance, has shown how avocats' briefs and other legal writings helped create and fuel a widespread interest in the law among French men and women during the seventeenth and early eighteenth centuries.[99] Following Hindle's lead, then, this study of Dijon's avocats explores the often-overlooked connection between the law and public opinion in France prior to the eighteenth century. In tracing the political careers, experiences, and ideas of the avocats who played a prominent role at Dijon's hôtel de ville, it builds on Karpik's observation that avocats were a "groupe charnière" situated at the nexus between state and civil society. The very nature of their profession, Karpik argues, made avocats mediating figures whose authority rested on their ability freely to determine and articulate the "public good" to both state authorities and individual clients. For Karpik, the avocats' "detachment" and their recognized ability to speak on behalf of others enabled them to emerge as spokesmen for the "public" during the eighteenth century and provided them with a degree of political influence out of all proportion to their wealth, status, and power.[100] Yet, although Karpik associates the profession's eighteenth-century politicization with its opposition to absolutism and its embrace of a liberal ideology, avocats, in fact, had a long tradition of advising, representing, and serving as members of the many privileged corporate bodies that constituted the early modern French state. By the end of the seventeenth century, avocats had long experienced a form of the "continuous administrative contact" that Habermas cited as central to the creation of a "public" in the eighteenth century.[101] Highly educated and immersed in the literate cultures of both humanism and the law, avocats pursued their professional and political activities in the world of the "intermediate" judicial and political authorities described by Montesquieu and Tocqueville as key elements of the ancien régime state and bulwarks against royal despotism. Avocats, such as those who dominated Dijon's city council, had a sophisticated understanding of the state's workings and a heightened sensitivity to changes in its structure and operation. They experienced up close the changes in the French state over the course of the seventeenth and eighteenth centuries and could articulate their views of these changes in juridically and rhetorically compelling ways.

As the following chapters will demonstrate, avocats such as those active in municipal governance in Dijon were at the heart of the "public sphere" of pre-eighteenth-century France. This "public sphere," it should be noted, was not Habermas's "bourgeois public sphere" of private individuals exercising reason and united by the circulation of printed matter. At the same time, however, it was by no means Habermas's seventeenth-century "representative public sphere," which absolute monarchs used to display their glory to a passive and obedient audience. Rather, this pre-eighteenth-century public sphere was a realm of critical political debate and discussion centered on the law, legal institutions, and the various privileged corporations through which a considerable number of individuals participated in the local workings of the French state. In many ways, this "legal public sphere" preceded and laid the foundations for the changes that took place in French political culture during the eighteenth century. A study of the political careers and writings of French avocats in the midst of the French state's evolution from a "judicial" to an "administrative" monarchy thus helps us develop a clearer picture of how those at the local level understood and experienced the process of state formation. It also helps us better comprehend the changing nature of French political culture over the course of the seventeenth century. The experiences of Dijon's avocats, I argue, demonstrate the existence of a "legal public sphere" of political debate and discourse at the local level in seventeenth-century France. As the monarchy's growing power and its creation of a larger and more elaborate administrative network transformed local politics and governance during the second half of the century, however, this "legal public sphere," and those it comprised, were increasingly forced to the margins. They did not, however, abandon their habits of political activity, analysis, and criticism. On the contrary, these evolved over the course of the eighteenth century, helping to give rise to the Habermasian "bourgeois public sphere" that came to dominate French political culture in the last decades of the ancien régime.

This study begins with a description of the municipal political system of seventeenth-century Dijon, focusing on the chronic conflicts between Dijon's powerful mairie and the city's other royal, provincial, and ecclesiastical governing bodies. To defend its longstanding powers from challenges by other authorities, the mairie continuously articulated, enacted, and defended its contested privileges. This, in turn, enabled many of the city's avocats to emerge as leading municipal political figures. The remainder of the first chapter shows how the city's avocats were, as they saw themselves, the ancien régime's exemplary "hommes politiques" and explains how they used their legal training and rhetorical skills to navigate and manipulate both governing institutions and informal networks of influence and patronage. Chapter 2 analyzes several disputes and recurring issues during the first half of the century in closer detail, concentrating on the tactics Dijon's avocats utilized to assert and maintain the city's privileges, jurisdictions, and autonomies. It traces how the mairie's avocats exploited the legal system and developed arguments justifying the mairie's traditional rights and interests while also examining how they used patronage networks to the city's benefit. The following chapter shows how the culture and practice of local government in Dijon was radically reconfigured through a combination of internal divisions and external pressures. These pressures shattered the cohesion and political effectiveness of the mairie and the avocats who were so important to its operations, making them completely dependent on the protection of Burgundy's royal governors. This development, combined with the growing assertiveness of the royal intendants, greatly enhanced the crown's ability to oversee local governance. This enabled the monarchy to greatly reduce the size and powers of the city council and limit accessibility to municipal offices, even in the face of opposition from a number of avocats and other notables. The fourth chapter examines the political marginalization of Dijon's mairie from local governance and the resulting exclusion of most avocats from their traditional role in municipal political life as Burgundy's governor, royal intendant, and their agents worked together to transform the mairie from a governmental institution with considerable local power into a small administrative corps with carefully circumscribed jurisdictions and competencies.

The final two chapters reconstruct how Dijon's avocats understood royal authority, the state, and their place within it during the seventeenth century. Chapter 5 looks at the impact of humanist education and legal training on the avocats' political thought while also exploring the importance of local identity, regional history, and political experiences. It shows that a "public sphere" of political discourse and debate, centered on the law and legal institutions, permeated Dijon's municipal political system in the first half of the seventeenth century and that the city's avocats were important participants in it. The avocats' writings show that they generally favored a strong monarchy and believed royal power to be "absolute," tending to downplay limits on it. In spite of this tendency, however, Dijon's avocats were also concerned with the proper limits and boundaries of royal power. In their view, the king was primarily a judge who was supposed to preserve existing political arrangements and ensure the proper distribution of power among various local authorities. The last chapter traces the political thought of Dijon's avocats in the wake of their marginalization from local governance and politics. It focuses on their return to more "constitutionalist" modes of political thought that stressed limits on royal power and reaffirmed the right of subjects to political participation through various corporate bodies and intermediate institutions. The final chapter begins by examining the increasing numbers of commentaries by Dijon's avocats on the customary laws of Burgundy. It closes with a detailed analysis of Claude Gilbert's utopian *Histoire de Caléjava, ou l'isle des hommes raisonnables* (1700). *Caléjava,* which offered a political system marked by widespread consultation, rational deliberation, and the active participation of the governed, anticipates the transformation of the seventeenth century's "legal public sphere" into the Habermasian "bourgeois public sphere" of the eighteenth century. Before looking at the avocats' political experiences and ideas, however, we must first examine the social, professional, and political worlds of seventeenth-century Dijon.

Chapter 1

Lawyers and Municipal Government in Dijon

The capital of the strategic crossroads province of Burgundy, seventeenth-century Dijon was a classic bonne ville and ville parlementaire. The city, along with the rest of the duchy of Burgundy, had been "reattached" to the French crown following the death of the last great Valois duke, Charles the Bold (d. 1477). Modest in size next to great provincial centers such as Lyon, Orléans, and Marseille, Dijon nonetheless outweighed these and all but a handful of other provincial cities as a governmental and administrative center. The 1 1/2 square kilometers inside the city's walls housed a full array of ancien régime law courts and government institutions, including the Parlement of Burgundy, a chamber of accounts, a bureau of treasurers, various lesser royal tribunals, and later the offices of the intendant of Burgundy. Dijon was also the permanent home of the Estates of Burgundy, which met every three years until the Revolution, and their standing committee, the chambre des élus, which supervised tax collection and other provincial affairs. The city itself was governed by a large, powerful, and active commune, the Mairie de Dijon, whose extensive jurisdictions and considerable autonomy over local governance dated back as far as the twelfth century. The mairie's strength in the late sixteenth century enabled those who dominated it to challenge the authority of Burgundy's Parlement and turn the city into a principal center of the Catholic League. And although many former League cities saw their privileges eroded in the early seventeenth century, Dijon's mairie maintained most of its powers intact.[1] To do so, however, it continuously had to battle Parlement, the city's other royal courts, and even the monarchy through the kingdom's many legal tribunals and informal networks of patronage and personal influence. Leading the defense of the mairie's privileges and jurisdictions were many of city's avocats, who played an increasingly prominent role at the hôtel de ville during the first half of the seventeenth century. By virtue of their professional expertise in law and rhetoric and their self-proclaimed personal qualities as defenders of justice and order, Dijon's avocats, like their counterparts across the kingdom, believed they had the right to participate in the workings of the state, even at the highest levels. Increasingly excluded from the royal magistracies they considered their due by the spiraling prices of venal offices, Dijon's avocats turned to the mairie to realize their political ambitions and to display their status as members of the local governing elite. The result was a sort of symbiosis between the avocats and mairie that lasted until Louis XIV's forced reorganization of the hôtel de ville in 1668. In the mairie, the avocats found an outlet to display their political talents and virtues, while the mairie benefited from the avocats' legal and rhetorical expertise, which enabled it to perform effectively its many functions and to maintain its privileges and jurisdictions largely intact well into the second half of the seventeenth century.

Dijon in the Seventeenth Century

Early modern Dijon was a strategic military, economic, and administrative center whose importance belied its relatively modest size (map 1). In 1602, Burgundy's capital numbered approximately fifteen thousand inhabitants; by the end of the century Dijon had grown to about twenty-two thousand, numbers that placed it on par with such important cities as La Rochelle, Grenoble, and Montpellier, but well behind others such as Rouen, Lyon, Toulouse, and Rennes.[2] Dijon was also an important communications and commercial crossroads. People and goods traveling from Paris to Lyon and points south passed through as they transferred from the Seine to the Saône river. In the opposite direction, individuals and commodities from as far south as Italy traversed Dijon on their way to Champagne, Paris, or the Low Countries.[3] More important, until the annexation of the Habsburg county of Burgundy (Franche-Comté) in 1678, Burgundy protected the eastern flank of the bassin parisien. Less than 50 kilometers from the frontier, Dijon was on the realm's forward line of defense. Historic, economic, cultural, and other ties between the duchy and the county also made the area a particularly sensitive frontier region.[4]

From 1363 to 1477, Dijon had been one of the principal capitals of the Valois dukes of Burgundy, whose territories stretched through much of eastern France, Luxembourg, parts of modern-day Switzerland and Germany, and as far north as Holland. For more than a century, the Great Dukes of the West were a dominant military and political force, surpassing the power and splendor of their nominal overlords, the kings of France. While France endured myriad crises, the Burgundian dukes–Philip the Bold, Jean the Fearless, Philip the Good, and Charles the Bold–extended their territories and sponsored one of the late Middle Ages' most spectacular periods of artistic and cultural activity. Although the dukes increasingly preferred to reside in their northern cities, their original capital hardly lapsed into obscurity.[5] Dijon's ducal council and Chamber of Accounts, which saw many of their functions limited by parallel institutions in the Burgundian Netherlands, continued to be the supreme governmental institutions for the duchy and

Map 1. France under Louis XIII. From A. Lloyd Moote, *Louis XIII, The Just* (Berkeley: University of California Press, 1989). Reprinted by permission of University of California Press.

county. Many of northern Europe's leading artists came to Dijon to work on the Chartreuse de Champmol monastery, which Philip the Bold founded just outside the city gates as a sort of Saint-Denis for the Valois dynasty, as well as a variety of other projects. Philip the Good had the ducal palace enlarged and remodeled even though he never set foot in the city after 1455. Although late medieval Dijon was not the Valois dukes' preferred capital, it was still the symbolic heart of the increasingly powerful Burgundian state and the capital of the dukes' southern territories.[6]

After Charles the Bold's death in 1477, Louis XI quickly "reattached" both Dijon and the duchy of Burgundy to the French crown. The neighboring county of Burgundy and the remaining ducal territories eventually fell to the Habsburgs. In return for Dijon's submission, Louis XI agreed to preserve the city's role as provincial capital and promised to maintain its existing institutions and privileges, a promise that his successors publicly renewed during their royal entries into Dijon throughout the sixteenth century.[7]

If the *Dijonnais* expected the crown to respect their "ancient liberties and privileges," it was in part because of the heavy price they incurred for their allegiance to France. Kathryn Edwards has provocatively described Burgundy as a "frontier"–a "hybrid zone or a 'middle ground'" where "relationships, institutions and attitudes [were] being renegotiated" in the wake of the partition of the duchy and the county after Charles's death. Burgundians on both sides of the new border maintained commercial, property, and familial ties, and pressed for a policy of neutrality that would permit persons and goods to flow freely between the two regions, even as Charles V reasserted Habsburg claims to the duchy in the first half of the sixteenth century.[8] The open border provided easy entry for Calvinist preachers and books into France while maintaining potentially unsettling links between Burgundians and the Holy Roman Emperor (Dijon's wine growers reportedly cried "Vive l'Empereur!" during a tax revolt in 1630). Habsburg troops repeatedly flooded across the border; French troops left devastation in their wake as they marched across Burgundy's fertile farms and vineyards to battlefields in Italy and elsewhere. In the middle of the sixteenth century, Jean Bégat reminded the king that "your cities of Burgundy," unlike those of other frontier provinces, "make a border and frontier without the other natural protections of sea or mountains, not only against one prince but several," including the "suspect" Germans and the "republican" Swiss.[9]

Burgundy's politically sensitive nature made it a favorite staging ground for rebellions against the crown. During the Catholic League (1589–95), Burgundy and Dijon were the duke of Mayenne's base of operations.[10] In the first half of the seventeenth century, three of the region's four royal governors–the dukes of Biron and Bellegarde, and the Grand Condé–sought to launch rebellions from the region. The fact that none was successful demonstrates the care that royal ministers exercised in their dealings with Burgundy and its capital. Careful intervention from Paris, combined with a general (if at times grudging) respect for provincial privileges, succeeded in preserving loyalty to the crown, though sometimes with little margin for error.[11]

Early modern Dijon was an ancien régime political and administrative center of the highest order, housing three sovereign courts and a host of other tribunals. The Parlement of Burgundy, created by Louis XI in 1480, was fifth in seniority after those of Paris, Toulouse, Grenoble, and Bordeaux. One of only seven in existence at the beginning of the seventeenth century,

Dijon's Parlement was the supreme court of appeals for the vast majority of civil and criminal cases in the region. It also had the right to register royal edicts before they could take effect in the province and to present remonstrances to the king that delayed the implementation of ordinances the magistrates found unacceptable. Parlement also had vaguely defined administrative powers over other areas concerning public order, health, and morality. By the early 1630s, Parlement consisted of nine presidents and sixty-six councilors divided into a *Grand'Chambre,* a *chambre de la tournelle,* which heard criminal cases; the *requêtes,* which judged cases involving those with *commitimus* (the right to be judged in the first instance and without appeal by royal *maîtres des requêtes*); and a *chambre des enquêtes,* ordinarily staffed by the newest and youngest judges, which primarily judged written appeals.[12] The Chamber of Accounts, founded by Philip the Bold in 1386, had ultimate jurisdiction over cases involving the royal domain, fiscal affairs, and the verification of royal officers' accounts. By the middle of the century, the Accounts consisted of ten presidents, three *chevaliers d'honneur,* twenty-eight masters of accounts, twelve correctors and seventeen auditors. In the 1620s, the chamber made a bid for local preeminence by purchasing a newly created jurisdiction over certain direct and indirect royal taxes (*aides et finances*) despite Parlement's objections. The violent confrontations that ensued eventually led to the chamber's exile for several years; jurisdiction over the aides et finances was eventually transferred to Parlement, consigning the Accounts to secondary status.[13] The Bureau of Finances, founded in 1577 to settle disputes involving royal taxation, consisted of three presidents, one chevalier d'honneur, twenty-one treasurers, and several receivers general. The jurisdiction of Dijon's bureau, like its counterparts throughout France, was whittled away to virtually nothing by the early seventeenth century and the office of trésorier was generally purchased only for the privileges it offered.[14]

A host of other lesser judicial and quasi-judicial bodies could also be found within the city's walls. The Bailliage of Dijon, composed of four lieutenants (one general, one civil, and two criminal) and seven councilors, heard appeals of criminal and civil cases from lesser courts in Dijon and the surrounding countryside. More specialized tribunals such as the *table de marbre,* which had authority over forests and waterways, and the *grenier à sel,* which had jurisdiction over the salt tax (the *gabelle*), were relatively small but enjoyed exclusive jurisdiction over their narrowly defined realms. Parlement and the Bailliage also had affiliated chancelleries that expedited and verified sealed royal letters.[15] Alongside these royal bodies were several nonroyal courts, such as the city's mayoral court, which had extensive first-instance civil and criminal jurisdiction, and ecclesiastical tribunals, such as those of the Abbot of Saint-Bénigne and the Sainte-Chapelle de Dijon, which had authority over their clerics and assorted religious and moral matters.[16] The

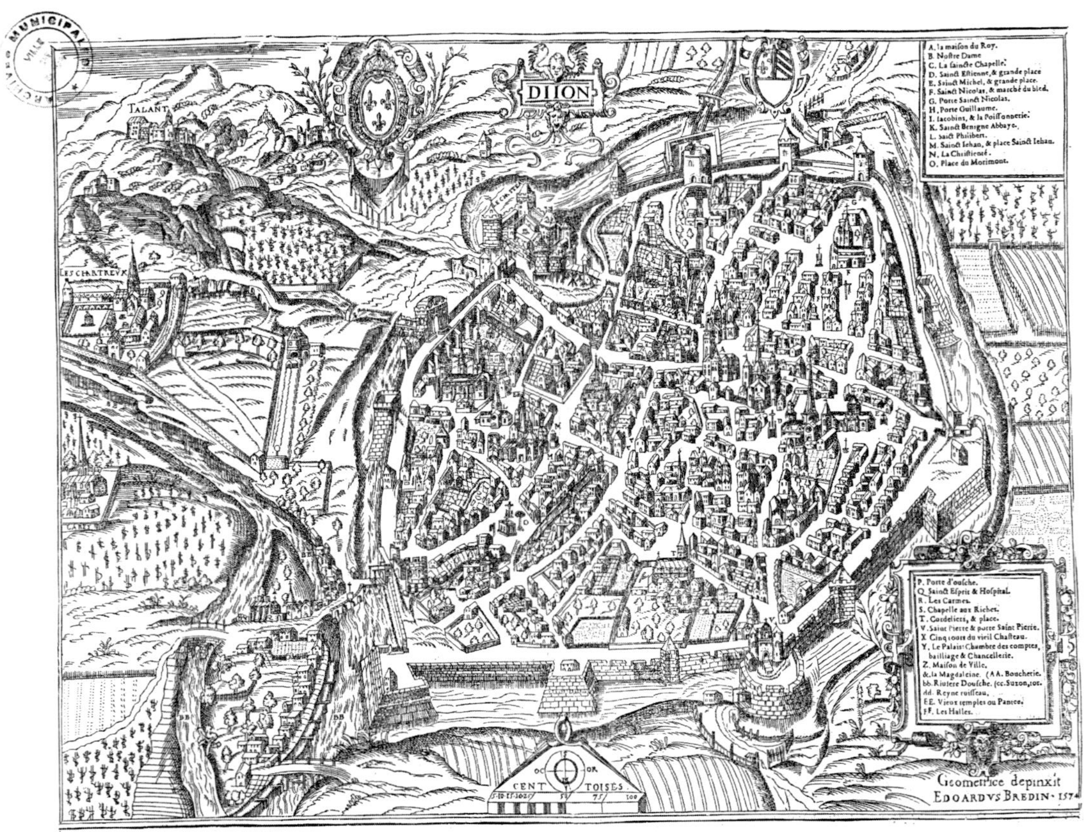

Figure 1. Dijon in 1574, by Edouard Bredin. Archives Municipales de Dijon.

Estates of Burgundy, which met every three years in Dijon, continued to negotiate taxes and other issues of provincial governance with the monarchy, while the chambre des élus supervised provincial administration and tax collection between assemblies.[17] This intense concentration of legal and governmental institutions had profound consequences for the city and the region. Dijon's artisans and shopkeepers increasingly specialized in luxury items coveted by the city's judicial officers and legal professionals, who in turn obtained most of their wealth from the vast rural territories they acquired in the sixteenth and early seventeenth centuries. "No longer simply the capital which directed the countryside," Gaston Roupnel observed, Dijon became "the center that absorbed it and contained it."[18]

Staffing this array of institutions were roughly six to eight hundred legal professionals. Taille rolls show that 765 of the 3,366 identifiable male heads of household in 1643 were affiliated with Dijon's legal and administrative institutions.[19] Members of this *monde judiciaire* ranged widely in socioeconomic status. At the pinnacle of regional society were the sovereign court magistrates. These sons of wealthy families were university educated, owned their offices, and usually enjoyed privileges including tax exemptions and ennoblement for themselves or their offspring. Their extensive rural land holdings underwrote their considerable political power and provided the wealth needed to construct and maintain impressive *hôtels particuliers* in the central parishes of Saint-Médard (near the palais de justice), Nôtre-Dame, and Saint-Jean (map 2). At the other end of the scale was the humble collection of *sergents* (bailiffs), *greffiers* (scribes), *huissiers* (tipstaffs), and others who kept the wheels of justice turning on a daily basis. These individuals drew modest incomes, had few privileges, and were relegated to a generally low status with limited possibilities for social advancement. Somewhere in between were the notaries and procureurs, whose "technical" professions required a greater degree of skill, literacy, and legal knowledge. Notaries recorded loans, leases, contracts, wills, sales, meetings, and any other activity for which an official record might be desirable. Procureurs managed the "mechanical" details of litigation: filing motions, drawing up court documents, maintaining records, engaging the services of an avocat (if necessary), and overseeing the other details of shepherding a *procès* through the courts. Successful individuals in these professions could build a decent fortune, acquire respectable rural properties, and associate with the city's elite, especially during the first half of the century.

Avocats did not fit neatly into Dijon's judicial hierarchy. Unlike procureurs and notaries, avocats were required to have a university education. Their profession was considered a "noble" one based on intelligence, ability, and merit rather than on "mechanical" skills. The most prominent avocats enjoyed reputations and social status, if not wealth, comparable to those of the city's parlementaires, who did not hesitate to marry their daughters to

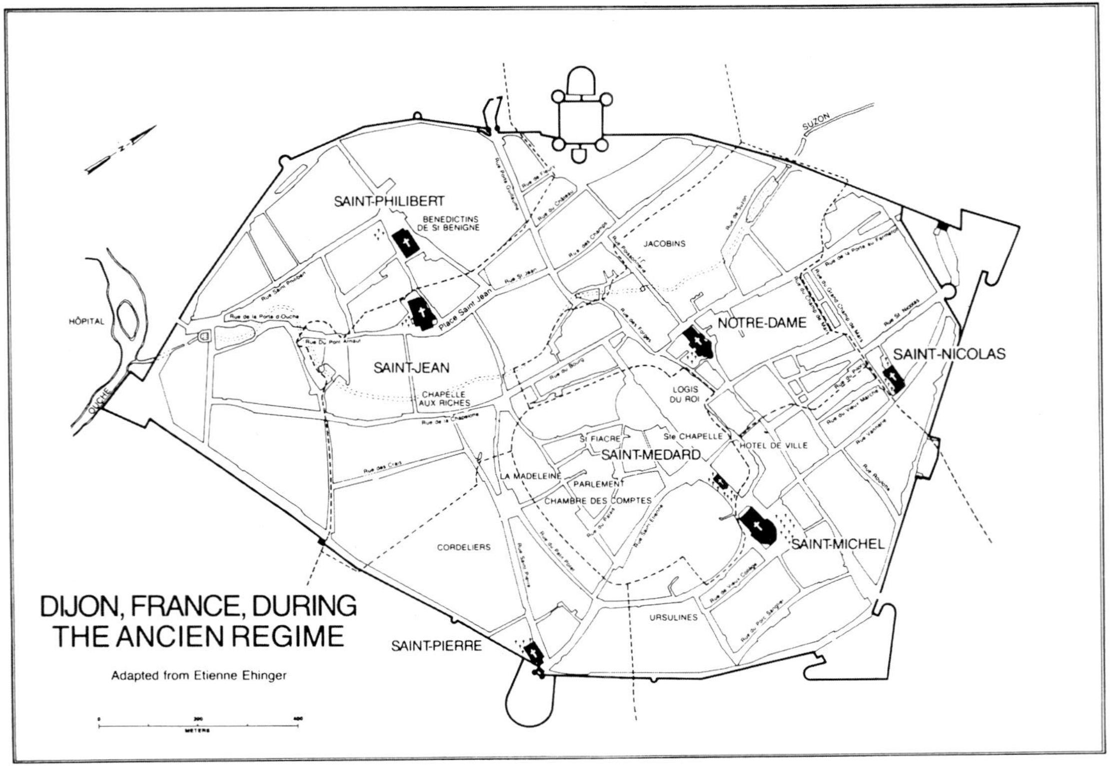

Map 2. Dijon's *ancien régime* parishes. From James R. Farr, *Hands of Honor: Artisans and Their World in Dijon, 1550–1650* (Ithaca, NY: Cornell University Press, 1988). Copyright © 1988 by Cornell University Press. Used by permission of the publisher, Cornell University Press.

avocats. Some lived alongside sovereign court magistrates in Dijon's central parishes and owned considerable estates and *rentes*. Most appear to have enjoyed a solid respectability, though some worked in obscurity and lived on the edges of poverty. Unlike the rest of the legal professions, whose places in Dijon's judicial, social, and economic hierarchies were relatively fixed, the avocats' profession was both independent and indeterminate. The avocats of Dijon, like their colleagues throughout France, saw their profession as a proving ground where individuals could use their talents and learning to gain glory, fame, and a reputation that would enable them or their descendants to obtain the highest offices in the region and the kingdom.

The Avocats' Profession

Formally defined, avocats were those who had obtained a university licence in law, undergone a character examination, and taken the avocat's oath before the Parlement of Dijon. Many who fulfilled these steps, however, had no intention of pursuing a career at the bar. Research for Paris and Toulouse indicates that only about one-tenth to one-third of those who took the oath exercised the profession.[20] The rest took the title "avocat" for a variety of reasons. After the Edict of Blois (1579), those wishing to hold a royal judicial office first had to undergo a (largely pro forma) stage at the bar. Others may have been procureurs and notaries looking to boost their careers. Finally, many were rentiers or minor officers who wanted to enjoy the prestige that came with signing their names as "avocats."[21]

For those who aspired to a career at the bar, the oath was a prelude to years of apprenticeship. As a result of French universities' heavy emphasis on Roman and canon law, young graduates were hardly prepared to begin practicing on graduation. Years of further study were essential to develop a command of the customary laws, parlementary arrêts, royal ordinances, and authoritative commentaries that made up the law in early modern France. The practical shortcomings of the university law curriculum were compounded by the widespread selling of law degrees, a practice that flourished until the Revolution.[22] To ensure the competence of its members, Dijon's bar, in concert with Parlement, imposed a mandatory multiyear apprenticeship for those wishing to practice before the city's law courts. During this *stage,* newly minted *avocats écoutants* (listening barristers) were required to attend all parlementary audiences under the supervision of senior colleagues and to familiarize themselves with the court's procedures and jurisprudence. Only after completing this apprenticeship was an avocat inscribed on the bar's *matricule* and allowed to practice within Parlement's jurisdiction.[23] These practicing avocats are the focus of this study.

According to contemporary descriptions of the profession, avocats were supposed to spend the prime of their careers as *avocats plaidants* (pleading barristers). Successful avocats earned the fame and reputation due their talents, study, and devotion to justice by displaying their oratorical skills and their command of French and Roman law in public court audiences. Unlike modern lawyers, early modern avocats, at least in principle, did not use the law to promote and defend their clients' interests. Rather, they were honorable gentlemen who spoke and wrote in the service of truth and justice. Much like their classical forebears, early modern French avocats sought to persuade their listeners to follow the correct course of action.[24] In a society that prized *l'art de bien dire,* a pleading by a renowned avocat became something of a public spectacle, with other avocats, their families, and interested persons flocking to the palais de justice to marvel at the beauty of an eloquent *plaidoyer.*[25] When age began to deprive an avocat of his memory, stamina, and strength of voice, he was supposed to enter the "honorable retirement" of an *avocat consultant.* Consulting avocats advised litigants, other avocats, and even Parlement, especially in complicated or obscure matters. Prominent *consultants* enjoyed the honor of sitting on the lower benches of Parlement; the city's six most senior *consultants* enjoyed the privilege of commitimus.[26]

Many practicing avocats, however, did not follow this classic career track. For one thing, a relatively small percentage dominated the business of pleading before Dijon's tribunals, leaving the rest to plead cases only sporadically, or not at all. Others simply lacked some of the skills needed to be a successful pleading avocat. Many of these individuals spent most of their careers as consulting avocats, a career path that, although perhaps less glorious, hardly implied obscurity. Charles Fevret praised the late-sixteenth-century avocat Jean Richard for his learning and erudition while remarking that he lacked the memory, energy, and eloquence required to be a successful pleader. François-Claude Jehannin, after an unsuccessful stint as a pleading avocat, developed a reputation for effective counsel and was nicknamed "the Papinien of Burgundy" after the legendary Roman jurist. Nicolas Perrier suffered from a speech impediment but nevertheless became one of the city's most sought-after consulting avocats in the late seventeenth century.[27]

Much like their modern counterparts, early modern avocats could use their legal training to pursue a range of professional trajectories and undertake a variety of functions. Some worked as judges in the many seigneurial and ecclesiastical jurisdictions in and around Dijon. The seigneurial justice of Magny-sur-Tille, a village 10 kilometers east of Dijon, was almost always held by an avocat from Dijon, and audiences usually took place in the avocats' hôtels. Some avocats, such as Philippe Midan, sought to accumulate multiple judgeships, both inside and outside the city. Others undoubtedly worked as informal arbitrators.[28] Avocats also served as counselors to institutions as the Estates of Burgundy and powerful noble families. Those who held these posts enjoyed considerable influence and numerous privileges, in many cases including exemption from the taille.[29]

Many of Dijon's avocats also sought to acquire lesser royal offices. In contrast with Paris, where practicing avocats could not hold office, those in Dijon could hold certain posts or perform specific functions. Jacques-Auguste de Chevanes continued to frequent the bar and developed a reputation for expertise in ecclesiastical matters while holding the office of audiencer in Parlement's chancellery. Claude Varenne became known as a leading pleader while simultaneously serving as controller in the same chancellery. Philibert de La Mare, Jehannin, Pierre Guillaume, and several others owned the office of *substitut du procureur-général* at Parlement while remaining active avocats. Charles Fevret, meanwhile, accepted a post as *secrétaire du roi au Parlement* from Louis XIII in 1630 (after refusing the offer of a counselorship) specifically because it would allow him to continue working as an avocat.[30]

Determining the exact membership of Dijon's bar for much of the seventeenth century is a difficult task. Although the avocats' Society of St. Yves kept an annual list (*matricule*) of active avocats, no copies are available before 1683.[31] Prior to this period, then, we must rely on the city's extensive taille rolls, as well marriage contracts, *inventaires après décès,* contemporary testimony, and other sources to identify Dijon's practicing avocats. An analysis of these records indicates that there were probably fifty to seventy-five active avocats in Dijon at any one time for much of the seventeenth century, and over one hundred throughout much of the eighteenth century.[32]

Like the bar of eighteenth-century Toulouse, Dijon's probably resembled a pyramid. Among the fifty to one hundred avocats active at any one time, a core of practicing avocats argued the vast majority of cases. A larger group comprised those who practiced only sporadically, or who used their legal training to act as judges, arbiters, or counselors.[33] Many "core" avocats can be identified from the testimony of contemporaries and later commentators, evidence of professional activity, and other factors such as dynastic persistence and family background. Although definitive figures are hard to come by, it is reasonable to estimate that roughly one-fourth to one-third of practicing avocats made up the core group–twelve to thirty-five at any given time. The remainder, however, should not be excluded from the ranks of active avocats. As Bell has observed, "it would be anachronistic to conclude that only those men who practiced full-time deserve treatment as full-fledged members of the profession."[34] Being an avocat was more than a simple *métier,* it was a *qualité*–a "state" of existence. This study, therefore, will examine the political experiences of all avocats active in Dijon, regardless of how frequently or in what manner they practiced law.

Those who envisioned their sons wearing avocats' robes had to start early, enrolling them by the age of eight or nine (if not earlier) in one of the many local *collèges* that had sprung up in sixteenth-century French cities.[35] In Dijon, the school of choice was the Jesuit Collège des Godrans, founded in 1581 with funds bequeathed by the Odinet Godran, a president in the Parlement of Dijon, and heavily subsidized by the municipal government. As elsewhere, the sons of Dijon's leading families (and those who aspired to enter their ranks) received an education that stressed Latin grammar, rhetoric, literature, philosophy, and history, with a small amount of Greek thrown in for good measure. The standard collège curriculum, known as the "Parisian Style" (*modus parisiensis*) centered on the writings of Cicero, Terence, Virgil, Ovid, Horace, Sallust, Livy, and other ancient authors, as well as works by more recent humanist scholars. French language and literature were not taught, and students were exposed to a minimum of history, geography, and science.[36]

From the perspective of families seeking to place their children in legal careers, royal offices and other "honorable" professions, the modus parisiensis was extremely practical. Students mastered the authors and works that formed the "culture of reference" for France's literate elites. Upper-level courses stressed eloquence and rhetoric, two important skills for future avocats. The emphasis on Latin language and literature, meanwhile, helped prepare students for the Latin-based law curricula of France's universities.[37] Avocats thus shared the educational background and moral outlook of the legal and judicial elites that were rising to preeminence across sixteenth- and seventeenth-century France and Europe. Like the judges of Dijon's royal courts before whom they argued their cases, avocats left school imbued with the values and culture of civic humanism, which, according to Georges Huppert "were drilled into memories, displayed in books, and blazoned on walls of the *collège*." The highly structured, ordered curriculum of the Parisian Style, Huppert observes, subjected students to "systematic assaults of rectitude. . . . The design of the buildings, the management of the schools, the books read in the classes all conspired together in this purposeful project, whose goal was nothing less than the nurture of a new type of man, a citizen of the Republic." It also conferred a "vaguely antique quality" to officeholding "as the only respectable position in the République in which wealth and virtue might easily be combined."[38] Inspired by the examples of classical antiquity, especially Cicero, avocats viewed knowledge as an "indispensable guide to civil life" and believed the union of eloquence and philosophy was essential to securing a just and stable political order. "An order of 'words' guaranteed by the example of Roman classicism," Marc Fumaroli observed, "would guarantee the solidity of public and moral 'things.'" Whereas seventeenth-century French ethics and philosophy increasingly counseled withdrawal from public life and promoted individualist ethics over civic virtues, Dijon's avocats continued to portray themselves in humanist terms that promoted the virtues of knowledge, persuasion, and the active pursuit of the public good. If they were not civic humanists in the classical sense, they were at the very least "civil humanists" according to Donald R. Kelley's apt definition.[39]

The prevalence of "civil humanist" and Neostoic values of discipline, hierarchy, moral probity, and the disinterested pursuit of reason and the public interest among Dijon's royal judges and avocats reflected a larger cultural shift taking place across early modern France and Europe during this period–the emergence of the "rule of law" as a core principle legitimating the distribution and deployment of state power and public authority. In the wake of the religious wars and social upheavals of the sixteenth century, William Bouwsma observed, "was a singular exaltation of law as an antidote to disorder."[40] Policing the boundaries "between the conventional world and the chaos beyond it," legal professionals emerged as agents of peace and stability, using human reason and pragmatic judgment to promise "a measure of security, both for individuals and for society as a whole."[41] "In the seventeenth century," James R. Farr has recently argued, "law was increasingly perceived by the ruling classes as the elemental substratum of a well-ordered state."[42] The consequences of this cultural shift, he argues, were not merely political but epistemological, for belief in the "rule of law" "grew from a reorientation of how men understood the meaning of order in general and their place in securing it." Judges and legal professionals such as the avocats at the heart of this study believed that adherence to legal norms and the provision of impartial justice were essential to preventing a return to the chaos and disorder that had ravaged Europe in the sixteenth century.[43] There were, to be certain, some disparities in the legal views and political outlooks of Dijon's judges and avocats that likely reflected the differences in their roles in the legal system and their positions with regard to the monarchy. As Jonathan Dewald has pointed out, judges took a more pragmatic approach to the law than avocats, who considered themselves experts in working through the law's legal complexities. Indeed, judges never explained the reasoning behind their arrêts. That was to be found in avocats' factums and plaidoyers, which circulated individually and in collected form both inside and outside the world of the palais de justice.[44] The judges' position as agents of royal authority and their property stake in their offices could also make them more conservative and less outspoken in their views on royal authority than avocats. Finally, as access to royal offices became more difficult and the robe took on increasingly aristocratic traits, royal judges came to place more value on high birth. Avocats, in contrast, continued to proclaim that their profession was open to all men of talent, as we shall see.[45]

Nonetheless, as Marcel Bouchard has pointed out, Dijon's robe and bar shared a common educational background, intellectual interests, and political concerns.[46] The differences between them were more superficial than fundamental, reflecting two facets of the same elite legal culture. "We are all in the same boat, avocats, even though our tasks are different; happy navigation is our common endeavor," declared Nicolas Brulart, Parlement's first president, during his harangue for *rentrée* of 1677.[47] Indeed, as we shall see, avocats considered themselves to be the true embodiments of this emerging legal culture and the truest champions of the "rule of law," even more so than the magistrates before whom they plead their cases. "Roman consuls sometimes stepped down from their positions to defend their friends at the bar," Pierre Legouz noted. In France, he continued, "it is often the opposite that happens . . . for it is the orators of the bar who express their ideas through the mouth of the leading magistrates whose harangues they compose."[48]

Prior to the founding of Dijon's law faculty in 1723, Dijon's aspiring avocats had to travel elsewhere to obtain their university law degrees once they completed their collège studies. No matter where they went, students followed a three-year program that focused on Roman and canon law. Training was extremely traditional and focused almost exclusively on textual exegesis, necessitating the *stage* described above. Only after the 1679 Ordinance of Blois was French law added to the curriculum and then only in the final year of study. Until the ordinance, the first year focused on Justinian's *Institutes;* and the last two years were devoted to the remainder of the *Corpus Juris Civilis* as well as to Gratian's *Decretals,* the principal canon law text. After 1679, the curriculum remained the same except for the addition of the French law course, which royal officials hoped would better prepare future avocats to use the actual law of the land. French law courses were taught in the vernacular rather than Latin and did not rely on established, authoritative texts such as the *Corpus Juris Civilis.* At the end of the third year, the student was supposed to defend his thesis publicly, though this was a mere formality.[49] Even in the late eighteenth century, French legal education remained virtually uninfluenced by contemporary intellectual movements such as Cartesian philosophy and the growing interest in natural law and public administration that swept northern Europe.[50]

On entering the profession, Dijon's avocats also joined a confraternity known as the Société de St. Yves. Founded in 1616, the société originally included procureurs, but after the latter left to form their own confraternity in 1655, the société appears to have taken on characteristics similar to the Parisian Order of Avocats.[51] Its activities ranged from the typical confraternal role of providing mutual aid to protecting the honor of the profession and its members.[52] The société also functioned as a sort of professional association, distributing printed copies of new royal edicts and even establishing an arrangement with the Parisian order allowing Dijonnais avocats to plead in the capital without first being inscribed on the Parisian tableau.[53]

In conjunction with Parlement, the société also attempted to control access to the profession. Prospective avocats had to be sponsored by an avocat with at least ten years standing and be approved by the bâtonnier. Finding a sponsor was usually not a problem, provided the candidate paid his *droit de la chapelle.* The société did try to prevent undesirables from joining its ranks, however. When Claude Ravey, who had obtained his licence after being expelled from the communauté des procureurs, attempted to take the oath, the société opposed his reception, albeit unsuccessfully.[54] Once an avocat was received, the société was responsible for verifying his status as a practicing avocat, maintaining a seniority list, and settling disputes between him and other members.[55]

The société, in tandem with Parlement, also worked to establish professional standards and to curb abuses. When judicial business stalled because of avocats' chronic absence at audiences, for example, Parlement turned to the société.[56] The société also took steps to prevent indecency and dishonesty in avocats' pleadings, tried to keep avocats from showing overt disrespect for judges, and worked to dissuade its members from signing judicial mémoires or factums they had not written.[57] Even dress was regulated by the société and Parlement. Avocats were required to wear long black robes and round bonnets at the palais de justice and to abstain from wearing lace, gold belts, or colored ribbons. Outside of court, avocats who wore "colorful or indecent" robes faced a fine of 100 livres for demeaning the dignity of the profession and its members.[58]

In spite of these activities, the Société de St. Yves never became a tightly organized, centrally run corporate body like the many guilds and professional corporations that dotted early modern France. Unlike Dijon's Community of Procureurs or even the royal courts before which the avocats practiced, the société could not formally discipline its members or represent the profession in a legally binding manner, and the société was never included in Dijon's *registres des corporations et confraternites.*[59] This is because the société was not a "corporation"–a legally constituted body responsible for representing the bar's collective interests. Rather, it was described by its members as an "order"–a free association of individuals that acted only by mutual consent of its members. As both Bell and Karpik have noted, the lack of a corporate structure and the need to act by mutual consent made the Parisian order a potent political organization during the Jansenist controversies of the early eighteenth century. At the same time, however, this flexibility also limited its ability to regulate the behavior of its members, who jealously guarded their professional independence. Avocats considered external controls on their behavior and arguments, even those imposed by other avocats, inherently incompatible with their calling to defend truth and justice as they saw fit.[60]

The avocat's independence, Lenard Berlanstein has pointed out, "was a mark of the high status of [his] profession: he was an intermediary between the law and the public."[61] Apologists emphasized that the avocats' independence, combined with their talent, unrelenting pursuit of justice, and political virtue, conferred "personal" nobility. "Who other than the avocat," François-Bernard Cocquard wrote in the early eighteenth century, "is more deserving of the *qualité* of noble, since he makes it known every day by his spirit and virtue, while the nobility that is called 'by birth' often remains buried in obscurity." An avocat, Cocquard concludes, "can always pass for a gentleman, but the reverse is not so."[62] The late-seventeenth-century avocat Nicolas Perrier asserted that "the function of the avocat is noble in and of itself," and that "as one acquires nobility by the sword, so does one acquire it through the science and function of an avocat."[63]

Avocats considered themselves equal, if not superior, to Dijon's sovereign court judges in terms of learning, merit, and probity. Cocquard repeated Loisel's early seventeenth-century dictum that "from a mediocre avocat one can make a good conseiller," and noted that "more spirit and talent is needed to compose and utter a mediocre plaidoyer than to say, coldly, in lifting one's bonnet . . . 'I am of the opinion of Monsieur So-and-so.'"[64] The avocats' sense of their professional dignity was such that the Société de St. Yves refused to send a deputation to welcome Brulart back from exile in the late 1650s because he insisted on being greeted as "monseigneur" rather than "monsieur."[65] Parlementaires regularly acknowledged the avocats' pride in their honorable calling even as they bristled at their pretensions. "You still have this advantage over us," Brulart told the avocats at the rentrée of 1666, "in that most of our activity takes place in the shadows . . . while you display openly and in plain daylight the great eloquence, erudition, and knowledge that you have acquired."[66] More than seventy-five years ago, Bouchard highlighted the avocat's ambiguous place in *Dijonnais* society, asking, "[W]hat place should we assign to the avocats, this order which was refused the highest rank but which refused to be content with the second?"[67]

Avocats prided themselves on being the heirs of Cicero and the Roman bar, and for being the tireless and selfless champions of truth, justice, order, and virtue.[68] "What is more beautiful than the profession of avocat!" Charles Fevret wrote in the mid-seventeenth century. "Its labors, its difficulties, its daily struggles which fortify the spirit and keep it always in good form." An avocat, Fevret told his son, "will remain valiant until his dying breath. . . . He has too much to do for others and for himself."[69] Nearly a half century later, the avocat-général Joseph Durand, a third-generation avocat who spent fifteen years at the bar before purchasing his office, proclaimed the avocat's profession the most honorable of all, requiring good sense, boldness, probity, eloquence, and a heroic commitment to the law–the "thorniest" and "most laborious" of the sciences.[70] The avocat, Cocquard wrote, often cannot find time to exercise all of his virtues in a single day. Avocats "defend peoples' goods, liberties, and lives, as well as their honor, which is dearer than life itself."[71] Avocats even portrayed the profession as more useful to society than the profession of arms, comparing the bar to a militia and noting that some of antiquity's greatest figures obtained glory at the bar as well on the battlefield.[72] Even Brulart pointed out that the military art was capable only of subduing those who troubled public order, whereas justice was its foundation. Indeed, Cocquard insisted, the avocat's profession was the very basis of civil society itself.[73]

These lofty ideals, of course, should not be taken as a literal description of the avocat's profession. Although the situation in Dijon did not exactly parallel that of the Parisian bar, which both Karpik and Fumaroli describe as being in a state of decline during the seventeenth century, avocats and parlementaires in Burgundy's capital also voiced their anxieties over the worsening state of professional standards and personal comportment among avocats. By the middle of the century, Charles Fevret was already lamenting the situation in his dialogue, *De claris fori burgundici,* pointing to venality, the immaturity of new avocats, and lost respect for ancient models of eloquence as main causes for the bar's decline.[74] Durand deplored the fact that the avocats of his day neglected eloquence in order to quickly learn the *routine du palais* and begin practicing, thereby sacrificing their "ambition" for glory and virtue to the "interest" of financial rewards. For Durand, this perversion of the avocat's ideal explained the "barbarity," "impoliteness," and "sterility" plaguing the bar, as well as a range of other abuses.[75] In their efforts to crack down on improper behavior among avocats, Parlement and the Sociéte de St. Yves also cited the breakdown of professional discipline and decorum.[76] The divergence between the ideals and the realities of the avocat's profession, nonetheless, does not diminish the significance of the values Dijon's avocats claimed to live by. Indeed, the avocats' professional values in many ways paralleled and reinforced the beliefs and ideals they honored as leading members of the city's notable class and municipal elite.

A Municipal Elite

Although Dijon's avocats came from a variety of familial backgrounds and financial situations, most clustered near the top of the city's socioeconomic pyramid. While not at the pinnacle of regional society, the avocats' comfortable wealth, reputable social status, and honorable profession generally placed them in the leading ranks of the city's notables. Although avocats moved with relative ease in the world of robe magistrates, royal officers, and provincial nobles, their status was based not on titles, offices, or clearly defined privileges. Instead, the avocats' status was based on more intangible factors such as talent, personal reputation, and professional expertise. Avocats, like other members of the city's municipal elite, emphasized their quality as gens de bien and sought to distinguish themselves from the uneducated, undisciplined, and potentially immoral urban masses. The avocats' ability to embody virtues of self-discipline, public service, and personal disinterestedness made them leading members of Dijon's municipal elite. Increasingly excluded from royal magistracies by the spiraling prices of venal offices, Dijon's avocats increasingly turned to the mairie to pursue their political ambitions. In the process, they became the leaders of, and spokesmen for, the city's notable class.

Although avocats boasted that their profession was open to all who possessed the requisite talent and training, the vast majority were sons of Dijon's legal professionals and royal officers. Out of a sample of 130 avocats received at the bar before 1700, over half (52.3 percent) were sons of avocats and another 23.1 percent were sons of royal officers. Most avocats thus belonged to the upper echelons of the Dijonnais notability, as is evident in their marriage patterns. The father-in-law's qualité can be determined in the cases of 58 avocats. Nearly 30 percent (29.2 percent) of these avocats married the daughter of a royal officer or seigneur, and slightly more than one-third (34.5 percent) of them married into the family of a fellow avocat. Another 13.8 percent married into bourgeois or liberal professionals' families. Only about one in four (22.4 percent) wedded the daughter of a procureur, notary, or other lesser legal professional. The avocats' honorable station in Dijonnais society is also evident in the marriages they arranged for their daughters. Out of a sample of 69 daughters of 57 different avocats, 33 (47.8 percent) married royal officers, with 18 (26.1 percent) marrying a sovereign court magistrate. Twenty-two (31.9 percent) wedded avocats, while another 7 (10.1 percent) married nobles or *seigneurs*. Only 3 (4.3 percent) avocats' daughters married lesser legal professionals, while another 4 (5.8 percent) wedded a "bourgeois." Although these numbers likely overstate the frequency with which avocats succeeded in marrying their daughters upward, they nevertheless show that the avocat's honorable status provided access to the highest levels of provincial society. Dijon's avocats, for the most part, were products of a rather close-knit group of families whose social and professional lives centered around the city's law courts and the leading elements of the urban notability.[77]

Although the glory days of the early sixteenth century–when the bar was the "vestibule" to the highest positions in justice and the royal administration–were past, the avocat's profession could still be a way station to higher offices for some families.[78] An analysis of the sons and grandsons of these

130 avocats shows that their descendants remained entrenched among the city's notables and that a considerable percentage was able to move upward socially and professionally. Of 182 known sons, the largest group (36.8 percent) pursued their fathers' profession. The remainder undertook other honorable vocations or moved up the social ladder. More than one-fourth (25.3 percent) became royal officers, with a little more than one in ten (11.5 percent) obtaining a sovereign court magistracy. Others joined the church (18.1 percent) or the military, or lived as seigneurs (3.3 percent each). Only one lived as a bourgeois and none appears to have adopted a humbler station in life, though such individuals would also have been likely to leave fewer traces for historians to track. A similar pattern is evident in the next generation as well. Just over one in five grandsons became avocats (21.8 percent). An equal number held royal office, with 15.4 percent gaining sovereign court magistracies. A larger percentage joined the military (11.5 percent) or lived as seigneurs (12.8 percent), while a slightly smaller percentage joined the church (12.8 percent). Overall, then, Dijon's avocats were established members of the city's notable class whose families had the potential to move up the ladder socially and professional in subsequent generations and rarely moved downward.[79]

The avocat's professional independence and the absence of a corporate regulatory structure resulted in wide variations of wealth. Albert Poirot's study of Parisian avocats in the late eighteenth century revealed that more than a third died with fortunes in excess of 100,000 livres, whereas a quarter left less than 15,000. In late-eighteenth-century Toulouse, the top 20 percent of the bar had fortunes in excess of 60,000 livres, whereas the bottom third owned less than 20,000 livres each.[80] The same disparities in wealth are evident in Dijon. In 1669, for instance, five avocats paid tailles of 75 livres or more, whereas fifteen paid 10 livres or less.[81] Most avocats fell in between and, like their counterparts in other cities, were "squarely in the upper middling ranks of society, better off than artisans and most tradesmen, but far below the glittering heights of the magistrature and *haute finance*."[82] James Farr has shown that procureurs were in the top quartile of the city's population throughout the seventeenth century, and most avocats probably fared better. The average avocat paid more than six and a half times the average taille in 1601. Although this ratio fell to 228 percent of average in 1690 before rebounding to just over three times the city average in the early eighteenth century, a portion of this decline can be attributed to the growing percentage of avocats who became exempt from the taille–almost one-third of avocats on the tableaux of 1690 and 1710 and close to half in 1699.[83] Most practicing avocats, then, were comfortably wealthy but not necessarily immune to financial stresses brought on by tax increases, economic downturns, and other circumstances, as we shall see.

A sampling of financial records such as marriage contracts and *inventaires après décès* also suggests that most avocats were financially secure but not wealthy. Like their colleagues in eighteenth-century Besançon and Toulouse, the average avocat probably enjoyed about one-tenth the wealth of the city's average parlementaire. Most avocats appear to have managed their wealth pragmatically. The avocat's lifestyle, Berlanstein has noted, "demonstrated a spirit of cautious spending. . . . Rich or modest, the barristers aimed for solid comfort and not much more."[84] Although some, such as Jean Guillaume, lived in impressive hôtels particuliers, most appear to have lived in houses that were spacious by the standards of the day but modest next to those of the city's sovereign court magistrates.[85] Jacques Bourée, a frequent member of the city government in the 1650s and 1660s, lived in a six-room house in Nôtre-Dame parish worth 1,900 livres that included a library, kitchen, and two bedrooms. Jean Derequeleyne's house consisted of five rooms (including an office), as well as a *grenier* and a *cave*. Chrétien Guillaume's two-story house, which included two *caves,* was valued at 4,900 livres.[86] Avocats appear to have spent their money on necessities such as food and wine; modest comforts such as furniture, tapestries, and decorations; and professional needs such as books, papers, desks, and *robes d'audience.* At his untimely death in 1655, for example, Chrétien Guillaume had a net worth of approximately 16,000 livres, which included a little more than 163 livres in silver coins and more than 700 livres worth of new and aged wine, as well as about 50 livres worth of flour. The rest of Guillaume's *meubles* consisted of kitchen supplies, clothing, a large number of chairs, numerous tapestries and curtains, three oak coffers, an oak bed, bedding, and assorted household supplies, all of which were estimated to be worth only 300 livres or so. Derequeleyne's belongings showed a similar practical bent. His *cave* contained 1,278 livres worth of new and aged wine (which may have come from his vineyards in nearby Fontaine-les-Dijon), accounting for roughly one-third of his movable belongings. The records give little sign of the kinds of conspicuous consumption and displays of wealth common among nobles and high-ranking officers during this period. Guillaume possessed only a modest library valued at 60 livres, two paintings–one of Juno, Athena, and Venus, and the other of the Four Parts of the World–worth a total of 18 livres, and some fine napkins worth a total of 27 livres. Derequeleyne's main indulgence appears to have been his many maps and paintings, including a map of Holland, several paintings of religious themes, a number of landscapes, and two portraits of Louis XIV (one with the queen). Many of the paintings were in gold frames; all of them were valued at a little more than 500 livres. He also had a library of 154 titles, most of which were legal, rhetorical, or religious works, with an estimated value of 338 livres, and two watches, including one valued at 60 livres.[87]

The avocats' conservative and practical attitudes toward wealth were also reflected in their preference for relatively secure investments, such as *rentes,* farms, vineyards, and other rural landholdings. All but roughly 1,275 livres of Chrétien Guillaume's wealth was in the form of either rentes or real property, including several plots of vines in nearby villages. Bourée died with a total worth of at least 30,000 livres, of which roughly 27,000 was in the form of rentes. He also co-owned a farm in the town of Arnay-le-Duc with his brother, which they rented to a M. Chamard. Bernard Deslandes, who died in the late 1660s, owned thirty rentes with a value of 7,526 livres; several domains that he leased out in the village of Desbarres; vines and other lands in Beaune, Pommard, Savigny, Chenôve, Bligny-sur-Beaune, and Besançon; and houses in Beaune, Rufay, and elsewhere.[88]

Many avocats did not derive the bulk of their income and wealth from professional activities. This trend was increasingly so during the latter part of century, when litigation levels declined throughout the kingdom.[89] Indeed, avocats emphasized the "disinterestedness" of their labor, noting that they offered their services freely. While avocats could receive honoraria, they insisted that these payments were gifts, not fees, and noted that avocats could not sue to recover unpaid honoraria (though at least one did try).[90] Although avocats at the top of the bar's "pyramid" undoubtedly earned sizable incomes from their professional activities, most likely earned only a modest sum.[91] The ideal of the avocat as a gentleman who used his leisure to serve justice thus corresponded at least partially with the professional reality of Dijon's bar. Most avocats drew their wealth primarily from other sources, most notably family settlements and dowries. Pierre de Villers received 30,000 livres from his father, the prominent avocat Philippe de Villers, at his marriage in 1603, including a house in Saint-Michel parish worth 8,000 livres, rentes totaling 18,000 livres, 1,000 livres in cash, and 3,000 livres to be paid in an unspecified form. Pierre's wife, the daughter of another avocat, brought a dowry of more than 34,000 livres in rentes, meubles, jewels, and various "droits paternels et maternels."[92] Philibert de La Mare, the son of a lieutenant-général in the Chancellery of Beaune, received half of his father's lands and seigneuries worth 13,400 livres, as well as 8,000 livres in rentes, rights to an inheritance at Beaune worth 5,400 livres, and 10,700 livres in "droits maternels échus." La Mare's father also agreed to pay off any debts his son incurred prior to the marriage's consummation. Although the "droits paternels et maternels" of La Mare's wife were not valued, they must have been considerable: the contract specified that the bride and groom would each contribute up to 6,000 livres to purchase meubles for their new household.[93] Not all avocats were so fortunate, however. Claude Bourrelier, the son of one of the city's best-known avocats, inherited only a small piece of land in the nearby village of Daix, three *queues* of wine from vineyards there, nine measures each of wheat and barley, one *feuille* of wine per year from a *vigneron* in Dijon, and rights to a debt of 27 livres owed by another vigneron. His wife, the daughter of a deceased avocat, brought only wedding clothes worth 120 livres and silver plate and fine napkins worth an additional 180 livres to the marriage.[94] Relative to most early modern Dijonnais, Bourrelier and his wife were hardly poor, but they were much less well off than De Villers and De La Mare. Although De Villers paid 60 livres in tailles in 1643, Bourrelier paid only 3 livres a quarter of a century later.[95]

As the seventeenth century progressed, Dijon's avocats, like the city's other legal professionals, appear to have come under mounting financial pressures resulting from higher tax burdens, a depressed economy, and declining caseloads. The city's procureurs, Farr has noted, dropped from the 87th to the 75th percentile in wealth over the course of the century.[96] The same erosion in financial status seems to have affected many avocats. In May 1669, the city pursued Bénigne Griguette for several years' worth of arrears on his tailles. Although the mairie eventually reduced his debt to 100 livres, this amount still had to be collected through a judicial seizure.[97] Between 1657 and 1678, at least six other avocats were pursued for back taxes totaling between 10 and 194 livres.[98] Others complained about excessive tax burdens and successfully petitioned for reductions. In July 1666, the mairie accepted Jean Humbelot's claims that he was being overtaxed and reduced his tax arrears to 50 livres. During the next two decades, the mairie reduced the tailles at least five other avocats.[99] Other instances suggest that many avocats felt pinched enough financially to evade their tax obligations. Three vignerons successfully sued the avocat Soyrot before the mairie in March 1666 when he failed to pay his levy for troop lodgings. In March 1674, the avocat Derequeleyne's refusal to pay an inheritance tax resulted in the seizure of his moveable goods.[100]

Despite these mounting financial pressures, avocats continued to enjoy an elevated status in local society, ranking just beneath sovereign court magistrates and above nonofficers and nonnobles in Dijon's social hierarchy.[101] Although avocats were not ennobled by law, the honor associated with their profession conferred a sort of cultural nobility that opened doors to the highest social and professional circles. Dijon's avocats prided themselves on the fact that nobles could and did exercise the profession without loss of status. They claimed that it conferred a "personal nobility" and evoked the glories of the ancients in describing their activities. "The function of avocat is noble in itself," Nicholas Perrier declared. "The avocat's function is so considerable that it cannot be subject to any charges nor to any act that derogates its honor." Cocquard evoked the status and privileges enjoyed by the Roman bar. "These Masters of the Universe," he wrote, "were not fooled when they called [the bar] the seminary of dignities; when they called its functions great, useful, necessary, praiseworthy, honorable, holy." Cocquard echoed other apologists for the avocat's profession by observing that high-ranking Roman officials considered it an honor to perform the avocat's functions and even left their magistracies or refused the consulship to pursue glory at the bar.[102]

The avocats' elevated social status, combined with their legal and rhetorical expertise, thus made them natural leaders of Dijon's urban notability.

Avocats derived their social status and authority from both their technical mastery of the law and the moral qualities associated with their supposedly tireless and disinterested pursuit of justice and the public good. Therefore, they were at the heart of an emerging legal culture that stressed the importance of the impartial and unbiased "rule of law." Although the workings of the legal system remained intractably bound up with private interests, patrimonial concerns, and profound external pressures from powerful, highly placed patrons, the norms of impersonal law and unbiased justice carried increasing cultural and ideological force during this period.[103] Indeed, Jeffrey K. Sawyer has shown how "many men trained in the law were seriously concerned about corruption and reform." Lawyers and judges, he argues, "could agonize over the complex problem of reconciling one's economic interests and one's conscience. Then as now, a self-image of the hard-working professional elite characterized men of the law, and a tone of moral superiority can be detected in the writings of many jurists."[104]

The social and moral values ascribed to the provision of impartial justice were increasingly central to the self-perception of these new legal and judicial elites and essential for legitimating their newfound power and status. Avocats thus shared the magistrates' belief that they served the "public good" by imposing discipline, hierarchy, and order on the rebellious, chaotic, and disordered society around them through their disinterested civic virtue and their commitment to the values of reason, moral probity, and the "rule of law." In return, their recognized mastery of the law and their abilities to use the disparate textual, conceptual, rhetorical, symbolic, and institutional components of this developing legal culture allowed many avocats to enjoy a much more respectable status and degree of influence than their wealth and social background might have otherwise allowed. Avocats' legal expertise, in short, enabled them to build connections with the royal judges and officers who comprised the majority of Burgundy's provincial elite. It also allowed them develop and utilize various political skills in institutions ranging from Parlement to the Estates of Burgundy to the Mairie de Dijon.

The attitudes of these legal professionals resonated with early modern elites who believed their society was "insecure, unstable, and too mobile" and that the masses they governed "were savages who had to be disciplined through laws determined by human reason."[105] The chaos engendered by the Wars of Religion and the influence of Counter-Reformation teachings led urban notables increasingly to distance themselves from the culture and behavior of their city's lower classes. Dijon's municipal elite shared the crown's obsession with reinforcing hierarchies, imposing moral and social discipline, and maintaining order and tranquility.[106] More than any other social group in the kingdom, notables found themselves on the frontline of governance. When the fragile state of order in their cities broke down, they were often the first to pay the price, from both above and below.[107]

Unlike that of nobles and royal officials, the authority of Dijon's avocats rested primarily on their personal qualities rather than any fixed powers or social rank.[108] In their minds, their legal expertise entitled them to participate in local governance. The Romans called avocats "the Authors of the Laws, Legislators, Ministers of the Republic, Fathers of the *Patrie* . . . Honored, Magnificent, Counts, Most Enlightened, Most Noble, Friends of the Prince, and even Kin of the Emperor," Cocquard noted. Avocats "ceaselessly employ law and reason" to reduce the pretensions of the great, to protect widows and orphans, to combat crime, and "to defend people's goods, liberties, [and] lives, and even their honor." The avocat's profession, Durand noted in the late seventeenth century, had long been the principal occupation of those who aspired to magistracies and dignities, and its current state of decline was attributable to the exclusion of avocats from political life.[109] Humanist beliefs in the political benefits of reason and persuasion were also cited to justify the avocat's political vocation. Influenced by Cicero and the Stoics, contemporaries believed the "virtuous orator" benefited a political community by persuading his listeners to pursue the causes of truth, order, and the public good.[110] "The orator," Durand claimed, "is still considered the voice of the people and the refuge of individuals," while the jurisconsult was "the oracle of his *pays* and the counsel of its citizens." Politics required eloquence, and the eloquent person was, by nature, a political one. "[W]ith the arms of reasoning and speech," Durand noted, avocats "fight before tribunals, sometimes for the preservation of goods or lives, and other times for the defense of honor and liberty." As the defenders of public order and tranquility, he observed, avocats merited the highest rank in "well-ordered states."[111]

The avocat thus incarnated many of the moral and political virtues embraced by Dijon's municipal elite. "Independence was only acquired and maintained by virtue," Karpik has noted, and only the avocat's "passion for the public good" enabled him to triumph over selfish interests.[112] Avocats were thus seen as defenders of social order, moral rectitude, and the cause of justice at a time when urban elites were obsessed with protecting a fragile social and moral order they believed was constantly threatened by those who could not contain their desires, ambitions, and interests. In a 1657 speech to the bar, parlement's First President Brulart told the avocats, "Justice has impressed upon you an implacable hatred against violence and tyranny, and she uses your mouths as eloquent organs with which to reestablish the truth and to confound vices." A few years later, he observed that "the security of states, the protection of the great, the defense of the weak, *honnêteté* in morals and all conditions" were the fruits of the avocats' labors on behalf of justice.[113] The avocat's disinterestedness and his constant self-sacrifice in the name of justice made him a quasi-sacred defender of the public good. Brulart cited the avocat's "assiduous and difficult service" to the cause of justice, while Cocquard traced the profession's roots back to Christ, who "deigned to make himself the avocat of the human race before God." Elsewhere, Cocquard noted that the avocat tirelessly "consecrates his ministry to public and individual needs, signaling every day the talents of a spirit regulated by the virtues of the soul.[114]

Apologists for the profession not only lauded avocats' personal and professional qualities, they also complained that the venality of offices increasingly excluded avocats from magistracies and other public charges to which they had once been entitled–charges they believed they merited more than those who now purchased them. "We no longer live in those times when men are sought out for offices because of their merit and valor," the Parisian avocat Antoine Loisel wrote in the early seventeenth century. Now those who could not use their wealth to advance themselves "stagnate in the dust of the palais."[115] Nearly a century later, Durand lamented that gold and silver "open the door to magistracies and dignities that were once purchased only with learning and virtue."[116] In the face of their exclusion from many sovereign court offices, Parisian avocats turned to the royal court to gain notice for their literary and rhetorical activities.[117] Dijon's avocats, in contrast, turned to an alternative institution to pursue their political interests, the Mairie de Dijon. Before looking at the avocats' prominence at the mairie and the city council's reliance on their legal, rhetorical, and political skills, however, we must first examine the mairie's extensive offices and jurisdictions in the first decades of the seventeenth century.

The Mairie de Dijon

Dijon's municipality traced its powers back to a charter granted by Duke Eudes III of Burgundy and confirmed by the French king Philip Augustus in 1183. By the end of the fifteenth century, the commune held the seigneurial rights of the viscounty of Dijon, exercised first-instance jurisdiction over most civil and criminal matters in the city and its banlieue, regulated commerce and other aspects of urban life, managed the collection and expenditure of certain tax revenues, and supervised the city's militia and defense. These powers were preserved when Dijon recognized Louis XI as its sovereign after the death of Charles the Bold in 1477. Although Parlement began sending deputies to observe the annual mayoral elections in 1559, the sovereign court never established firm control over the municipality, as became evident during the Wars of Religion. In 1579, the mairie acquired the moribund royal prévôté, giving it the power to inflict the death penalty. When Dijon opened its gates to Henri IV's armies in May 1595, it did so only after Henri promised that the municipality's cherished privileges would remain intact.[118] The Dijonnais, as one of Henri's advisors remarked, "were particularly devoted to their privileges."[119]

The mairie's most important officer was the vicomte-mayeur, who prior to 1611 was elected annually by all male heads of household. After this date, only those who paid 4 livres per year in tailles for three consecutive years were eligible to vote, although it appears that others continued to participate in the elections as well.[120] The vicomte-mayeur presided over the city council and had considerable patronage powers, including the right to nominate six échevins for retention as *anciens*. He also named lieutenants to staff the mayoral court and filled other minor posts. The mayor held the city's seals and insignia, guarded the keys to the city gates, and commanded the urban militia in the absence of the royal governor and the lieutenant-géneral. The mayor of Dijon was also ex officio president of the Third Estate of Burgundy and a permanent member of the chambre des élus. By the early seventeenth century, the mayor's office was so important that individuals could serve no more than two consecutive terms, after which they could not be returned to office for three years.[121]

Joining the mayor were twenty échevins who were selected annually by the outgoing city council.[122] To ensure continuity, six échevins were continued each year, if they had not already served more than two consecutive terms. Anciens were nominated by the new mayor and selected by the outgoing échevins, who could substitute their own choices. Fourteen new échevins were then selected according to a formula that fixed the representation of the city's seven parishes.[123] As representatives of the urban community, échevins performed a wide range of duties, sometimes at their own expense. Their oath required them "to well and loyally guard and help to guard, with all of their power, the rights, privileges, franchises, and liberties of [Dijon] without hindering them in any possible manner."[124] This meant defending the city's interests when dealing with the king, provincial governors, Parlement, and others. Collectively, the échevins issued ordinances concerning public works, urban commerce (especially the sale of bread and wine), *la police* (public order and morality), municipal finances, public health and safety, and any other issue that might affect "le bien public." Individually, échevins were charged with overseeing the city's professions, sanitation, defense, and record keeping. Échevins also acted as intermediaries between their parishes and the mairie, collecting information, helping to draw up taille rolls, overseeing the potentially unstable world of cabarets and hotels, and ensuring the execution of municipal and royal ordinances.[125]

Aiding the mayor and échevins in their functions were the secretary, receiver, and the *procureur-syndic*. The duties of the municipal secretary and receiver need no further elaboration here. Neither appears to have been particularly influential, but both posts were lucrative enough to have been sold off in the early seventeenth century. The procureur-syndic, on the other hand, continued to be chosen annually by the mayor (subject to confirmation by the échevinage), and remained a significant figure in municipal politics. Chosen from the city's procureurs, the syndic and his substitutes recommended ordinances and other actions to the city council, supervised the municipal watch, prosecuted miscreants before the mayoral court, executed judicial seizures of goods, and drew up the civil documents that fell under the mairie's jurisdiction. The syndic also acted as the city's official solicitor, managing the technical aspects of the mairie's constant flurry of lawsuits.

As the city's solicitor, the syndic frequently sought the aid of the *conseils et avocats de la ville de Dijon*. The number of conseils was theoretically limited to four (six after 1649), but the mairie often employed more.[126] Appointed for life, the conseils were established avocats who had distinguished themselves at the hôtel de ville and/or the bar. In return for a 50 percent taille reduction, exemption from militia service, an annual honorarium of five livres, and fees ranging from a few to 100 or more livres per year, the conseils performed the bulk of the mairie's legal work. They advised the syndic and city council on lawsuits, wrote mémoires and factums, and pled for the city before Parlement and other tribunals.[127] The conseils also served as official advisors and were summoned to all council meetings and assemblies where important matters were discussed. Although the conseils lacked any formal powers, their legal expertise, familiarity with municipal affairs, lengthy tenure, and considerable influence made them important figures in Dijonnais politics.

Urban defense and the maintenance of order were ensured by the parish-based *milice bourgeois*. Parish officers–captains, lieutenants, and ensigns–generally served until death, resignation, or (more rarely) destitution. They commanded sizable contingents of armed men, marched at the head of their parishes in public processions, and were highly visible local figures who attended mass and dinner every Sunday with the mayor. They participated in city council deliberations concerning defense and public safety, and could bring disturbers of the peace before the mayor or his lieutenants for trial.[128] Unlike many other cities, where urban militias were in a state of decline, Dijon's frontier location meant that parish officers continued to exercise important and highly sensitive functions in the early seventeenth century.

Civil and criminal justice within the city and its immediate surroundings fell under the jurisdiction of Dijon's mayoral court, and the mayor and échevins regularly heard cases during their audiences.[129] For the most part, however, justice was administered by the *lieutenants de la mairie,* who were nominated annually by the mayor. Lieutenants had to be Catholic and hold a university law degree; they also had to have already taken the avocat's oath.[130] Most were young avocats at the beginning of their careers, and a 1645 deliberation noted that they were named, in part, "to become familiar with and capable in affairs of legal practice and the instruction of civil and criminal cases."[131] Quite a few also had ties to the incumbent mayor, échevins, or other prominent local figures. To ensure that young avocats had an opportunity to enjoy this judicial apprenticeship, the mairie in 1645 began limiting lieutenants to three consecutive terms, after which point they could not serve for three years.[132] Lieutenants heard cases and rendered judgment on minor ones that needed no further inquiry. Other instances required the mayor's presence for a judgment to be pronounced. Lieutenants were allowed to collect fees from parties in all but the most insignificant cases, but they appear to have received no other payments or privileges.[133] Nevertheless, the lieutenants appear to have been a significant patronage resource, as can be seen in the dramatic expansion in their numbers from two in the early years of the seventeenth century to as many as twenty-five in the mid 1660s, despite attempts by Parlement and the Bailliage to impose limits.[134]

The mairie's extensive authority and considerable autonomy had two significant consequences for the political participation of Dijon's avocats in the first half of the seventeenth century. To perform its many functions effectively, the mairie needed individuals with the necessary wealth, status, education, and legal training to staff positions ranging from échevin to lieutenant de la mairie. At the same time, the mairie's wide-ranging jurisdictions placed it in chronic conflict with Dijon's other institutions, which often challenged the mairie's authority and sought to undermine it. These conflicts will be examined in greater detail in the chapters that follow. For the moment, it is important to note that the mairie depended on the avocats in its ranks to defend its jurisdictions and autonomy from "encroachments" by other authorities. Dijon's mairie thus relied heavily on the city's avocats, both to carry out its day-to-day operations and to defend its position in the complex web of authorities that made up the early modern French state. The avocats, in turn, depended on the mairie to provide the opportunities to participate in local governance to which they believed themselves entitled by virtue of their professional "nobility" and their status as leading members of the municipal elite.

The Avocats and the Mairie

Dijon's avocats were convinced that their professional training and personal qualities made them "political men" par excellence. By the late sixteenth century, however, the soaring prices of most royal offices placed them beyond the reach of most avocats. The offices of the Mairie de Dijon, which were filled through election and cooptation, by contrast, remained open to avocats (and other notables with the requisite talent, merit, and connections) throughout the first half of the seventeenth century. Avocats thus turned to the hôtel de ville to realize their political ambitions and to reaffirm their status, to the point that Henri Drouot could describe the late-sixteenth-century mairie as "the avocats' local dictatorship."[135] The city government, meanwhile, profited from the avocats' expertise in law, rhetoric, and the institutional and informal workings of the early modern French state. The relationship between Dijon's avocats and the mairie prior to 1668 was thus a symbiotic one, as the avocats helped the mairie carry out its many functions while also working to protect its increasingly contested jurisdictions and autonomy. It is hardly a surprise, then, that Dijon's avocats were a large and growing presence at the hôtel de ville and played a leading role in municipal politics throughout the first half of the seventeenth century.

The careers of two individuals illustrate how the legal and rhetorical expertise of Dijon's avocats enabled the mairie to perform its many functions and defend its contested jurisdictions. The son of a greffier and procureur, Etienne Bréchillet was received at the bar in 1610 and entered the hôtel de ville roughly a decade later as a lieutenant de la mairie. In 1626, he was selected as an échevin from St.-Michel parish and was twice retained as an ancien, serving as *garde des évangiles* in 1628. He served six more terms as échevin, including another three-year stint in the late 1630s, and was named conseil de la ville in 1629. Bréchillet's political career prospered in all political conditions and he appears to have enjoyed the trust and respect of a broad cross-section of the municipal elite. At the height of the Dijonnais Fronde, for instance, Bréchillet was named to the échevinage by the outgoing Condéan regime and was one of the few retained when the anti-Condéans installed a new city council a few months later. Bréchillet helped design the Grand Condé's entry ceremony in 1648, but also welcomed Condé's successor (and soon-to-be enemy of his clientele), the duke of Epernon, on behalf of the mairie when he first arrived at Dijon.[136]

During his many years at the hôtel de ville, Bréchillet's legal skills were put to use in a number of ways. When Louis XIII announced his visit to Dijon in 1629, Bréchillet was charged with drawing up a list of the city's privileges for ratification. The same year, he helped write legal briefs for a lawsuit against Dijon's *patissiers* at the Chamber of Accounts.[137] As conseil, he advised the city on legal matters ranging from its judicial rights over the nearby towns of Fontaine-les Dijon and Chenôve, disputes over the collection of the local wine tax, and lawsuits against the abbot of St.-Bénigne and the city's notaries. He also provided written plaidoyers for the city's lawsuit against the merchant judges, or *juges-consuls,* and wrote at least two *conclusions definitives* for criminal trials held at the Mairie.[138]

Bréchillet was also active as a negotiator, lobbyist, and spokesman for the mairie. He was one of the city's two deputies to the provincial estates in 1626, though he lost his bid to speak for the city. The following year, he was part of a deputation sent to Paris to lobby (unsuccessfully) against the exile of the Chamber of Accounts to Autun. Despite his modest background, Bréchillet was also chosen to present the city's gift of a diamond cross to Louis XIII and to address him on the city's behalf during his royal entry in 1629. When the city council learned that Louis was displeased with this gift, Bréchillet was dispatched to Beaune and then Grenoble to present the king with another. During his journeys, which also took him to Valence and Paris, Bréchillet met with Louis, Richelieu, and Marillac to press for ratification of the city's privileges and to lobby for the continuation of the octrois on salt, wheat, and iron.[139] Nearly a decade later, Bréchillet won Condé's support for Parlement's return after an outbreak of plague. In 1651, Bréchillet presented the city's case for the demolition of the Château de Dijon to the provincial Estates.[140]

In addition to defending the city government's interests before the monarchy and other institutions, Bréchillet was a frequent spokesman for the mairie to the general populace. As garde des évangiles in 1628, he addressed the electoral assembly on the evils of electoral "*brigues et monopoles*." He designed the *entrées* of Louis XIII and the Grand Condé in 1629 and 1648, as well as other festivities, such as the fireworks for the majority of Louis XIV.[141] Bréchillet also wrote several pieces for the *mère folle,* a "misrule" group of notables and middling inhabitants who performed comedic plays during Carnival and other important occasions. The plays, written in a mixture of Burgundian *patois* and French, were a unique opportunity to translate the urban elite's philosophy into the terms of the city's lower classes.[142]

Little is known about Jacques Rousseau's background, though he may have been the son of the Master of Accounts Charles Rousseau. This would explain his rapid entrance into the municipal government soon after his reception at the bar around 1641. During the 1640s, Rousseau served five years as a lieutenant and was also named conseil de la ville–apparently with the support of the future Grand Condé.[143] He was not selected to the échevinage, however, until the mairie was controlled by the opponents of Condé's former clients. After being named échevin in June 1657, Rousseau served three consecutive terms and was named garde des évangiles in 1658 and 1659. Although Rousseau never again sat on the city council, he remained conseil de la ville until his death in 1671. Unlike Bréchillet, Rousseau also sought office outside the mairie, purchasing a position as *substitut du procureur-général au parlement* in 1657.

Unlike Bréchillet, Rousseau does not appear to have been a major spokesman for the municipal regime; most of his significant work for the mairie took place during his three terms as échevin. Rousseau was an extremely active deputy, lobbyist, and negotiator who traveled considerably to maintain the city's relationship with the governor, to pursue its interests at the royal court, and to oversee its many lawsuits before various tribunals. When Epernon's son died in February 1658, Rousseau and another avocat were sent to convey the city's condolences. While at Paris, they tended to the city's lawsuits at the Parlement of Paris and the royal council, requested letters renewing the city's octrois, and successfully lobbied Epernon to restore the échevinage, which had been temporarily reduced to six, to its traditional size of twenty.[144] In June 1657, Rousseau was part of a deputation that asked Epernon to intervene with the élus in a dispute over the taille. When the élus attempted to exclude the mayor from the chambre des élus the following year, Rousseau and three others met with the chancellor when he passed through the city. By 1659, the conflict had led to a lawsuit at Paris, and Rousseau was sent to lobby the *trésorier de l'épargne* for his support.[145] During his three years as échevin, Rousseau also made repeated trips to Paris and Rouen to manage the city's lawsuits against (among others) the heirs of the abbots of St.-Bénigne and St.-Etienne, the city's privileged inhabitants, the Ursulines, the widows of the city's huissiers, the city government of Châlon, and a certain Sieur Baudot, who had insulted the city magistrates. Rousseau obtained consultations, had factums published, sought to have cases evoked to more favorable jurisdictions, secured favorable arrêts, and even convinced Condé to mediate some of the more intractable disputes shortly after his restoration as governor in 1660. For good measure, Rousseau used some of his time in Paris in an attempt to have Dijon exempted from the taille in return for an annual payment, though this ultimately proved fruitless.[146]

Given the mairie's ample need for the avocats' legal and rhetorical skills, both for its day-to-day operations and to defend against encroachments on its political privileges, it is not surprising that avocats occupied a significant and growing percentage of seats on the city council prior to 1668. Avocats were naturally suited to be lieutenants de la mairie and the conseils de la ville and dominated in those offices, where their legal expertise was indispensable. For many avocats, the post of lieutenant could be an important stepping stone to further municipal offices. More than 41 percent of those who served at least one term as lieutenant between 1595 and 1660 became échevins prior to 1668, and two-thirds of the 145 avocats who became échevins during this period had prior service as lieutenants. If the office of lieutenant was a stepping stone, then posts as conseils de la ville were rewards for service to the city: most conseils were experienced avocats who had already served as échevin or mayor.[147]

Avocats also made up a significant percentage of those holding leading positions at the mairie prior to 1668. As table 1.1 shows, avocats were the single most widely represented group among the 1,398 échevins who served during this period, accounting for more than 31 percent of those who held the office. Moreover, avocats held an increasing number of positions in the échevinage as the century progressed. Table 1.2 illustrates that the city council contained only three or four avocats per year immediately after the Wars of Religion, when many *ligueur* avocats would have been excluded from office. By the 1630s, however, members of the bar often made up a sizeable plurality of échevins and in some years even comprised a majority of the échevinage.[148]

Table 1.1. Dijon's échevins, by *qualité* (1596–1667)

Qualité	Number	Percent
Avocats	442	31.6
Royal officers	184	13.2
Sovereign court	4	0.3
Inferior court	74	5.3
Financial	106	7.6
Liberal professions	50	3.6
Other legal	235	16.8
Bourgeois*	306	21.9
Merchants	116	8.3
Other	39	2.8
Unknown	26	1.9
Total	1398	100

* Includes individuals listed as "*honnorables hommes.*"
Source: AMD B-235–B-306

Table 1.2. Percentage of échevinage held by avocats (1595–1670)

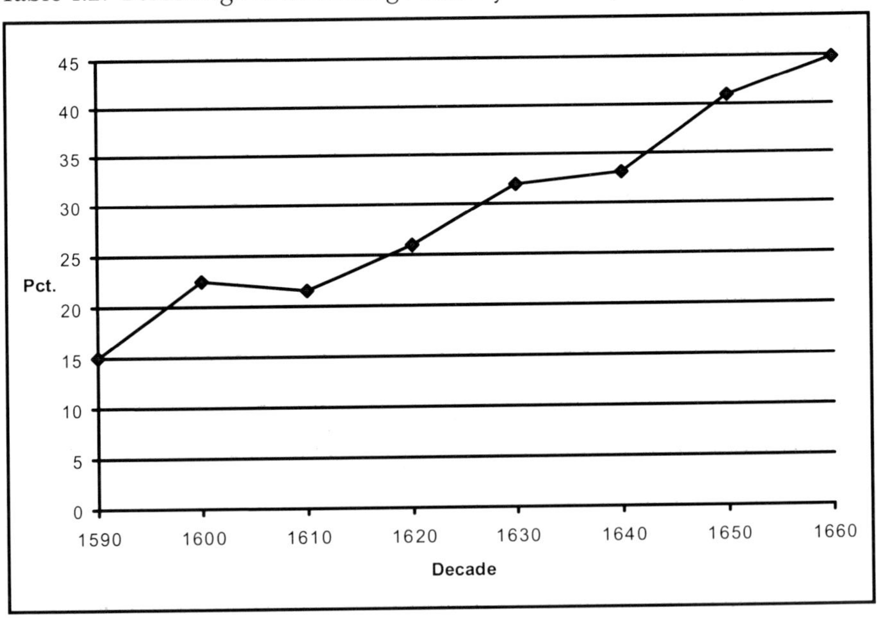

Note: Decade marked 1590 begins in 1595.
Source: AMD B-234–B-307

The thirty-eight individuals who held the post of mayor between 1595 and 1670 formed an elite group in which royal officers outnumbered avocats.[149] Nonetheless, Dijon's avocats were well represented in the city's most important office. Nearly one in three vicomte-mayeurs prior to 1668 was an avocat, and avocats served more than one-third of all mayoral terms during this period. Moreover, avocats often headed the hôtel de ville at moments of crisis and political instability. Bernard Coussin was mayor in 1599 when Parlement attempted to undermine the city's traditional electoral privileges. Following the death of the controversial mayor Chrétien Le Masque in 1608, the city council turned to the avocat Jean Defrasans to complete his term. Bénigne Euvrard headed the mairie during the Lanturelu revolt in 1630, which temporarily cost the city its political privileges. When these were restored in 1631, the first mayor chosen was Defrasans's son, Jacques, who was so effective that Burgundy's new governor, the prince of Condé, personally asked Parlement to allow him a third consecutive term, one of only two times the two-term limit was violated prior to 1668. In all, the younger Defrasans would be elected mayor eight times before dying in office in April 1663. At the height of the Fronde, the rival factions chose the respected avocat François Malteste as a compromise mayor. In a similar vein, two-thirds of the nine individuals named *commis à la magistrat* by the échevins to complete the term of a mayor who had died or was otherwise unable to complete his term were avocats. As with the échevins, the presence of avocats in Dijon's highest municipal office increased after 1630. Prior to this year, only five of twenty-four vicomte-mayeurs were avocats (20.8 percent), and these individuals filled only 30.1 percent of mayoral terms. After 1631, however, eight of eighteen mayors (44 percent) were avocats, and members of the bar filled almost half (48.7 percent) of all mayoral terms, the same percentage as the nine royal officers who served as mayor during this period (table 1.3).

Scarcely a dozen avocats donned the vicomte-mayeur's robe from 1595 to 1668, but almost three times as many did assume the mairie's second most important position, the garde des évangiles. The garde, who held the Gospels and other symbols of the mayoralty, was elected annually by the outgoing échevins to assure the interim between the end of the mayor's term (usually around 14 June) and the selection of a new échevinage (usually on 23 June). For this ten-day span, the garde filled the mayor's functions, presiding over city council meetings, judging cases, and, perhaps most important, overseeing the mayoral elections and the selection of the new city council. Although most gardes fulfilled their mandates without incident, the post was a sensitive one. Gardes directed the municipal government at the most delicate time of the city's political year. The smooth transition of the municipal regime could depend on their ability to insure the peaceful operation of the electoral process. When election results were disputed, gardes could remain in office until the matter was resolved.[150] They also had to take the lead in

Table 1.3. *Qualités* of vicomte-mayeurs and commis à la magistrat (1595–1670)

	Number	Percent	Terms	Percent
Avocats	12	31.6	26.5	34.2
Royal officers	19	50	43.5	56.1
Sovereign court	10	26.3	19	24.5
Inferior court	5	13.2	15.5	20
Financial	5	10.5	9	11.6
Liberal professions	1	2.6	0.5	0.6
Other legal	1	2.6	0.5	0.6
Bourgeois*	2	7.9	5	6.4
Merchants	2	5.3	1.5	1.9
Total	38	100	77.5†	100

Note: All partial terms = 0.5.
* Includes individuals listed as "*honnorables hommes.*"
† In 1608–9, both the mayor and one commis à le magistrat died in office, meaning that three individuals held the city's chief magistracy. All three have been credited with serving half a term.
Source: AMD B-234–B-307

defending the city's privileges against Parlement and the bailliage, which occasionally sought to take advantage of this interim period to challenge the Mairie's authority and autonomy.[151]

The post of garde des évangiles, even more than that of échevin, was dominated by members of the bar. As table 1.4 indicates, 54.7 percent of gardes between 1595 and 1668 were avocats, whereas just over 17 percent were royal officers. Here, too, the avocats' control grew markedly. After 1631, 82 percent of gardes were avocats; no other profession had more than two individuals hold the post. The powers and symbols of Dijon's highest office were thus frequently in the hands of the city's avocats during the first seven decades of the seventeenth century; in sensitive or troubled times, Dijon's municipal elite often placed their trust in the political skills of a member of the bar.

Although no one year can be described as representative, the mairie's average composition during this period highlights the avocats' importance. The vicomte-mayeur was likely to be a royal officer, though the odds that an avocat would be in charge of the hôtel de ville were hardly insignificant. An avocat would likely be responsible for overseeing the selection of a new mairie and ensuring the smooth transition from one regime to the next. In

Table 1.4. *Qualités* of gardes des évangiles (1595–1668)

	Number	Percent	Terms	Percent
Avocats	35	54.7	41	56.9
Royal officers	11	17.2	13	18.1
Sovereign court	2	3.1	2	2.8
Inferior court	6	9.4	7	9.7
Financial	3	4.7	4	5.6
Liberal professions	1	1.6	1	1.4
Other legal	7	10.9	7	9.7
Bourgeois*	9	14.1	9	12.5
Merchants	1	1.6	1	1.4
Total	64	100	72	100

* Includes individuals listed as "*honnorables hommes.*"
Source: AMD B-234–B-306

an average year, the six avocats who sat on the city council were an influential group, capable of dominating debates and handling much of the mairie's most sensitive business. Their influence would be compounded at important sessions by the reputation and expertise of the conseils de la ville, who generally numbered six in spite of the Parlement's repeated ordinances. At times, several more avocats might also be present in their capacity as parish officers. Finally, the mairie would employ roughly twelve young and less prominent avocats as lieutenants to staff the mayoral court. Many of these lieutenants, in turn, could be expected to enter the échevinage and continue the avocats' domination of the mairie.

The importance of the mairie and its offices to Dijon's avocats can be seen in the latter's willingness to risk professional repercussions for their actions as municipal officers. Disputes between Parlement and the hôtel de ville frequently put avocats in the cross-fire. Parlement forbade Mayor Bernard Coussin to exercise his functions as an avocat in retaliation for his opposition to the court's plan's to change the procedures for electing the vicomte-mayeur in 1599. Three decades later, Parlement prohibited avocats and procureurs who were serving as échevins from practicing their professions before the court in retaliation for the mairie's attempts to prevent the Chamber of Accounts' exile. In the early 1650s, meanwhile, Antoine Calon was similarly prohibited from pleading before the court after publicly protesting Parlement's registration of a royal edict declaring his friend Marc-Antoine Millotet ineligible to run for mayor.[152]

Ironically, the same factors that motivated early seventeenth-century avocats in their tenacious defense of the mairie's authority and autonomy sometimes brought them into conflict with the city council. Their belief in their "personal nobility" and the superiority of their profession prompted several precedence disputes at the hôtel de ville. The most significant and protracted of these occurred in 1633 when the Order of Avocats filed a lawsuit at Parlement claiming precedence at public events for all avocats over échevins who were not members of the bar. Although Mayor Jacques Defrasans and the five avocats serving as échevins denied any knowledge of the lawsuit, neither they nor the eight conseils de la ville would agree to take up the mairie's cause. Only when compelled by Parlement did the senior conseil, Antoine Changenet, agree to assist the procureur-syndic. Not surprisingly, the mairie appears to have lost the case.[153] In the late 1640s, a precedence conflict arose between the conseils de la ville and the échevinage that ultimately required the Grand Condé's intervention.[154] Finally, in June 1658, a protracted precedence conflict broke out when the médecin Guibaudet proposed ranking the large number of first-time échevins selected that year according to the traditional criterion of marriage date. The avocat Bénigne Boullier protested that "neither sieur Guibaudet nor any other doctor should proceed or claim a place that is not behind all the avocats of the Chamber." Avocats, Boullier asserted, "must proceed médecins at all assemblies." Three years later, the issue remained unresolved and when the marriage date standard was again proposed, the avocat Jean Derequeleyne walked out of the chamber in protest, later informing the council that he would appeal the proposed decision with the Order of Avocats' support. Although the final outcome of the dispute is difficult to determine, the rolls of échevins from 1662 until the reorganization in 1668 generally list avocats ahead of other échevins, with the exception of royal officers.[155] Ordinarily, the municipal government relied on the avocats in its ranks to organize and articulate its resistance to external "encroachments" on its rights and jurisdictions. When the avocats turned against the mairie, however, the latter found that the former could utilize the ancien régime's legal institutions and channels of informal influence against it just as successfully.

In the end, however, such disputes were never a veritable threat to the mairie's place in the early modern French state. Avocats might quarrel about their status and seek to assert their preeminence, but they were also dependent on the mairie and its offices. The avocats' conflicts with the mairie were, above all, signs of the city government's importance to the members of the bar, who did not try to diminish its independence or prerogatives. On the contrary, the avocats relied on the political opportunities and affirmation of status that accompanied municipal offices, while the mairie benefited from the avocats' legal knowledge, rhetorical abilities, and expertise as the "institutional technicians" of the early modern French state.

Politics in seventeenth-century France primarily took the form of lawsuits and legal arguments over privileges, jurisdictions, and precedents. Such disputes occurred before the kingdom's many legal tribunals, which were the French state's principal governmental institutions. Contests of authority and competing claims over the legitimate exercise of public power were also played out in personal interactions among social and political elites. The early modern French state's ambiguous and fluid jurisdictional boundaries and procedures thus placed particular importance on the legal, rhetorical, and political skills associated with the avocat's profession. Avocats were the technical experts of this creaky, often confusing, system and their familiarity with the arcana of French law and the eloquence of classical antiquity enabled them to manipulate France's legal system and informal patron-client networks. Although the venality of offices barred many avocats from the high-ranking sovereign court posts to which they once aspired, Dijon's avocats found they could exercise the civic humanist virtues of learning, eloquence, and active pursuit of the public good through Dijon's powerful and largely autonomous municipal government. The political opportunities provided by the Mairie also enabled Dijon's avocats to demonstrate their status as leading members of the municipal elite and their continued membership in the "political nation."[156] A sort of symbiosis thus developed between Dijon's leading avocats and the hôtel de ville. The mairie's effectiveness as a local governing body depended increasingly on the avocats' legal skills. Defense of the mairie's jurisdictions against challenges by the city's other authorities, meanwhile, came to rely on the avocats' ability to use legal procedures and rhetorical appeals to frustrate "encroachments" on the city's privileges. Members of the bar became increasingly prominent within the municipal regime, occasionally provoking conflict with other members of the municipal elite. Ultimately, however, the prevalence of avocats at the mairie is one reason that Dijon successfully maintained most of its privileges intact at a time when many other French cities saw theirs whittled away. The next chapter will examine at greater length the avocats' role in using the institutional and informal networks of the ancien régime state to protect a municipal political system that ensured the authority of Dijon's mairie and the urban notables who staffed it, as well as the gradual transformation of this system during the first half of the seventeenth century.

Chapter 2

The Avocats and the Politics of Local Privilege (1595–1648)

At the local level, the ancien régime French state was embodied primarily in the panoply of royal, seigneurial, municipal, and clerical law courts that dotted rural and (especially) urban communities. This fact had significant consequences for early modern French politics. David Parker has noted the period's "all-pervasive legalism," marked by "a constant preoccupation with the extent and limits of the liberties of the subject as sanctified by custom."[1] Even at the height of Louis XIV's reign, Parker argues, contemporaries viewed royal authority primarily in terms of distributive justice. The main obligations of the king and the royal council were "to ensure a fair and proper distribution of justice, and the harmonious operation of legal procedures." Although the legal system and the state were hardly autonomous, they were also not entirely captive to the interests of the ruling classes. Rather, they were "a mechanism for conducting and regulating the incessant struggles for power, status, and wealth among the great families, clienteles, and corporations that dominated French society."[2] French law and legal institutions, in short, were an indispensable source of legitimacy for virtually all political actions.

At the local level, the early modern French state was also characterized by a bewildering complex of overlapping jurisdictions and institutional rivalries. Disputes over jurisdictional boundaries and sociopolitical status were endemic in a political system whose framework had been cobbled together from widely disparate local institutions, royal innovations, and temporary expedients implemented over several centuries. New offices were created with jurisdictions similar to those of old ones that were not abolished. Administrative institutions exercised judicial functions, while judicial companies had administrative powers. Broadly worded charters and vague legal customs meant that several authorities could usually claim jurisdiction over any given matter. Individuals and institutions rarely enjoyed unquestioned and unrivaled power in any domain. Political authority in France's urban centers was divided, uncoordinated, and ambiguous.[3]

At the level of municipal government, then, the French state in the early seventeenth century was marked by "[a]n uncertainty about who should obey whom in what circumstances." Sharon Kettering, for one, has compared urban centers to "living political organisms." "Within a framework of national, customary, and local law" she says, political life "ebbed and flowed around the governors, intendants, estates, sovereign courts, nobles, and municipal officials in a bewildering complexity." Cities were thus subject to frequent "crises of command" that could lead to paralysis, as competing jurisdictions faced down each other in contests of authority.[4]

Overlapping jurisdictions and loosely defined political boundaries left a considerable amount of space to local actors. The pull of competing authorities and the sheer multitude of laws, edicts, ordinances, customs, arrêts, and other directives–many of which conflicted with each other–allowed officials such as Dijon's mayors and échevins considerable freedom of action. The disparate elements of French law provided both justifications for their claims to legitimately exercise political power and the institutional and ideological means to oppose efforts by other authorities to deprive them of it.

Although disputes over the exercise of political power were framed in legal language and resolved according to "'legal-procedural' tactics and style," the legal process was by no means entirely rule driven. Most disputes were determined as much by social factors, especially the status, influence, and *crédit* that each party and their backers could bring to bear, as they were by the legal process itself. This is not to say that we can dismiss legal procedures and arguments as irrelevant façades. The pervasive legalism of early modern political culture and the widespread influence exercised by the law and legal professionals meant that in the vast majority of cases, resolutions had to respect the limits imposed by accepted notions of law and procedure. At the same time, however, the breadth and flexibility of early modern law meant that strong legal arguments were rarely enough to ensure a favorable outcome. Moreover, legal institutions were generally slow, cumbersome, and unpredictable, making the support and influence of well-connected and socially prominent patrons essential to moving cases along and securing a positive judgment. Political success in early modern France thus rested on the ability of institutions and individuals simultaneously to "mobilize an array of technical judicial tactics," and to "invoke the intervention of the great who . . . would be favorably or unfavorably inclined in proportion to the skill with which the game of patronage had been played."[5] The early modern state worked not by ascertaining right and wrong, or by establishing clear jurisdictional boundaries and hierarchies. Rather, it sought to resolve disputes among its constituent authorities effectively. In this sense, political disputes were not much different from those between ordinary individuals. Litigation was one element in a broader range of dispute-resolution techniques, including negotiated settlements and arbitration.[6] Disputes over jurisdiction and the exercise of political power were often settled informally through negotiations and/or arbitration. "Confrontation, crisis, and compromise was part of the way the political culture worked," Peter Campbell has observed.[7] Brinkmanship and strident assertions of rights violated or authority outraged were usually preludes to negotiations that took place within a broadly accepted social and institutional framework that commanded the legitimacy necessary to make effective the resolutions it brokered. Although the system was certainly inefficient, it was also practicable given the constraints imposed by early modern French institutions and society. It helped to obtain the willing compliance to authority that, far more than forcible compulsion or the threat thereof, was essential to effective governance in the early modern period.

In many ways, then, political activity in the early modern French state was well suited to the particular skills and qualities associated with the avocat's profession. Avocats, by virtue of their training and professional experience, possessed the expertise needed to frame political disputes in legal terms and to develop persuasive arguments that not only justified claims to political authority but also ensured the intervention of relevant legal tribunals, even if they did not always rule favorably. In addition to having legal expertise, avocats were also skilled in the arts of persuasion, which could be extremely useful in negotiating informal settlements or obtaining the support of powerful patrons. As Jeffrey Sawyer has observed, "it was common in the seventeenth century to view politics as a process whereby one gained or lost influence through managing the perceptions (*impressions*) of others."[8] Perceptions were managed not only through public spectacles and printed pamphlets, but also behind the scenes through letters, deputations, oral addresses, legal arguments, and a host of other techniques. And avocats, with their experience in pleading cases, formulating legal arguments, and writing factums, had extensive experience in managing perceptions. Finally, although many avocats were not themselves nobles (though some were), the honorable status accorded their profession conferred a social prestige that enabled them to serve as effective spokesmen and intermediaries on behalf of lesser authorities, such as Dijon's municipal government, in their frequent interactions with the monarchy, great nobles, and high-ranking provincial authorities.

This chapter will examine several of the ways avocats helped the mairie negotiate its relationship with other authorities in order to assert and maintain the city's privileges, jurisdictions, and autonomies in first half of the seventeenth century. It will explore how avocats used the possibilities afforded by the ancien régime's legal system to respond to repeated attempts by other authorities to assert control over the hôtel de ville or to encroach on municipal jurisdictions. The following sections will show how the avocats used their legal expertise both to exploit the legal system and to develop arguments justifying the preservation of the mairie's traditional rights and powers. At the same time, we will also examine how the mairie and the avocats used informal networks of patronage and influence to the same end, most notably by cultivating the protection of Burgundy's governors, especially the princes of Condé. In order to do this, we will look at the mairie's operations and the avocats' activities in several domains where municipal authority was contested during the first half of the century: preserving the procedures for electing Dijon's vicomte-mayeur and maintaining the composition of its city council, defending the mairie's jurisdictions and symbolic status, protecting the mairie's authority (if not independence) over the naming and supervision of municipal officials, and the pursuit of municipal interests, especially in the face of opposition from the city's other authorities.

Defending the Elections

In 1607, one of the deputies sent by the Parlement to observe the annual mayoral election told the crowd waiting to cast their votes, "[T]he privileges conceded to the . . . city [are] most beautiful . . . ; there are only four cities in all of France that [have] similar ones."[9] Dijon's principal privilege was the right its inhabitants had enjoyed since the thirteenth century to elect their mayor.[10] Whereas the chief magistrate of most early seventeenth-century French cities was elected by a small oligarchy or chosen by the king from a list of nominees, all male heads of household in Dijon could vote for the mayor, a right they often exercised regardless of wealth or status.[11] Efforts by the municipal elite to choose the mayor by cooptation or by royal officials to do so by controlling the election were limited. The Chamber of Accounts had the right to cast the first vote, the "vote of the king," and representatives of the governor or the lieutenant-général had the right to make recommendations, but these efforts to sway the outcome enjoyed limited success in the early seventeenth century. The outgoing city council could also try to influence the election by voting as a bloc for a particular candidate. This too was not always effective.[12] Successful mayoral candidates in Dijon had to mobilize support among the city's many wine growers and artisans. Candidates often plied voters with wine, food, and even coin to win their votes. Anywhere from eight hundred to nearly two thousand individuals voted in the early seventeenth century, and a candidate needed only a simple plurality to win election.[13]

The electoral system, and the city's privileges more generally, enabled the avocats, procureurs, notaries, minor royal officers, and other well-to-do bourgeois who made up Dijon's municipal elite to dominate local affairs, even if they often clashed among themselves in the process. They also created mounting conflicts with the city's other authorities, especially Parlement, in the years after the Wars of Religion. Many parlementaires refused to forgive the mairie for Jacques La Verne's reign of terror during the Catholic League, when many of the sovereign court's magistrates were chased from the city in a wave of arbitrary expulsions, confiscations, and executions.[14] Parlement also saw the mayor's power as an affront to its authority and dignity as Burgundy's highest tribunal.

From 1595 to 1611, the Parlement of Dijon and the city's other sovereign courts repeatedly sought to establish their control over the mairie. Citing the chronic scandals and electioneering ("*brigues et monopoles*") that accompanied the annual mayoral elections, they sought to bring the city's political system in line with their conception of proper social order and discipline.[15] Although the courts' efforts met with a considerable amount of sympathy, as members of the municipal elite had been trying to rein in the disorder associated with the elections since the late sixteenth century, the mairie ultimately resisted all attempts to "innovate" or "encroach" on its privileges.[16] The mairie, and especially the avocats in its ranks, played a vital role in fending off challenges by Parlement and the other sovereign courts. The avocats' ability to mobilize support against the sovereign courts' initiatives and to develop acceptable legal justifications for their resistance, combined with their persistent opposition, made it possible for Burgundy's governors to intervene and to preserve Dijon's municipal system. Although there can be no doubt that the mairie would not have succeeded without gubernatorial support, the importance of effective local opposition cannot be underestimated. For all their power and influence, Burgundy's governors needed a viable mairie whose composition and authority commanded legitimacy among Dijon's political classes to ensure effective municipal governance. This provides at least one possible reason for their willingness to protect the existing municipal regime.

In September 1595, Mayor René Fleutelot, a moderate procureur who had helped broker the city's recognition of Henri IV as king, died in office, setting off a battle over the naming of an interim mayor. This was to be the opening event in a decade-long struggle between Parlement and the hôtel de ville for control of municipal government. To defend its privileges and autonomies, Dijon's mairie alternately negotiated with and exploited the tensions between the other main poles of authority operative within the city, especially Parlement, the provincial governor, and the monarchy itself.

After Fleutelot's death, the greffier Jacques Colin, the senior échevin and a prominent ex-ligueur, emerged as a leading candidate to replace Fleutelot. To block Colin, the sovereign court asked the city's deputy, the avocat Claude David, to take the post of commis à la magistrat. Although David had also been associated with the Catholic League, he was nevertheless considered "a man of honor and merit" according to the parlementaire Gabriel Breunot. David declined the honor, urging the magistrates not to intervene and "to not take it wrongly if [the mairie] seeks to conserve its privileges." When Parlement named one of its presidents, Bénigne Fremyot, a leading royalist, as commis à la magistrat, Colin denounced its interference with the mairie's right to name the interim mayor from within its ranks, saying that the arrêt "deprived the people of its privilege in all points to elect its magistrates in the future, so that finally they will be made into perpetual offices which will be purchased by those who employ themselves the most to obtain them and those whom the king favors most." Despite these objections, Fremyot was installed. In his speech to the assembled échevins, he assured them that Parlement did not intend to violate the city's privileges, but was concerned only with ensuring the mairie's loyalty to the king. At the same time, however, he made it clear that Parlement considered the hôtel de ville an inferior body that should rightly be under the sovereign court's control.[17]

Shortly after Fremyot left the municipality in June 1597, Parlement began considering plans to change the electoral format in order to reduce corruption and to make the mairie easier to control. In November, the court informed the chancellor of widespread brigues during the June elections and lobbied for changes. Leading the opposition to the Parlement's moves was the avocat Bernard Coussin, a former ligueur and deputy to the Estates-Général of Blois (1588), who had been named commis à la magistrat the previous month. At Coussin's prompting, the hôtel de ville hastily dispatched a letter to the chancellor, asking him "not to permit a breach to be made in the privileges sworn to by the king."[18] When Coussin succeeded in having himself named garde des évangiles the following June, the avocat du roi, Marc-Antoine Millotet, a former royalist who supported Coussin's rival, immediately appealed to Parlement, which declared that it "had never seen such dirty and sordid *brigues* as those which are seen being committed publicly this year." In response, the mairie dispatched two of the city's leading barristers, Jean de Souvert and Claude David, to argue on Coussin's behalf. Although the first president cut Souvert's plaidoyer short, the mairie prevailed, even though Parlement ordered the rules modified to prevent a repeat occurrence.[19] Coussin was named "candidate of the king" by the Chamber of Accounts and received the unanimous support of the outgoing échevinage on his way to being elected mayor with 1,240 out of 1,710 votes.[20]

The following May, Parlement decided to take the initiative and remake the city's political system on its own authority. The mairie was ordered to produce copies of all records concerning its privileges, a move that was usually a first step in challenging traditional rights. The mairie, under Coussin's direction, responded that the city's male heads of household had always elected the mayor and that "the exercise of this right [serves as] a title according to the law." Yet, although the mairie presented Parlement with copies of fourteenth-century titles upholding its claim, a parlementary commission ruled that the mayor should henceforth be chosen by lot from the three highest vote getters.[21] To mobilize support against the arrêt, Coussin summoned an assembly of notables at the hôtel de ville, where he declared "in a loud and intelligible voice" that his oath as mayor "required him to the defend the city's privileges, even against the king and his officers." Coussin persuaded the notables to support the preservation of the existing system. Parlement responded by declaring the assembly illegal, summoned the recalcitrant mayor to explain his actions, and forbade him to exercise the functions of avocat. It also dispatched letters to the provincial governor, the duke of Biron, as well as the chancellor and Président Jeannin of the Parlement of Paris.[22]

In response, Coussin and his supporters appealed to Biron as well, hoping to take advantage of his deteriorating relationship with the sovereign court. Biron's support helps explain why Henri intervened to protect the city's privileges while also trying to broker a settlement. Proclaiming, "I want the authority of my Parlement to be conserved, and the privileges of my city of Dijon in no way diminished," Henri decided that he would choose the mayor that year from the top three vote getters.[23] Henri's advisers were aware that the Dijonnais were "particularly devoted to their privileges," which may explain why the king passed up an opportunity to remake Dijon's city government along the lines of other cities.[24] Instead, he decided that an assembly of delegates from Parlement, the Chamber of Accounts, and the mairie would meet under Biron's direction to settle the conflict.[25] The failure of the edict to reach Dijon by 20 June, however, lead to the postponement of the elections and continued conflict between the mairie and Parlement. Parlement declared that the mairie's failure to hold elections meant its judicial powers were forfeit to the Bailliage, an order Biron promptly annulled.[26] With the governor's support, the mairie was able to control the assembly ordered by the king and secure a recommendation that the electoral format remain unchanged. Parlement, however, refused to concede and issued orders to arrest Coussin, the garde des évangiles Jean Jacquinot, and several others. Biron's influence, though, was apparently sufficient to keep them out of prison.[27] In early September, Biron obtained lettres de cachet ordering the elections to be held "according to the old custom." When Parlement refused to register the assembly's decision, Biron obtained *lettres de jussion* annulling all relevant parlementary arrêts so that "in the future, the parlements will be more restrained in giving arrêts contrary to [His Majesty's] will and to the liberties and privileges of his subjects.[28]

Biron's influence at court was ultimately the deciding factor in the city's triumph, but the importance of Coussin's ability to mobilize swift opposition to the Parlement's coup cannot be understated. According to at least one contemporary account, the city council had initially been divided over whether or not to accept Parlement's arrêt.[29] Had the échevins acquiesced to the sovereign court's demands, Biron would likely have had less room to intervene and uphold the traditional municipal system. Although the governor enjoyed considerable authority in the province, he was still constrained by various social and political concerns. Not only did Parlement, as the province's highest royal court, have an equally weighty claim to authority, but its members were also among Burgundy's wealthiest, highest-ranking landholders. Any move to overturn the court's ruling arbitrarily would have risked alienating a large majority of the judges and would have compromised Biron's ability to keep his crucial frontier province pacified. To act legitimately within the context of Dijonnais and Burgundian politics, Biron needed the opportunities afforded by the mairie's appeal and the justifications provided by the mairie's legal arguments opposing Parlement.

Biron's arrest and execution for treason in June 1602 deprived the municipal government of its patron and provided a new opportunity for Parlement and the other royal courts to establish control over the mairie. In January 1603, Parlement and the Chamber of Accounts each put forward new reform plans designed to strengthen their oversight of the municipal regime. The Accounts proposed reducing the échevinage to seven and limiting mayors to two consecutive terms, followed by six years of ineligibility for city office. Parlement, meanwhile, pressed for reducing the échevinage to twelve, limiting the franchise to those paying 1 écu of taille per year, and selection of the mayor by lot from the three top vote getters. Once again, there appears to have been support for these changes within the mairie's ranks. In late January 1603, the conseillers Grange and Sayve informed Parlement that when they had presented Parlement's proposal to the city council, it had "been approved by all present," and that, "everything took place very calmly and without disturbance." After another general assembly, however, the mairie once again refused to concede. On 5 May it sent deputies to remind Parlement that the royal letters confirming its privileges "have always been considered as inviolable laws."[30] In one concession to the sovereign courts, the mairie agreed that three-term mayors could not be reelected for three years; the following year, it limited mayors to two consecutive terms.[31]

Parlement's efforts did not end there. Three years later, it overturned Pierre Buatier's election as garde des évangiles, and declared both him and Jacquinot ineligible to stand for election. To protest, the city dispatched the avocat Claude Bouhardet and three others to Parlement. There Bouhardet, who spoke for the mairie even though he was a first-time échevin, convinced the magistrates to restore Buatier's eligibility. Rumors that Parlement was plotting to have one of its own elected mayor prompted the court to issue an arrêt invalidating any votes received by its members.[32]

After a decade, little had changed in the contest for control over the municipal elections. Parlement's legal and institutional maneuvers were repeatedly rebuffed by the city and its avocats. In this context, it is not surprising that Parlement would decide to assert its supremacy by intervening directly in the electoral process itself. At the electoral assembly in June 1608, Parlement's deputies denounced three candidates as brigueurs and read an arrêt declaring them ineligible.[33] Parlement's coup divided the votes of the outgoing chambre de ville among the avocats Jean Richard (11), Jean Defrasans (3), and Claude Mochet (3); the merchant Chrétien Le Masque (4); and three others (1 vote each). When the confusion settled, Le Masque, a former ligueur, won with only 42.4 percent of the nearly sixteen hundred votes cast, the lowest percentage of any winning candidate since 1595.[34] The outgoing mayor appealed the election, but Parlement ordered Le Masque invested with his marks of office.[35]

Parlement had secured the election of its candidate for mayor, but was still far from controlling the mairie. Although the mayor could nominate six échevins as anciens, the outgoing échevinage was free to disregard his choices when naming its own successors. Aware of this fact, Parlement dispatched two deputies to oversee the selection of the new échevinage on 23 June, a clear violation of the city's privileges. Despite the parlementaires' assurances that they "did not want to derogate or in any way alter the city's privileges," the conseil de la ville Bernard Martin challenged the deputies' presence as soon as they entered the chambers.[36] Despite the deputies' presence, the outgoing échevins refused to elect several of Le Masque's nominees, naming instead the outgoing mayor, Etienne de Loysie; Etienne Humbert, whom Parlement had named as a *brigueur;* and four others. Parlement promptly voided the proceedings and ordered Le Masque's son-in-law, the bourgeois Desnoyers, and the avocat François Bastonnier retained, with the four remaining anciens to be chosen in the traditional manner. Despite this, the échevins again rejected Desnoyers and Bastonnier. Of Le Masque's nominees in the second election, only Jean Richard, who had received the most votes for mayor from the outgoing échevinage, was retained. Parlement's coup was thus thwarted by a solid bloc of opposition among the outgoing échevins. Several months later, the mairie, with the help of the baron de Lux, the lieutenant-général, obtained an arrêt from the royal council restoring the six échevins whom Parlement had removed from office.[37]

Parlement's efforts to take control of the mairie fell apart less than two weeks later, when Le Masque suddenly died. Though divided over who should succeed Le Masque, the échevins made sure not to provide the court with a new justification for intervening in what was supposed to be a purely internal affair. Two prominent avocats, Jean Richard and Jean Defrasans, both claimed the right to serve as commis à la magistrat. The debate between one former candidate for mayor and the cousin of another threatened to reinvigorate the factional disputes of recent elections. Instead, Defrasans and Richard agreed to let the échevins, conseils de la ville, and parish officers choose between them. Defrasans was selected, and a potentially destructive situation was defused.[38]

Although Henri IV intervened in the politics of other former Catholic League towns, he had honored his word to respect the Dijonnais' privileges for more than a decade. Only after a decade of escalating struggles between the Mairie and Parlement did the king move to establish greater control over the mayoral elections in Dijon. But although royal changes to civic elections and government in the sixteenth and seventeenth centuries were almost always permanent, those that Dijon experienced were short-lived and had limited consequences for the urban political system.[39] Although the mairie's successes may have been due partly to luck, they were at least partly due also to the timely and persistent opposition of the mairie, led by the avocats in its ranks.

Although Parlement's 1608 coup ultimately failed, the hostilities prompted Henri to bring the selection of Dijon's mayor under greater royal control. Shortly after the controversial 1608 elections, Henri declared that he would henceforth choose Dijon's chief magistrate from the top three vote getters, and though the mairie reluctantly carried out Henri's orders under Bellegarde's supervision in June 1609, it immediately sought to have them reversed. In the wake of Henri's assassination in May 1610, the mairie again followed the new procedure but also began to lobby for restoration of the old system.[40] In August, it received letters for an assembly of delegates from the mairie, the sovereign courts, and the Bailliage to debate the future of the municipal regime. The monarchy proposed making the mayoralty an "annual office," reducing the échevinage to ten (plus two ecclesiastics, instead of six) and "several other things," the council's registers noted, "which are entirely contrary to the privileges granted and conceded . . . by the dukes of Burgundy [and] confirmed by the kings." The Bailliage favored implementing Parlement's 1599 arrêts; the Accounts also wanted an unspecified reduction in the number of échevins. On 23 February 1611, a general assembly of municipal and Bailliage officers "and a good number of bourgeois and other inhabitants of the parishes of this city" voted for restoration of direct mayoral elections.[41]

The task of defending the city's position in its negotiations with the royal courts fell to the avocats Nicolas Jachiet and Philibert Grostet. At the conference that followed, deputies from the Accounts and the Bailliage held to their positions, while First President Berbisey accused the mairie of packing the general assembly with its supporters. Jachiet and Grostet replied that the city had fulfilled its obligations and that the matter was settled. The sovereign courts continued their efforts to impose changes on the mairie, prompting the latter to announce that it would not send Jachiet and Grostet to the next scheduled meeting on the grounds that "they cannot and do not desire to participate in any resolutions which the said assembly wishes to make for the change of the . . . upkeep of the . . . city's privileges." A parlementary arrêt finally compelled Mayor Humbert, Jachiet, and Grostet to attend, but they expressly protested the "prejudices" being committed against the city's privileges.[42]

Frustrated by the obstinacy of the sovereign courts, the mairie sent Jachiet and Grostet to take its case directly to the regent. Deputies from the Parlement, meanwhile, obtained an arrêt from the royal council delaying the elections of 1611 for three months. In the end, the task of wading through the conflicting reports and choosing an electoral format fell to Bellegarde, who on 26 July obtained the restoration of direct mayoral elections with one important condition: henceforth, only those who paid annual tailles of

4 livres in each of the previous three years could vote, a requirement that disenfranchised most vignerons and lesser artisans. For Bellegarde, the mairie, and Parlement, the tax requirement (which the city had previously promoted) made elections more orderly by reducing the need for electioneering and facilitated the election of mayors acceptable to all parties.[43] Within a decade, elections became predictable, essentially preordained events where the official nominee was consistently elected by overwhelming majorities. Effective, obedient mayors could generally count on a second term. Such an arrangement, it should be stressed, was not seen as a violation of the mairie's privileges, but rather as an effective compromise that served the interests of the monarchy, the city's other authorities, and the municipal elite. The crown obtained a stable and obedient local government, the sovereign courts saw an end to electoral disorders that offended their sense of order, and the municipal elite retained control over the distribution of most local offices and a large degree of autonomy in governing the city. Even the consequences of the lower classes' exclusion from the elections should not be overstated. Although the number of those casting votes for mayor declined temporarily, by the mid-1630s they began once again to approach the levels of the late sixteenth century, suggesting that vignerons and artisans remained a significant, if now chastened and obedient, element of the electorate.[44]

In the end, more than fifteen years of attempts by Parlement, the other royal courts, and the monarchy to do away with Dijon's traditional municipal system had relatively little impact. Dijon's municipal elite, unlike its counterparts in many other cities, preserved the core of the city's political privileges intact. Larger political rivalries (such as those between the Parlement and Biron), fortuitous events (such as Henri IV's assassination in 1610), and the city's strategic location on France's vulnerable eastern frontier were undoubtedly significant factors in determining the outcome of the conflicts described above. Of equal, if not greater, importance, however, was the ability of many of the mairie's avocats to use their legal and rhetorical training to exploit to the full the political opportunities created by these conditions. By skillfully working the early modern French state's formal and informal networks of power, the avocats helped to preserve the political status quo–and their own political opportunities–at a time when many other cities were coming under increased royal control.

Protecting Municipal Autonomy

"A municipality which failed to defend [its] privileges," Richard Bonney once observed, "could expect nothing but trouble."[45] Throughout the early seventeenth century, Dijon's mairie worked tirelessly to defend its privileges from "encroachments" by other authorities, including the city's three sovereign courts, its Bailliage, and its many ecclesiastical tribunals, among others. The avocats at Dijon's hôtel de ville helped direct the seemingly endless waves of litigation produced by chronic jurisdictional disputes and developed the arguments used to defend mayoral prerogatives. Outside the formal legal system, avocats played central roles in negotiating settlements with other authorities. Their ability to fashion persuasive legal, historical, and political arguments also helped them shape the way disputes were understood, contested, and (often) resolved. Finally, the avocats' honorable status, rhetorical skills, and intellectual training made them effective emissaries to the great nobles, royal ministers, and regional elites on whom the mairie relied for protection.

The extent of the mairie's legal jurisdictions and police powers made conflict with other local institutions almost routine. One of the city's chief rivals, Dijon's Bailliage, frequently challenged the mairie's rights to draw up inventaires après décès, affix seals, conduct judicial sales, and perform a host of other routine legal activities.[46] These disputes produced a torrent of litigation between the two corporations. In a 1627 pleading before Parlement, the avocat Pierre Guillaume noted that more than thirty suits between the two had been filed at Parlement or the royal council in the past three or four years. Litigation between the mairie and the Bailliage was so routine that the mairie often added complaints about the Bailliage's new "encroachments" to cases already pending.[47]

The constant sparring with the Bailliage was echoed by frequent conflicts with other authorities. When officials of the Table de Marbre confiscated and sold a deer without the aid of a municipal sergeant, the mairie promptly objected to the violation of its privileges.[48] Conflicts with the many ecclesiastical jurisdictions within the city walls were also commonplace. In 1631, the city appealed to Parlement after officials of the justice of St.-Etienne affixed seals and inventoried the belongings of the church's deceased canon, claiming that his house was under the city's jurisdiction. The following year, it challenged the Sainte-Chapelle's right to try a man for stealing a chalice, arguing that "the sieurs de la Sainte-Chapelle have no jurisdiction in the said church nor anywhere else in the city."[49]

Overseeing this steady stream of litigation were the Mairie's avocats—both the conseils and those in the échevinage. In 1625, the mairie sent one of its échevins, the avocat Louvain Gelyot, to Parlement to argue against parlementary and Bailliage interference with municipal justice. Four months later, Gelyot returned to defend the city before the Grand'Chambre for having arrested an official of the abbot of St.-Etienne for murder. In 1631, the city refused demands by the clergy of the Sainte-Chapelle to turn over one of its chaplains after he was arrested for nocturnal "insolences et divisiones," and sent the avocat Jean Casotte, an échevin, to respond to the Sainte-Chapelle's appeal to Parlement.[50] Jurisdictional disputes also kept the city's conseils busy. Antoine Morisot's records of his activities in 1607 show that he consulted and pleaded several cases against the Bailliage for interfering with the mairie's jurisdiction. In 1611, Morisot and the conseil Richard Maire consulted in a case against officers of the abbot of St. Etienne for affixing seals in the home of a parlementaire. During his long career as a conseil, Pierre Malpoy advised and pleaded numerous jurisdiction cases against the Bailliage; the seigneurial justice of nearby town of Chenôve; and the clergy of St. Etienne, St. Bénigne, and other religious orders.[51]

Effective public authority under the ancien régime depended far more on symbolic resources than on coercive force. Although the bitter contests that individuals and corporations waged to secure recognition of their status, to maintain or advance their rank in public forums, and to defend their honor from even the slightest insult may seem excessive to modern eyes, they actually had considerable political significance. If a company's place in the order of a procession or the costume its members could wear changed, such a change would be interpreted as a sign of growing or diminishing power and status. The right to speak at the beginning of an assembly was not only a sign of respect, it enabled one to influence the debate far more effectively than subsequent speakers. It is hardly surprising then, that the mairie defended its status within Dijon's panoply of authorities as vigorously as it did its formal jurisdictions and powers. To retain its place as a significant local authority and to secure its continued ability to participate in the French state, the mairie constantly had to ensure that its political rights were recognized by other local and national authorities, as well as by the populace as a whole.

Securing frequent and public recognition of city's privileges was critically important to maintaining the mairie's symbolic authority. Public confirmations of Dijon's privileges, as well as other ceremonies and rituals, helped support the mairie's claims to the legitimate exercise of public power. Like other cities, Dijon maintained extensive archives of the grants, charters, and confirmations on which its privileges were based. Not only were these frequently cited in the many legal conflicts between the mairie and other authorities, but they also served a symbolic function as tangible reminders of the municipality's history and the traditional rights it had always enjoyed.[52] As the mairie's "institutional technicians" and leading spokesmen, avocats were crucial to protecting the symbolic potency of Dijon's privileges. When Louis XIII announced that he would make his royal entrée into Dijon in January 1629, the council deputized four avocats to draw up a request to have the king confirm the city's privileges on the basis of records in the municipal archives. Shortly thereafter, it dispatched two échevins, the avocats Guillaume and Blanot, to Troyes to inform the king of plans for the ceremony and to urge him to perform its "central act"–swearing to uphold the city's privileges at the altar of St.-Bénigne cathedral. Although Louis ultimately demurred, offering instead to confirm Dijon's privileges once the keeper of the seals had received copies of the city's titles, the mairie continued to pursue the matter. A little over a month later, Blanot and Bréchillet were sent with four other échevins to show the necessary documents to Marilliac. They were then instructed to pursue the matter at the conseil d'état. A few months later, the city received royal letters patent confirming its privileges.[53]

The mairie also reacted swiftly and vigorously to perceived threats to its honor and status. When two parlementaires accused the échevins of stealing from funds for the poor, Blanot reported the insult to the mairie, which dispatched him and the échevins responsible for distributing alms to protest to the first president. A few days later, Parlement's syndic personally apologized to the mayor, assuring him of the court's "very good opinion" of the échevins. Several times during the first half of the century, the mairie asked avocats in its ranks to draw up requests and mémoires supporting the acting mayor's right to sit in the chambre des élus when this right was challenged.[54]

Symbolic affronts to the mairie's authority were generally perceived in the same terms as jurisdictional conflicts and usually prompted the same kind of response from the mairie. Legal historians have long noted that many civil and criminal suits during this period concerned insults and disputes over honor.[55] The same was true of conflicts between institutions. One of the most significant and protracted conflicts pitted the mairie against the Bailliage for control of the right to invest new mayors with their symbols of office. Every year on 24 June, the newly elected mayor and échevins, accompanied by a large crowd of inhabitants, assembled in the cemetery of St.-Bénigne to watch the new mayor take the oath of office. The oath was typically administered by the lieutenant-général of Dijon's Bailliage, after which the new mayor received the gospels and seals symbolizing his office's authority from the garde des évangiles. Controversy broke out at the 1626 investiture ceremony for the avocat Jacques Defrasans when the Bailliage's lieutenant-général and avocat-général refused to attend, claiming the right to present the mayor with his symbols of office. After several hours, the two eventually arrived, accompanied by an intimidating contingent of royal sergeants and halberds. The lieutenant-général, with the avocat-général's encouragement, refused to accept the gospels and administer the mayor's oath until he was given the seals as well. Defrasans, in turn, ordered the garde to refuse on the grounds that "this was a novelty that the sieurs du Bailliage want to establish." On the advice of one of the city's *prud'hommes* (advisors), the avocat Nicolas Folin then administered the oath and presented Defrasans with the symbols of office. The following day, the mairie filed suit against the Bailliage officers; a few weeks later one of its conseils, Pierre Malpoy, pleaded the city's case at Parlement.[56] The immediate outcome of the mairie's lawsuit is unclear, and the matter was apparently still unresolved in June 1627. Less than a week before the election, the mairie sent the avocat Pierre Guillaume to ask Parlement to prevent a replay of the previous year's events. In his speech, Guillaume noted that the Bailliage officers' pretensions, "which at first glace seem unimportant, would, if permitted, destroy the Mairie." If the lieutenant-général were given possession of the seals, even if only for a symbolic moment, "he could then claim that in this instance of confirmation, he holds the magistracy and that it ceases to exist outside of his person." If this were to happen, Guillaume continued, the municipality itself would cease to exist, since the lieutenant-général could demand the city's keys and do away with the mairie's halberds and sergeants. In the event of an incumbent mayor's death or a contested election, moreover, the Bailliage could simply appoint the mayor. Giving the seals to the lieutenant-général, Guillaume concluded, would make him governor of the city. The first president, who was still upset with the mairie for boycotting the annual Sainte Hostie procession because of its dispute with the Bailliage, reproached the city for "having poorly pursued the matter," adding that "he desired more time to remedy the situation."[57] In the end, though, Guillaume's efforts were successful. The city government retained the right to invest new mayors with their symbols of office, thereby reaffirming the mairie's autonomy from the Bailliage.

Naming Municipal Officials

Crucial to the mairie's continued authority was the preservation of its right to name and oversee its own officials according to traditional procedures. Although governors, royal courts, and even the monarchy increasingly sought influence over the naming of mayors, échevins, and other municipal officials, open interference with the mairie's authority to name and confirm its own officials often met with resistance. Twice in the early seventeenth century, the monarchy tried to gain control over the selection of the mayor, as it had in many other cities. In the wake of the Lanturelu revolt of 1630, it also tried to reduce the échevinage to a smaller, more manageable size. Both efforts failed in the face of the municipal elite's persistent hostility.[58] Although overt threats to municipal autonomy met with vigorous opposition, subtler attempts to influence the composition of the hôtel de ville by recommending candidates were generally more successful because they did not challenge the mairie's authority. Thus, Henri IV recommended Bénigne Fremyot's reelection as mayor in 1596, "only if this is not contrary to your liberties and privileges." In 1641, the procureur-syndic Barthelemy Moreau resigned and nominated Pierre Taisand as his successor, citing instructions from the governor during his recent visit. Taisand was then elected unanimously after the city council noted his "fidelity, vigilance, and affection for the affairs of the city." Henri de Bourbon's recommendation that Pierre Terrion be reelected mayor in 1642–one of the few such instances recorded in the mairie's deliberations during the first half of the century–was couched in the language of request and favor.[59]

In light of such instances, it is naturally tempting to see municipal officials of this period as mere clients of central authorities, installed by the region's governors and their local brokers, and lacking any real agency or independence. The oft-cited claim of the avocat-général Marc-Antoine Millotet that all of Burgundy's royal and municipal officials owed their positions to the Condés, only reinforces this impression.[60] This view, however, is not wholly supported by the city's registers. On a number of occasions, the mairie named officials without awaiting external input and at times even acted in defiance of it, citing its traditional practices and procedures as justification. The dynamic was thus much more complicated than Millotet and some historians of early modern urban politics have realized. The notables who staffed Dijon's mairie were aware of their need for support from other authorities, most notably Burgundy's governors. At the same time, however, they were eager to defend the privileges and prerogatives that gave municipal offices meaning. The city's avocats helped the mairie negotiate the delicate balance between acquiescence and resistance to other authorities as it sought to maintain its authority to name and oversee municipal officials.

Although choices for these important offices were undoubtedly influenced by royal governors and their local brokers–most notably Parlement's first president–overt interventions appear to have been rare. In 1641, Condé asked the mairie to name Hughes Jannon, a former lieutenant in the Bailliage of Auxonne, as garde des évangiles. At the selection of the new échevinage in 1643, Mayor-elect Pierre Comeau, the lieutentant-criminel of Dijon's Bailliage, produced a letter from Condé listing those he wanted named to the new city council.[61] More frequently, however, disputes over municipal offices were handled internally, as happened in 1637 when a proposed échevin was challenged or when échevins absent from the election of the garde des évangiles were disqualified from voting on the next year's council.[62] Other disputes were referred to Parlement, as was the case in 1635 when a new échevin was excluded on the grounds that his uncle had served the year before.[63] Far from intervening actively in municipal elections during this period, though, Parlement appears to have confined itself to hearing disputes brought to it by the mairie and disaffected claimants for municipal office.[64] From the reform of the mayoral elections in 1611–12 until the Fronde, the city government's right to select and oversee its mayors, gardes, and échevins was generally respected by Burgundy's governor, Parlement, and other authorities.

The same was true for other municipal officers as well. As a letter from Bellegarde to the mairie in July 1622 made clear, governors expected to be consulted on the selection of parish officers, and they sometimes also made their preferences known when vacancies occurred. In August 1641, the avocat Jean Bourrelier was named ensign of St.-Jean Parish on Condé's recommendation. Five years later, the prince wrote to inform the mairie that "he would be agreeable" to the election of the avocat Bénigne Soyrot as captain of St.-Philibert. The prince's preferences went beyond the mere naming of officers, moreover. In 1636, he ordered the mairie to refuse Jacques Defrasans's resignation as captain of Nôtre-Dame.[65] Governors also influenced the selection of other officers, most notably the procureur-syndic. Most of the time, however, the mairie selected parish officers, conseils, and other municipal officials without the kinds of interventions by the Condés and their brokers that became routine in the second half of the century.[66]

Even when governors and their brokers made their wishes known, the mairie did not hesitate to substitute its own judgment or defend its right to do so. When Condé recommended Jannon as garde des évangiles in 1641, the échevins instead elected Antoine Moreau, a minor fiscal officer. When Moreau refused the post, perhaps out of fear of offending the prince, the mairie wrote to Condé to justify its actions. It also sent the avocat Paul Mailly to complain to Parlement and expelled Moreau from the council. Jannon, for his part, filed suit against the mairie as well. Rather than deciding the case, Parlement simply ordered the outgoing mayor to remain in office and restored Moreau to the échevinage in time to participate in the upcoming election. In a similar fashion, controversy erupted in 1643 when a bloc of échevins rejected Mayor Comeau's nomination of the avocat Antoine Bouchard as ancien in favor of the bourgeois Jean Boulier. When Comeau protested, citing Condé's express wishes, Boulier replied that "the Prince is so just and so equitable" that he would never be upset with the city for deviating from his list of nominees. Condé, he explained "will not find this to be a bad thing, since it would not be contrary to his intention to name and elect *gens de bien*." After seeing a large portion of his slate systematically voted down, Comeau finally stormed out of the chamber, accompanied by his allies, among whom were four of the council's five avocats. A few weeks later, Parlement, which had initially refused to intervene, ordered new elections. Even then, it did so in a way that minimized its involvement. Without ruling on the legality of the previous election itself, the court persuaded the five contested anciens to resign and then threw out the lawsuit. When new elections were held in early July, most, though not all, of Comeau's original nominees were elected. Perhaps more tellingly, concern with adhering to the city's established procedures appears to have been greater than the desire to accommodate the prince's wishes: all five échevins who had been nominated and elected after the departure of Comeau and his allies were retained on the city council.[67]

Boulier's claim that Condé would not mind if the mairie rejected his nominees in favor of other "gens de bien" was not mere rhetoric; on the contrary, it expressed a widely held belief among Dijon's municipal elite about their relationship to the governor and other authorities. Throughout this period, the mairie was given considerable latitude in selecting its own officials, as long as those chosen were considered reputable and responsible. Henri de Bourbon's nomination of Soyrot as captain of St.-Philibert once again illustrates the limits of external influences in the face of municipal traditions and procedures. Ordinarily, when an officership in the civic militia became vacant, subordinate parish officers were promoted and a new ensign named. Condé's request would have forced the mairie to override this practice and install Soyrot ahead of the current lieutenant and ensign. The mairie's response was to try to chart a middle road that protected municipal practices while respecting the prince's wishes, promoting the two current officers and making Soyrot ensign, a decision that appears to have drawn little protest.[68] Another case three years later further illustrates the complicated relationship between the mairie and the governor. When the city council assembled to name a new lieutenant of St.-Jean Parish, the syndic requested a delay, noting the mayor's absence and the need to consult Condé. At the same time, another échevin presented a request from the merchant Nicolas Deschaulx, who held letters from both the Grand Condé and his late father promising to name Deschaulx ensign when a vacancy occurred. In spite of this, the assembled échevins elected the avocat Jacques Baudot lieutenant, pending the decision of the ensign, Jean Bourrelier, to accept the promotion. When Bourrelier exercised his option three days later, Baudot objected, claiming that his and the council's honor had been impugned and that he had the support of the prince's *secrétaire des commandements*. Deschaulx meanwhile, appealed the entire proceeding to Parlement as a violation of the prince's authority. Ultimately, the council decided to follow its traditional practices, naming Baudot ensign and writing Condé to ask his approval. In this instance, however, the prince could not tolerate the affront to his authority. Noting that he had not been consulted and that he had given another person reason to expect the position, Condé replied that he could not accept the mairie's decision, though he was also clear in pointing out that he was not passing judgment on Baudot's suitability. The prince stopped short of ordering Deschaulx's installation as ensign, however. Instead, he instructed the city simply to "proceed to the election of a person capable of filling the said place of ensign." The mairie then elected the avocat Antoine Fevret in Baudot's place.[69] After Condé's arrest by Mazarin the following year, Baudot was restored as ensign of St.-Jean and eventually rose to the captaincy, where he remained well into the second half of the century.[70]

These types of conflicts between the city government and rival local corporations–especially the Bailliage–continued to be a chronic feature of Dijonnais politics. Unlike during the first decade of the century, however, these ongoing disputes were generally kept within limits through the mediating–and moderating–influence of Burgundy's governors, who were prepared to intervene and broker a cessation of hostilities whenever the situation appeared ready to get out of hand. As a rule, therefore, clashes between the mairie and other local corporations tended to become much more routine. Jurisdictional lawsuits against the city's rivals and deputations to Paris and elsewhere to oversee them while currying favor with those in positions of influence became as basic a function of municipal government as cleaning the streets or regulating the taverns and markets. The resulting balance between Dijon's various local institutions, with their overlapping jurisdictions, intertwined personnel, and long-standing professional jealousies was perhaps not a model of efficiency or stability, but it managed to work well enough. Supported by the avocats' effective use of litigation, negotiation, and persuasion, the Mairie de Dijon managed to coexist rather well with the city's Parlement and Bailliage after the settlement of 1612.

The Pursuit of Municipal Interest

The avocats' skills at manipulating legal arguments and the legal system, as well as their ability to serve as effective negotiators and intermediaries, were also crucial to the mairie's ability to pursue its own interests when dealing with other authorities. Many historians tend to see the late sixteenth and early seventeenth centuries as a time when municipal governments lost their political agency. Municipal interests, they argue, were subordinated to those of the monarchy and its agents as urban elites abandoned Renaissance civic consciousness in favor of a more aristocratic and hierarchical worldview.[71] This was not entirely the case in Dijon. As Hilary Bernstein has shown for sixteenth century Poitiers, even royal officers were capable of defending and promoting municipal interests and traditions while members of city governments, even if this put them at odds with their fellow royal officers.[72] Although the civic consciousness that flourished in the sixteenth century was certainly waning in the first half of the seventeenth, it was by no means extinct. Throughout this period in Dijon, the mairie, and especially the avocats in its ranks, repeatedly invoked traditional concepts of urban community and shared responsibility in their ongoing and occasionally successful attempts to get the city's clergy and privileged inhabitants to help bear the mounting fiscal burdens facing the city. In other areas as well, it is clear that the avocats and others who staffed the mairie continued to take their obligations to pursue the city's interests seriously well into the 1630s and 1640s, even if this sometime put them at odds not only with local authorities, but even with Burgundy's governors and the monarchy as well.

Like most French cities, Dijon emerged from the Wars of Religion with its financial affairs in ruins. The costs of dealing with the chronic crises of the early seventeenth-century–outbreaks of plague, poor harvests, troop movements, urban defense, and so on–meant that fiscal pressures only mounted throughout the period. A quick examination of the city's accounts reveals just how precarious its finances were. In any given year, the mairie might borrow thousands, even tens of thousands of livres from wealthy inhabitants (usually royal officers), securing the loans with funds from various royal octrois. Despite these infusions of cash, the Mairie usually ended up with annual deficits of roughly 2,500 livres in the late 1620s to 20,000 livres per year in the 1640s. In some years, the city's receiver found himself without any cash on hand before the end of the fiscal year. Although the mairie usually had little difficulty securing loans, its officials undoubtedly worried that any interruption in the city's access to royal and provincial tax revenues would threaten its access to the credit needed to sustain its activities.[73]

In these circumstances, it is hardly surprising that the mairie sought to tap the considerable wealth of Dijon's clergy and privileged royal officers whenever practicable. The two groups had always been *contribuable* for certain expenses essential to the well-being of the city as a whole, most notably defense and plague relief.[74] By the late sixteenth century, however, the clergy and royal officials began to consider themselves separate from the urban community and increasingly refused to contribute to traditional levies they had willingly paid a century earlier. Throughout the early seventeenth century, the mairie repeatedly tried to enforce traditional tax claims against the city's clergy and privileged inhabitants. Although the need for resources was clearly one motivating factor, the mairie placed equal, if not greater emphasis, on defending a more expansive and inclusive concept of civic community that affirmed not only the clergy's and privileged inhabitants' status as inhabitants of the city, but also the mairie's authority over them under certain circumstances. Thus, when the mairie dispatched deputies to negotiate a settlement with some of those whose houses had been damaged after Lanturelu, it specifically instructed them that any settlement must note that "all of the city's corps, ecclesiastical as well as secular" were liable for the sums agreed to, "since all are included in the arrêt and condemnation under the collective name of inhabitants."[75]

Through their use of formal legal procedures and informal channels of influence, the mairie's avocats helped the hôtel de ville pursue its rights to levy all inhabitants regardless of their status and to defend the traditional notion of urban community on which the mairie's authority rested. When the clergy refused to pay its "free gift" in 1626, the mairie sent Jean Guillaume, a conseil de la ville and one of Dijon's most prominent avocats, to plead its lawsuit at Parlement. Two years later, the mairie and the clergy again clashed, this time over the formula used to calculate the latter's contribution for poor relief. Citing a 1455 ordinance of Duke Philip the Good, the city's conseils advised the mairie that the clergy owed an additional 450 livres and that the matter should be pursued at Parlement. During an outbreak of plague in 1632, Parlement and the clergy suggested that the city's *chambre de charité* request a doubling of the octroi on wheat to support loans needed to pay the extra expenses. The city refused, claiming that its honor would be slighted and, on the advice of its conseils, rejected tax increases in favor of contributions from the clergy and royal officers "as has been done in similar occasions in the past." In 1632 and 1648, the mairie tried to get the privileged and the clergy to pay part of the costs associated with the entries of Henri and Louis de Bourbon, citing sixteenth-century precedents. In the mid-1630s, meanwhile, the mairie was involved in a protracted dispute with the royal officers and clergy over funds to repair the walls and purchase gunpowder for the city's defense in the midst of heightened Imperial military activity in Burgundy.[76]

Such efforts, of course, were not always successful. The clergy and officers refused to contribute to Condé's entries, forcing the city to borrow thousands of livres each time. Sometimes the mairie's efforts produced more mixed results, as in the dispute over the clergy's free gift. After Guillaume's plaidoyer, Parlement ordered the clergy to pay the city more than 1,800 livres. Soon thereafter, however, the matter was evoked to the royal council. The Mairie first dispatched two échevins–the avocat Pierre Guillaume and Jean Thomas, a councilor in the Bailliage–to manage the case. A month later, Mayor Defrasans pursued the affair while in Paris on behalf of Burgundy's estates. The dispute was finally settled in November 1626 when Defrasans, citing the case's excessive costs, dispatched Guillaume and the ex-procureur Valot to negotiate a compromise with the clergy.[77] Negotiations over paying for plague costs in 1632 apparently failed as well. The matter went before the royal council, which decided to double the octrois on wheat rather than compel the clergy and officers to contribute. Although this was a loss for the city, the additional revenue from the octrois likely cushioned the blow.

On the other hand, the mairie succeeded in winning recognition for its claims on a number of occasions. The most obvious example of this occurred when the mairie tried to get privileged inhabitants to pay for repairs to the walls and other defense-related costs in the mid-1630s. In a letter to Condé in January 1636, the mairie lamented that it owed workers more than 15,000 livres and had no money to pay them. It asked the prince to order the royal officers to help defray the costs or at least to allow the city divert funds from the octrois on wheat. The mairie also complained about the sovereign courts' attempts to usurp its fiscal and police functions, "in which they want to destroy the magistracy." Six months later, the mairie sent the avocats Bourrelier and Desnoyers to visit Condé at the siege of Dôle and ask him to order the clergy and privileged to help pay for the purchase of munitions. The sovereign courts, in turn, tried to force the mairie to borrow 12,000 livres and also tried to take over administration of the city's octrois. When the mayor and two échevins, all avocats, learned of the plan, they again protested that it would "destroy" the city government and also complained that the courts' plan would shift the costs onto the city's overburdened populace.

A few days later, Condé sided with the mairie and ordered the clergy and privileged to contribute according to their abilities, prompting a guarded response from Parlement's first president. A week later, Parlement wrote to the prince complaining that the mairie had rejected its "appropriate and most expedient" proposal to fund the purchase of munitions. The mairie countered by writing to inform Condé of the poor state of the city walls and asking him to order all inhabitants, including the clergy and privileged, to take turns working on them.

Under the direction of Mayor François Moreau, the mairie consistently outmaneuvered the clergy and officers to position itself as the loyal and obedient defender of the city in a time of military exigency. In December 1636, Condé took the highly visible step of personally addressing the city council in its chambers, where he praised the mairie for its devotion to the king's service. The following March, Condé again visited the city. This time, he chastised the three sovereign courts before an assembly that included more than two hundred inhabitants, the city council, conseils, prud'hommes, and parish officers. He also produced royal lettres patentes and an arrêt from the Council of State declaring the clergy and privileged contribuable for the costs of improving the fortifications. Although the case dragged on for several more years and it appears that the mairie never actually collected any money, the city still triumphed in several important ways. The municipality received royal validation of its claims that the clergy and privileged were part of the urban community and obligated to share certain burdens concerning the city's well-being. This was not a trivial point. At the same time as this dispute was taking place, the mairie was also asserting that Dijon's clergy and privileged had to help the city pay damages owed to those whose property had been damaged in the Lanturelu revolt, on the grounds that the king made all "inhabitants of the city" liable.[78] Perhaps even more important, the mairie strengthened its relationship with Condé considerably, ensuring that it would have an important protector in future disputes with the city's other authorities and even the monarchy.

Avocats were also crucial to ensuring the mairie's ability to pursue its interests in its interactions with the monarchy. As the hôtel de ville became increasingly dependent on royal tax concessions to maintain its solvency in the seventeenth century, avocats served as vital intermediaries in securing grants either directly from the monarchy or, more often, through the intercession of powerful patrons. Following Louis XIII's entry in 1629, for example, Bréchillet and Blanot were sent to follow the royal court to obtain a number of concessions. Although they failed to gain either ennoblement for current members of the mairie or the city's exemption from the taille, they obtained a number of fiscal concessions. When the Chamber of Accounts balked at registering the royal letters confirming these taxes, the mairie sent Boisselier to the court's home in exile at Beaune to pursue the matter. After the city was ordered to reimburse those whose homes had been damaged in the Lanturelu revolt, several avocats, including Defrasans, Guillaume, Pérard, Malpoy, and Simon Bourguignon helped contest what the city saw as the excessive claims made by the "interessez" and convinced Condé to negotiate a more moderate settlement. Malpoy and Defrasans, with Condé's help, also gained the permission for the city to divert 50,000 livres from provincial revenues and the right to levy a new tax on wine entering the city to pay off the damage claims.[79] The extent to which Dijon benefited from royal largess was thus at least partly due to the assiduousness with which the avocats in the mairie's ranks pursued fiscal grants for the city both at court and in their frequent meetings with Burgundy's governors and other authorities.

Although Dijon's city council usually sought the support of Burgundy's governor, Parlement, or other authorities to aid their defense of municipal interests, the mairie and its avocats did not hesitate to pursue what they perceived as the city's interests in the face of opposition as well. A decision to open new roads in 1623 met with hostility from Bellegarde, who was upset that the mairie had not consulted him in advance. The city council replied that it had felt no need to inform him, since a project so "full of justice and useful for public convenience" would certainly meet with his approval.[80] When the Council of State exiled the Chamber of Accounts four years later, the mairie vigorously opposed the action, even though this brought it into open conflict with Parlement, with whom the Accounts were embroiled in a major controversy, and the crown.[81]

Even as the mairie became increasingly reliant on the protection of the princes de Condé in the late 1630s and 1640s, it still went against the princes' wishes when it believed those wishes conflicted with municipal interests. In April 1638, the city government under Mayor François Moreau, avocat, refused the prince's request to pay for the new intendant's lodgings, protesting that the unprecedented expense "would result in consequences that would be gravely prejudicial" to the city. When Condé renewed his request three years later, the mairie again demurred, claiming that the funds would have to come from revenues dedicated to the city's fortifications and that the Chamber of Accounts would not approve the expenditure. Only in 1642 did the mairie finally begin paying for the intendant's lodgings.[82] In the midst of the city's 1638 conflict with the clergy and privileged, Moreau asked the council to send him to court to seek Condé's help, but then agreed to defer his trip after a request from the first president, deciding to write to the prince instead. Two days later, however, the échevins affirmed their resolution to send the mayor to court, but Moreau now protested that the mairie should await Condé's response. Concerned that other corporations had deputies at court, the city council named another avocat, the échevin Louvain Gelyot, to take Moreau's place but agreed to await Condé's letter. When the prince's response arrived, it included instructions that the city not send a deputy, but the échevins–over the objections of the mayor and another avocat, Jean Humbert–dispatched Gelyot to court, citing the affair's importance and the need to have someone at the royal council to oversee the city's affairs. Although we might expect that the mairie would have paid a high price for disobeying the prince's orders, this was not the case. According to Gelyot's reports, the prince continued to support the city's cause at the royal council and had several helpful meetings with him. Only the prince's departure from court to command royal armies in Guyenne, he added, had prevented a successful resolution of the matter.[83]

Throughout the first half of the seventeenth century, the avocats who dominated the Mairie de Dijon played a central role in its ability to effectively pursue and defend its interests, even when those interests set the municipality at odds with other authorities, including the provincial governor. The avocats' mastery of law and rhetoric enabled the mairie to navigate the early modern state's parallel and overlapping structures of power and dispute resolution to ensure that the city's–or at least the mairie's–interests were recognized and maintained. But although the mairie and the avocats were able to exploit the system with considerable success in the initial decades after the Wars of Religion, they were also in many ways unable and even unwilling to do much about long-term trends that undermined municipal autonomy and rendered the mairie increasingly dependent on the protection of Burgundy's governors. This dependence proved an effective means of securing municipal interests in the 1630s and 1640s, but in the long run it left the mairie's unity and authority extremely vulnerable in the absence of a strong and effective regional governor.

The Changing Nature of Local Politics

The municipal political system that emerged after the settlement of 1612 was quite stable throughout the first half of the seventeenth century. With the exception of the year following the 1630 Lanturelu revolt–when Louis XIII restricted the franchise to a small group of notables, reduced the échevinage to six, and ordained that he would choose the mayor from the top three vote getters for the next six years–the mairie's privileges were never overtly called into question. And although Louis intended his changes to be permanent, the municipal elite's persistent efforts to have the city's privileges restored succeeded in reviving the traditional system less than a year later.[84] But if the mairie's right to participate in the local functions of the early modern state was not questioned, the precise scope and limits of its authority were constantly challenged. The tension and friction between the mairie and Dijon's many other local authorities was characteristic, and even fundamental to the operations, of the ancien régime state.

In this type of municipal political system, the mairie had continuously to negotiate the boundaries of its authority with, and play off the tensions between, other authorities: the monarchy, the governor, Parlement, and a host of other tribunals. Frequently it employed lawsuits, or at least the threat of litigation, as a response to perceived "encroachments" on municipal rights and privileges. At the same time, the mairie continued to cultivate and maintain its place within patronage networks and other informal channels of influence in order to benefit from the protection of high-ranking and well-connected elites. Of primary importance in this regard was the mairie's ability consistently to secure the support of Burgundy's royal governors, most notably the princes of Condé. The avocats on Dijon's city council during the first half of the seventeenth century played an indispensable role in helping the mairie negotiate and exploit the ancien régime state's delicate system of tensions and balances to preserve its privileges, jurisdictions, and authorities. Municipal politics thus provided Dijon's avocats with an ideal environment to exercise their self-professed vocation as hommes politiques.

The key figure in the municipal political system was the provincial governor, the ultimate representative of royal authority in the region. Although Burgundy's governors made only occasional visits to the province and generally relied on correspondence and local intermediaries to make their presence felt, their active involvement helped make the local political system reasonably stable and effective. This, in turn, enabled the mairie to use the framework provided by existing institutions and accepted legal principles to resolve its chronic conflicts with those who contested its privileges and authority. Throughout the first half of the century, but increasingly so under the princes of Condé, all sides increasingly looked to the governor to arbitrate disputes over authority. During the mairie's lengthy dispute with the clergy and privileged over payments for munitions and fortifications maintenance, both sides wrote and sent deputies to make their cases to Condé.[85] When the chambre des élus sought to exclude the city's commis à la magistrat from its deliberations, Condè was asked to arbitrate. The mairie, then, became increasingly dependent on the governor to protect its authority and to make the institutional apparatus of the early modern state function effectively. Louvain Gelyot, the mairie's deputy to court in 1638, learned this first hand. As soon as the prince left Paris, he reported, the progress of the mairie's cases at the royal council came to a complete halt.[86] This sense of dependence can also be seen in the mairie's practice, beginning in 1642, of sending 12 feuillets of the best new wine to the prince and 4 feuillets to his secretary and later other members of his household as well as to the provincial intendant (who was a client of Condé's). As the council noted in its deliberation of 22 October 1644, the wine was meant to thank the prince and his agents for "the graces and favors they perform daily for this city of Dijon and to oblige them to continue them in the great and important affairs which the city has before the royal council."[87] This language of obligation was even more evident in the words of one mayor, who described Condè as "this tutelary angel of the province and this city of Dijon" and noted that under his administration, "the magistracy will only have to occupy itself with matters of police and financial administration."[88] The mairie also turned increasingly to the princes for help in settling its internal disputes. When Jacques Jacquinot, a corrector in the Chamber of Accounts and a first-time échevin, refused to take his place on the city council unless he was ranked directly behind the mayor, the mairie fined him 1,000 livres, prompting Jacquinot to obtain an arrêt in his favor from the Accounts. After more than a month of wrangling, the prince settled the matter, ordering Jacquinot to return to the city council at the traditional rank. The mairie was instructed "to cause him no difficulties," and both sides were directed to "drop all legal pursuits in this matter and to discuss it no further."[89] In the midst of a precedence dispute with the rest of the mairie three years later, the conseils de la ville wrote to ask the Grand Condé to arbitrate during his next visit to Dijon to save the mairie the expenses of a lengthy lawsuit.[90]

Many historians of early modern France have identified the multitude of overlapping, vaguely defined, and poorly coordinated local authorities as the weak point of the ancien régime state at the local level. Although this problem certainly existed in Dijon, gubernatorial authority generally prevented "crises of command." The Condés and their clients, in particular, helped to coordinate the activities of Dijon's many authorities and to delineate their proper spheres of authority within the city. On the whole, this worked to the mairie's benefit. In 1632 and again in 1636, for example, Condé upheld the mayor's right to command the civic militia against the claims of Parlement's first president. In the latter instance, Condé's response shows just how careful he was to maintain a precise division of powers among the competing authorities. He noted that the first president had power over pressing and extraordinary matters while the mairie enjoyed power over ordinary concerns. The guarding of the city, the prince concluded, fell in the latter category. "I will never breach your privileges," the prince assured the mairie, instructing the city council to show his letter to the first president and to pay their respects, "your privileges and customs having been saved." Throughout the first half of the seventeenth century, both Henri de Bourbon and his son appear to have kept their promise to prevent any "breach" in the city's privileges.[91]

The mairie's reliance on gubernatorial protection led to a gradual transformation in the nature of municipal politics during the first half of the seventeenth century. By mid-century, the relationship between the two had become increasingly routinized and standardized. Sometime in the late 1630s or early 1640s, the mairie began to compile its requests into lengthy mémoires. In two mémoires dated 1646 and 1647, for example, the mairie asked the princes to obtain funding to repair two of the city's bridges, to overturn a recent judgment exempting certain inhabitants from the octrois on wine, and to settle its precedence dispute with one of the substitutes of Parlement's procureur-général. The mairie also asked the princes to defend the city against the governor of the chancellery, who was seeking damages at Parlement for lands he claimed had been lost when the city built a new bastion near the porte d'Ouche, and to name new parish officers to replace the captain and lieutenant of St.-Pierre, both of whom no longer lived in the city. The princes, in return, would comment on the mairie's requests and return the mémoires to the city council with responses ranging from brief promises of support to lengthier directions on how to proceed.[92] According to some historians, clientage ties and personal bonds of loyalty became increasingly impersonal, formulaic, and even "bureaucratic" during the late seventeenth and early eighteenth centuries.[93] Although the mairie's practice of presenting its collected requests to the princes in written mémoires was not impersonal and bureaucratic in and of itself, it does appear to have been a step in that direction.

At the same time as the mairie's interactions with the princes were taking on this more routinized, almost bureaucratic character, the Condés and their brokers were intervening more frequently to install their clients in key municipal positions. Again, the situation was a far cry from the second half of the century, when the Condés supervised virtually all municipal appointments; nevertheless a trend was beginning to take shape.[94] Still, most municipal appointments prior to the Fronde do not appear to have been directly influenced by the governors or their agents, and as I argued earlier in this chapter, the princes' control over the mairie was far from complete. It would be more accurate to say that the princes enjoyed mounting influence over an increasingly deferential and dependent mairie. Thus, when Mayor Jean Tisserand died in office in September 1635, the mairie visited Condé as a body and asked him to choose a commis à la magistrat, "out of the respect which is due to the honor of his command." Recognizing the Dijonnais' attachment to their privileges, Condé thanked the city council for the honor and declared that he would "leave the chamber in its liberty, not wanting in any way to innovate on that which has been done in the past nor to prejudice the said chamber."[95] The relationship between the mairie and the prince was thus based on a delicate balance of give and take. The Condés recognized the importance of municipal sensibilities, while the mairie acknowledged its dependence on the princes and the consequent limits on its freedom of action.

Gubernatorial authority and protection became even more important to the municipal system's stability in light of mounting signs of internal tensions at the hôtel de ville. Although Millotet's assertion that all mayors and échevins were hand picked by First President Bouchu appears considerably exaggerated, his remarks nevertheless testify to a perception that the mairie was increasingly dominated by clients of the Condés and their brokers in the decade leading up to the Fronde. The controversy over the selection of ancien échevins in 1643, as well as Parlement's removal of the procureur Julien Chevalier as ancien in 1646, reflect increased conflicts at the hôtel de ville. The same could be said of Baudot's removal as ensign of St.-Jean in 1649. It is worth noting that Baudot was restored to his position after Condé's arrest in 1650, and that Chevalier was a leading figure in the *frondeur* mairies of the early 1650s.[96] At the same time, it would be wrong to describe the mairie's factional conflicts as simply a struggle between a pro-Condé clique and their opponents. Many of the protagonists of the 1648–49 controversy over the conseils de la ville, which saw the mairie decide to use avocats on the échevinage to the exclusion of the conseils, were either direct or indirect clients of the Condés.[97]

The emergence of such disputes had considerable significance for the ability of Dijon's municipal elites to protect the mairie's privileges. The municipality's success in defending them was due in large part to the fact that the many avocats who played prominent roles at the mairie remained committed to preserving the city's privileges, even when they were divided by their desire to enjoy their fruits. By the late 1640s, however, this fundamental commitment to protecting the traditional municipal system seems to have been in decline. Increasingly, it appears, only the authority of "monseigneur le prince" and his agents was sufficient to keep the mairie's internal conflicts from spiraling out of control.

The consequences of the mairie's increasing dependence on the prince and the increasing tensions in its ranks became more evident in the following decades. Condé's arrest by Mazarin in 1650 and his eventual replacement as governor by the largely ineffective duke of Epernon resulted in a series of political crises that undermined the viability of the municipal system as it had developed in the first half of the seventeenth century. Condé's removal unleashed a decade of bitter factional rivalries marked by the increased willingness of both sides to seek the intervention of outside authorities in order to gain control of the hôtel de ville. The 1650s in Dijon were marked by a series of coups and countercoups that eventually undermined the viability of the traditional municipal system by depriving it of its internal cohesion and the ability to pursue its interests independently. This, in turn, made it easier for others to challenge and undermine municipal authority. From there, as the next chapter will demonstrate, it was only a small step to marginalizing the mairie as a legitimate political actor, a development that ultimately deprived most of the avocats in its ranks of the ability to participate in the local working of the French state.

Chapter 3

The Collapse of the Municipal Political System (1649–68)

At the end of April 1643, Dijon's city council received a report that one of its conseils, Pierre Guillaume, had asked Parlement to prohibit the city's counselors from consulting with the municipal syndic in a lawsuit against the damoiselle Des Millieres. Guillaume also asked the court to forbid the mairie to use anyone other than the conseils to handle its legal affairs. In response to Guillaume's obvious attempt to hamstring the city in its dispute with Des Millieres, the city council affirmed that "as long as there are avocats among the échevins who would like to plead or write for the city's affairs and lawsuits, they will be employed and the procureur-syndic will not be obliged to seek the assistance of the conseils."[1]

Although it unclear whether Guillaume's request was ever granted or whether the mairie enforced its deliberation in the years that followed, the relationship between the six conseils de la ville and the échevins continued to deteriorate. At an assembly to discuss the doubling of an entry tax on wine in January 1648, another conseil, the former mayor Jacques Defrasans, was asked to recuse himself for an alleged conflict of interest. A few days later, the conseils asked Parlement to order that they be summoned to all general assemblies and allowed to sit with the chamber de ville, "as has always been done." The city council responded by describing the conseils as a "corps extraordinaire" to be summoned only at the council's pleasure. The next day, the conseils refused to take their place at another assembly when they were summoned to sit as "notables" rather than as conseils, and by mid-January they had filed a separate suit against the échevin Claude Grillot, a conseiller in Dijon's Bailliage court. Another échevin, the avocat Jacob Chesne, was instructed to handle the case on the city's behalf. Despite the city's success in having the matter evoked to the royal council, Parlement issued a provisional ruling in early February ordering the mairie to summon the conseils to all assemblies and to seat them in their customary location. The following month, Condé issued an ordinance confirming Parlement's ruling.[2]

Despite the prince's involvement, tensions between the échevinage and the conseils continued to run high. In early February 1649, acting on the advice of the échevin Jean Guillemet, a minor official in the Chamber of Accounts, the city council decided that it would enforce the deliberation of 30 April 1643 and utilize avocats in the échevinage rather than the conseils to handle the city's legal affairs. In his report, Guillemet alluded to the city's difficulties with Defrasans the year before. Defrasans, in return, reported that he had been summoned before Parlement to respond to an appeal concerning the doubling of the octrois and announced his intention to sue the mayor and échevins as individuals. On 25 February, the échevin Jacques Baudot, an avocat who had defended the city's exclusion of the conseils before Parlement, reported that Guillaume had "pled his appeal in terms that were offensive and injurious to the honor of the magistrates."[3] A little less than a month later, Parlement issued an arrêt forbidding the municipal syndic to employ anyone other than the conseils for the city's legal matters on pain of a personal fine. As it had the year before, the mairie appealed to the royal council. The conseils, in turn, sought Condé's intervention. In mid-July, the prince reaffirmed his earlier order. Without addressing the conseils' precedence claims, he ordered the execution of Parlement's arrêt requiring the city to use the conseils for all of its legal affairs.[4]

The dispute between the conseils and the échevinage in the late 1640s reveals the mounting tensions among the ranks of Dijon's notables and the growing political divides among ranks of the city's avocats. In 1633, for instance, no avocat would defend the mairie when the Order of Avocats claimed precedence for its members over all *non-gradué* échevins, requiring Parlement to compel the senior conseil de la ville to work with the procureur-syndic on the city's behalf.[5] In the late 1640s, in contrast, a number of avocats, including Jacob Chesne and Jacques Baudot, supported the mairie's position against the conseils.[6] Although it is tempting to see this as the result of conflicts among rival factions vying for control of the hôtel de ville, the evidence does not seem to warrant such a conclusion. Two of the central figures in the conflict, Defrasans and Guillaume, were well-established members of the municipal elite with significant ties to the Condés and their local brokers. Defrasans, whose father had served as vicomte-mayeur in the early seventeenth century, had served seven terms as mayor since the mid-1620s. In 1633, the Grand Condé's father had personally asked Parlement to permit Defrasans to serve a third consecutive term as mayor, despite the longstanding prohibitions against doing so.[7] Guillaume, for his part, had served three terms as échevin in the late 1620s; his cousin Chrétien was a current member of the hôtel de ville.

"Messieurs les princes, father and son, have governed Burgundy with complete authority for more than twenty years," the avocat-général Marc-Antoine Millotet wrote in his oft-cited *Mémoires* on the Burgundian Fronde. Although Millotet might justly be accused of exaggerating the extent of the Condés' control over Dijonnais politics, his comments do draw our attention to an important feature of the conflicts between the conseils and the échevinage in the late 1640s.[8] The dispute was not one between a group of insiders attempting to control access to municipal offices and the benefits that accompanied them. Rather, it was a conflict among those who were already inside the municipal political system. Guillaume and Defrasans had relatives in the échevinage; another of the conseils, Antoine Vallot, was himself an échevin.[9] And the controversy appears to have stemmed from a series of almost mundane disputes over status, precedence, and influence within an otherwise functional system of municipal governance. If anything, the conflict between the conseils and the échevinage was the product not of factional divides, but rather of the growing fragility of the cultural and institutional frameworks that made up Dijon's municipal political system. The growing tendency of local political actors to look to the governor to resolve disputes and prevent crises of authority weakened the ability of local institutions, procedures, and cultural values to perform these functions.

The events of the 1650s—most notably the Grand Condé's arrest in January 1650; his later departure as governor of Burgundy; and the heavy-handed and ineffective management by his replacements, the dukes of Vendôme and Epernon—exacerbated disputes among Dijon's avocats and other local political actors. They also helped to transform internal conflicts among the city's municipal elite into factional divides between increasingly militant rival parties.[10] This can be seen in way the conseils' dispute reverberated over the course of the following decade. Following Millotet's controversial election as mayor in June 1650 and the forcible installation of his slate of échevins by Vendôme the following month, Guillaume was once again accused of insulting the mayor and échevins. This time, however, he was removed from his post as conseil, no doubt in part because of his perceived sympathies for the prince and Millotet's opponents.[11] Shortly after Millotet returned to office as mayor in the summer of 1652, the mairie ordered the suppression of the conseils de la ville, ostensibly as a cost-saving measure, declaring that "there are ordinarily in this chamber a number of avocats who can serve the city, as has been done before, without collecting any fees." Although the deliberation also noted the advantages the mairie would obtain by being able to use the services of whichever avocat it wished, as well as the fiscal benefits of removing the conseils' partial tax exemption, this decision also allowed Millotet to distance several supporters of the rival *condéen* party, including Defrasans (who had run for mayor against Millotet the previous year) from the city government, a tactic he had already employed against several parish officers suspected of sympathizing with the province's former governor.[12] Jacques Rousseau, by contrast, became a leading figure at the hôtel de ville in the 1650s; Pierre's cousin Chrétien served several terms as échevin prior to his untimely death in 1655.[13] Not until Condé's return as governor in 1660 were the six conseils restored to their old positions, and then only after agreeing to forego any claims to back wages and agreeing to pay any tailles that had been levied on them during the intervening period.[14] With the prince and his agents firmly back in control, Defrasans and Guillaume, the mairie's bitter opponents during the 1650s, took turns as vicomte-mayeur in the 1660s.

In the case of mid-seventeenth-century Dijon, at least, factions did not create political conflicts so much as political conflicts created factions. For more than two decades, the Condés had provided the structure within which Dijon's avocats and other local actors could wage politics by using their "tactical power" resources to contest the distribution and utilization of power and status within the confines of the municipal political system.[15] Although it is true that this system showed considerable signs of tension during the late 1640s, they remained largely contained thanks to the authority of "monseigneur le prince" and the influence his brokers and clients exercised over Dijon's many governmental bodies. The Grand Condé's removal from the province and his replacement by the ineffective Vendôme and Epernon completely upset the delicate balance of municipal politics that had evolved during the first half of century, resulting in a decade of coups and countercoups that undermined the mairie's political legitimacy as well as the cohesion of city's avocats in their defense of municipal privileges and interests. As intraelite disputes evolved into bitter and protracted rivalries between factions of *condéens* and *frondeurs,* both sides did not hesitate to appeal to the "absolute" authority of the crown and the power of the governors and other external figures in their quest for control over the hôtel de ville. Although both parties, as well as the many individuals who were not firmly committed to either side, claimed to be acting in defense of municipal privilege, the mairie's authority was increasingly revealed to be utterly dependent on gubernatorial favor over the course of the 1650s. Indeed, when the outgoing échevins refused to name one of the mayor-elect's candidates to the échevinage in June 1656, Epernon simply had the city council reduced from twenty to six and imposed his own candidates on the hôtel de ville.[16] A blank arrêt from the royal council dated 7 June 1659, authorizing Epernon to strike down the election of an unnamed prud'homme for "brigues, monopoles and bad intentions for service to the king" shows just how ready the Grand Condé's successor was to intervene in favor of those loyal to him–in this case an apothecary named Goujon.[17] Throughout the 1650s, Epernon's treatment of the mairie was a far cry from that of first two Condés, who were tactful, even deferential, in their treatment of Dijon's city council. Little wonder then, that the city rejoiced when it learned of the prince's return to the governorship of Burgundy in January 1660.[18]

Although the Grand Condé's restoration appeared to signal a return to the status quo ante, it actually served as little more than a prelude to the wholesale reorganization of the mairie and a sweeping transformation of local political practice, culture, and participation later in the decade. Amid all the turmoil at the hôtel de ville, a new figure had emerged on the local political scene, one who would play a leading role in the transformation of governance and politics and Dijon. Although Claude Bouchu was not Burgundy's first royal intendant, he was far more active and ambitious in performing his functions than any of his predecessors. Bouchu's lengthy campaign to verify and liquidate the debts of Burgundy's communes (including Dijon), his near constant presence in the city and growing surveillance over the mairie's actions, and his role in clarifying and streamlining the complex and often contradictory channels of power and authority that the mairie's avocats had exploited so effectively in the first half of the century—all undermined the municipality's claims to an active and autonomous role in local governance. The growing power of the intendant, combined with the Condés' increasingly careful supervision of the mairie and the persistence of factional divides among the avocats and the rest of the municipal elite, all paved the way for Louis XIV's dramatic reorganization of Dijon's city government in 1668. After several unsuccessful attempt by the monarchy to reduce the size and limit the authority of Dijon's mairie over the course of the seventeenth century, Louis finally succeeded in reducing the hôtel de ville from a large, fairly open body with a significant role in local governance to a small group of hand-picked notables who served largely as administrative agents of the crown and its officials. In the process most of Dijon's avocats, who had long participated in the governance of their city through the Mairie, found themselves excluded from urban politics and participation in the local workings of the French state.

The 1650s: A Decade of Crisis

By the late 1640s, Burgundy had been transformed from a region "rife with popular unrest" into one where "scarcely a rumble of discontent could be heard."[19] Compared with other peripheral regions, such as Provence and Guyenne, Burgundy remained generally calm during the mid-century upheaval of the Fronde (1649–53). This was especially true during the "parlementary Fronde" of 1648–49. The Grand Condé's influence and extensive regional clientele network, as well as by now ingrained habits of obedience to the crown, kept Parlement, other regional bodies and the Mairie de Dijon loyal to Mazarin and the regent, Anne of Austria. Even after Condé's surprise arrest in January 1650, neither Parlement nor the mairie threatened to revolt, despite powerful currents of support for the prince in both bodies.[20]

Dijon's seeming tranquility next to cities such as Paris, Aix, and Bordeaux belies the fact that the Fronde and the entire decade of the 1650s were actually a period of profound political conflict within the walls of Burgundy's capital. Despite its limits, Dijon's municipal political system had functioned effectively for almost four decades under the protective wing of the region's powerful yet largely distant governors, who were in turn supported by an increasingly strong monarchy. The crown's weakness during Louis XIV's minority and Mazarin's controversial ministry, the sudden removal of the Grand Condé as governor, and his replacement first by the duke of Vendôme and then the duke of Epernon brought the system's weaknesses to the fore. A series of miscalculations by the two new governors, neither of whom had the temperament or the skills to manage Dijonnais politics as effectively as the Condés, allowed the divisions that had been simmering among the city's notables to erupt into the open. As a result, Dijon's mairie lurched from one crisis to the next throughout the decade. Groups competing for control of the municipality, in particular the factions known as the Condéens and Frondeurs, readily appealed to the absolute power of the monarchy and the authority of Burgundy's governor and Parlement in their efforts to gain (and maintain) control of the mairie. This is not to say that the notion of municipal privilege disappeared from local political discourse. On the contrary, it was regularly invoked as justification by both those in power at the hôtel de ville and their opponents. Municipal officials, meanwhile, continued their predecessors' efforts to defend the mairie's jurisdictions and status. But a decade of repeated coups and the willingness of many avocats and other notables to override the mairie's privileges by invoking royal and gubernatorial authority when events warranted revealed that Dijon's "beautiful privileges" and venerable traditions were losing their potency as a principle of local political ideology and as a source of unity around which Dijon's notables could rally. The city's avocats, who had long been united in their commitment to defending the city's privileges, were deeply divided as well.

As was the case during the first decade of the seventeenth century, Dijon's municipal elections became a focal point for local political conflict following the Grand Condé's arrest in January 1650. External interventions in the selection of the vicomte-mayeur, échevins, and other municipal officials, which had been sporadic and limited from 1612 to 1649, became almost routine during the 1650s as Vendôme and then Epernon sought to ensure that the mairie remained in the hands of their local supporters. The cycle of coups and countercoups, combined with repeated invocations of external authority and extraordinary procedures, exacerbated divisions among Dijon's notables, including the city's avocats. The nearly constant state of crisis prolonged existing disputes and provoked new ones. In the end, the events of the 1650s helped undermine the unity of Dijon's municipal elite and their commitment to the defense of the city's privileges. Instead, the city's avocats and other notables became almost completely reliant on gubernatorial and royal authority to preserve local order and stability.

News of Mazarin's surprise imprisonment of Condé (along with the princes of Conti and Longueville) sent ripples of fear throughout the leading ranks of Burgundy's capital. Mayor de Mongey described the reports as a "fascheuse nouvelle." The procureur-général Pierre Lenet reported that First President Bouchu burst into tears, fearing that Mazarin would have the prince killed in prison.[21] Both the prince's adversaries and his supporters believed Dijon and Burgundy were likely rise in revolt to support their popular governor. In April 1650, Mazarin and Anne brought the young king Louis XIV to Dijon in an effort to ensure the city's loyalty. Lenet, meanwhile, expected a "general revolution" against Mazarin, writing that he believed that "it would not be difficult to get the Parlement, the cities, and the province to rise up against [Mazarin]."[22] These expectations, however, turned out to be unfounded, as the mairie showed every sign of remaining obedient to the crown, even as it deplored the princes' arrest. After some initial hesitation, the mairie moved in collaboration with Parlement "to ensure the city's security in obedience and service to the king." A few weeks later, the council ordered the avocat Jean Bourrelier to investigate three youths for shouting, "Vive Condé!" The council noted that they "could not remain unpunished, since it is a question of serving the king." In April, Mazarin assured the assembled council that the king and his mother were "greatly satisfied" with the city's loyalty. "Never did one see more tranquility" than reigned in Dijon and Burgundy, Lenet observed, "which by all appearances should be beginning a civil war, and which are the city and province which causes the royal court the greatest apprehension."[23] Nonetheless, Condé's removal from the scene created a vacuum that allowed the emergence of a faction centered around Président Nicolas II Brulart (whose family Condé had removed from the first presidency in favor of the Bouchu clan), the avocats-généraux Millotet and Gaspard Quarré d'Aligny, "and several others who had been distant from M. le Prince."[24] The Frondeurs, as they came to be known, became a focal point for the energies of those notables who had found themselves increasingly marginalized at the hôtel de ville under the Condés.

The power vacuum in Dijon was only exacerbated by the fact that Condé's replacement, César de Vendôme, enjoyed neither the title nor the powers of a provincial governor. Vendôme's charge as supreme military commander in Burgundy was much more limited in scope. The seemingly temporary nature of his mission meant that he had little leverage with local political leaders, most of whom anticipated that Condé (who remained governor even during his imprisonment) would eventually return.[25] Convinced that he would never win over Condé's supporters or ensure the city's loyalty as long as they dominated the mairie, Vendôme threw his support behind the Frondeurs, especially Millotet, who was known to be a leading opponent of Condé's local clientele.[26]

The first sign of impending trouble came over the nomination of the garde des évangiles in June 1650. Vendôme wanted the surgeon Etienne Buisson (who denied that he had sought the duke's favor) named to the post and had requested that the selection be delayed until his arrival at Dijon. De Mongey, however, refused to do so, citing his need to leave the city for personal business. Another échevin, the bourgeois Jacques Chauvrenault, tried unsuccessfully to halt the proceedings, which ultimately resulted in the election of the elderly physician Alexandre Rapin.[27] By that point, the procureur Genreau noted in his memoirs, Vendôme had already decided that he would ensure Millotet's election and spared little effort in support of his new client, making sure that he received the "king's vote" from the Chamber of Accounts and even diverting royal revenues to purchase votes, declaring that "it would be better for the king to lose a hundred thousand écus" than to lose the election.[28] Millotet eventually triumphed with nearly 1,400 votes (compared with a mere 81 for De Mongey) in an election marked by numerous irregularities, most notably the widespread participation of individuals who did not meet the tax requirements for voting established in 1611. Both Rapin and Lenet appealed Millotet's election, but Vendôme obtained an arrêt from the royal council confirming its outcome as well as lettres de cachet ordering Rapin and the avocat Jean Bourrelier, another of Millotet's opponents, to come to Paris to explain their actions, a trip that would cost the elderly Rapin his life.[29]

Condé's release in February 1651 not only exacerbated tensions within the city; it also resulted in a countercoup that entirely reversed the political situation in Dijon. News of the prince's liberation prompted a massive nocturnal celebration. Large groups of armed inhabitants marched through the streets, led by Defrasans, Bourrelier, and other leading Condéans, beating the *toscin,* throwing stones at the homes of the mayor and his allies, and shouting "Vive Condé!" Bouchu held a magnificent ball where, one of Millotet's supporters recounted, everyone wore the colors of Condé and the Spanish. The jubilant Condéans also built a large *feu de joie* in the place St.-Jean and had a "Te Deum" sung at St.-Etienne Church, openly challenging the legitimacy of Millotet's regime by appropriating ceremonies the mairie used in its public celebrations.[30] A few months later, despite Millotet's attempts to curry favor with Condé, the prince obtained a new arrêt from the royal council striking down Millotet's election. On 11 May, Bourrelier was named commis à la magistrat. In his speech, he thanked the prince for "reestablishing the city's privileges." The following day, the Mairie sent three avocats and a procureur to thank Parlement for its help in having the city's privileges restored.[31]

While all this was going on, Condé engineered an exchange of governorships with the duke of Epernon, whose ineffectiveness and high-handed methods were at least partially responsible for driving Guyenne into revolt during the Parlementary Fronde. While using his vast clientele to maintain de facto control over Burgundy, Condé planned to launch a rebellion from Guyenne and drive Mazarin from the kingdom. At first, Epernon tried to placate the city's notables, especially the prince's supporters. He promised the mairie that he would "contribute everything that depends on the authority His Majesty has given me for the conservation of your privileges," and that he would not seek to impose a candidate at the upcoming election.[32] The Frondeurs' initial appeals to the new governor met with little success. Epernon refused Millotet's offers of support, noting that he had promised Condé that he would not allow Millotet's reelection. Rather, he insisted, his goal was to "restore to the people this liberty to elect their mayor, following their privileges," and he was personally "indifferent" to the ultimate outcome. Although he asked the mairie for information about individuals "who can be useful in the service of the king and the public" in order to "help you make choices in the next election," Epernon conceded that he could not offer much advice before reaching Dijon and simply admonished the mairie to prevent "factions, brigues, et monopoles," to ensure that the elections were carried out in the "customary manner," and to make sure that only individuals of known quality were elected. As with Vendôme, however, Millotet was ultimately able to play on the new governor's fears of an uncontrollable mairie dominated by the prince's supporters. Shortly before the elections, Epernon threw in his lot with the frondeurs, provoking a new electoral crisis.[33]

The mayoral elections of 1651 were arguably the most contested and chaotic since the early seventeenth century. Condé's supporters rallied behind Jacques Defrasans, an established figure in municipal politics who had already served seven terms as mayor. "All of the city's inhabitants were divided," the Auditor Gaudelet wrote in his journal, as Defrasans and Millotet engaged in widespread bribery and solicitation in an attempt to gain control of the hôtel de ville.[34] Bouchu spoke openly of the "disorder" in the city and accused the frondeurs of heightening the risk of "sedition." The mairie, citing the spread of "scandalous words tending towards sedition" and "several illicit assemblies both day and night" instituted a curfew and a ban on public gatherings. Less than a week before the election, Bouchu obtained an arrêt from the royal council that restated the requirements of 1611 and declared Millotet ineligible to run for mayor, prompting reports that the populace was threatening to set fire to the city if the avocat-général was not elected.[35] Millotet's supporters, meanwhile, accused Bouchu of attempting to buy the votes of the procureurs. Epernon secured a lettre de cachet declaring both Defrasans and Millotet ineligible. On the morning of the election, seven avocats and the avocat-général Quarré entered Parlement with news that a large number of vignerons were threatening violence if they were prevented from voting.[36] With the threat of a popular uprising hanging over them, both sides searched for compromise candidates. Condé's supporters put forth Bourrelier, whom even the conseiller Malteste (generally a supporter of Millotet) described as "a man of honor and spirit." The Frondeurs, meanwhile, turned to Malteste's father, the avocat François Malteste, whose "great reputation, and . . . known probity and prudence" (if his son is to be believed) made him an excellent candidate to pacify the warring factions. In the end, Bourrelier withdrew, and Malteste was elected almost unanimously with over 1,800 votes (many of which came from ineligible vignerons, as Parlement noted).[37]

With Epernon's open backing, Millotet was again elected mayor in 1652 and 1653. Five years later, Epernon again tried to return Millotet to the vicomte-mayeur's office, provoking a new electoral crisis that laid bare the divisions among the city's notables. On 13 June, the échevinage met to select a garde des évangiles. Hughes de La Croix, a *trésorier et payeur des gages* who does not appear to have been closely aligned with any faction, had been commis à la magistrat for the previous two months while Mayor Comeau was in Paris. La Croix suggested that he should continue to hold the gospels and seals, and that electing a garde des évangiles under the current circumstances would be contrary to the city's privileges.[38] According to Gaudelet, however, Millotet had already persuaded a majority of échevins to name one of his friends and allies, the avocat Jacques Rousseau, to the post. To avenge the insult, La Croix decided to challenge Millotet and quickly gained the support of a considerable portion of the city's notables and populace. In his journal, Gaudelet recounts how a divided Chamber of Accounts initially voted to give La Croix the "king's vote" before reversing itself under intense pressure from Epernon. The governor also sent the outgoing échevinage a letter requesting their support for Millotet's candidacy, while the procureur-syndic Gillet opened an investigation into alleged "brigues et monopoles" by La Croix. Just prior to the election, Millotet published a counterfeit royal ordinance threatening those who did not vote for him with a 100-livre fine.[39]

The behavior of Millotet and his supporters, according to Gaudelet, prompted many to believe that "he wanted to violate [their] liberty and deprive them of their privileges." La Croix was elected handily by a margin of 1,090 to 318 but never took office. Ironically, Millotet appealed to Parlement, accusing La Croix of buying votes from the wine growers and the poor, accusations that Gaudelet and later city councils both rejected. The garde des évangiles Rousseau refused to let La Croix assume office in spite of Parlement's orders to the contrary. Meanwhile, Epernon obtained an arrêt from the royal council annulling the election. His efforts to have Millotet named mayor, however, were frustrated by Mazarin, and Comeau was instead continued in office for a third term. The following year, following the Grand Condé's return as governor of Burgundy, La Croix was once again elected vicomte-mayeur by an overwhelming margin.[40]

As we saw in chapter 2, the mairie vigorously defended its right to name its members–especially échevins–throughout the first half of the seventeenth century. During the 1650s, however, groups vying for control of the hôtel de ville, along with Vendôme and Epernon, repeatedly invoked the authority of the royal council to name échevins sympathetic to their cause. Such conflicts were even more frequent, more protracted, and more destabilizing to the cohesion of the city's avocats and other notables than external interventions in the mayoral elections.

The first controversy erupted in June 1650 when Millotet, with Vendôme's assistance, obtained a lettre de cachet naming all twenty échevins. When Millotet presented the letter to the outgoing échevins, who had assembled to choose their successors, all but two (those who had earlier opposed Rapin's nomination as garde des évangiles) protested that the letters violated the city's privileges. One of those present, the procureur Genreau, later wrote in his journal that Millotet "wanted to demolish the city's privileges."[41] Over Millotet's objections, these échevins (including nine who had voted for him), proceeded to choose a provisional échevinage, pending remonstrances to the king.[42] The following afternoon, an assembly of notables summoned by the outgoing échevins met in the presence of "a large number of inhabitants of all conditions" to debate further measures. With the conseils de la ville and many of the parish officers in attendance, the assembly voted to send a deputation with the city's remonstrances to the regent. The only recorded opposition to this decision came from the avocat Claude Dorge, ensign of St.-Michel Parish.[43] Such maneuvers, however, only delayed the inevitable. On 21 July, Vendôme entered the hôtel de ville armed with a new lettre de cachet and accompanied by one hundred soldiers to install an échevinage named by the regency. Proclaiming that the city's privileges were not being trampled, he chastised the recalcitrant échevins, saying, "His Majesty finds it very strange that a company such as this one has the audacity to override his orders." A majority of the échevins left the council chambers in protest and marched to Parlement where, according to Genreau, Bourrelier delivered a "wonderful" speech denouncing Vendôme's coup. The court, however, refused to intervene, in spite of Bouchu's vigorous lobbying.[44]

Following the Grand Condé's release, Millotet's échevinage was thrown out of office along with its mayor, as the prince obtained an arrêt from the royal council reestablishing the city council of 1649. The naming of échevins after Malteste's election the next month appears to have taken place without incident, especially since Malteste, in what may have been a gesture of conciliation, named several Condéans to the council. Three months later, however, Epernon obtained a royal arrêt reestablishing the échevinage that had served under Millotet, with several alterations. At this point, as the conseiller Malteste noted in his *Anecdotes secretes,* even Millotet's staunchest supporters were growing uneasy with such repeated external interventions in the naming of municipal officials.[45]

Epernon's inability to manage Dijon's divided municipal elite led to a new crisis in the summer of 1656, and the governor's heavy-handed response demonstrated just how tenuous the mairie's political privileges had become. The trouble began when the avocat and mayor-elect Jean Siredey presented his slate of anciens to the outgoing city council. After ratification of the avocat Philibert Huissier, who as garde des évangiles was automatically continued, the échevins rejected Siredey's nomination of the avocat Issac Quarré in favor of another avocat, Jacques Baudot. Siredey accused Baudot of purchasing his election and stormed out of the hôtel de ville along with Quarré, the avocat Bénigne Griguette, and six others. After Siredey refused Epernon's summons to settle the matter, Huissier and the remaining échevins proceeded to elect the remaining eighteen échevins *par provision*.[46] This provisional council apparently never sat, however, because Siredey and his followers obtained a parlementary arrêt continuing the outgoing council pending the outcome of their appeal. On 4 July, Parlement ordered new elections, which Epernon's secretary attempted to halt by claiming that the governor had obtained an arrêt from the royal council. When he failed to produce a copy, Quarré, Griguette, and their allies carried out new elections; they were retained as anciens, while Huissier and Baudot were voted out. A week later, the arrêt du conseil cited by Epernon's secretary arrived. Rather than simply naming a set of échevins for the year, it ordered a radical overhaul of the municipal regime, reducing the échevinage to six, who were to be named by Epernon.[47]

The échevinage was restored to its traditional size in 1658, due in part to lobbying by Rousseau and Huissier.[48] The following year, however, brought more gubernatorial intervention. Even before the La Croix–Millotet controversy arose, Epernon secretly obtained an arrêt from the royal council authorizing the new mayor (presumably Millotet) to name all twenty échevins. When the arrêt was presented to the outgoing échevins along with a second one overturning La Croix's election, five avocats and two other échevins walked out of the council chambers, protesting that the arrêts violated the city's privileges. In spite of this, the garde des évangiles Rousseau, who presided over the session in the absence of Mayor Comeau, named the new échevinage in the presence of the remaining échevins as well as the intendant and the governor. The following year, Condé obtained a similar arrêt empowering La Croix to select all twenty échevins. "It is true that this was against the ordinary forms," Gaudelet commented in his journal, "but there were no other easy means to prevent divisions between Sieur De La Croix and the outgoing échevins."[49]

Other conflicts and controversies throughout the decade also fostered divisions among the city's notables. In some cases, the divisions reflected larger social tensions within the city. Millotet and the Frondeurs, for example, regularly exploited their popularity with the city's disenfranchised lower classes in their conflicts with Condé's supporters.[50] Other conflicts dragged on for years, often before the royal council and far-flung parlements. In October 1650, for example, the mairie revived accusations that Pierre Guillaume, one of Condé's leading supporters, had insulted the mayor and the échevins at Parlement a year and a half earlier and ordered him removed from office. In retaliation, Parlement suspended Millotet from his functions as avocat-général, prompting the mairie to send the avocat Calon to protest to the royal council. For the next six years, the mairie was forced to defend itself against repeated litigation by Guillaume at the royal council and the Parlement of Grenoble.[51] Although the Mairie won the vast majority of its legal skirmishes with Guillaume, it finally decided to settle with him to avoid additional legal costs, creating a rente in his favor paying 110 livres per year.[52]

The mairie's conviction of the avocat Pérard of speaking and writing "words of scorn against the honor of the city's magistrates" also resulted in drawn-out litigation between a leading avocat and municipal political figure and the mairie. Pérard appealed to Parlement, where he had several relatives, but the case was transferred, first to the privy council, then to the Parlement of Grenoble, and finally to the *requêtes de l'hôtel.* After an unfavorable decision in late 1656, Pérard allegedly compounded his offense by accusing the mairie of lying in its case and of deliberately failing to present him with an arrêt ordering him to pay the court costs. Unlike Guillaume, Pérard appears to have had more success against the mairie in court. In December 1658, he obtained permission from the royal council to sue two current and two former échevins personally before the Parlement of Aix. A few months later, the mairie, perhaps once again fearful of rising legal costs, agreed to arbitration with Pérard.[53]

The weakening of the municipal political system was also reflected in several lengthy conflicts between the mairie and local authorities, most notably Parlement and the chambre des élus. Throughout the decade, but especially during Millotet's terms as vicomte-mayeur, the mairie and Parlement clashed on matters large and small. In a calculated insult, Parlement dispatched a huissier to summon Millotet to the palais de justice in Jan. 1651 to hear its orders that the Mairie surrender the deliberation ordering Guillaume's destitution as conseil de la ville. In response, the city council sent six avocats to protest that the mayor should be summoned by a greffier and to complain that Parlement was interpreting the Mairie's actions "sinisterly and . . . in a negative light."[54] The mairie also complained that Parlement was interfering in its oversight of the night watch; refusing to pay certain taxes it owed for poor relief, defense, and mud removal; and interfering in the selection of municipal officials, among other things. The mairie also protested that

Parlement was abusing its judicial authority by issuing over fifty groundless arrêts against it on the reports of biased commissioners without ever bothering even to summon the city's procureur-syndic and by suspending all of the mairie's avocats and procureurs from their professional functions. The royal council responded with a declaration chastising the sovereign court and its members for using its authority "more to avenge their own quarrels and those of their relatives and friends than to render justice," and First President Bouchu in particular for acting daily "to the prejudice of [Dijon's] rights and privileges" by creating false controversies as a pretext for intervening in municipal affairs–most notably the naming of city officials. Despite this rebuke, difficulties between the two bodies persisted for much of the decade in the form of a protracted dispute over seating arrangements at the Jacobin convent for the mass preceding the mayoral election.[55]

The mairie's difficulties with the chambre des élus appear to have started when the élus had the échevin Monnyot imprisoned in the midst of a dispute over the method for calculating Dijon's taille obligations. Although Parlement ordered Monnyot released and attempted to broker a resolution, the elus obtained an arrêt from the royal council ordering Monnyot reimprisoned, pending payment of 102,000 livres. The city also sought Epernon's help in negotiating a solution, but its repeated entreaties seem to have garnered little response prior to late June, when Epernon instructed the élus to reach an amicable solution. The mairie, meanwhile, named six of the city's "most famous" avocats to fashion its response. Epernon's attempts to broker a resolution personally failed when the mairie rejected the élus' demands that the mayor and échevins be held personally liable for the 10,000 livre difference between the two methods of calculating the taille. Eventually, the governor ordered the mairie to pay the sum provisionally and gave it three months to raise 6,000 livres.[56] Epernon's orders hardly brought an end to the dispute, however. When the old method of calculating the taille was restored in late 1658, the mairie sought to have its 10,000 livres refunded. The élus, in turn, sought to have the vicomte-mayeur excluded from the chamber until the city paid other sums the élus claimed were owed. Various lawsuits and other conflicts between two bodies lingered into the early 1660s.

The constant electoral disputes and other conflicts of the 1650s brought divisions among the city's avocats into the open. Many of those who had been established at the hôtel de ville in the 1630s and 1640s, such as Pierre Guillaume, Jacques Defransans, and Jean Bourrelier, sided with the Condéans. Others, such as Calon and Jean Godran des Chasans sided with the Frondeurs. Some avocats, meanwhile, appear not to have been closely aligned with either faction, or to have moved between sides as events warranted. The clearest indication of this can be seen in the échevinages of 1650 and 1651. Three échevins elected provisionally by the city council in June 1650–the avocats Paul Mailly and Bernard Grusot and the bourgeois

Jean Garnier—were retained on the échevinage by the royal council. The following year, three avocats from the échevinage chosen in June—Mailly, Etienne Bréchillet, and Maurice David—were retained when the crown replaced the échevinage in September.[57] Rousseau, who had been named conseil de la ville under Condé, meanwhile, allied with Epernon and Millotet in the late 1650s.

The divisions among the city's avocats and other notables can be seen in their use of competing discourses of obedience to the king and defense of municipal privileges to justify their actions, with rival parties adopting the position that best suited their interests as events warranted. After Millotet's election in June 1650, the outgoing échevins protested the royal patent letters naming the new city council. Millotet insisted that the king's letter had ended the outgoing council's authority and that it "does not prejudice the city's privileges, which are much different than the right of nomination which the said échevins pretend to have." The outgoing échevins retorted that "if His Majesty had been advised of the privileges accorded the city for the nomination of échevins, confirmed by the kings his predecessors and followed without violation, he would have never derogated from them."[58] A few days later, the avocats Bourrelier and Guillaume Berruchot were sent to ask Parlement "to give its protection to the conservation of the city's privileges," while the conseil de la ville Bénigne Guenebault was instructed to write Vendôme, Mazarin, the Marshal Villeroy (the king's personal guardian), and Secretary of State La Vrillière "to ask them to impart their favors to maintain the city in its privileges . . . and [in] the immemorial possession of the said city for the nomination of échevins."[59] When Vendôme visited the hôtel de ville the following month to execute the royal orders, Rapin and Bourrelier insisted that the mairie's privileges gave it the right to name its own officers, prompting Vendôme to order "those who do not wish to obey the king's will" to leave the chamber.[60] When his election was overturned the following May, Millotet declared himself ready to "gaily cast off a heavy burden I never sought" since "it is an absolute necessity in all affairs to blindly obey the king."[61] His opponents, meanwhile, celebrated "the reestablishment and conservation of the city's privileges," deputizing the avocats Berruchot, Louis Jannon, and Claude Colin as well as Genreau to thank Parlement for its help.[62]

The following month, the situation reversed itself after the royal council disqualified Millotet from running for mayor. Millotet's friend the avocat Antoine Calon cited the city's privileges in a request to have the avocat-général's candidacy reinstated, while Conde's supporters invoked royal authority to justify his exclusion.[63] When Parlement ordered the election of a new échevinage in 1656, the garde des évangiles Huissier protested that although he had come to the council chambers prepared to carry out the court's arrêt, he could not do so "because [Epernon] has received orders from the king, which must necessarily be obeyed." When Epernon's greffier failed to produce a royal arrêt, however, Quarré and Mayor-elect Sirey insisted on the need to elect new échevins "in light of the urgent necessity of political affairs."[64] Three years later, the avocats Baudot and Bourée, both of whom had been supporters of Epernon, stormed out of the council chamber along with five other échevins (three of whom were members of the bar) on hearing the royal council's arrêt permitting the mayor to name all twenty échevins for the year. Proclaiming that they "were ready, as always, to obey His Majesty's orders," they nonetheless opposed "[these] arrêts obtained . . . by surprise and without the parties having been heard" and declared that they "could not consent to this nomination, which is directly against the privileges of the city." At the same time, La Croix asked the Parlement to block the arrêt's execution, claiming that "the privileges of the city would be entirely obliterated." The garde des évangiles Rousseau countered by asking the remaining échevins if "they were ready to obey the King's will" and carried out the arrêt with their support despite Parlement's express prohibitions.[65]

In spite of these divisions, avocats and notables from all political persuasions did not entirely abandon their defense of the mairie's interests and powers throughout the decade. The most obvious example of this was François Malteste's term as vicomte-mayeur at the height of the Fronde. Malteste appears to have worked to build consensus among the competing factions. He permitted the election of several of Condé's supporters to the échevinage and refused to subordinate the city's interests to Epernon's orders, pressing efforts to have Dijon's château destroyed despite Epernon's opposition. At the same time, Malteste also led the mairie in refusing Condé's request to give the château's commander military authority over city, saying that to do so would "shock the city's most noble and ancient privilege and would tend to ruin the magistracy's authority."[66] In 1653, the mairie refused to turn over its registers to Parlement, which claimed the authority to remove offensive deliberations from them. As it had done before the Fronde, the mairie continued to challenge attempts by the Bailliage and other authorities to encroach on its rights and jurisdictions and moved swiftly to quash "evil rumors against the honor of the magistrates."[67] In 1655, the mayor and échevins pledged their personal belongings to cover the city's debts. The following year, the mairie sent the avocat Bénigne Griguette and another échevin to protest that Epernon's nominee for procureur-syndic had not been a resident of the city long enough to hold the post. The avocat Rousseau, meanwhile, spent much of 1659 traveling to Paris and Rouen to oversee the mairie's litigation against the city's Ursulines, the heirs of the abbot of St. Bénigne, the privileged inhabitants of the city, and the élus.[68]

Overall, however, the mairie's dependence on gubernatorial authority became almost total over the course of the 1650s. There was hardly any protest when Epernon had the échevinage reduced to six in 1656. When the mairie sought to have the council restored to its original size, it lobbied the governor. Although the mairie protested Epernon's candidate for procureur-syndic, it quickly backed down in the face of the governor's intransigence.[69] Throughout the decade, the mairie looked to Epernon for protection in matters large and small. When one of the lieutenant du roi's sergeants marched in front of the garde des évangiles during a procession, the mairie wrote to ask Epernon "not to suffer that the magistrate be troubled in its rights and privileges." Shortly thereafter, it wrote that the parish officers had violated the city council's authority by seeking full exemption from the taille rather than the 50 percent reduction the mairie had requested from the crown. "We ask your protection," the mairie wrote, "so that the said officers do not remove themselves from obedience which they owe the chamber and that [our] authority no be diminished."[70] Throughout its dispute with the élus, the mairie repeatedly asked Epernon for his "intentions," his protection, and his help in resolving the conflict. In early 1659, meanwhile, it successfully appealed to the governor to have the troops lodged in the city removed and the exiled Parlement returned.[71] As we shall see in the next section, this trend continued after the Grand Condé's return as governor in 1660, helping to pave the way for the crown's definitive reorganization of the mairie and local politics in Dijon in the summer of 1668.

The End of the Old Municipal Regime

On the surface, the eight years following the Grand Condé's return as governor in 1660 appear to have marked a return to the municipal political system of the pre-Fronde years. Elections for the mayor and city council all took place without incident. The day-to-day workings of the city government settled back into the patterns that had developed during the first half of the century. The initial period after Condé's return also saw a winding down of some of the conflicts of the previous decade. The deposed conseils de la ville, as noted earlier, were restored to their positions through the prince's mediation. The city council, meanwhile, made a formal effort to have the 1659 arrêt alleging "brigues et monopoles" by La Croix overturned as "contraire à la verité," and prejudicial to the mairie's honor and future reputation.[72]

This apparent continuity, however, masked several subtle but important shifts in the networks of power, both local and national. Condé, although still a prestigious war hero and a formidable figure, had returned from his Spanish exile chastened. His weakened position made him less able to defend provincial interests at court. At the same time, he and his agents were also more active in supervising the municipal regime, regularly nominating candidates for vicomte-mayeur.[73] The mairie, in turn, became even more dependent on Condé's intervention to protect its authority and to help it manage its conflicts. When the mairie removed the avocat Soyrot from the captaincy of St.-Philbert Parish for refusing to lead its inhabitants under arms during an important annual procession, the mairie asked Condé to support its decision and to name a replacement as quickly as possible.[74] Shortly after the prince's return in 1660, the mairie asked Condé to help settle disputes with the royal treasurer Jannin, the chambre des élus, and the city's Ursulines. When the various parties failed to resolve their differences, the mairie sent the avocat Boullier to ask the prince to continue "the benefits which the city has always received from Your Highness's protection." Condé agreed, promising to write in favor of the city's claims. When the Parlement of Rouen moved to judge Jannin and the élus' suits against the city the following year, the mairie asked Condé to use his influence with one of the élus or to ask the *rapporteur* at Rouen to delay the Jannin case, claiming that "this affair is capable of ruining this poor city . . . and has already cost more than 15,000 livres for travel and legal costs." A few weeks later, the case was suspended. The dispute with the élus was finally resolved in 1663 when Boullier and Bourrelier negotiated a settlement on behalf of the mairie with Condé's help.[75]

An even more significant change was the growing power and activity of an important new local political figure, the royal intendant, Claude Bouchu (1655–83). The once-established view of intendants as bureaucratic administrators who supplanted the great nobility and venal officeholders has been replaced in recent years by a more nuanced understanding of these royal commissioners as informants and mediators who coordinated, rather than circumvented, the actions of governors, royal officers, and other local authorities with those of the crown. Although intendants are no longer seen as agents driving the French state's political modernization and centralization, even revisionist historians believe that their regular presence in the provinces had significant consequences for local political cultures and practices. By extending the "sovereign gaze" and projecting royal authority more fully into the provinces, intendants helped cut through the conflicting jurisdictions and institutional confusion characteristic of the state at the local level in the first half of the seventeenth century, elevating the importance placed on law and royal interests in the conduct of provincial affairs.[76]

Although Dijon had housed intendants since the 1630s, Bouchu's predecessors played only a minor role in local politics. Burgundy's first three intendants–Charles de Machault (1635–38), Jacques Mangot (1638–44) and Louis de Machault (1644–50)–were all Condéan clients who acted as auxiliaries of the governor. To be sure, they were not mere figureheads; Charles de Machault presided over a commission investigating municipal debts and in 1637 held a lit-de-justice to force registration of contentious fiscal edicts.

On the whole, however, they were so unobtrusive that the Parlement of Burgundy was one of the few not to demand their withdrawal in 1648.[77]

Claude Bouchu, who became intendant of Burgundy at the age of twenty-eight and served until his death in 1683, differed from most intendants, who were generally outsiders with few local connections, limited mandates, and relatively brief terms of residence (six years, on average).[78] Claude, by contrast was the product of an established Burgundian parlementaire family; his father, Jean, had been Parlement's first president from 1644 to 1653. While a client of Condé's, he also received Mazarin's secret support and protection during his early years. Indeed, the cardinal's choice of Bouchu as intendant was in keeping with his preferred strategy of playing rival local factions off one another. Epernon had removed the Bouchu clan from the first presidency after Jean's death, but the Bouchu clientele remained a formidable regional network.[79] In choosing Bouchu to assist Epernon, Mazarin gained an agent who would watch the governor carefully. Not surprisingly, then, the intendant quickly became a controversial figure. In 1660, for example, Parlement sent deputies to ask Condé to have the post of intendant suppressed in Burgundy, or at the very least, to remove Bouchu. The following year, the chambre des élus protested that Bouchu's commission for the verification and liquidation of communal debts "will ruin the privileges, sap the foundations, [and] ruin the order and economy of the province."[80] The mairie, however, seems to have had few problems with the intendant. By the beginning of the 1660s, it was sending regular deputations to pay the city's respects and it regularly presented him with gifts of wine.[81]

Beginning in the early 1660s, however, the mairie saw its fiscal liberties increasingly eroded by the growing power of the royal commissioner. The city's financial situation, already precarious prior to the Fronde, became increasingly dire during the 1650s. In 1653, an assembly of notables approved selling the office of municipal secretary to raise money. The elimination of the conseils de la ville was also proposed as a cost-saving measure, at least on the surface. In 1655, the council resolved to verify the city debts and retire them when possible to free its revenues for other needs. At the same time, it also required the mayor and échevins to pledge their moveable and immoveable goods as security for the city's debts. That same year, the municipal receiver was forced into hiding to avoid arrest by officers of the Bailliage. The mairie had outstanding debts of over 17,841 livres but had no cash at all on hand.[82] By early 1663, when Bouchu began verifying and liquidating Dijon's debts, these totaled almost 459,462 livres. In contrast, the city's annual revenues averaged only about 31,200 livres per year, of which 18,000 went to ordinary annual expenses.[83]

Bouchu's increased activity in local politics and government was not limited to the fiscal realm, however. After Epernon had the échevinage reduced to six in 1656, Bouchu was ordered to investigate "factions and disobediences," in Dijon. During the controversial election between Millotet and La Croix three years later, Bouchu was again ordered to investigate possible "brigues et monopoles" and to ensure that the arrêts continuing Mayor Comeau in office and allowing him to name the échevinage were executed.[84] The mairie also increasingly interacted with the intendant in the course of its regular business and disputes. When the mairie ordered unauthorized construction by the Ursulines torn down in 1659, it asked the intendant not to intervene and sent Rousseau to discuss the affair with him. When the Ursulines obtained an arrêt against the city from the royal council, Bouchu urged both sides to work out their differences informally. Several years later, the mairie asked the intendant to deliver an arrêt from the royal council concerning the taxation of privileged inhabitants.[85] Not all interactions between the city council and the royal commissioner were so cooperative, however. In 1662, the mairie asked Bouchu to rescind his order that the mairie pay for the transport of a prisoner condemned to the galleys. A little more than a year later, meanwhile, Bouchu obtained a royal arrêt limiting the mairie's longstanding authority over collecting the taille.[86] Once a figure of negligible importance in local politics, by the mid-1660s the intendant figured frequently in the mairie's deliberations and activities. This trend would increase even more after the monarchy radically reconfigured the size, composition, and authority of Dijon's city government in June 1668.

By all outward appearances, the mayoral election of June 1668 was thoroughly ordinary. As had become his custom, Condé wrote the city magistrates in advance requesting the reelection of the incumbent mayor, the Master of Accounts Jean Joly. The avocat Jacques Chesne was selected garde des évangiles and took possession of the gospels, seals, and other marks of the mayoral office five days before the election. The only sign that anything might be out of the ordinary came on the eve of the election, when the mairie ordered an investigation into alleged "brigues et monopoles" despite the apparent calm in the city. The next day, the election took place without incident, and Joly was returned to office. This would be the last time that Dijon's municipal elections followed the traditional format dating from the ducal era.[87]

Two days later, Bouchu informed the mairie that he would attend the next day's session when the outgoing échevins were to name their successors so that he could "inform [them] of the King's will," and carry out an arrêt from the royal council. The arrêt, which had been obtained in April by Mayor Joly, ordered the échevinage reduced from twenty to six and did away with the traditional system of parish-based representation and the selection of échevins by cooptation. Henceforth, échevins would be chosen by the vicomte-mayeur without regard for parish residence. Future elections would take place every two years instead of annually and term limits were also changed for échevins, allowing those retained as anciens to serve for four consecutive years.[88] To forestall opposition, the king named the six échevins for the following two years by lettres de cachet. When two of those named were unable to serve, Bouchu selected their replacements.[89]

Several factors help to explain why the crown decided to undertake such a radical transformation of Dijon's mairie. The arrêt of 20 April justified the royal council's actions on both fiscal and political grounds. The size of the échevinage, it stated, created an unnecessary tax burden because échevins paid reduced tailles while in office. The arrêt also accused the échevins of using their power over the taille rolls to favor their friends. Indeed, the reforms included an overhaul of the collection of the taille. Instead of having échevins draw up taille rolls for their parishes every six months, the royal council ordered the échevinage as a group to compile the parish rolls once a year. The intendant also suspected the hôtel de ville of wasting municipal revenues on frivolous deputations to Paris, gifts to patrons, and other unnecessary matters. The arrêt also claimed to rectify "the many difficulties [created by] the great brigues et monopoles" that result during in the naming of échevins, disorders which, the arrêt continued, threatened the city's tranquility since "la police, which is the principal function of the said échevins, is poorly performed."[90] Louis XIV's profound mistrust of cities capable of resisting his authority, as they had done during the 1650s, was likely another factor. A smaller city council whose membership turned over less frequently would ultimately prove much easier to control. Finally, it appears that Mayor Joly may have played an important role as well. In a letter to the intendant Nicolas Auguste de Harlay almost two decades later, the merchant and former échevin Dupelu claimed that Joly, fearing that he would not be reelected in 1668, obtained the arrêt to ensure that he would remain mayor.[91]

As the preceding chapter demonstrated, however, Dijon's notables, especially the avocats who dominated the hôtel de ville, had a long history of successfully blocking efforts to change the form of the mairie and the elections. They had used litigation, negotiation, and the lobbying of powerful patrons to block or reverse at least four significant attempts to alter the mairie's privileges in 1599, 1608, 1630, and 1656. In the past, these techniques had been effective in suspending changes or at least mobilizing opposition while the mairie worked relentlessly, sometimes over the course of several years, to preserve the city's privileges. More often than not, the mairie successfully sapped its opponents of critical momentum while it rallied local support, and its persistence enabled it to find the allies it needed to maintain or restore the status quo. It is hardly surprising, then, that the mairie turned to the same strategy once again. Perhaps forewarned of the arrêt, the avocat Antoine Calon announced to those present that he had been charged by several "notable inhabitants" to oppose its implementation.[92] The monarchy, however, had clearly anticipated such opposition, as the arrêt ordered Condé, the lieutenants-généraux, Bouchu, and all other royal officials in the province to execute its provisions regardless of any opposition. Mayor Joly read a letter from one of the secretaries of state indicating that the changes had Condé's full support and that "any deputation on this subject would be useless and disagreeable to His Majesty." Bouchu, meanwhile, instructed Calon to give his appeal and procuration to his secretary, who would forward them to the royal council, which definitively quashed the appeal five months later and prohibited all other royal tribunals from intervening.[93] Still, some avocats and notables refused to surrender quietly. In early December, a city council deliberation noted the circulation of "seditious words against the magistrature of this city," and "against the service of the King, the public good, and the authority of the magistrates." When the mairie ordered a *monitoire* published to uncover the identity of those slandering the new regime, a large number of vignerons gathered at St. Michel Church, "although this was not their custom" to drown out its proclamation.[94] While we have no direct evidence to suggest that some of the city's notables may have been trying to foster a popular uprising against the new mairie, only a week later the conseil de la ville Jean Siredey informed the city council that he had been empowered by more than one hundred fifty notables to seek the arrêt's revocation, as well as a general exemption from the taille for the city, and asked the magistrates to join his efforts. The following February, the city's doctors, procureurs, and notaries asked Parlement not to register the royal patent letters confirming the échevinage's reduction on the grounds that the arrêt had not included them among the ranks of eligible officeholders.[95] Ultimately, however, Siredey was prevented from pursuing his appeal by another arrêt from the royal council, while the doctors, procureurs, and notaries were reassured by the city council that they were eligible for municipal offices as either gradués or bourgeois.[96]

Why did Dijon's mairie fail to beat back the arrêt of 20 April 1668 when it had successfully done so many times in the past? Divisions among the city's notables, and especially the avocats, were undoubtedly a major factor. As noted earlier, the arrêt had been solicited by Mayor Joly. And although avocats such as Calon and Siredey led the opposition to it, others, such as Chesne, quickly emerged as defenders of the new regime. In October, the city council ordered his factum justifying the changes at the mairie in response to Calon's appeal printed and distributed to the populace, the intendant, and the governor.[97] Several more avocats–among them Etienne Malpoy, Pierre Monin, and Claude Gauthier–were willing to serve on new city councils in the years immediately following 1668. Such collaboration between members of an urban elite and the crown, of course, was hardly unique to Dijon. As David Parker has noted, "[T]he price of absolutist politics was the confirmation of the social status, influence, and wealth of those able and willing to betray their corps, community, or province."[98] Such appears to have been the case in Dijon.

Bouchu's presence was another determining factor. As an effective and unassailable representative of royal authority, the intendant, by his very presence, transformed the ground rules for political activity in Dijon. Until 1668, the mairie benefited from the confused, overlapping, and poorly defined networks of power that made up the municipal political system. The avocats' skillful use of the legal system and informal networks of influence enabled the mairie to preserve much of its autonomy and authority over local affairs. The avocats' abilities also made it easier for the city government to interpose itself as a mediator between the monarchy and the urban populace. Bouchu's constant surveillance and his unquestionable authority as an agent of the king helped to clarify jurisdictional boundaries and reinforce local hierarchies. Most important, he closed off many of the avenues of opposition and resistance that the mairie had long used to preserve its status as a legitimate local political actor. Thanks to the intendant, the king and his ministers were now better able to project their authority onto the Burgundian capital. The intendant's ability to provide reliable and independent information to the royal council also undermined the mairie's role as a key intermediary institution. Dijon's traditional mairie had been rendered superfluous, and once it was no longer able to manipulate the legal system or gain the support of powerful protectors, it simply could no longer protect its privileges and traditional practices. As a result, the mairie and most of the notables who staffed it ceased to be legitimate participants in local politics and the workings of the French state. Of course, the monarchy still needed agents who could manage day-to-day affairs in the city and ensure the execution of orders from Paris and Versailles. That is why, in the decades that followed, Dijon's once-powerful city government would be gradually transformed into an arm of the local royal administration.

Whatever the reasons behind the arrêt and its successful implementation, its implications were dramatic. Curtailing the size of the échevinage and reducing the frequency of elections resulted in nothing less than the mairie's political marginalization. For decades, Dijon's city council had been an integral part of the state and its operations at the local level. Through the mairie, the city's notables and especially its avocats, who believed their personal and professional qualities made them hommes politiques, were able to participate in local governance and the workings of the French state. Although these opportunities did not disappear altogether after 1668, they did decline precipitously. Placing the selection of the échevinage in the hands of the mayor, invariably a client of the Condés, transformed municipal offices into the domain of a small, hand-picked circle of trusted clients, friends, and allies. The mairie was also deprived of most of its political authority, agency, and status. In July 1668, another arrêt of the royal council forbade the mairie from dispatching deputations without informing the intendant of its "purpose and necessity," and obtaining his approval."[99] These restrictions, which appear to have been enforced quite consistently, were restated in 1678 and 1683 as the monarchy extended them to almost all of the kingdom's cities. Although the crown justified these moves as cost-cutting measures, they also had enormous political implications. In addition to closing off one of the most effective methods of protest and resistance available to the mairie, it also widened the distance between the city's notables and the crown. No longer part of the body politic, the mairie and the city's notables could no longer communicate directly with the king and his ministers. This intermediary role was now filled by the intendant, while the mairie was reduced to a minor entity under the tutelage of the crown.

The mairie's greatly reduced autonomy and authority was also evident in the intendant's *tutelle* over the city's finances. The ability to control its own purse had been a cornerstone of the mairie's continued vitality during the first half of the century. Its ability to use its patrimonial revenues, tax income, and borrowing capacity enabled it to pursue litigation, send and maintain representatives at the royal court, bribe influential officials, and display its position in the local political order through expensive gifts and lavish ceremonies, such as those staged for the entrées of kings and governors.[100] In 1669, less than a year after the reorganization of the municipal government, Bouchu was given the power to oversee Dijon's revenues and fixed expenses. The city's ordinary expenses, which had never been less than 18,000 livres per year, were now fixed at a little over 11,000 livres. The mairie was also prohibited from levying any new taxes or raising old ones without royal approval; nor could it borrow money without the prior authorization of a general assembly, the provincial élus, and the chancellery. Colbert's edict of April 1683 expanded the powers of intendants throughout France to fix ordinary municipal expenditures and required their authorization for all extraordinary expenses. Dijon's mairie was prohibited from floating new loans except to pay for the lodging of troops, lost necessities, and the restoration of church steeples. Loans that were approved had to be subscribed by an assembly of "la plus saine partie" of the city.[101]

Conclusion

Throughout the first half of the seventeenth century, Dijon's mairie had successfully defended its traditional political privileges and jurisdictions against "encroachments" by Parlement, Burgundy's governors, and the monarchy. Their repeated efforts to reduce the city council to a more manageable size, to change the format for electing municipal officials, and to limit the scope of the mairie's powers and jurisdictions had all been largely unsuccessful. This was in large part because the avocats who figured prominently in Dijon's municipality were able to use a combination of legal strategies and the influence of powerful patrons to block changes to the mairie or to have them rescinded quickly when they did occur. They were able to exploit the fragmented character of governmental authority in the ancien régime French state to preserve the hôtel de ville's powers largely intact. The delicately balanced municipal political system that evolved during the first half of the seventeenth century unraveled under the internal and external stresses of the 1650s and early 1660s. The removal of the Grand Condé as Burgundy's governor created a power vacuum that ultimately led to the collapse of the structure in which municipal politics in Dijon took place. The inability of Condé's replacements, Vendôme and Epernon, to fill this vacuum adequately allowed intraelite conflicts to escalate and to harden into deep factional divides. One result of these divisions was that the city's avocats and other members of the civic elite no longer rallied around the defense of the mairie's privileges and the preservation of the city's political identity as they had in the past. Instead, they often turned to the king's "absolute" power and to the external authority of governors and others in their attempts to gain and maintain control of the mairie.

While Dijon's urban notables were becoming more divided, Burgundy's royal intendants and, after 1660, the Condés and their agents, effectively supplanted the mairie and those who staffed it as the primary intermediaries between Dijon and the crown.[102] When the arrêt of 20 April 1668 was made public, several of the city's avocats once again turned to their old strategies of resistance only to find that they no longer worked in the face of a more coordinated and determined set of royal authorities. In addition, a number of other avocats worked to counter local opposition to the arrêt and its transformation of the city government. The mairie was now largely marginalized from the local state apparatus in Dijon. The notables who dominated it were, for the most part, excluded from local governance.

According to William Beik, France's towns "became less independent" under Louis XIV, "but the people who ruled them had a better hold over them."[103] This appears to have been the case in Dijon. In the wake of the 1668 reorganization of Dijon's municipality, a few individuals benefited from increased protection from the Condés, the royal intendants, and their local agents. These individuals also saw their social status and prestige enhanced. Shortly after the arrêt of 20 April 1668 was executed, Louis issued patent letters permitting the city magistrates to wear red robes in public, and the mairie promptly set about obtaining the necessary materials for the magistrates' new outfits.[104] But as the next chapter will show, those who remained at the mairie exercised far less political power and initiative than their predecessors. After an initial period of transition, Dijon's city government was reduced to a small administrative body whose membership and actions were closely supervised by the Condés, the royal intendant, and their agents. The arrêt of 20 April 1668 also had devastating consequences for political participation by the city's avocats. Dijon's avocats, like urban notables across the kingdom, were the big "losers" of Louis XIV's reign. Where they had once been minor, but by no means insignificant, members of the French "political nation," they now found themselves écartés from the French state and deprived of the roles in local governance to which they had long been accustomed. The nobles, officers and great landholders who "basked in the sun" of Louis XIV's reign did so at the expense of those like the avocats of Dijon, who learned the hard way that their services as intermediaries between city and crown were no longer necessary.

Chapter 4

From Local Government to Royal Administration (1669–1715)

The situation in Burgundy's capital after 1668 seems to bear out Nora Temple's claim that the later Bourbons "transformed municipal officials into the petty agents of the bureaucracy," and reduced them to the status of "simple executives, responsible to the royal government." A number of other historians have echoed this view. Roland Mousnier, for instance, concluded that "cities and communities were increasingly administered from Paris, then Versailles, by a multitude of arrêts du conseil rendered on the basis of intendants' reports."[1] Robert Harding argued that although the intendants did not supplant regional governors, they did transform the crown-town relationship from an exchange of reciprocal favors into a routine administrative tutelage. Peter Wallace observed that in the newly acquired city of Colmar, "Royal absolutism ushered in a profound change in the political ethos of the men who served in municipal office. They continued to administer day-to-day civic affairs, but now as bureaucratic agents of the crown." "Individual urban economies and oligarchies did indeed prosper," Beik noted in his study of Languedoc, "but, in terms of power, the consulates were at the bottom of the provincial pecking order, and everyone else's gain was their loss."[2]

Dijon thus fits into a much larger trend in seventeenth-century French state formation. Although not exactly representative, for the situtation in no ancien régime city was ever fully representative, the changing relationship between the municipal government of Burgundy's capital and the crown broadly captures the changing balance between center and periphery in the French state. The events of 1668 and developments in the years that followed led to profound and sweeping changes in the character of the mairie and its officials. After an initial period of transition, Dijon's municipal officers were quickly subsumed into the larger structures of the emerging "administrative monarchy." The mairie's activities were closely monitored by Burgundy's governors, the royal intendants, and their agents, who selected the mairie's officials from a small circle of well-connected and obedient notables. The new regime did work to defend the mairie's remaining jurisdictions and the status of its officers, resorting to litigation when necessary. On the whole, however, it appears to have developed a much less adversarial relationship with Dijon's other authorities. This was due, in large part, to changes in the way local political disputes were resolved. Instead of applying "judicial" methods such as litigation, which were so prominent in the early seventeenth century, the mairie and other bodies now settled many of their conflicts "administratively," through queries to higher authorities–most notably the intendant and the governor. This clarification of the channels and limits of authority, however, came at a price for the mairie, which became much less insistent on preserving its rights and jurisdictions inviolate as it had in the past.

Although the arrêt of 20 April 1668 transformed municipal political life in Dijon, it did leave some traditional elements in place, most notably the fiction that the mayor and échevins continued to be elected according to traditional methods. This final link with the past was shattered with the sale of municipal offices to a small group of notables in 1692. Although the city government tried to portray the "repurchase" of its offices as a means of preserving its privileges, in reality the event marked the consolidation of municipal power in the hands of the few individuals who financed the city's payments to the king. As the final section of this chapter will show, the transformation of Dijon's mairie after 1668 and the closing of the hôtel de ville after 1692 had a profound impact on the political careers of Dijon's avocats. Once active participants in local governance, they now found themselves largely excluded from the political nation and from participation in the workings of the early modern French state.

Structuring a New Mairie

Although Dijon's city government was fundamentally transformed in the aftermath of 1668, the new municipal system emerged only gradually over the course of the following decade. The first selection of new échevins in June 1670 resulted in multiple controversies as rival kin groups maneuvered to dominate the newly diminished city council. When the incoming mayor, the conseiller Jean Catin, named the controller Marc and the avocat Gautier as senior échevins, the garde des évangiles Chesne protested that they were both ineligible, having already served for three consecutive years. He and the three other outgoing échevins then elected four new city council members, including Chesne's in-law, the avocat Antoine Morelet, and the bourgeois Cuisinier, an uncle of one of the other four outgoing échevins. When Marc and Gauthier named a rival slate of their own, Chesne and his supporters threatened to appeal their retention as senior échevins. Catin, meanwhile, protested that his powers were being usurped and threatened to appeal Cuisinier and Morelet's elections, prompting Chesne and his backers to withdraw their threat. This accommodation appears to have been short lived, however. A few days later, the merchant Claude Dupelu appealed the election of Cuisnier and Morelet to Parlement while Chesne and his followers appealed Marc and Gauthier's retention. On 10 July, Parlement struck down Cuisinier's election and the mairie named Dupelu in his place.[3] In late September, the royal council ruled Marc and Gauthier ineligible to serve as senior échevins, although the mairie apparently did not learn about the arrêt until the beginning of January when Chesne and his supporters presented it to the intendant. Instead of conceding, however, the mairie quickly dispatched Marc, Gauthier, and Dupelu to Paris to find out if the judgment had been obtained with Condé's knowledge. Bouchu, meanwhile, helped to calm the situation in Dijon by brokering an agreement with Marc and Gauthier not to attend city council meetings while the dispute remained unresolved. In mid-March, Condé's personal intendant, Thésut de Ragy, informed the mairie that the prince and his son both wanted Marc and Gauthier reinstated and secured the city council's agreement.[4] This did not resolve the matter, however. A month later, the three other échevins–Morelet and the avocats Pierre Monin and Bénigne Desnoyers–began to boycott city council meetings, declaring that "they could not suffer having them [Marc and Gauthier] sitting in the chamber" when the royal council had forbidden them to do so. For several weeks, the three rejected repeated entreaties to end their holdout, with Monin and Desnoyers even refusing to serve as envoys to greet the Grand Condé's son, the duke of Enghien, in advance of his official entry as Burgundy's new governor. Only after Enghien met with the entire city council at the logis du roi was the matter settled. Morelet, Monin, and Desnoyers agreed to accept Marc and Gauthier's presence and "to live in peace with and to render all honors due to monsieur le vicomte-mayeur."[5]

Such conflicts, however, quickly became a thing of the past when Burgundy's new governor, Henri-Jules de Bourbon, and his local agents took control over the naming of all mayors, échevins, conseils, and parish officers during the early 1670s. Although Burgundy's governors occasionally intervened in the selection of city officers during the first half of the seventeenth century, they usually limited themselves to nominating the mayor and parish officers.[6] After the Grand Condé returned as Burgundy's governor in 1660, he regularly nominated candidates for vicomte-mayeur who were invariably elected with near unanimity. This pattern continued after 1668, as when Henri-Jules routinely informed the city council of his choice for mayor well before the scheduled elections. By the end of the 1670s, if not earlier, the governor also began to name the entire échevinage. His letter of 19 May 1679 is typical. "The renewal of your city's magistracy is to take place on the next St. Jean's day," he wrote the mairie. "To fill the place of the four who must leave [the city council], one cannot make a better choice than . . ." In two other letters also dated 19 May 1679, Henri-Jules instructed the outgoing council to cast their votes in the mayoral election for the conseiller Baudinot de Selvres, who had previously served as mayor from 1674 to 1677, and informed Selvres which échevins should be retained in office.

The governor also named the city's procureur-syndics and conseils de la ville. Syndics were usually named around the same time as new mayors and échevins, whereas conseils were nominated as needed. In June 1687, for example, the prince wrote to inform the mairie that one of its conseils had settled in Paris with no intention of returning and advised the council to name the avocat Normant in his place.[7] Such nominations, of course, do not necessarily reveal the intense behind-the-scenes lobbying of Condé's local agents by those seeking municipal positions, as the process for naming a new conseil after the untimely death of Aimé-Joseph d'Azincourt indicates. Both Condé's personal intendant and the city council recommended Jean Gault over two other candidates. At the same time, however, another avocat, Philippe Midan, obtained the backing of the royal intendant. Reluctant to undermine either his agent or the king's, Condé sought to work out a compromise. A week later, Midan's blind and elderly older brother agreed to resign as conseil, allowing both Gault and Philippe Midan to be sworn in as conseils. Thésut de Ragy's logic in promoting Gault's candidacy, meanwhile, also shows that the Condés and their agents tried to distribute offices as widely as possible. Although the two other candidates were both worthy, Thésut de Ragy wrote, both were subdelegates of the royal intendant and thus already enjoyed the exemption from lodging troops conferred on the conseils. Gault's ability, the support of his fellow échevins, and his need for the position's benefits all figured in Thésut de Ragy's ultimate decision.[8] Those who aspired to municipal office in Dijon after 1668 were thus, as Beth Nachison has written, "well-advised to apply directly to the governor's intendant," who funneled information about various candidates and their abilities to Chantilly, relayed the prince's decisions to the mairie, and helped to ensure that they were carried out.[9]

The complete control that Condé and his agents enjoyed over the selection of municipal officials also enabled them to keep loyal and effective mayors and échevins in office beyond the limits established by the arrêt of 20 April 1668. After 1676 and until the monarchy's sale of municipal offices in 1692, compliant city councils were often continued in office beyond their two-year terms. In 1676, 1683, and 1686, for example, the intendant went to the hôtel de ville in person to deliver arrêts postponing the elections for a year and continuing the current échevins in office unless, as was the case in 1683, some of them had already served four consecutive years. In 1689, the intendant ordered the elections delayed until an arrêt from the royal council could be obtained postponing them for another year.[10] Two years earlier, the crown not only delayed the elections, which had not taken place since 1684, for nearly a month, it also ultimately issued an arrêt naming the mayor and échevins.[11] Thus, as the flow of information and commands between Dijon and Chantilly grew in scope and became increasingly regular and routinized, the prince and his agents were increasingly able to impose their will on local institutional practices and procedures.

Had Burgundy's governors and intendants simply named municipal officials directly, some elements of the pre-1668 municipal political system dominated by Dijon's avocats might have remained in place. However, external control of the hôtel de ville went much further, as the mairie found itself under consistent surveillance by the Condés, their agents, and the royal intendant. In November 1668, for example, Bouchu personally supervised the registration and execution of a royal arrêt against the Jansenists. When intendants did not attend the mairie's meetings in person, they left no doubt that they were still following events at the hôtel de ville carefully. In a letter dated 3 May 1678, for instance, Bouchu instructed the mairie to register the royal edict forbidding cities to send deputations without prior approval from the intendant. "Do not fail to execute it point by point," he admonished the city council, directing it to "justify its registration and publication to me within two weeks in conformity with my ordinance." In a stern letter to the syndic in 1689, the intendant Florent d'Argouges warned, "above all I recommend a great deal of diligence, because if you take too long to render account to me of what you have done, I will be obliged to inform the king of it."[12] The year before, Argouges compelled the mairie to remove the municipal secretary from office, which it did without apparent complaint. He also asked the city to send him biweekly accounts of grain prices and to draw up a list of all municipal officers, including the dates they entered office, their wages, and all vacant posts.[13]

Throughout the first half of the seventeenth century, the mairie benefited from a distinct lack of coordination among the various institutions and authorities that made up the local state in early modern Dijon. As we saw earlier, the many avocats active at the hôtel de ville were able to take advantage of these jurisdictional conflicts and ambiguities to protect the mairie's privileges and political power. By the final decades of the century, however, the mairie found that it had little room to maneuver in the face of extensive cooperation between other local and regional authorities. Although the Condés were essentially absentee governors, Nachison has shown that they maintained an active correspondence with their agents and were closely involved in managing provincial affairs. Letters from Bouchu, the greffier des états Rigoley, and others show the extent to which the governor, his agents, and the intendant cooperated in their supervision of the city. In one letter to Colbert, for instance, Bouchu noted that the prince had already written twice to inform him of his desire to have the city magistrates ask for a continuation of certain octrois to finance several urban improvement projects. In two letters in August 1681, Rigoley informed the mairie that the intendant had charged him with sending the city copies of an arrêt ordering the suppression of octrois on the Saône river and two other ordinances. In return, he ordered the mairie to send him the *procés-verbaux* and attestations of their registration and publication. In 1682, Condé asked Rigoley to send copies of Dijon's privileges and instructed him to write Bouchu about the recent declaration on the *crües* that he had sent to Colbert. Later that year, he informed Rigoley that he saw no need to change the mayors and échevins of several unnamed towns because Bouchu was happy with them and noted his support for the intendant's plan to "completely do away with deputations, as they are useless and have already been dealt with by general arrêts." In January 1684, Condé wrote to Rigoley to say that the pavement of Dijon's streets could be improved and that the intendant would determine where repairs should start. Five years later, he told Rigoley that until he had met with the intendant he could not decide what to do about the mairie's claims that its patrimonial revenues had declined. At the same time, he ordered Rigoley and Argouges to cooperate on a response to the city's request for 1,600 livres to pay for repairs.[14] Under these circumstances, the city council's decision in December 1670 to have portraits of Louis XIV and his father, as well as those of Enghien and his father and grandfather, hung in the council chamber seem especially revealing. It was now as if the mairie's every move literally took place under the watchful eyes of France's kings and the region's royal governors.[15]

By the late 1670s, Dijon's municipal officials had been reduced to little more than local agents of the royal administration and the provincial governor. One of the mairie's principal activities in the years after 1668 was to publish and execute orders of the royal council, Burgundy's intendants, and other authorities.[16] Increasingly, the Condés, their agents, and the royal intendants became the driving force behind the mairie's activities and directed the governance of the city through their hand-picked officials at the hôtel de ville. In 1675, Bouchu directed the mairie to compel the city's masons and laborers to work on the fortifications of the town of Auxonne. In 1686, Harlay ensured that the mairie executed royal orders to expel Protestant ministers from the city. Seven years later, Argouges sent the échevins to nearby villages in order to secure grain supplies for Dijon at "reasonable prices."[17]

The extensive efforts to pave the city's streets and generally embellish the urban landscape show both the extent to which the prince and royal agents were involved in municipal affairs and the mairie's general lack of initiative or political agency during this period. Although Bouchu described the city streets in 1678 as "so deformed and so dirty that it is nearly impossible to traverse them," noted that the hôtel de ville "was on the verge of ruin," and said the Suzon was "so polluted that it almost constantly gave rise to malignant fevers that could degenerate into the plague," it was Condé and not the mairie who proposed an ambitious plan to confront these problems. In a letter to Rigoley in January 1684, the prince even detailed the kind of repairs he wanted made and the types of stones to be used. Later that year, he asked Rigoley to oversee the street repairs being undertaken as well as for a map with the name of each street written on it. In January 1687, he asked Rigoley to redo the map because it was not accurate in several places. He also requested that the new map be color-coordinated according to both the types of stones used for paving and the current state of repair.[18] When the mairie did act, it generally sought the guidance and approval of the governor, the intendant, or their agents. This was partly a consequence of the mairie's loss of control over its revenues and expenditures. The result of all these changes was no less than the mairie's political transformation from an active member of the corporate order of the realm into a legal minor under the tutelage of the monarchy and its agents. Those who staffed the mairie were similarly transformed from active participants in the workings of the French state and local governance into simple agents acting on behalf of, and largely at the behest of, other authorities.

The Remnants of Municipal Authority

Although the mairie became increasingly passive and more dependent on the prince and the intendant, the mayor and the échevins continued to exercise and defend their authority in a circumscribed realm. Freed from the larger political concerns that had occupied so much of its attention prior to 1668, the city council became much more meticulous in its attention to the mundane details of urban life, including the collection of taxes and the behavior of the city's artisans and vignerons. With the support of the intendant, the mairie also continued to supervise daily areas of concern closely, such as the prices of grain, bread, and other necessities; the activities of city's various métiers; and the maintenance of public areas. Finally, it continued to resist vigorously attempts by the city's other tribunals to encroach on the one privilege that had been left relatively unchanged after 1668–its right to dispense justice in the city and its immediate surroundings.

Jurisdictional conflicts between the mairie and other tribunals remained common in the decades after 1668. The right to affix seals and inventory the belongings of the recently deceased remained a constant source of friction between the mairie and the Bailliage throughout the period. In December 1682, the royal tribunal claimed the right to affix seals in the homes of officers and other privileged individuals who had not yet attained perfect nobility. When the city's attempts to seek a mediated resolution failed, it sought permission to use 1,000 livres from the *deniers d'octroi* to pursue the case at the royal council and dispatched an échevin to follow the case at court. The dispute was finally settled by the intendant Harlay, who tried to split the difference. In 1686, he ruled that the Bailliage would have jurisdiction over the *anoblis* themselves, while the mairie would continue to exercise authority over their wives, family members, domestics, and other household members. Harlay's decision was ratified by an arrêt of the conseil privé on 11 March 1688.[19]

Although there is no direct evidence to show that the Bailliage sought to profit from the mairie's 1668 reorganization, the two bodies contested each other's authority in other areas as well. In June 1676, for instance, the mairie sued the lieutenant-criminel of the Bailliage for usurping its jurisdiction in a case between the procureur Chantrier and his wife. Three years later, the mairie and the Bailliage became embroiled in a jurisdictional dispute over the theft of some lamps from Nôtre-Dame Church, which the royal court claimed was a sacrilege and thus a *cas royal.* When the mairie asserted its authority to try the murderers of a huissier of the Requêtes du Palais and to investigate several thefts from the churches of St.-Lazare and the Jesuits, the Bailliage (now the Présidial of Dijon) filed suit at the Great Council. In 1697 and 1698, meanwhile, the mairie appealed two lawsuits concerning the présidial's encroachments on its judicial privileges to the royal council.[20] Although the mairie lost some ground to the présidial in the final decade of the seventeenth century, it successfully maintained much of its judicial authority within the city.[21]

As was the case in the first half of the century, challenges to the mairie's authority did not come from the Bailliage alone. When officers of the justice of St.-Bénigne affixed seals in the house of a recently deceased huissier in the Cour des Monnaies, the mairie quickly filed suit at Parlement, alleging that the church's officers had also affixed seals in several other houses abutting the monastery of St.-Etienne or located in its courtyard.[22] For at least two decades, the mairie waged a running battle with the Degaud family for the high justice rights over the nearby village of Fontaine-les-Dijon. When the body of a man who was struck by lightning was removed from Fontaine before the mairie's officials could examine it, the city council dispatched two échevins to Parlement to pursue the matter and to press the city's case with the reporting judge. After a public brawl, the mairie ordered the officials of Fontaine's medium and low justices to halt their investigation or face a fine of 20 livres.[23] Dijon's city council also endeavored to preserve its "immemorial rights" to administer justice and the bans de vendage in the nearby village of Chenôve as well.[24]

The new regime also sought to defend and even to augment the mairie's political status and symbolic authority when possible. During the ceremonies honoring the anniversary of the city's surrender to Henri IV in 1669, the auditor Gaudelet noted, the Bailliage dispatched its huissiers to guard the bench of the *fabriciens* of St.-Michel Church after learning that the city government had planned to occupy it. The mairie, in turn, sent its sergeants to remove the Bailliage's men forcibly, leading Parlement to prohibit both bodies from sitting at the bench in question. A decade later, the mayor complained to the first president of the Chamber of Accounts when one of the court's correctors refused to yield to him on the street. The first president assured the mairie that there was no "plot" on the part of the correctors and that "if this corrector had failed to yield to [the mayor], it was because he did not see him coming, since he has very poor vision [*ayant la vue très-basse*]." When the Estates of Burgundy passed several decrees challenging the precedence of the two échevins who accompanied the mayor as Dijon's Third Estate delegates, the mairie convoked an assembly of notables and then asked both the governor and the intendant to quash the Estates' decrees.[25]

Although the mairie still sought to protect its status and defend its remaining powers and jurisdictions, its tactics underwent an important and revealing shift in the years after 1668. Litigation at Parlement, the royal council, and elsewhere did not disappear, but it did become noticeably less frequent as the mairie turned increasingly to Burgundy's governors and intendants to resolve its disputes with other individuals and corporations. In January 1679, for example, a number of the city's inhabitants complained that the élus were collecting money to pay for étapes for royal troops and forcing innkeepers to lodge soldiers, all in violation of the city's privileges. When the élus demanded that their orders be executed without delay, the mairie insisted that they suspend their actions until it had a chance to inform Condé and receive his instructions.[26] Similarly, when the Bailliage's officers claimed the right to affix seals in the homes of anoblis under the terms of a 1643 settlement, the city council "invited" the royal court to allow Condé to "resolve our differences." Although the mairie was unsuccessful in this instance, the arrêt of 11 March 1688, which settled the dispute, stipulated that the intendant would judge all future disputes over the affixing of seals.[27] That same year, the city immediately sought to have a lawsuit at Parlement by the officers of the Monnaie over their inclusion on the taille rolls transferred to the intendant.[28] In the years after 1668, the intendant was also called on to settle a conflict between the mairie and the Chartreux monastery over the monastery's attempts to enclose the waters of the *fontaines et cours du Renne;* to adjudicate a jurisdictional dispute between the mairie and the *juges-consuls;* and to hear lawsuits against a notary and scribe who refused to turn over minutes of the tax rolls to the mairie's greffier, a *fermier du domaine* concerning the weights used in the city's *halles,* and messieurs de la Sainte-Chapelle.[29] An inventory of ongoing lawsuits by the city compiled in 1688 shows that six of the mairie's eight pendng cases were scheduled to be heard by the intendant, whereas only two were being pursued at Parlement.[30]

There are several reasons that the mairie may have turned to the governor and intendant rather than the courts, as it had in the past. The potentially high costs of litigation were undoubtedly not appetizing to a city council that no longer controlled its own finances and was constrained to operate within a limited budget. Indeed, as noted earlier, the mairie had to seek permission from royal commissioners to pay the costs of pursuing before the royal council its conflict over the affixing of seals with the Bailliage. Going directly to the governor or intendant probably also offered a quicker and more efficient way of resolving disputes between the mairie and other authorities. Furthermore, since the mairie's lawsuits were often resolved through the extrajudicial mediation or arbitration of the governor and other influential figures, even during the first half of century, the mairie's change in tactics may simply have been the formalization of what had already become an established, informal procedure.

Regardless of the cause, it seems fair to say that jurisdictional disputes and other conflicts between the mairie and other bodies became less "judicial" and more "administrative" in nature during the final decades of the seventeenth century. This can be seen in the way jurisdictional conflicts–a chronic problem of local governance–were handled. Disputes that would have resulted in protracted conflicts and prolonged litigation during the first half of the century were now settled, often quickly, by queries to the governor or the intendant. When Parlement claimed jurisdiction over a female domestic who "had conspired against the sacred person of the king" in 1670, the mairie decided that it would wait for Enghien's instructions before proceeding further, even though it had already interrogated the prisoner. Ten days later, the mairie quietly transferred the case to Parlement on the governor's instructions.[31] Nearly a decade later, the governor gave the mairie jurisdiction to hear the valet of Prieur de Baize's accusations against the prince's guards for insults, even though the valet had initiated proceedings before the lieutenant-criminel of the Bailliage.[32]

Even the dispute between the mairie and the Bailliage over the affixing of seals, which made it to the royal council, was settled by the intendant in a fraction of the time it took to resolve a similar conflict during the first half of the century. Indeed, the manner in which the case was settled is quite revealing. In the spring of 1686, Harlay wrote to the controller-general to inform him of his investigation into several inhabitants whose claims of nobility were being contested by the mairie. Although he initially considered this case to be separate from the city's dispute with the Bailliage, Harlay reported, Dijon's mayor had convinced him that the two were in fact inseparable. In addition to opposing those who claimed nobility before the intendant, the mairie was also constrained to respond to the Bailliage's claims before Parlement. Citing the Parlement's bias in favor of the Bailliage and the prohibitive cost of evoking the case to another jurisdiction, Harlay asked for jurisdiction over the city's dispute with the Bailliage. Later that year, he ruled that although the mairie's rights were better established, the Bailliage would have jurisdiction over the anoblis themselves, while the mairie would retain it over their families and other household members.[33] Although the mairie succeeded in getting the intendant to resolve the case relatively quickly, it did not obtain the confirmation of its jurisdiction that it undoubtedly desired. Instead, the result was a quick clarification of the relative authority of the city and the Bailliage, one the intendant conceded was motivated by pragmatic rather than legal concerns. In spite of the outcome, the mairie seems to have accepted Harlay's decision without protest, leaving the impression that it preferred a speedy clarification of its powers to the kind of tenacious defense of traditional rights and prerogatives that had characterized the city council's actions during the first half of the century.[34]

The post-1668 mairie comes across as much less insistent on preserving its rights and jurisdictions and far less belligerent in its relationship with other authorities than its predecessor. This can be seen in its dealings with the Chartreux monastery mentioned above. When the mairie first learned of the monks' plans to enclose the marsh, which was under the city's jurisdiction, it summoned a general assembly to discuss how to proceed against this violation of its "immemorial rights." A month later, however, the mairie received a letter from Condé directing the city to reach an accommodation with the Chartreux and offering to mediate personally during his next visit to Dijon. The matter appears to have lain dormant for a while, but eventually the city conceded part of its "immemorial rights" to the monastery. In a deal brokered by Bouchu, the mairie allowed the Chartreux to enclose part of the marsh while leaving the waters' source free and under the mairie's jurisdiction.[35] Similarly, when Parlement excluded échevins who lacked university degrees from judging criminal cases carrying afflictive penalties, the mairie did not object to Parlement's infringement on its corporate rights. Instead, it temporarily suspended the three such échevins in its ranks while it mustered evidence to present to Condé and the intendant. Six months later, Condé resolved the matter, ruling that échevins *non-gradués* could continue to hear such cases, but that they could no longer carry out the initial investigations into them.[36] Indeed, the mairie may have even been deferential to a fault at times. In 1694, for instance, the president of the Tournelle complained to the controller-general that the mayor had refused to investigate a brawl that recently occurred "on the streets in the middle of the day," but instead had ceded jurisdiction to the intendant. The mairie, he claimed, even refused Parlement's orders to take up the case, as "its fear of and respect for M. the Intendant has prevailed over its duty and the obedience it owes to Parlement's arrêts."[37] As we shall see below, it appears that those outside the hôtel de ville may have been more assertive in defense of the mairie's rights than the city council was on its own behalf.

The few instances when the city's traditional privileges were invoked after 1668 show how completely the mairie had been co-opted by the Condés, the intendants, and their agents. They also suggest that Dijon's avocats had largely ceased to be active public defenders and spokesmen for the city's privileges, perhaps because they had shifted their attention to the kinds of legal scholarship and other writings that will be discussed in chapter 6. When the scheduled elections for the new mayor had not been held by the end of June 1687, for instance, the merchant and former échevin Claude Dupelu complained to the intendant that "many of our principal inhabitants cannot suffer that in the capital city of our Province, the election of their magistrates be deferred without any reason." In an enclosed mémoire, Dupelu accused the Master of Accounts Jean Joly, who had been mayor in 1668, of wanting to monopolize the post of vicomte-mayeur. Nearly twenty years before, Dupelu charged, Joly obtained the arrêt of 20 April 1668 out of fear that he would not be elected to a second term. Now, he continued, the eighty-four year-old Joly "wants to never leave this charge," but that

> he cannot be mayor this year, at least not without violating the arrêts and letters patent verified in Parlement, and assuredly he would never be mayor by the voice of the people, both because of his age and because of the continual novelties that he introduces against the arrêts that he himself has obtained. He is trying to obtain an arrêt that will make him mayor without the suffrage of the inhabitants and to abolish their privileges. In order to be master of the Chamber, he also wants to name the échevins and procureur syndic . . . which should have been done on the twentieth of this month.[38]

Dupelu's stirring rhetoric in defense of the city's privileges, most notably the inhabitants' right to elect their mayor, recalled the headier days of the late sixteenth and early seventeenth centuries, when the mairie successfully fended off repeated outside efforts to encroach on its electoral privileges. The outcome of Dupelu's appeal, however, showed just how much things had changed in Burgundy's capital. Harlay promptly ordered Dupelu's arrest, characterizing his request as "tending toward sedition," especially since a recently published royal order had delayed the elections. Dupelu, it appears, escaped prison only by throwing himself on his knees before the intendant and begging his forgiveness. Harlay also forced the recalcitrant merchant to go to the hôtel de ville and apologize in person before the city council. Two weeks later, an arrêt from the council of state named Joly mayor and selected the échevins and syndic for the following two years as well. As if to highlight its subservience to the crown and its agent, the mairie decided to post the arrêt at the city's intersections before even reading its contents. The garde des évangiles, the avocat Mamet Chevaldin, then thanked Harlay "for all his kindness and the pains which he has taken" and reiterated the mairie's "respect, submission, and obedience" to the king and his commissioner.[39] Any ambiguities about the intendant's control over municipal governance in Dijon were dissipated with the brevity of Dupelu's protest and his complete humiliation over the elections of 1687. Chevaldin, unlike many of his predecessors at the mairie, made no attempt to contest this reality but rather quietly acquiesced to it.

Within the corridors of power as well, the mairie ceased to be an active participant in debates over its own powers, depending on others to defend its prerogatives on its behalf. In 1689, Controller-General Pontchartrain floated a proposal to create a lieutenant-général of police and several auxiliary officers in Dijon as well as in other towns in Burgundy that housed Bailliage courts.[40] Pontchartrain's plan was supported by the intendant Argouges, who wrote that it would improve the administration of justice, as "the mayors and échevins who have exercised it until now have done so badly." The intendant added that Dijon's mayor rarely held judicial audiences any more, preferring to turn them over to young avocats and that urban officials "only think of helping out their friends" while in office.[41] First President Brulart, in contrast, objected in phrases that echoed not only Dupelu's arguments but also those of the mairie during the first half of the seventeenth century. The controller-general's plan, he protested, "would change and reverse the province's ancient usage, where popular magistrates have always held the exercise of these jurisdictions." The right of the people to elect their magistrates annually, he continued, "is so ancient that in some cities its origin is no longer even known." Brulart also complained that urban officials' jurisdictions had been confirmed by France's kings, who long before had exempted Burgundy's towns from the Ordinance of Moulins (1566). Brulart also noted that it would be difficult to find qualified individuals to serve as mayors if the controller-general's plan was executed–a situation that could have serious implications for the regional Estates. Finally, Brulart argued, the new offices "would greatly upset" the inhabitants of Burgundy's towns. "Nothing is more dear to them than their privileges," he wrote. "Each person believes he has obtained and preserved them by his affection and fidelity, and regards the advantage of choosing his magistrates and changing them from time to time as an honor and a good."[42] A half century earlier, such arguments were commonplace at the hôtel de ville and issued forth regularly from the avocats on Dijon's city council. That they were now expressed by Parlement's first president and not by the mairie on its own behalf is testimony to the cultural as well as the institutional transformations wrought by the arrêt of 20 April 1668.

By the late 1680s, the Mairie de Dijon had become fully integrated into a new kind of power network–an "administrative monarchy" that more closely linked royal officials at the center with local agents in the provinces in a vertical relationship of command and obedience. A small group of individuals, hand picked by the Condés, the royal intendants, and their agents, now handled the city's affairs. Dijon's municipal officers, like those across the rest of France, "became less independent," but "had a better hold" over their city governments."[43] The enhanced status of those who now staffed the hôtel de ville could be seen in their fine new robes and the new portraits of the mayors and échevins that hung in the city council chambers after 1669.[44] In return, however, they enjoyed far more limited jurisdictions and were much more tightly supervised in their functions. Real political authority and initiative in the city now lay elsewhere, in the hands of the governors, the intendants, and their agents. After 1668, the Mairie de Dijon ceased to be an active component of the local state in any meaningful sense.

Urban magistrates, like many others who held office during the second half of Louis XIV's reign, soon found themselves subjected to intensive fiscal extortion by an increasingly authoritarian crown, desperate to fund its wars against the rest of Europe. John Hurt has recently shown how Louis XIV was repeatedly able to coerce the kingdom's parlementaires into paying *augmentations des gages* and other forced loans that eventually drove some magistrates into bankruptcy.[45] Not surprisingly, those who staffed Dijon's hôtel de ville, like their counterparts across France, were all but defenseless before the fiscal demands of the crown.[46] Any pretense that Dijon's traditional political privileges had survived dissipated with the sale of municipal offices beginning in 1692, to the point that soon thereafter, the vicomte-mayeur himself was publicly accused of "selling the city's privileges."

"Icy se vendent les privilèges de la ville"

As profound as the monarchy's 1668 transformation of the mairie was, it did at least leave intact some familiar elements of the previous regime. Chief among these were the assemblies to elect the vicomte-mayeur, which were now to be held every two years rather than annually. By the 1680s, as we noted earlier, the elections had effectively become triennial events, as compliant city councils were regularly continued in office for a third year. Nonetheless, as Dupelu's 1687 protest demonstrated, many Dijonnais notables still clung to these rights. Even after Harlay spectacularly crushed Dupelu's complaints when the 1687 elections were not held as scheduled, the inhabitants of Burgundy's capital could still claim to have some meager role in the naming of municipal officials. As Brulart informed Pontchartrain:

> If we object that they have deprived themselves of this freedom of choice by the great regard they show towards the governor's recommendations for the nominations of those he proposes, one can respond that they have not given him the right to elect, that a recommendation is not a command, that they have the advantage of changing their magistrates every two years, that the best men [plus honnetes gens] are honored by these positions, which each individual obtains according to his merit.[47]

The last remnants of this fiction disappeared with the monarchy's sale of city offices at the end of the seventeenth century, an event that completed the transformation of municipal politics and Dijon's mairie. In the early 1690s, as the monarchy struggled to keep its armies in the field against the combined forces of England, the Dutch Republic, Austria, and the Holy Roman Empire, it began aggressively to tap the wealth of France's towns, selling virtually all existing municipal offices and creating new ones for sale.[48] In August 1692, Louis XIV created offices of "perpetual mayors" along with new *assesseurs* in all walled cities except Paris and Lyon. The threat of losing control over their city's principal office, it appears, was enough to motivate the leading inhabitants of many major cities, including Dijon, to pay the crown's asking price, often 100,000 livres or more. Elsewhere, intendants ensured that the mayoralty was sold not to the highest bidder, but to the most powerful local institution, such as the présidial in Troyes, the bishop of Beauvais, and the archbishop of Reims.[49] Other cities allowed their chief magistracy to fall into private hands although some, such as Toulouse, quickly repurchased the office at the first possibility. Burgundy's smaller cities, unlike Dijon, saw their mayoralties purchased by the provincial Estates, which henceforth controlled their sale and transmission in conjunction with the princes of Condé. In January 1704, the monarchy sold off some city council seats in each town.[50] Once again, Dijon and a number of other major cities purchased exemptions.

Throughout the period, the Condés and their local agents actively mediated the steady transfer of wealth from the mairie and its officers to the crown so that the city could retain nominal control over the naming of municipal officials. Although the prince and the magistrates claimed they were protecting the city's privileges by repurchasing offices, in reality their actions only furthered the narrowing of political participation that had started in 1668. Municipal offices came to be monopolized by a small group of individuals who were willing to provide the necessary financing and who could maintain the approval of the governor and his local agents. This arrangement only enhanced the city council's near total dependence on, and submission to, Condé, his agents, and the royal intendant, once again furthering a trend dating back to 1668 and even earlier. Those who dominated the mairie after 1692 were obedient and compliant local administrators who usually acted on the initiative of the prince or governor and rarely performed any but the most mundane actions without their approval. In return, Condé protected the mairie's status and even defended its limited police and judicial jurisdictions. The small circle that controlled the hôtel de ville after 1692, meanwhile, used the princes' authority to protect their dominant position and to ensure their control of the small number of offices available at the mairie. As a result, access to offices at the mairie declined even further throughout the last two and a half decades of Louis XIV's reign.

The mairie's handling of the August 1692 edict creating perpetual mayors and assessors typified its response to royal attempts to sell off municipal offices.[51] In late 1692, Condé informed the city council that he had obtained an arrêt du conseil permitting the city to repurchase the offices of mayor and assessors, and invited the magistrates to put up the necessary sum. The following month, the mairie convened an assembly of notables, which decided to "very humbly thank" Condé "with one voice for the continuation of his good-will" and to authorize the mairie to borrow 142,000 livres to repurchase the offices, as well as the recently created position of *commissaire particulier aux revûes et logements de gens de guerre.* The same day, the mayor, échevins, procureur-syndic, secretary, and municipal receiver loaned the city a total of 105,100 livres toward the repurchase of the mayoralty in return for rentes on the city's patrimonial revenues and octrois. At the same time, six other individuals loaned the city 7,700 livres each to repurchase the offices of assessor, which they were then awarded by a grateful mairie. In May 1693, Louis XIV issued lettres patentes reuniting the offices of mayor, assessors, and commissioner for reviews and lodgings to the municipality of Dijon.[52] In theory, at least, the vicomte-mayeur would continue to be elected according to the provisions of the arrêt of 1668, and the assessors would be chosen by the city council. When the monarchy converted three of six seats on the échevinage into hereditary posts a decade later, the city council purchased them, as well as the newly created office of *concierge de l'hôtel de ville,* for 58,300 livres.[53] By the early eighteenth century, the burden of repurchasing the plethora of new offices that the monarchy created had clearly taken its toll on municipal finances. By 1707, according to one estimate, the city had issued rentes totaling more than 780,000 livres to help suppress offices such as the *garde-scel des sentences, jugements et autres actes;* the *jurés visiteurs et mesureurs du bois à brûler et du charbon;* and the *jurés crieurs d'enterrements et cris publics.*[54] To meet its extraordinary obligations, the mairie even created and sold offices such as the largely honorific post of *garde des titres et papiers de la ville,* which the elderly avocat Jean-Baptiste Perruchot purchased for 500 livres.[55]

The Condés and their agents often took the lead in directing the mairie on how to raise the sums needed to repurchase newly created offices. In May 1693, for example, Condé followed the lead of Thésut de Ragy, his local intendant, and suggested that the mairie purchase two offices by levying the parish officers, the conseils de la ville, the substitutes of the procureur-syndic, and the captain and lieutenant of the walls for the necessary sums. Those who could not or would not pay, the prince advised, were to be replaced by others who would. Later that year, he instructed the mairie to offer municipal offices in return for loans needed to pay off 4,000 livres owed to a *traitant.* And when the monarchy created the office of *lieutenant de police,* Condé wrote to one of his local agents to ask "by what means you believe we can find the money to do for the lieutenant de police as we did for the office of mayor."[56] As a result, access to municipal office in Dijon came to depend on financial factors, much like the venal royal offices that had been beyond the reach of so many of Dijon's avocats during the first half of the seventeenth century. Those who held, or desired, a municipal post now had to loan the necessary funds to the mairie. They were then named to the post until they resigned, died, or were removed for incompetence. Entry into the city council had a fixed price, ranging from 25,400 livres for the post of vicomte-mayeur to 5,300 livres for a seat as échevin, the cost of reimbursing one's predecessor for his contribution to the repurchase of the mayorship.[57] The three other principal offices–syndic, secretary, and receiver–were even more expensive, since those who acquired them had to pay for the office itself and for the finance on the mayoralty. Those already in office had to pay to keep their positions as well. In 1694, for instance, the mairie borrowed 26,400 livres to repurchase the offices of the urban militia; it then ordered the current officeholders to finance their offices or resign. In some instances, the mairie made little effort to hide the fact that its members were actively involved in the buying and selling of city offices. Such was the case in December 1692, when the avocat and first échevin Claude de La Loge "reimbursed" the receveur-général de la ville Parisot the 30,000 livres he had paid to finance the office. La Loge wanted to resign as first échevin in order to assume the receivership, but was prevented from doing so by Condé. Stuck with a post that he could not exercise because of its incompatibility with his position as échevin, La Loge ultimately reached an arrangement allowing his older brother, Pierre, to serve as receiver until he was free to do so.[58]

The sale of municipal offices only reinforced royal and gubernatorial control over the mairie, its officials, and their activities. Through their local agents, the Condés monitored the performance of city officials and gathered information about possible successors and replacements. "I do not believe there is any reason to change the magistrates of Dijon," Condé informed Claude Rigoley, secretary of the Estates of Burgundy and one of his local advisors, in the spring of 1696. "We will see at the Estates this coming year if any measures will be necessary in the future."[59] When changes were to be made in the échevinage, Condé wrote either to his local agents or to the city council directly with his orders, often relying on reports from his local agents.[60] The new mayor and four new échevins selected in 1703 had all been recommended by either the royal intendant or Thésut de Ragy, Condé's personal representative in Dijon. Mayoral elections continued to be held after 1693, but only on an irregular, ad hoc basis. Following Mayor Jannon's death in office in September 1694, for example, an arrêt from the council of state ordered elections for a new mayor held in less than a week. The arrêt also named Baudot as the king's candidate and overturned all legal impediments to his election, most notably the fact that the required four years had not yet elapsed since his last term of office. When a new election needed to be held in 1703, the royal council delayed it until August. When Mayor La Botte died in July 1714, elections for the new mayor were held the following month.[61]

Those who bought their way into the city government acknowledged their near complete dependence on the prince, his agents, and the intendant. The new municipal officers named in 1703 immediately wrote to thank the prince and his son, the duke of Bourbon, for their offices and to offer their "entire devotion to [your] service and perfect submission *in all orders that it pleases you to confer to us for execution.*"[62] Decorations with the prince's coat of arms, such as those placed over the entrance to the *jardin de l'arquebus,* and the gold-framed portrait of the prince that the mairie purchased for the council chambers testified to this state of dependence.[63] Not surprisingly, during this period the mairie enjoyed little political agency of its own. The magistrates demonstrated an almost deliberate passivity, awaiting orders from above before acting on anything but the most routine matters. During the early 1690s, the mairie waited for the intendant to order échevins to go to neighboring villages and bring grain to market to alleviate a shortage in the city. Following the death of Mayor Jannon, the échevins refused to name a commis à la magistrat until they had received Condé's orders. The following year, the Mairie asked the prince's permission to borrow nearly 74,000 livres to repurchase several newly created offices. A decade later, Condé gave the échevin La Rue permission to visit Paris for the city's affairs, but ordered him to consult the intendant first. At the height of the famine of 1709–10, it was the duke of Bourbon who wrote the mairie, directing it to take all necessary measures to relieve the suffering of the poor and ordering the mayor to work with the presidents of the superior courts and leading members of the clergy.[64]

In exchange for this "entire devotion to [your] service and perfect submission in all orders," the Condés protected the mairie's status and limited authority. When Parlement objected to the mayor's right to wear a velvet robe in public, the prince sided with the city, noting that the mayors of other important cities enjoyed this right and that parlements elsewhere had no objections. In 1699, when the monarchy created new offices of lieutenants de police, Condé instructed one of his local agents to tell those Burgundian mayors who held police rights to make an effort to keep them. "I hope to have these charges attributed to them," he wrote, for "if this charge is removed from that of mayor, they will lose one the greatest jurisdictions they have."[65]

After 1692, those who performed their duties to the satisfaction of the intendant and the governor were generally able to serve well beyond the customary term limits. Gubernatorial decrees continuing the terms of incumbent magistrates became routine in the 1690s. When Condé continued the incumbent council for yet another year in 1698 and the years that followed, the mayor was deputized to inform the heads of the city's superior courts "as he customarily does in such cases."[66] Indeed, the entire échevinage of 1692 remained in office until 1703. Three of the new échevins named that year remained in office until 1711, as did three others who were named in 1705. The Master of Accounts François Baudot, who became vicomte-mayeur in 1694, also served until 1703. His successor, the conseiller Julien Clopin, served until 1711. In June 1703, the royal council effectively abolished term limits on municipal offices by giving the mairie "permission to continue those magistrates that it elects in the future in those cases where it judges this to be advantageous."[67] However, Condé easily forced out those whose cooperation or efficiency were lacking, sometimes on the advice of their colleagues on the city council.[68]

By cooperating with the governor and effectively carrying out orders from above, municipal officials were actually able to use the prince's authority further to consolidate their hold on offices at the hôtel de ville. In April 1694, for example, the city council asked Condé to keep them in office beyond their two-year term limit, citing their contributions to financing the repurchase of offices. The mayor and the échevins even went so far as to suggest that no arrêt would be necessary, since those who financed the offices could not be removed without first being reimbursed. And although the Condés, their agents, or the intendant generally named officials to vacant posts, the small group that dominated the mairie after 1692 used their access to the prince to obtain additional offices when these came available. When a position as conseil de la ville came open in 1705, for instance, the mayor and the échevins recommended one of their own, the échevin Jean-François de La Rue, a suggestion the prince promptly ratified. Similarly, when the conseil Calon passed away in 1714, the mairie "took the liberty of advising" the prince to name the échevin Jean Tisserand in his place. "The personal merit of this échevin, known at the bar, and the continuous services he renders the city, of which we are very content, makes us hope that Your Serene Highness will have the kindness to give his agreement." Noting these "bons temoignages," Condé ratified the council's recommendation.[69]

As Peter Wallace observed for Colmar, "Investment in public debt marked a boundary of commitment to a new political order and separated insiders committed to a new regime from supporters of the old civic system."[70] Dijon's notables recognized this fundamental distinction, even as Condé and the city magistrates repeatedly represented their actions as preserving the city's privileges.

Those who did not belong to the small circle that monopolized the hôtel de ville saw the turn of events after 1692 as a betrayal, not a defense, of municipal privilege. One night in the beginning of March 1694, large placards appeared on the walls of Mayor Jannon's house reading "Icy se vendent les privilèges de la ville" ("The city's privileges are for sale here") and "Janon [sic] vend les privilèges de la ville" ("Jannon sells the city's privileges"). Evidently, the sentiments of this anonymous figure were shared by a significant portion of the populace. According to the Mairie's records, *libelles diffamatoires* against the hôtel de ville circulated throughout the city, as did complaints "in several places and houses of this city that he [Jannon] sells and abandons the city's privileges." The mairie considered these rumblings serious enough to warrant obtaining monitoires against those responsible for them.[71] Although it appears that those responsible for these attacks were never found, the placards' size and elaborate design (which included official-looking emblems such as fleurs-de-lys and halberds) suggest that they were produced by members of the city's notability who now recognized that the city's once large and accessible mairie was now essentially closed to them. Although powerless to alter this new reality, those who posted the placards, circulated the *libels,* and whispered rumors refused to acquiesce silently in their political disenfranchisement.

The Political Fortunes of Dijon's Avocats

The arrêt of 20 April 1668 entailed a dramatic reduction in the number of political opportunities for avocats and other notables at the hôtel de ville. Previously, fourteen slots on the échevinage became available every year; after 1668, only four slots opened up every two or, more often, three years. Changes in the method for selecting the échevins further limited access to a select few, and Louis XIV's 1692 sale of city offices only exacerbated this trend. There was an increase in some minor offices such as the lieutenants de la mairie, but on the whole an ever smaller group of notables tended to dominate municipal officeholding at the end of the seventeenth century. Although more avocats did obtain royal offices after 1668, these were generally minor, honorific posts that offered little in the way of power or political opportunity. Except for the few wealthy and well-connected individuals who continued to serve at the mairie, most avocats found themselves excluded from local governance after 1668. Furthermore, even those who remained at the hôtel de ville enjoyed little authority or political agency, instead serving primarily as local administrators carrying out orders from afar.

On the whole, avocats hoping to participate in municipal politics after 1668 faced much longer odds than their predecessors, as can be seen by the precipitous decline in available seats on the city council. From 1668 to 1715, avocats filled only 8.5 percent (4 of 47) of all mayoral terms, compared with 34.2 percent under the previous regime.[72] Following the end of Pierre Monin's term in June 1679, no avocat held the city's chief magistracy again under Louis XIV. By the end of the seventeenth century, royal judges and officiers monopolized the post of vicomte-mayeur, as they did throughout much of France.

The respectable socioeconomic standing of many avocats ensured that some would continue to pursue seats on the city council, even a significantly weakened one. Avocats willing to cultivate the favor of the Condés and their local agents (and to put forth the sums needed to finance city offices after 1692) could still hope for a career at the mairie. Philippe Papillon, a first-generation avocat whose father had been the Grand Condé's goldsmith, parlayed his family's connections into a seat on the échevinage from 1684 to 1690. Jacques Chesne, who played a critical role in the coup of 1668, took a more circuitous route. Likely the son of the avocat Jacob Chesne, who enjoyed a brief career as échevin and conseil de la ville before his early death in 1650, Jacques made his debut at the mairie as an échevin under Millotet's Frondeur government. The taint of his anti-Condéan associations may explain why Chesne did not reappear at the mairie until he was named échevin again in 1667. By then, however, he had clearly gained the trust of Condé and his agents. As garde des évangiles in June 1668, Chesne helped implement the arrêt of 20 April, and his once modest career soared under the new regime. Chesne served three separate terms as échevin for a total of seven years between 1668 and 1679. When the first post-1668 mayoral elections were held in June 1670, he once again served as garde des évangiles. Around the same time, Chesne was also named conseil de la ville, a post he held until his death in 1683.[73]

One factor that does not appear to have played a major role in Chesne's political success was money. His taille levy of 21 livres in 1669 was below the average of 28.74 livres paid by nonexempt avocats that year.[74] In contrast, Claude de La Loge's success at the hôtel de ville in the 1690s and 1700s apparently resulted from his willingness to use his wealth to secure municipal office. The son of a minor royal official from Saulieu, Claude moved to Dijon sometime in the late 1660s with his older brother, Pierre, who had obtained his father's office as a controller in the chancellery. The La Loge brothers' entry into municipal government was a modest one, with each serving one term as lieutenant in the early 1670s. For the next two decades, their presence at the hôtel de ville appears to have been negligible. Pierre sold his office at the chancellery in 1675, and the two likely pursued their careers as avocats, appearing consistently on the tableaux from 1683 onward. Since Pierre and Claude were both exempt from the taille, we have little direct information about their wealth. However, we can infer that the two were financially well off from the fact that they each had sole possession of two seigneuries. Named échevin in 1690, Claude proved to be a ready source of money for the financially strapped city council. He loaned the city 30,000 livres in December 1692 to finance the office of receveur-général de la ville, which Pierre exercised until 1703.

A month later, Claude put up 5,300 livres to help repurchase the mayoralty, while his brother loaned another 33,000 livres. In May 1693, Claude helped the destitute mairie borrow 3,300 livres to help buy the *jurés crieurs d'enterrrements et cris publics.* The following year, he advanced 57,500 livres to buy back the position of *receveur des deniers patrimoniaux;* in June 1696, he contributed another 6,000 livres to help repurchase the office of *controlleur des deniers communs.*[75] In return for investing more than 102,000 livres in municipal offices in less than four years, Claude was allowed to serve as échevin for thirteen years, including eleven as first échevin. He also served as interim mayor briefly after Jannon's death in September 1694 and as garde des évangiles during the 1703 elections.[76] Even after he left the échevinage in 1703, Claude remained part of the mairie, assuming the position of receiver-general that he had conferred on his brother in 1692. Along the way, Claude evidently achieved his dual goals of maintaining his fortune while proving his worth to the Condés and their agents. One of his sons became a conseiller at the Parlement of Dijon, while another purchased an army commission as captain in the Régiment d'Enghien.[77] Clearly, service at the hôtel de ville continued to provide an avenue to social mobility for those few families who possessed the wealth, good fortune, and political connections needed to obtain municipal office.

For the vast majority, however, the period after 1668 saw a sharp drop in the availability of political opportunities to which their predecessors had been accustomed. Although avocats actually controlled a greater percentage of seats on the échevinage, the sheer decline in available positions meant that a much smaller percentage of avocats held the post even once in their lives. Under the pre-1668 regime, just over half of the city's avocats (166 of 330) served at least one term as échevin at some point in their careers. After 1668, only about one in eight (24 of 191) did so. From 1692 to 1715, only eight avocats sat on the city council. Of the seventy-nine avocats whose names appeared at least once on the tableaux of 1690 and 1699, only six (7.6 percent) ever served as échevins during the last twenty-three years of the Sun King's reign.

Another way to measure the consequences of Louis XIV's actions on the municipal careers of Dijon's avocats is to examine the échevinage's openness to newcomers. As table 4.1 shows, Dijon's city council was quite accessible to members of the bar prior to 1668. Between 1600 and 1670, anywhere from seventeen to thirty-two avocats per decade made their debut at the échevinage, for an average of 23.7. After 1630, these numbers were even more impressive, as the number of new échevins hailing from the bar averaged 27.5 per decade and never dipped below twenty-five. After 1670, in contrast, the number of avocats making their first appearance on the city council in a decade never reached double figures, ranging from nine in the 1670s to one in the 1700s and 1710s, for an average of 3.8 per decade. Thus, although a small number of avocats continued to work their way into the city

Table 4.1. Avocats entering the échevinage for the first time (1600–1715)

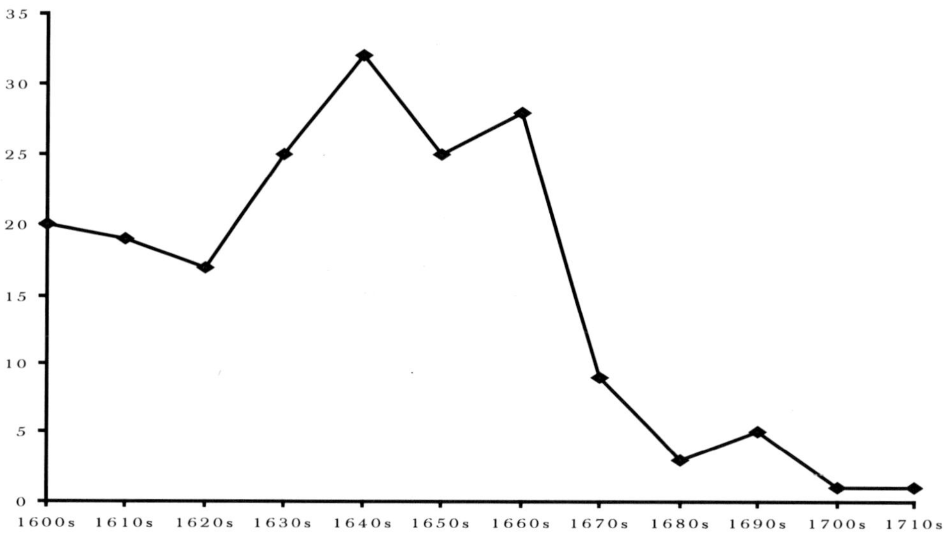

Source: AMD B-238–B-351

council after 1668, the end of the old municipal regime and the later sale of city offices closed off the échevinage to the vast majority of avocats, severing the once close link between membership in the bar and access to municipal office. One of the most striking consequences of this turn of events is that unlike their counterparts in the first half of the century, many of the city's most prominent avocats never served a single term on the city council.

Although they were largely excluded from the échevinage after 1668, the avocats' expertise continued to make them valuable to the hôtel de ville in certain legal and technical capacities. During the first two decades after 1668, the average number of avocats staffing the mayoral court rose dramatically. Between 1670 and 1681, the mairie employed an average of 25.6 lieutenants per year, with the number dropping to just over nineteen in the following decade.[78] Indeed, the mairie may have expanded its employment of lieutenants to compensate for the loss of other offices. In 1669, for example, Joly dramatically increased the number of lieutenants from eleven to nineteen, ostensibly "to expedite justice." Beginning in 1672, the city council instituted a weekly rotation, converting to a monthly one in 1684.[79] These changes, which helped open up more positions, might suggest an expansion of municipal justice, but other evidence indicates that this was not so. Citing a shortage of cases, the mairie ordered lieutenants to reduce their weekly sessions from four to a maximum of three in August 1687. Nevertheless, it maintained a sizable contingent of eighteen lieutenants, up from the previous year's twelve.[80] Even this effort to keep municipal positions available appears to have been undone by the financial stresses of the 1690s and 1700s. From a high of twenty-eight in the mid-1670s, the number of lieutenants plummeted to six (1694–1703) before rising to an average of 11.8 in the final decade of the Sun King's reign.[81]

The nature of the lieutenants' office also appears to have changed as well. Prior to 1668, lieutenants were generally avocats at the beginning of their careers for whom the post was a brief apprenticeship and an initial taste of municipal service. On average, lieutenants under the old municipal regime served just over three years and only three served ten years or more. Indeed, a municipal deliberation in 1645 specifically limited lieutenants to three-year terms, followed by a three-year period of ineligibility, so that more "young avocats" could benefit from the experience of serving at the municipal court.[82] After 1668, lieutenancies were increasingly filled by established avocats who served substantially longer terms, averaging almost eight years.[83] Of the sixty-six lieutenants between 1668 and 1700, fifteen (22.7 percent) served ten or more years, and some even appear to have become career lieutenants. Bénigne Deslandes, for example, held the office from 1668 to 1710, with only a brief interruption between 1672 and 1674. Philibert Paressot held his post without interruption from 1668 to 1691. Although some avocats served only briefly before rising to higher municipal office, the ranks of these municipal judges increasingly came to be dominated by a core of individuals who spent a sizable portion of their careers in this capacity.

The office of conseil de la ville underwent a similar transformation. Although no new posts were created, there once again appears to have been some effort to expand the availability of the limited number of remaining offices at the mairie. Under the old municipal regime, conseils were generally avocats with records of distinguished prior municipal service. Of the thirty-four individuals who held the office between 1596 and 1667, twenty-eight (82.3 percent) had previously served on the city council. After 1668, on the other hand, the clear majority of conseils (fifteen of twenty-five) never served as échevins; four of the remaining ten were named conseils within two years of entering the échevinage. Indeed, it appears that some avocats even tried to invert the traditional progression by citing their activities as conseils to obtain seats on the city council. Such was the case with Claude Ravey, who invoked his experience "pleading all of the causes that [the mairie] has in Parlement" in an unsuccessful bid to be named échevin in 1702.[84]

Although there may have been efforts to spread remaining municipal offices around, especially in the immediate aftermath of 1668, a countervailing tendency arose for offices to become concentrated in the hands of certain individuals, a trend that appears to have grown over time. In addition to serving as échevin for much of the 1670s, for example, Jacques Chesne was also a lieutenant de la mairie from 1672 to 1674 and a conseil de la ville from 1670 to 1682. Jean-Baptiste Midan sat on the échevinage from 1672 to 1674 and later served simultaneously as lieutenant (1677–84) and conseil (1676–91). By the last decade of the seventeenth century, at least four avocats served simultaneously as lieutenant and conseil. One of the four, Jean Tisserand, also sat on the échevinage while serving as lieutenant. Jean-François de La Rue, meanwhile, was both échevin and conseil de la ville from 1705 to 1711.

In an apparent effort to compensate for declining opportunities at the hôtel de ville, a larger percentage of avocats obtained royal offices. Based on the sample used in chapter 1, a comparison of avocats received before and after 1660, also shows a noticeable change in officeholding patterns. Whereas the percentage of avocats holding both royal and municipal offices dropped slightly among avocats received after 1660 (from 17.9 percent to 14.6 percent), the percentage of avocats obtaining only royal offices increased from 22.6 percent to 36.6 percent.[85] Although it might be tempting to interpret this change as a shift from a localistic to a national political identity, most of these offices were minor ones that frequently conferred tax exemptions and other privileges but offered little in the way of actual powers or political opportunities. Although two avocats obtained parlementary seats by 1720, most acquired relatively low-level positions such as auditor or controller in the chancellery or substitut du procureur-général in one of the sovereign courts. Avocats also obtained minor fiscal offices with some frequency. These offices, as David Bien noted, usually involved trivial functions and brought little income. The same was true of many of the new offices created to fund Louis XIV's later wars, such as the *chauffe-cire et scelleur hereditaire* in the chancellery and the *controlleur extraordinaire des guerres,* which a number of avocats also purchased.[86]

Some of Dijon's avocats also availed themselves of a new opportunity in the latter part of the seventeenth century, serving as subdelegates to the intendants of Burgundy. According to Henri Moreau, subdelegates first appeared in Burgundy as part of Bouchu's campaign to verify and liquidate communal debts. By the end of the ancien régime, Hilton Root claims, Burgundy had thirty-four subdelegates, more than any other province. The history of the intervening 130 years is sketchy, but it does appear that fixed territorial subdelegations were well established in Burgundy by the early 1690s, and quite possibly earlier.[87] Burgundian subdelegates, as Moreau has noted, were recruited almost exclusively from the ranks of the men of law. The twenty-three individuals who have been identified under Bouchu included eleven avocats, seven royal judges, three royal notaries, and two procureurs.[88] Not surprisingly, however, most of them appear to have come from areas other than Dijon, and I have been able to identify only about a dozen Dijonnais avocats who served as either temporary or general subdelegates at some point during their careers. At least some avocats viewed the position of subdelegate as a viable outlet for their political ambitions in spite of the inherent limits on the nature of their duties and prerogatives. As "correspondents" and *hommes de confiance* of the royal intendant, avocats who served as subdelegates were, in many ways, no different from those who held office at the mairie after 1668. They were not participants in the local government of their city and region; they were administrators working on behalf of, and in the name of, a remote central authority.

In the aftermath of 1668, then, many of Dijon's avocats found themselves exchanging real political authority and active participation in local governance for honorific alternatives. At the same time, a larger percentage of avocats and their families found themselves completely excluded from public life altogether under Louis XIV. Among avocats received prior to 1660, only 23.6 percent held no offices at all; after 1660, that number rose to 34.1 percent. Although this increase may not appear significant, it is important to keep in mind that it occurred at a time when the size of the bar was undergoing a substantial decline. Thus, although there may have been only half as many practicing avocats in Dijon at the end of the seventeenth century as there were at the beginning, those who remained found still fewer political opportunities available to them. Those that did remain consisted largely of honorific royal offices that conferred little authority or opportunities to participate in local governance. The select few who continued to find their way into the city council, meanwhile, exercised far less authority and had much less agency and autonomy than their predecessors prior to 1668. Carefully supervised by the governor, the intendant, and their local brokers, these avocats were reduced to little more than local agents of the expanding administrative monarchy, responsible primarily for putting into effect decisions made at the royal council, the prince's château at Chantilly, the intendant's mansion, or other locations largely removed from the hôtel de ville.

Conclusion

The avocats of Burgundy's capital, like urban notables and other middling groups with histories of active participation in local governance, found themselves largely excluded from public life in the second half of the seventeenth century as Louis XIV's authoritarian brand of rule restricted political activity to a much narrower and more easily managed circle of aristocrats, commissioners, and venal officeholders. The small remnant of lawyers, bourgeois, and other notables who continued to pursue political careers at the mairie of Dijon and elsewhere found their authority and autonomy substantially limited.

Stability at the upper reaches of early modern France's sociopolitical structure demonstrated by recent revisionist studies should not blind us to the profound significance of the changes in political practice and experience that took place at the local level. The growth of the "administrative monarchy," whether or not it can be accurately termed "absolute," resulted in the disenfranchisement of many mid-level notables whose activity in privileged local corporations such as the Mairie de Dijon had made them participants in the local workings of the state. This tendency, which was already evident in the first half of the Sun King's reign, accelerated after 1690, as the experience of Dijon's avocats shows. The changes Louis XIV implemented may have been more personal than structural in nature, but that did not prevent groups such as the avocats of Dijon from perceiving them as a profound and fundamental change to a system that had served their personal, political, and professional interests for more than a century.

The efforts by the Condés, their agents, and members of the mairie to distribute posts such as mayoral lieutenancies and municipal counsellorships to help compensate for the sharp decline in political opportunities on the city council itself should not divert our attention from the dramatic impact of the arrêt of 20 April 1668 and of the sale of municipal offices on the careers of most Dijonnais avocats. Both the lieutenants and the conseils were auxiliary officers whose primary function was to perform tasks that were already the avocats' preserve. They conferred neither the power nor the prestige enjoyed by the mayors or échevins of the pre-1668 regime. Nor did they provide avocats with the kinds of opportunities to fulfill their vocations as "political men," as their predecessors had done. Before 1668, avocats sitting in the échevinage might well be called on to address the first prince of the blood, the king's ministers, or even the king himself on behalf of a corporation that played a small, but integral, part in the governance of the realm. They could expect to make important decisions concerning local affairs and see them through, even at times over the objections of Parlement or other royal bodies staffed by their socioeconomic and professional superiors. After 1668, the avocats could expect only to hear minor cases in the name of municipal justice, prepare legal briefs and pleadings on the mairie's behalf, or, if they were lucky enough to obtain a coveted seat on the échevinage, to oversee the day-to-day administration of the city while carrying out directives from the intendant and the governor. The sale of municipal offices at the end of the century simply completed the cycle. In the beginning of the seventeenth century, the Mairie de Dijon had provided a nonvenal outlet for the political ambitions of avocats unable to afford the spiraling costs of royal offices. After 1692, avocats who lacked the wealth and connections necessary to enter the charmed circle of Dijon's city council saw that option taken away from them as well. The consequences of this turn of events were not lost on contemporaries, such as the avocat-général Joseph Durand, who associated the closing of the hôtel de ville with the declining caliber of the bar of Dijon in a speech before the Parlement in 1699. Drawing an obvious comparison between the Burgundian capital in the late seventeenth century and the societies of classical Greece and Rome, Durand noted that the ancients cultivated the study of eloquence only as long as it led to higher honors and dignities. As soon as the bar ceased to be a way station to higher offices, he observed, both eloquence and the legal professions fell into a state of decline.[89]

Durand's observations bring us back to the main question that was raised in the beginning of this chapter: what were the consequences of Louis XIV's policies for the powerful cities and for urban notables who once played an important role in local governance? Although it is true that Dijon's experience was partially shaped by particularities of local customs, institutions, history, and personalities, the Burgundian capital nevertheless fits into a much larger pattern of change that swept across urban France from the late sixteenth to the early eighteenth centuries. The main characteristics of this trend included the curtailing of municipal political privileges and autonomies by royal officials; increased central oversight of municipal administration, usually facilitated by the presence of a royal intendant or subdelegate; and the political disenfranchisement of large segments of the urban population, usually by a small portion of the local oligarchy who preferred to throw their lot in with the monarchy rather than with the local inhabitants. These changes occurred at a gradual, uneven pace throughout the kingdom, subject to a multitude of local variation and vagaries. A good number of cities had seen their privileges effectively curtailed by the time of Henri IV. Among these were Orléans, Limoges, Lyon, Abbéville, Amiens, and Troyes. Others, such as La Rochelle and Metz, saw their privileges undermined during the reign of Louis XIII. In addition to Dijon, during the first decades of the Sun King's reign many cities that had managed to defend their privileges finally gave in to royal pressure; Toulouse, Angers, Colmar, and Marseille figured most prominently in this group. A few, such as Nantes, managed to hold out a little longer, until the stresses of Louis' later wars proved to be too much. Among this group were some of Louis' recent acquisitions, such as Lille and Strasbourg, which gradually saw their autonomies eroded, if not always breached, by agents of their new monarch.[90] Dijon, then, fared better than many French cities in preserving its political privileges during the seventeenth century. Ultimately, however, it too succumbed to the "developmental logic" of the territorial state described by Chevalier.[91] When it did, the city's avocats figured among those whose fortunes and interests suffered the most in the process. The second part of this book will examine how Dijon's avocats sought to comprehend the political changes that were taking place around them. It will also explore how their understanding of the early modern French state did, and did not, change as they found themselves excluded from local government and political life.

Chapter 5

Legal Culture and Political Thought in Early Seventeenth-Century Dijon

"The jurist," François Baudouin wrote, voicing a position widely recognized in early modern France, "is a political man."[1] In the first four chapters of this book, we have analyzed the political activities of Dijon's avocats in the seventeenth and early eighteenth centuries. We have shown how the avocats used the opportunities provided by the city's large and powerful mairie to satisfy their political ambitions. At the same time, we have demonstrated how the avocats' legal and rhetorical expertise helped Dijon's embattled hôtel de ville maintain its jurisdictions and governing authority for more than seven decades after the Wars of Religion. The preceding chapters have also shown how the avocats responded to the dramatic decline in political opportunities available to them after the 1668 reorganization of the city government. Although some avocats continued to find outlets for their political ambitions–at the scaled-down mairie, as subdelegates to Burgundy's intendant, or as minor royal officers–most found themselves excluded from local politics and governance, roles which they believed they were to entitled by virtue of their professional training and personal qualities.

This chapter and the one that follows will examine the other principal component of Dijon's avocats' political experience–the conceptual framework they used to understand the French state and their place within it. Although absolutist ideology theoretically made governance the *secret du roi,* restricted political thought and analysis to the king and his advisors, and reduced all others to passive spectators of royal majesty, the reality was quite different.[2] Considerable evidence shows that Frenchmen (and women) of all social levels sought to stay abreast of local, national, and even international events. They also had strong opinions about the proper order of things and regularly debated and criticized the actions of the monarchy and local officials.[3] Although it would be going too far to describe such analysis and debate as constituting a "bourgeois public sphere" along the lines described by Jürgen Habermas, it is also clear that his neat distinction between the "representative public sphere" of the seventeenth century and the "bourgeois public sphere" of the eighteenth does not hold up to careful scrutiny, especially in the case of Dijon.

Political debate and discourse in seventeenth-century France was conducted primarily using the language and concepts of the law. For most French men and women, the law courts were a principal point of contact with the state. Even those of relatively modest social standing exhibited a great deal of interest in and knowledge of the law. The "public sphere" or "civil society" of seventeenth-century France thus existed primarily in the realm of the law and legal institutions.[4] Avocats were central figures in this early modern civil society in two significant ways. First, they were important members of the urban notability, which had traditionally played a key role in local governance. Second, their intellectual training and experience with governmental institutions and practices gave them the expertise needed to understand and critique the actions of the monarchy and other authorities.[5] Avocats were not only active participants in the developing legal culture of this period, they also considered themselves its leading exemplars and most able practitioners.

Although avocats belonged to the social world of robe officials and parlementary magistrates, as noted in chapter 1, they were (for the most part) not officeholders with financial and familial ties to the monarchy. These traits have prompted considerable interest in avocats' political thought during the eighteenth century but have not led to the same level of examination for preceding periods.[6] How did legal training, culture, and experience shape the political consciousness of Dijon's avocats during the seventeenth century? How was their political awareness defined by the dramatic changes in the city's political landscape and the avocats' own political experiences over the course of the seventeenth century?

An examination of the avocats' writings and other works show that their political imagination consisted of three main components: the king, the city (or region), and the law. Other elements influential among political thinkers of the time, such as religion and Reason of State theory, played much less prominent roles in the avocats' view of the French state. Although the avocats did not share a single, monolithic understanding of the relationship among king, city, and law–different elements received varying levels of prominence at different points during the century–these provided the basic framework of the avocats' political consciousness. Overall, the avocats favored a strong, "absolute" monarch whose power was nevertheless limited by the existing social and political order. They did not believe that the royal will was the only source of law or social order, and they deemphasized the notion that sovereignty consisted of the right to command and legislate. Instead, they viewed the king in traditional terms as a judge whose function was to maintain the proper distribution of authorities and to preserve existing political arrangements. Dijon's avocats also believed that royal authority was mediated by historical and contractual relationships that ensured the city's and the region's political privileges and established their roles as intermediate authorities. They also claimed that regional customs, as the province's "natural law," limited royal prerogatives in Burgundy. The king's power, they held, was not that of a divine-right sovereign but was rather akin to that of a feudal lord. Underlying the avocats' political thought was their belief that they and other members of the municipal elite had the right to participate in the French state through governance of the city and the exercise of its longstanding political privileges and jurisdictions.

The political views of Dijon's avocats, it should be emphasized, did not remain unchanged over the course of the century. As historians have noted, early modern French political discourse oscillated between "constitutionalist" ideals of limited royal power and devolved authority, and "absolutist" theories that held that the king's power was primarily legislative and that his ability to command was the only guarantee of social order. The experience of the Wars of Religion, continued regional instability in the early seventeenth century, the mounting influence of Bourbon-absolutist ideology, the city's increasing dependence on powerful protectors, and mounting internal divisions within the municipal elite helped prompt a more "absolutist" turn in the political thought of Dijon's avocats through the middle of the century. At no point, however, did the avocats fully embrace the absolutist theories emanating from Paris and Versailles. Instead, their ideas continued to show the influence of juridical conceptions of limited royal power, devolved authority, and the importance of an immutable social and political structure that guaranteed the rights of intermediate bodies and local elites to participate in the governance of the realm.

Political Thought in Seventeenth-Century France

Fashioned from a wide range of legal, historical, and other sources, seventeenth-century French political thought was filled with ambiguities and tensions. Views of the monarchy and the king's role within it generally drew on the same body of authorities, principles, and concepts, but fell between poles stressing the king's unfettered authority and the limitations distinguishing royal power from tyranny. As Adrianna Bakos has argued, concepts of "authority" and "limitation," which had been intertwined in French political thought during the sixteenth century, increasingly moved apart in the seventeenth. This resulted in the emergence of what might be called "absolutist" and "constitutionalist" discourses. Although such terms can be problematic when used to discuss early modern French politics, they can also be an effective shorthand to distinguish thinkers who stressed unlimited royal authority from those who called attention to restraints on that authority.[7] The boundaries between constitutionalists and absolutists, it should be stressed, are not always clear. Both drew on a common store of legal references, authorities, historical examples, and language. Moreover, as Bakos notes, there was a considerable amount of cross-fertilization between the two schools of thought, although this was most often "[to] make lightning raids into enemy territory to steal or sabotage polemical weaponry" than to reconcile their differences. Absolutists might still accept the theoretical value of devolving authority to intermediate bodies, whereas constitutionalists would not deny that the king enjoyed "puissance absolue." And although the mainstream of French political thought clearly shifted towards the absolutist pole in the seventeenth century, elements of constitutionalist thought remained viable and influential, especially outside of Paris.[8]

"The splendid constitutions of France," wrote Bernard du Haillan in the late sixteenth century, permit nothing to the king "except what is just, reasonable, and prescribed by the ordinances themselves."[9] Constitutionalists such as Du Haillan stressed several important themes. Although accepting that kings were "absolute" and not bound by the laws, constitutionalists limited royal discretion to the narrow realm of positive law. The king's "absolute" power was circumscribed by divine and natural law, the kingdom's fundamental laws, long-standing customs and traditions, and the dictates of reason and religion. Thus, the *bordelais* jurist Pierre de Lancre concluded in 1617 that kings were subject to the same laws of justice as all other humans. In the same year, the Toulousain parlementaire Bernard de La Roche-Flavin declared, "Our monarchy of France is not an absolute kingdom, where the will of the king is law, his word an arrêt." More than three decades later, Claude Joly, avocat-général of the Parlement of Paris, wrote, "The power of kings is not absolute and without limits . . . [it] is bounded and limited and . . . they may not dispose of their subjects according to their will and pleasure."[10]

Constitutionalists also highlighted the judicial nature of royal power, emphasizing the king's obligation to maintain the proper balance within the body politic and the correct distribution of authorities, privileges, and honors. Early modern French people imagined their polity as "an order, an arrangement, a disposition of things in the manner of a body's composition."[11] Jean Bacquet argued that political rights and privileges were beyond the royal prerogative, and nobles justified their rebellions as defenses of this "half-customary, half-written" arrangement against changes they believed would undermine 'the laws of the kingdom,' its 'statues,' its 'constitutions,' [and] its 'police.'" Not surprisingly, constitutionalists also placed great emphasis on the role of intermediary corporations and authorities.[12] As Roland Mousnier observed, they believed "the rights of subjects were guaranteed by their participation in legislation, in the "police" or administration, and, to a lesser extent, in the government by the intermediary of diverse orders and corps."[13]

Finally, constitutionalists stressed the dual nature of kingship, distinguishing the office and person of the king. In their eyes, kings did not have a personal or dynastic claim to power but governed in accord with the kingdom's laws and traditional political structure. Guy Coquille, for instance, stressed the reciprocal relationship between monarch and populace, claiming that the latter retained ultimate legislative authority.[14] Charles Loyseau, whose works straddled the constitutionalist and absolutist camps, defined the king as a public "officer" and contrasted his power with the unrestrained and arbitrary private power of a seigneur. Joly, meanwhile, observed that kings were made for people and not vice versa. "There have always been people without kings," he noted, "but never kings without people." "The king," he concluded "is not absolute master of the law and may not ruin and destroy it whenever he pleases, since by the contract the people submitted to him only on condition that he preserve and maintain the law."[15]

Seventeenth-century absolutists, in contrast, freed royal power from the restraints of institutional checks, traditional political arrangements, and all but the most theoretical legal restraints.[16] For Bodin, the king was the sole legislator and thus above all human laws, including his own and those of his predecessors. Although Bodin conceded that royal actions that transgressed divine and natural law were illegitimate, he also rejected the possibility of any legitimate resistance. Jacques-Bénigne Bossuet declared that the king need not render account for his acts to anyone and that resistance to his will was akin to sacrilege. In a similar vein, Jean Domat noted that although the king should observe the laws as an example for his subjects, "no man has the right to call him to account for his conduct."[17]

Absolutists also stressed the king's capacity to make law and to command his subjects. In their eyes, the king was legislator, not judge. For Bodin, sovereignty consisted in the ability to "give laws to the subjects in general without their consent" and without the approval "of any other greater, equal or lesser than himself." Bossuet considered the king's power to legislate and command the sole source of order. "Royal power constitutes the kingdom, holds it all in its condition as God holds the world together. . . . [I]f authority were to cease within the kingdom, all would be in confusion." Domat, meanwhile, claimed that it was the "universal obligation of all subjects in all cases to obey the ruler's orders without assuming the liberty of judging them."[18]

Although absolutists allowed a role for intermediate authorities and corporations, they downplayed their significance, instead emphasizing the king as the sole source of order. Bodin and Cardin Le Bret both declared sovereignty indivisible, inalienable, and eternal. And although Bodin encouraged estates and other bodies where subjects could voice opinions and grievances, he also proclaimed the monarch "above all subjects."[19] Bossuet affirmed that the king was the sole source of order and that magistrates were mere agents of his will. "Consider the prince in his cabinet. From thence flow the commands which coordinate the efforts of magistrates and captains, of citizens and soldiers, of provinces and armies. . . . It is the image of God, who directs all nature from his throne in the highest heaven." For absolutists, all other institutions and authorities were mere emanations of the royal will with no independent power or agency.[20]

Absolutist thinkers also tended to blur, or even efface, distinctions between the office of the king and its incumbent. Whereas constitutionalists stressed that the crown devolved in accordance with established laws and customs, absolutists stressed personal and dynastic elements that turned sovereignty into the king's proprietary right. When the young Louis XIII held a lit-de-justice in the wake of his father's assassination, he violated the ceremonial protocol whereby the new king avoided public appearances until after his predecessor's burial. The old ceremony's emphasis on "the king's two bodies" was replaced by a vision of the king as a phoenix rising from his predecessor's ashes. The old "ceremonial interregnum" gave way to a new emphasis on immediate succession. *Le mort saisit le vif,* a private-law maxim pertaining to inheritance, was increasingly invoked to describe the succession, further conflating the crown with the monarch's personal possessions.[21] Absolutists such as Le Bret and Bossuet also stressed the monarch's singular, heroic qualities, which they considered a product of his quasi-divine calling.[22] The notion that the king and his "crown-worthy" male relatives were different from the rest of humankind–chosen by Providence for the "greatest of all secular dignities, the French crown"–found expression in a new "dynastic mystique" of the "princes of the blood" and the *sang royal.*[23]

These, then, were the principal poles of the political discourse within which Dijon's avocats lived, worked, and thought. Before we examine the nature of the avocats' political thought and the changes it underwent during the seventeenth century, it will be helpful to determine who the leading thinkers of the Dijonnais bar were, the kinds of works they produced, and the impact of their political experiences, especially at the mairie of Dijon, on their writings and ideas.

Dijon's Avocats as Political Thinkers

How did Dijon's avocats view the French state and their place in it? Historians have long recognized jurists, especially avocats, as being among the leading political thinkers of the early modern period.[24] Only in the late seventeenth century, according to William Church, did they lose their preeminence as political theorists in France. Even this is questionable, as chapter 6 will show.[25] Avocats were among the era's few "vocational intellectuals," and the inherently politicized nature of their profession made complete withdrawal from political thought highly unlikely, even if the nature of their ideas changed.[26] This section will look at the influences on the political thought of Dijon's avocats, the political experience of the bar's leading thinkers, the nature of their output, and the unsystematic and circumstantial character of the avocats' political thought.

The avocats' shared legal education and training provided much of the framework for their views of the state, the nature of royal power, and the role of other authorities. Although French university law courses were not explicitly politicized, their curricula were based on implicit assumptions about France's political order. The law curriculum was thus "a forum in which the burning questions of early modern political thought were judged and analysed."[27] Professors frequently expounded a mélange of absolutist and constitutionalist ideas. On the one hand, they insisted that royal authority was in no way limited by customary law, estates, or parlements. On the other hand, they espoused contractualist theories, claiming that kings derived their authority from the people and approving passive resistance to violations of natural and divine law or the common good. Law school thus may not have provided avocats with a fully articulated system of political thought, but it did give them the principles, maxims, and terms they used to understand the operations of the French state.[28] The avocats' rhetorical training, meanwhile, made them natural candidates to deliver the many speeches, *harangues,* and *discours* that were part of public life, especially during the first half of the seventeenth century.

If education provided Dijon's avocats with concepts and vocabulary, then the social and professional environment of the palais de justice exposed them to many of the era's key issues. Avocats frequently dealt with fundamental problems concerning property rights, jurisdictional boundaries, custom, and precedent, and a host of other issues in their pleadings and consultations. The world of the palais, where avocats worked, socialized, and made important personal and familial connections, also shaped their political consciousness. In Dijon, as in many other French cities during the late sixteenth and seventeenth centuries, local culture and society were increasingly dominated by the world of the law courts and the judges and legal professionals who staffed them. As Dijon evolved into a primarily legal and administrative center, it is hardly surprising that the city's intellectual and cultural life centered around the law courts and came to be dominated by royal magistrates and other legal professionals, especially the city's many avocats.[29] The juridically based culture that emerged was noteworthy for its profound conservatism; particular emphasis was given to the value of precedent, custom, and tradition. "Conservative by instinct" and "conservative in theory," the members of Dijon's robe responded to the monarchy's innovative theories and designs "by invoking the *mos majorum* in the Estates' decrees and the Parlement's remonstrances."[30] Leading parlementaires, Bouchard has shown, maintained a juristic and particularistic interpretation of France's political order that had more in common with that of their Renaissance predecessors than with theories of absolute royal power emanating from Versailles. "It was in the name of the region's particular customs that the *robins* rose up against innovations, it was as the region's natural defenders that they opposed any revolutions."[31] For them, the monarchy remained an essentially judicial institution that was bound to respect local privileges and authorities. When kings or their agents transgressed these bounds, parlement's leading magistrates often resisted in word as well as deed. One year after Dijon's surrender to Henri IV, First President Denis Brulart reminded the king that Burgundy's sovereign court was "like a barrier between the monarchy and the people, to defend the latter against extraordinary impositions and charges." The entire parlement was exiled for nearly a year in 1637 after refusing to register a series of fiscal edicts, and twelve leading parlementaires were exiled in 1658 when the court attempted to prosecute a scribe for the "crime" of following the chancellor's orders to provide extracts of edicts that had been registered "*du très exprès commandement du roi*" during a lit-de-justice in November of 1658.[32] Even a conseiller such as Claude Malteste, who sided with the royalist faction in Parlement during the Fronde and wrote in his *Anecdotes secretes* that Parlement's only duty was to secure Conde's submission to the king, continued to highlight the sovereign court's role as an essential mediator between the monarchy and the people. "It is true," he wrote, "that parlements are set between kings and the people in order to carry subjects' complaints to the sovereign, and the master's commands to the subjects."[33] Given the extent of daily personal and professional interactions between many avocats and royal judges, it is highly likely that parlement's conservative, legalistic political attitudes and its hostility to change inspired the avocats, or at least supported and encouraged them in expressing similar views.

The third major influence was the avocats' experience in local political life, especially at the mairie prior to 1668. The connection between municipal political experience and the avocats' political thought is evident when we look at those who left records of their political ideas. If we consider known works of a potentially political nature (including those now lost), as well as references by contemporaries and later historians, we find that approximately forty-eight avocats–roughly 25 to 50 percent of the avocats active between 1595 and 1660–left any trace of their political attitudes.[34] Of these, almost all (89.6 percent) had a political career of some sort, and more than three-fourths (77.1 percent) had some connection with the hôtel de ville. The links between the mairie and these avocats were strong, as two-thirds of the avocats served at least one term as échevin or held another major municipal office at some point in their career.[35] The question then becomes, What were these avocats writing? The abbé Philibert Papillon's eighteenth-century bibliography of Burgundian authors, one of the best guides to Burgundian literary output prior to 1750, records a total of 172 works (2.26 per year) by Dijonnais avocats between 1595 and 1667, of which 119 (1.6 per year) were published.[36] Forty-three (23.6 percent) works from the pre-1667 sample can be categorized as "public," theatrical or historical. Another forty-four (24.2 percent) were legal works, including fifteen in the form of plaidoyers or commentaries on civil and ecclesiastical law. When we include works of biography (seven, or 3.9 percent) and political philosophy (six, or 3.3 percent), it becomes clear that more than half (55 percent) of the works produced by Dijon's avocats prior to 1668 were in genres that made them well suited to political commentary, as we shall see below.[37]

The 1668 reorganization of the hôtel de ville, which excluded most avocats from the municipal posts that had long been their prerogative, combined with the "cultural absolutism" of Louis XIV's reign, led to a decline in overt political commentary by avocats. This is clearly reflected in the changing identity of avocats who left traces of their political attitudes. The eighteen such avocats received between 1660 and 1715 were still largely involved in public life, as two-thirds still held some sort of office during their careers. The nature of their offices, however, changed markedly. Only one-third of the post-1660 group ever held municipal office, compared with more than three-fourths of the pre-1660 group. Of the six who did serve at the mairie, only two were ever mayor or échevin. The other four, who included the distinguished avocats Jean Melenet and Claude Varenne, only served as conseils de la ville. And although half of the eighteen held royal offices (three held both royal and municipal offices), most held minor posts such as secrétaire du roi in the chancellery or substitute of Parlement's procureur-général. Prior to 1668, the leading political thinkers among Dijon's avocats had been at core of local political life and were extremely well represented at the mairie. After 1668, such thinkers were on the margins of municipal government and local politics.

The consequences of this marginalization can be seen in the declining output and changing nature of avocats' writings in the decades after 1668. Papillon records only fifty-six works by avocats from 1668 to 1720 (1.06 per year), of which only thirty-three (0.62 per year) were published. In the wake of the 1668 reorganization of the mairie, Dijon's avocats published only one-third as many works and produced less than half the amount of writings on an annual basis as they had previously done. Public, theatrical, or historical texts, which made up nearly a quarter of the pre-1667 sample, practically vanished, with only three (or 5.36 percent) appearing after 1667. Biographies remained nearly constant (3.57 percent), but only one work of political philosophy (1.79 percent) was produced. Legal works grew to 39.29 percent of the avocats' total output, but unlike the pre-1667 sample, most took the form of more narrowly focused, technical works on regional customs and jurisprudence. Only five of the twenty-three works recorded were the more publicly accessible plaidoyers or commentaries.[38] On the whole, Dijon's avocats appear to have turned away from works with explicit political messages after 1668. Even when overtly political works were published, they did not always reflect a desire to engage in public debates. Guillaume Raviot's condemnation of the Jansenists' use of the *appel comme d'abus,* for instance, was published entirely without the author's involvement or consent.[39] These trends would seem to support Church's perception that jurists increasingly avoided political discussions under Louis XIV in favor of more "technical" legal works. As we shall, however, the changing literary output of Dijon's avocats did not necessarily imply their depoliticization. Rather, it simply meant that Dijon's avocats continued to express their belief in limited royal power, the judicial nature of the monarchy, the importance of intermediate authorities, and the rights of subjects to participate in local governance in different forms.[40]

One of the distinguishing features of the avocats' political thought was its eclectic nature. The avocats' intellectual background and the character of their writings combined to reinforce the seemingly unsystematic features of their thought. When thinking about the French state and their city's place within it, the avocats could not turn to an established set of principles. Rather, they had to grapple with ambiguous and at times contradictory authorities ranging from classical antiquity (including Roman law) to medieval jurisprudence, French customs, and "immemorial" traditions. Like their colleagues across early modern Europe, Dijon's avocats found themselves in a creative enterprise that required them to fashion legal, social, and political meaning in highly contingent responses to specific problems and cases.[41] The avocats' political eclecticism was enhanced by the fact that most expressed their political views through *pièces de circonstance*–writings, speeches, and other works created in response to specific events and concerns. Their works, for the most part, were devoted to narrow issues and were not intended to present comprehensive and systematic legal and political theories.[42] Avocats' writings were meant to persuade, inform, impress, and even entertain audiences ranging from the urban populace that attended the carnival plays of the *infanterie dijonnoise,* to parlementaires, royal governors, ministers, and even the king. Nevertheless, the assumptions and general principles implicit in many of these pièces de circonstance reveal the avocats' underlying attitudes about the French state and the nature of royal power. Though not always consistent, the avocats showed a remarkable adherence to a few basic principles throughout the century, most notably the limitations on royal power, the importance of intermediary authorities to the French state, and the right of subjects to participate in governance through long-established local and regional institutions.[43]

The political thought of Dijon's avocats was organized around three main conceptual poles–the king, the city (or region), and the law. By configuring the relationship between these three in different ways and with varying points of emphasis, the avocats could tilt their view of the state toward either the absolutist or the constitutionalist pole. Over the first half of the seventeenth century, the political thought of Dijon's avocats gradually shifted towards the absolutist pole. At no point, however, did the avocats fully embrace absolutist thought in all of its implications. Despite some shifts in emphasis, Dijon's avocats remained committed to constitutionalist ideals and a juridically based view of the monarchy that limited royal power and insisted on a governmental role for intermediate corporations and authorities.

Royal Authority: "Absolute Power" and Its Limits

Dijon's avocats believed that strong royal power was necessary to guarantee peace, order, and the public good. In spite of this, there were important differences between the avocats' understanding of the king's "absolute power" and that of theorists such as Le Bret and Bossuet. Whereas absolutists reduced limits on royal authority to self-imposed restraints and emphasized the monarch's legislative capacities, the avocats continued to point to the limited scope of "absolute" royal power and the judicial nature of the king's authority. Nonetheless, the avocats' treatment of royal power displayed some increasingly absolutist tendencies during the first half of the seventeenth century, most notably in adopting the rhetoric of Bourbon-absolutist hero worship and the dynastic mystique of the sang royal. This shift toward the absolutist pole, however, was always tempered by underlying juridical conceptions of monarchy that limited the avocats' willingness to embrace fully the absolutist vision of an unfettered sovereign whose will was the only source of order.

The desire to restore order was one of the most basic elements of early seventeenth-century Dijonnais political consciousness. The Wars of Religion had devastated the region's agricultural output, saddled towns with heavy debts, and divided provincial elites. The Thirty Years' War saw Burgundians forced to house and feed troops headed for the frontier while their crops, houses, and villages were repeatedly destroyed. Dijon and other cities endured shortages of food and other resources while sheltering rural inhabitants behind their walls. The Grand Condé's rebellion in the middle of the century brought more troops and violence to the province. Such recurrent hardships made a strong monarchy capable of ending such disorders highly desirable.[44]

The tumultuous local situation was not the only reason avocats supported a strong monarchy. The period also witnessed an effort by the early Bourbons to reinforce their claim to the throne by refashioning traditional principles of divine-right monarchy and hereditary succession to create a rhetoric of absolutist hero worship that celebrated the singular virtues and superhuman capabilities that the royal family enjoyed by virtue of its *sang royal.* Bourbon-absolutist rhetoric built on the Renaissance use of classical gods and heroes such as Jupiter, Apollo, Hercules, and Augustus to praise the semidivine qualities of the king and the royal family. Their superhuman virtues were depicted as the only guarantees of peace and order in a chaotic and disorderly world. In elevating the king above society and "putting kings off the page," Bourbon-absolutist propaganda reduced the rest of the populace to the passive role of spectators who could only praise the herculean triumphs of the king and his relatives while recognizing the benefits they received as a result.[45] Gradually, the rhetorical trends emanating from Paris and the royal court affected the way Dijon's avocats described their city's relationship with the king and its place in the kingdom, as the following section will make clear.

For virtually every avocat, a monarchy capable of ensuring order and prosperity required a king who wielded "absolute power." In 1605, Jean de Souvert reminded the Estates of Burgundy that its role was to advise the king. Requiring the sovereign to obey his subjects, Souvert claimed, was equivalent to "mutilating the crown itself."[46] Etienne Bréchillet's speech to Louis XIII in 1629 praised the monarch as the source of all good and noted the "infinite distance" between "the king's glorious and august head" and "the humble quality of his subjects."[47] In his account of Condé's entrée a few years later, Pierre Malpoy noted the populace's "absolute" dependence on their kings.[48] Avocats even used "absolute power" to describe nonkings and even nonpersonal qualities. In the mid-1640s, Bénigne Griguette credited the "pouvoir absolu" of Abbot Suger and François, duc de Guise, with protecting the kingdom and the Catholic faith.[49] In a series of stanzas celebrating the Grand Condé's military triumphs, Jean Casotte noted that the prince's "glory and absolute power / force audacity and insolence / to restrain their violence / to the terms of a just duty."[50]

Avocats portrayed absolute power, whether wielded by the king or another, as the source of peace, order, and a host of other benefits. Above all, it was associated with *le bien public*. Griguette, for example, linked Epernon's "absolute power" with the restoration of the city's liberty and public well-being. A few years earlier, Bréchillet assured his readers that the young Louis XIV would "lead us to enjoy the sweet calm of peace." "Good kings," Charles Fevret wrote, should "pacify that which is divided, reunite that which is in discord, soften by love that which is inflexible, forcibly subdue that which is in rebellion, draw advantages from disorders, resolve differences through Justice, put an end to usurpations through authority, and regulate the functions of officers."[51]

The king's power to legislate and command also found its way into the avocats' discussions. Souvert, for example, said the king's principal duty was "to teach his subjects how to be obedient." A half century later, Fevret wrote that sovereignty consisted of the power "to make laws, edicts, and regulations, with injunctions to their subjects to obey and observe them, regardless of their qualité."[52] Overall, though, the concept of legislative sovereignty remained a relatively minor theme in the avocats' discussions of royal power.

In spite of these absolutist tendencies, most avocats continued to understand "absolute power" in a more traditional sense. They highlighted limits that absolutists downplayed, such as divine and natural law, reason, and the dictates of the "public good." For Souvert, the subject's duty to obey the king was mirrored by the monarch's obligation to obey the law of nature, making "the law mistress of one and the other, or, as Pindar says, the queen."[53] Fevret, a half century later, drew a less than subtle parallel between the papacy's authority over the French church and royal power in general. "All of those who have spoken of the absolute power of sovereigns," he asserted in his *Traité de l'Abus,* "have been of the advice that it should reduce itself to the name of reason and the law of equity. . . . [A]ll other interpreters have regulated absolute power, for they have all, by their writings, reduced it to right reason and equity."[54]

The king's obligation to pursue the "public good" was central to the avocats' conception of royal power. It allowed them, like most contemporary thinkers, to distinguish "absolute power" from "tyranny." Absolute monarchs, they believed, could use their power only in a rational and restrained manner that promoted the public good. Tyrants, in contrast, made unrestrained and irrational use of their powers to satisfy personal desires. Perhaps the most extended meditation on this distinction was Griguette's tragedy *La mort de Germanic Cæsar.* Griguette dedicated his play to Henry of Lorraine, a leading participant in the comte de Soisson's 1641 revolt against Richelieu, whom the rebels denounced as a corrupter of the kingdom's "traditional order."[55] The play recounted Tiberius's supposed assassination of his adopted son and heir, Germanicus, which would have been familiar to contemporaries from Tacitus's *Annals,* a touchstone for seventeenth-century discussions of political authority and morality.[56] Tacitus portrayed Germanicus as an exemplar of lost Roman virtues who might have restored the Republic if given the opportunity. Tiberius, in contrast, was an archetypal autocrat, corrupted and rendered a tyrant by unlimited power.[57] If anything, Griguette drew the distinctions between Germanicus and Tiberius in even starker terms. Tacitus, for instance, reports Germanicus's belief that he was poisoned, but also notes that contemporaries were uncertain as to the truth of this charge. Tiberius's role in his adopted son's death is similarly unclear: Tacitus implies that any foul play was likely the product of Germanicus's rivalry with the arrogant, impetuous Piso (or Pison in Griguette's tragedy).[58] These quintessentially Tacitean ambiguities, however, are nowhere to be found in *La mort de Germanic Caesar.*

Griguette's play begins with the proconsul Pison receiving orders to kill Germanicus, who is described as a budding tyrant and usurper. It soon becomes clear, however, that it is Tiberius who is the true tyrant, a jealous and irrational figure who wants only "to reign alone in his authority."[59] Tiberius's agents–Pison, his wife Placine, and their friend Domitius–embody the unregulated personal ambition, treachery, and disorder symptomatic of tyranny.[60] Placine, for instance, tells her husband that "blind obedience" is needed to maintain Tiberius's authority."[61] The three conspirators employ a sorcerer to poison Germanicus while Pison continues to act as his loyal friend, even after the plot has been exposed by the young prince's allies.[62]

Germanicus, on the other hand, embodies "absolute power" in the positive sense. Unlike Tiberius, he acts for the good of the empire by pacifying rebellious provinces and deposing tyrants.[63] A model of respect for law and legitimate government, Germanicus points out the dangers inherent in unrestrained power. "When we usurp that which we find so sweet / Honors being charming, we take license / to render ourselves absolute when we have the power / But these frail grandeurs do not dispense us / from suffering trespasses on a pomp-filled throne." The differences between the tyrant Tiberius and the absolute prince Germanicus are evident in Pison's son's denunciation of the conspiracy, which prompts Pison to remark that his son is caught in "the apparent splendor of an absolute power," while conceding that "Tiberius is no longer but the shadow of a Monarch."[64]

The character of Pison *fils* drives home the play's principal theme: the limits of legitimate royal authority. Pison and his conspirators believe Tiberius's authority is limitless and beyond question. In the opening scene of the final act, the younger Pison confronts his disorderly mother, berates her counsel of "blind obedience," and dismisses Tiberius's *secret du roi* as a justification for her actions. Pison's son is not the only one to invoke the limits of royal authority, moreover. Alluding to the traditional argument that kings should not alter the existing political order, the dying Germanicus implores his friend Sentius and his followers to ignore Tiberius's "new laws," to defend their "liberties," and to avenge his death.[65]

In addition to seeing royal authority as absolute yet limited, Dijon's avocats continued to view it as more judicial than legislative. For Souvert, the kingdom's peace and stability rested on the monarch's ability to arbitrate disputes and distribute honors, rewards, and privileges justly. Any attempt to change traditional laws and customs were inherently suspect.[66] Three decades later, Pierre Guillaume lauded the justice of Louis XIII's reign in a speech before Parlement. In *La mort de Germanic Caesar,* Germanicus resists calls to mete out a punishment stiffer than exile once Pison's plot is discovered, declaring, "I am, here, a judge without passion." Moreover, Germanicus explicitly links his "absolute power" with his function as a judge. In a similar fashion, Griguette remembered Henri IV for "[m]aking justice shine in the spirits of the French / Ordering each to observe the laws," and described him as an "*arbitre absolu*."[67]

Although constitutionalist ideals of limited royal power and judicial monarchy remained a vital part of the avocats' political consciousness, we can detect a gradual shift toward the absolutist pole during the first half of the seventeenth century. This is especially evident in the avocats' adoption of the rhetoric of absolutist hero worship. Jean Casotte declared that the Grand Condé's efforts were the sole cause of the province's happiness. Bréchillet declared that kings are "the living statues of divine majesty," singled out by heaven for adoration from the moment of their birth.[68] The mystique surrounding the *sang royal* also found its way into the avocats' writings. In a *harangue* before Condé in 1632, Jacques Defrasans thanked the king for placing Burgundy under the command of the first prince of the blood. Bénigne Pérard attributed Condé's mastery of the "art of commanding well" to his inherited virtues. The blood that runs through Bourbon veins, Fevret said before Parlement, "is animated by other spirits, and the hearts that beat in their chests are of an entirely different movement than all other men." A decade later, Griguette described Henri IV as "this phoenix reborn from the debris of its ashes."[69]

These ideas, it should be stressed, did not suddenly transform Dijonnais political discourse during the first half of the seventeenth century. Nonetheless they did have a gradual impact, especially in the context of increasing divisions among the municipal elite and the oligarchy's growing dependence on the princes of Condé. The avocats' discussions of local identity reflect their changing conception of the city's relationship to the king and Dijon's place in the kingdom's political order. We can see this transition most notably in the gradual changes in the avocats' representation of Dijon as "the city of the gods" in the first half of the seventeenth century.

Local Identity: The City as "Sacred Center"

In a 1662 journal entry, the procureur Pierre Genreau wrote, "Dijon, how I cherish you! Dijon, how lovable you are! Dijon, may God bless you!. . . . May it please the living God that Dijon never dies and that its goods, piety, justice, police, and splendor increase always."[70] The seventeenth century, according to many historians, saw urban elites abandon local traditions, cultural forms, and identity in favor of values, behavior, and language emanating from the court and Paris. Although this was true to some extent in Dijon, the avocats' conception of the city's relationship with the king remained grounded in local history, institutions, and memory.[71] This grounding was most evident in the image of the "city of the gods," which portrayed Dijon as "sacred center" and an active participant in the corporate French state. Increasingly bitter factional divisions, combined with the influence of Bourbon-absolutist rhetoric and ideology, pushed the avocats' view of the city-king relationship toward the absolutist pole. Nevertheless, Dijon's avocats never fully accepted the implications of absolutist theory. By the latter part of the century they had turned to regional customs and history to express their belief that royal power over Burgundian institutions was limited and that local elites and authorities enjoyed the right to participate in local governance.

Dijonnais municipal identity drew on three central elements, the first of which was the city's Roman origins. Educated inhabitants of Burgundy's capital proudly traced their city's origin back to the Gallo-Roman period. Local legends often associated Dijon's founding with the third-century emperor Aurelian (270–75 C.E.), with Pierre de Saint-Julien's *De l'origine des bourgongnons* (1581) providing a typical account. According to Saint-Julien, Aurelian founded Dijon to appease the tutelary gods of the Celtic settlement he had recently destroyed. The new city was founded on the same spot with the most favorable of auspices and was named Divio in their honor. Others, meanwhile, traced the city's roots as far back as Trajan (98–117 C.E.).[72]

Writers also cited Dijon's history as the capital of the duchy of Burgundy and its subsequent "reattachment" to the French crown to explain the city's particular importance. Descriptions of post-1477 Burgundy as "the First Peerage and Duchy of France" were commonplace while the ducal period continued to attract attention from avocats throughout the century.[73] In addition to works on Burgundian customs and jurisprudence, avocats produced antiquarian treatises on the Valois dukes, Philip the Good's Order of the Golden Fleece, and Dijon's ducal Sainte-Chapelle.[74] The mairie protested the exile of the Chamber of Accounts in 1627 as "directly contrary to the establishment of the Court of Accounts in this city of Dijon four hundred years ago by the dukes of Burgundy."[75] When the mairie marched out to greet Epernon before his 1656 *entrée,* it carried a pennant given to it by one of the dukes of Burgundy. Although the late-seventeenth-century conseiller Philibert de La Mare remarked on the fading memory of the Valois dukes, several inhabitants successfully petitioned the Mairie in 1682 to authorize "a chariot representing the ancient dukes of Burgundy, Madame la Dauphine, and the new-born prince" to celebrate the birth of the dauphin's son, the duke of Burgundy.[76]

Municipal identity also reflected the city's continued preeminence in regional affairs. Institutions such as the Estates of Burgundy still inspired localistic sentiments. When Dijon's monopoly on hosting the provincial estates was threatened in the early seventeenth century, Jean Defrasans assured the mairie, "I will omit nothing to preserve this privilege, which I consider one of the city's and magistracy's most important." The presence of numerous royal sovereign courts and other royal institutions was another source of civic pride. The first ceremonial archway designed for Louis XIII's 1629 *entrée* included a figure dressed in a scarlet robe "because of the Parlement with which the city is honored." The mairie considered the removal of any sovereign court as an offense to local privilege and dignity. The entire échevinage, for instance, went before Epernon in 1659 to ask for the exiled Parlement's return "because the entire city suffers enormously and its authority declines greatly because of this interdiction."[77]

Works by many prominent avocats portrayed the urban community as a valued inheritance to be preserved for future generations. In a 1609 eulogy for Defrasans, the young avocat Louvain Gelyot lamented the current state of "Dijon, our mother city," and decried rampant electoral corruption as "[a] monster, which might have put / our DIJON to an end."[78] Two decades later, Charles Fevret juxtaposed the city's illustrious past and troubled present in a speech after the 1630 Lanturelu rebellion. Invoking the Valois dukes, Fevret lamented that Dijon's "luster [no longer] ravishes the admiration of other cities." The following year, Fevret thanked the region's new governor for preserving "the only title of honor remaining to us to mark the fidelity of our predecessors, this beautiful and excellent privilege of being a pays d'état."[79]

The most common and persistent expression of municipal identity was the image of Dijon as "the city of the gods." *La ville des dieux* was a humanistic play on the city's Latin name, Divio, which appears to have become commonplace by the late sixteenth century.[80] In first half of the seventeenth century, the ville des dieux theme appeared most notably in a series of four royal and gubernatorial *entrées* for Louis XIII (1629), Henri II de Bourbon, prince of Condé (1632), his son Louis II (1648), and Bernard de Foix de la Valette, duke of Epernon (1656). The entry decorations and programs were designed by three of the city's leading avocats: Bréchillet (1629 and 1648), Malpoy (1632), and Jean Godran des Chasans (1648 and 1656). Bénigne Griguette, meanwhile, wrote the elaborate commentary commemorating Epernon's 1656 entry.

In representing Dijon as "the city of the gods," Dijon's avocats expressed two fundamental elements of local political culture and their city's relationship with the king. The first was that Dijon's social and political order was sacred and worthy of defense. The second was that the city's relationship with the monarchy, though unequal, was nevertheless reciprocal and governed by rules of honor and respect. Dijon's obligations to the king were those of a vassal to his lord and not a subject's unqualified submission to an absolute ruler. Over the first half of the century, depictions of the ville des dieux underwent significant changes as a result of both local events and the influence of Bourbon-absolutist rhetoric. An examination of the *entrées* shows the declining importance of municipal political identity as the ville des dieux became an increasingly minor and passive aspect of the entry programs. Even so, the surprising persistence of the ville des dieux theme into the middle of the seventeenth century reveals a great deal about the avocats' view of municipal identity in the face of growing internal divisions and Bourbon-absolutist rhetoric during the early seventeenth century.

Bréchillet's design for the first archway of Louis XIII's 1629 royal entry called attention to the unequal yet reciprocal relationship between city and king. It portrayed a mounted figure of Louis XIII greeted by Cybele, the mother of the gods. Crowned with towers and dressed in a scarlet robe signifying Dijon's status as the seat of a parlement, the "city of the gods, mother and capital of the entire province" handed Louis a key to the city. In contrast with the obedient but unbowed Cybele, a figure of fidelity "humbled herself before the king." The wishes and submission of Dijon, meanwhile, simply appeared at the king's feet without explanation. Cybele's position relative to these other two elements called attention to the city's relative equality to the monarch. Latin and French verses on the archway praised Louis' military triumphs and pledged the city's fidelity but stopped short of proclaiming the king to be the embodiment of the state or the sole guarantor of peace and order.[81] The four remaining archways said little about Dijon's relationship with the king, focusing instead on Louis' recent victory at La Rochelle.[82] Although Bréchillet's glorification of the king echoed Bourbon-absolutist rhetoric, his *entrée* program did not embrace its underlying assumptions. The city was positioned as the king's *serviteur*–a relationship that lesser nobles used to verify their status and their inclusion among those entitled to participate in political life.[83] Dijon pledged its fidelity and obedience to the king much as a vassal would to a lord, but it pointedly did not humiliate itself as a passive subject. Furthermore, by making the city, as well as Louis, divine, Bréchillet also decreased the symbolic distance between the two. While acknowledging Dijon's inferior status, Bréchillet also reaffirmed its membership in the corporate French polity.

Malpoy's archways for Henri de Bourbon's 1632 *entrée* stressed the theme of restoration and made particularly prominent use of the ville des dieux theme. The procession's first archway featured *le bon événement* welcoming Condé to the city of the gods, followed by a large *théâtre* in which Malpoy replaced Cybele with five deities–Minerva, Mars, Ceres, Bacchus, and Mercury–surrounding an empty chair to be filled by the province's new governor. The final archway depicted a young man playing a lyre, "raising and rebuilding your capital city," in a manner "worthy certainly of a god, and of a city of the gods."[84]

When compared with Louis XIII's *entrée,* Malpoy's decorations appear somewhat more absolutist in tone, although elements highlighting the reciprocal relationship between city and king remained. The *sang des Bourbons,* absent in 1629, made an appearance, as did references to the new governor's status as first prince of the blood. In addition, Condé was also portrayed as a protector and source of renewal, although usually in the more traditional language of the patron-client relationship than in the heroic glorification typical of Bourbon-absolutist rhetoric.[85] On the other hand, Malpoy's entry explicitly paralleled Conde, the "god," and Dijon, the "city of the gods." The

Figure 2. Pierre Malpoy, *Entrée de très haut et très puissant Prince Henry de Bourbon, Prince de Condé*... (Dijon, 1632). Second archway: Minerva, Mars, Ceres, Bacchus, and Mercury welcome Condé to *la ville des dieux*. BMD, Breuil III-1. Photo: Bibliothèque Municipale de Dijon.

Figure 3. Pierre Malpoy, *Entrée de très haut et très puissant Prince Henry de Bourbon, Prince de Condé* . . . (Dijon, 1632). Fifth archway: Condé as Apollo rebuilding Dijon with his lyre. BMD, Breuil III-1. Photo: Bibliothèque Municipale de Dijon.

five gods welcomed the prince and "turned over to him the government of this city which they have had from its foundation, leaving him with all authority."[86] Once again, la ville des dieux was neither passive nor submissive. On the contrary, it voluntarily handed over its authority to the prince in a manner reminiscent of the Roman people in the *lex regia*.[87] Although the city was subordinate to the prince, the scene on the second archway expressed the avocats' belief that Dijon remained a privileged and politically active member of the realm.

Bréchillet's and Godrans' archways for the Grand Condé's 1648 entry diverged from those in 1629 and 1632 by stressing the virtues and quasi-divinity of both the new governor and the young Louis XIV. They portrayed the king and his representative as sources of order, protection, and social benefits. In summarizing the meaning of the third archway, which showed Louis as Jupiter receiving the adulation of his hopeful subjects, Bréchillet described the king as the conqueror of war, discord, and avarice, and praised the "*jeune soleil*" as the source of a new "golden age." Of the king, Bréchillet wrote, "[H]e is the living source of his subjects' happiness just as the sun is of light; they cannot subsist without the communication of his graces." The fourth archway, meanwhile, featured an allegorical figure of Condé's virtue carrying a pomegranate that symbolized good laws and civic unity, demonstrating "that the virtue of this great prince will preserve the king's subjects in concord and unity."[88]

Concepts such as the *sang royal* and the hereditary transmission of royal virtues, minimal in 1629 and 1632, dominated in 1648. The Grande Condé's status as first prince of the blood was repeatedly invoked, as was his Bourbon ancestry, which made the new governor "heir of merit and of blood." One of the 1648 ceremony's innovations was a "*théâtre d'honneur*" where Saint Louis and illustrious members of the Bourbon line recognized that the prince united their separate virtues, "making him the miracle of the century." Malpoy, by contrast, had mentioned Henri de Bourbon's status as first prince of the blood only a few times, and then usually to point out the honor Burgundy had received.[89]

Whereas the 1629 entry took pains to show the city as subordinate but not passively submissive, Bréchillet's 1648 *entrée* unambiguously showed the city's three orders giving Condé their submission and obedience. The 1648 entry did not abandon the "city of the gods," image but it did make the ville des dieux's role much more passive. Dijon was depicted not as a sacred person (or group of persons), but as a sacred place–a temple from which three figures, Religion (clergy), Honor (nobility), and La Politique (Third Estate) exited, accompanied by a cupid offering three hearts to the new governor. The theme of the "city of gods," which had previously personified the city's reciprocal, though subordinate, relationship with the monarchy, was now used increasingly to glorify the Bourbon kings and governors.[90]

In spite of this, Bréchillet's 1648 entry continued to invoke, albeit in a muted fashion, the reciprocal relationship between king and city as well as the latter's role in the French state. The second archway evoked the metaphor of a corporate society in which each member has its own function and status. Whileas other elements of the entry expressed the Bourbon-absolutist position that the royal will was the only source of order and social cohesion, Bréchillet's commentary described the three orders' "natural" and "indissoluble" bonds of "union and obedience," echoing the constitutionalist argument that society prefigured the king, not vice versa. Bréchillet also depicted the Third Estate as La Politique–an amalgam of Justice, *police,* and the Arts.[91] The compass in the figure's hand, Bréchillet observed, represented "the moderation required in all political actions" and was the symbol of reason required for all human actions. The scales she carried in the other hand, meanwhile, stood for equity in both commutative and distributive justice. Bréchillet thus assigned two of the principal functions of government–justice and *police*–and one of the main attributes of the absolute monarch–reason–to the Third Estate rather than the king. In so doing, he rejected the notion that government was the crown's sole prerogative. The second archway thus undermined, at least partially, the absolutist rhetoric celebrated in the rest of the entry. "The prince, as well as the Magistrate," Bréchillet wrote about a scene on the fourth archway, "is a bright light who lights the way for and leads the rest of the people, exciting them to imitate his [its] virtue. . . . "[92] In associating the magistrate (most likely the mairie) with the prince, Bréchillet reinforced his claim that Dijon's Third Estate and municipality had a legitimate and indispensable role to play in governing the city.

Jean Godran de Chasans returned to the allegory of Cybele in his design for the duke of Epernon's 1656 *entrée,* which took place amid the factional hostilities lingering after the Burgundian Fronde. The entry's archways celebrated Epernon as the restorer of peace and unity and highlighted his authority as the only way to heal the city's divisions. Epernon's arrival, according to Griguette, "like a blazing sun has dissipated the stormy nights of our internal divisions, defeated our enemies, and reunited our wills in His Majesty's service so that we may long enjoy the advantages of peace."[93] The ongoing hostilities between the Condéans and their opponents prompted Godran de Chasans and Griguette to adopt an absolutist tone whose fulsome praise of Epernon and emphasis on the city's passivity went well beyond Bréchillet's 1648 program. For Godran des Chasans and Griguette, the ville des dieux was no more than another component in a pageant of absolutist hero worship.

The differences between the Cybeles of 1629 and 1656 show how the avocats' understanding of Dijon's relationship with the monarchy had changed. Both portrayed Cybele as a matronly figure presenting the city's keys to the entering dignitary. In 1629, however, Cybele wore scarlet to signify that Dijon was home to a parlement. In 1656, by contrast, she wore Epernon's

Figure 4. [Etienne Bréchillet]. *Description et interpretation des portiques erigés à l'entrée de très hault et très puissant prince, Louis de Bourbon, Prince de Condé . . . en la ville de Dijon, le 6 mars 1648* (Dijon, 1650). Second archway: Religion, Honor, and La Politique welcome Condé to *la ville des dieux*. BMD, Breuil II-43. Photo: Bibliothèque Municipale de Dijon.

Figure 5. [Etienne Bréchillet]. *Description et interpretation des portiques erigés à l'entrée de très hault et très puissant prince, Louis de Bourbon, Prince de Condé . . . en la ville de Dijon, le 6 mars 1648* (Dijon, 1650). Fourth archway: Condé's virtue carries a pomegranate, symbolizing good order. BMD, Breuil II-43. Photo: Bibliothèque Municipale de Dijon.

colors to emphasize her dependence on the governor. The profound fissures in Dijon's body politic meant that order and stability had to be imposed by Epernon and the "city of the gods" was reduced to complete passivity and submission.[94] Dressed in Epernon's colors, la ville de dieux could only surrender her keys, "once the symbol of power, but now . . . the true mark of her submission and obedience."[95]

Bréchillet's use of the temple and the figure of La Politique in 1648 expressed the belief that the city and its elite continued to play a role in the French state, despite the *entrée*'s generally absolutist tenor. Such ideas were totally absent in 1656. The little cupids surrounding Cybele represented the citizens of Dijon, whose love for Epernon "reciprocally and insensibly attaches" them to the prince's heart, "so they may afterwards enjoy the favors they hope to receive from him."[96] Epernon, Griguette wrote, "knew how to use this authority to establish peace and assure the repose of this province under the happy commandments of the king." Following the entry, a fireworks display showed Epernon as an angel of peace who "disposed the hearts and wills of our citizens to mutual love, Union, and Concord."[97]

Although Godran de Chasans and Griguette could not evoke Epernon's royal blood, they nonetheless stressed his kingly personal qualities. Their first archway, for example, called attention to the House of Foix's alliances with "all the princes of Christendom." Echoing the *théâtre* of Condé's ancestors, an elaborate tableau on the procession's final archway celebrated Epernon's many virtues, inherited from his illustrious forebears."[98] Indeed, in trying to establish the unpopular Epernon as the equal of his popular predecessor, Godran de Chasans and Griguette amplified the absolutist tenor of their *entrée* well beyond Bréchillet's 1648 program. In the hands of the author of *La mort de Germanic Caesar,* Epernon became a paradigm of "absolute power" while Condé's many supporters were cast as "tyrants."

Portrayals of Dijon as la ville des dieux, especially the earlier ones, highlighted the avocats' view of Dijon as a "sacred center."[99] Although this view waned gradually during the first half of the seventeenth century, the persistence of such a municipal identity is significant at a time when the monarchy asserted that it was the kingdom's sole source of legitimate authority. In representing Dijon as the "city of the gods," the avocats recognized the mairie's subordination to the king, but also called attention to its political authority and place in the French state. The "city of the gods" motif also expressed an older understanding of the monarchy as a series of reciprocal relationships between "sacred" centers such as Dijon and the ultimate "sacred" center–the king. If Louis XIII and the Condés were Hercules or Augustus, then Dijon was Cybele, or an association of deities. And even if it was not portrayed as one or more divinities, it was still a sacred place–a temple or Pantheon. The ville des dieux motif thus reduced the symbolic separation of status between Dijon and the entering king or governor. Kristen Neuschel's study of noble

Figure 6. [Bénigne Griguette]. *Les armes triomphantes de son altesse Monseigneur le duc d'Espernon pour le sujet de son heureuse entrée faite dans la ville de Dijon, le huictième jour de May 1656* (Dijon, 1656). First archway: "The People's Love for the Duke," with Cybele, mother of the gods. BMD 18164. Photo: Bibliothèque Municipale de Dijon.

Figure 7. [Bénigne Griguette], *Les armes triomphantes de son altesse Monseigneur le duc d'Espernon pour le sujet de son heureuse entrée faite dans la ville de Dijon, le huictième jour de May 1656* (Dijon, 1656). Third archway: The victories of the duke of Epernon. BMD 18164. Photo: Bibliothèque Municipale de Dijon.

culture has shown how unequal exchanges benefited the inferior party by validating its privileged status.[100] In a similar fashion, Dijon submitted to its king or governor not with the subservience of a powerless subject, but with the respectful obedience that a privileged, honorable member of the realm owed to its legitimate superior. Increasing factional divisions among the municipal elite, combined with the growing influence of Bourbon-absolutist rhetoric and ideology, gradually recast the boundaries of legitimate political participation in Dijon during the first half of the seventeenth century. As the distance between the king and rest of body politic grew, the "city of the gods" ceased to be an honorable subordinate with a recognized place in the kingdom's political life. Instead, it became an increasingly passive, submissive, and minor voice in a chorus celebrating the heroic virtues of the king and his governors, and the benefits of peace and order they conferred.

Conclusion

As Dijonnais municipal identity waned, it was replaced during the second half of the century by a new attention to regional customs and particularities. Burgundy's customs and institutions were generally seen as predating the region's rattachement to the crown in 1477. Every edition of the Coutumes de Bourgogne, for example, reprinted Philip the Good's original lettres patentes and identified his approval as the ultimate source of their legal authority.[101] Legal precedents and ordinances from the ducal era were cited alongside more recent cases without any distinction.[102] Even though nearly three hundred years had passed since the death of the last Valois duke, Dijon's avocats saw no historical or legal rupture.

Another important theme was the concept of Burgundian "liberty." Late-sixteenth-century writers such as Saint-Julien had insisted that Burgundians were "perpetually free" and that "if some princes have ruled over them (as is certainly the case), it is because [the Burgundians] have chosen to accept them rather than because they were forced to take them." In the early seventeenth century, Souvert encouraged deputies to "retake their ancient liberty" by defending the province's privilege to hold Estates.[103] Such ideas were revived in the late seventeenth century. Pierre Taisand claimed that Burgundians were unique among humankind for having never lost their personal liberty. François Perrier, in a late-seventeenth-century plaidoyer, argued that villagers should not be forced to buy their salt from a more distant grenier because "we are in a region of liberty and freedom." Gabriel Guillaume and Pierre Petit, conseils of the Estates of Burgundy, asserted during the 1690s that Burgundian custom, in contrast with those of many other places, had "an air of freedom and liberty for persons and possessions." As far as Dijon's avocats were concerned, then, Burgundy retained its distinctive character and institutions. French kings, as successors of the Burgundian dukes, were bound to recognize the same liberties, privileges, and customary arrangements as their predecessors had.[104]

Throughout the first half of the century, the avocats considered the city a "sacred center" and a participant in workings of the corporate French state. By mid-century, the ville des dieux theme faded from the avocats' political discourse as a result of growing factionalism and the persistent influence of Bourbon-absolutist rhetoric and ideology. Although the avocats' writings demonstrate a gradual shift towards the absolutist pole of political thought, they never fully embraced the implications of absolutist theory. They continued to believe that royal authority was constrained by and mediated through local customs, traditions, and institutions. The only difference was that by the late seventeenth century, regional particularism and liberty had replaced municipal identity as the avocats' primary frame of reference, as the following chapter will demonstrate.

"Right down until the last decades of the seventeenth century," David Parker has argued, "the ambiguities in French thought continued with its paradoxical emphasis on both an undivided supreme power and the important, indeed essential function, performed by a multiplicity of institutions. The notion of sovereignty as absolute, yet restrained, remained powerful . . . because such a view continued to make reasonable sense of the world in which Frenchmen lived."[105] This was certainly the case among the avocats of seventeenth-century Dijon. And although the avocats tended to highlight the king's "absolute" power as the ultimate source of political order and social benefits, especially as the urban notability grew increasingly divided, they never abandoned their belief that royal power was limited by reason, custom, and a corporate political order that gave the kingdom's gens de bien the right to participate in the legitimate exercise of public authority. In the wake of Louis XIV's transformation of Dijon's municipal political system in 1668, the second half of the century saw Dijon's avocats shift back toward more "constitutionalist" ways of understanding the French state.

The next chapter will examine the many continuities in the avocats' political thought during the second half of the seventeenth century. Although royal theorists increasingly emphasized the king's "absolute" and irresistible authority, many of Dijon's avocats remained committed to a juridically based view of the monarchy that posited a contractual relationship between the city or region on the one hand and the crown on the other. At the same time, chapter 6 will also examine a far more sweeping critique of ancien régime monarchy and society in a utopian travel account written by one obscure Dijonnais avocat. Whether they looked to past customs or distant, fictional shores, Dijon's late-seventeenth-century avocats began to reconceptualize their relationship to a state and a political system of which they were no longer active members.

Chapter 6

Custom, Reason, and the Limits of Royal Authority

As French political thought became decidedly more absolutist in tone during Louis XIV's reign, Dijon's avocats displayed a more traditional, constitutionalist view of the king as a "judicial monarch." Though accepting such commonplace absolutist notions as "le mort saisit le vif," "qui veut le roi, si veut la loi," and "le roi est empereur en son royaume,"[1] Dijon's avocats also called attention to the independent development of regional laws and institutions. They described these things as expressions of Burgundy's "natural law," thereby placing them beyond the royal prerogative. They also called attention to the contractual relationship between king and province, again limiting the monarch's ability to alter regional laws, institutions, and practices unilaterally. Finally, Dijon's avocats also described the king not in Bossuet's terms, as "the image of God" whose will was the sole source of order and peace, but rather as a feudal lord whose role was to maintain the complex balance of devolved authorities that made up the French state.

This chapter will begin by examining the intellectual world of Dijon's avocats and other legal professionals during the late seventeenth century. Next, it will analyze the significance of the rapid expansion in the number of commentaries on Burgundian custom and other areas of private law in the late seventeenth and early eighteenth centuries. It will then show how the avocats' enduring belief in the limited scope of legitimate royal authority was tied to their attitudes about the right of worthy individuals to participate in local governance. From there, I will examine how one Dijonnais avocat combined his legal background with Cartesian philosophy, deism, and other late-seventeenth-century intellectual currents to imagine a radical alternative not only to the reign of Louis XIV, but to ancien régime monarchy and society as a whole. In so doing, I will try to indicate how the avocats' exclusion from the political nation after 1668 altered their relationship to the French state and their conception of politics, helping to transform the law-centered "public sphere" of the seventeenth century into the more familiar "bourgeois public sphere" of the eighteenth century. In this new "public sphere," where reason and political judgment would be exercised outside the confines of the state rather than within it, the avocats' mastery of law, reason, and eloquence would once again entitle them to play a legitimate role in public life and the governance of the realm.

Obedience and Opposition at the Palais de Justice

Even at the height of Louis XIV's reign, Dijon's Parlement remained a reservoir of historical traditions and legal theories that envisioned the French state as a corporate polity with a delicately balanced traditional constitution. Though outwardly compliant and even docile, Burgundy's highest court nurtured an undercurrent of criticism of and hostility to the king and his policies that was rooted in the region's legal customs and historical traditions.[2] At the same time, some parlementaires appear to have been receptive to new influences linked to Cartesianism and the works of Pierre Bayle, John Locke, and other similar thinkers–intellectual trends that also fostered a highly critical view of the monarchy and its actions. Ensconced in the "civil humanist" legal culture of the palais de justice, Dijon's avocats shared many of the magistrates' criticisms of Louis XIV's policies and the theories that supported them, as we will see.

The Parlement of Dijon, much like its counterparts throughout France, was essentially tractable and compliant throughout most of Louis' reign. The "taming" of Burgundy's high court, to a large extent, even preceded the beginning of Louis' personal reign. In November 1658, the young Louis held an unprecedented lit-de-justice in person to compel registration of several fiscal edicts. Although the magistrates complied, they did not hesitate to demonstrate their opposition to the king's tactics. Shortly after Louis' departure, Parlement voided the registered edicts on a technicality and vowed to send new remonstrances to the king. The magistrates also stripped the greffier-en-chef of his office for expediting a false document and insulting members of the court. Louis responded by summoning First President Brulart and four conseillers to explain their actions and then promptly exiled them to Perpignan. The royal council then voided all of Parlement's measures and imposed an interdiction that lasted until June of the following year. Brulart himself was not allowed to return to Dijon until January 1660.[3] The threatened creation of a *chambre souveraine* for Bresse and Bugey in the early 1660s, which would have meant a substantial reduction of Parlement's already small jurisdiction, gave the monarchy even greater leverage over the recalcitrant magistrates. For the remainder of the century, Louis kept Burgundy's supreme court in line by using the tactics of supervision and negotiation described by Albert Hamscher in his study of the Paris Parlement.[4] If anything, Burgundy's Parlement appears to have been among the kingdom's most obedient and submissive tribunals. In August 1667, for instance, it registered Louis' sweeping ordinance reforming civil procedure without complaint after hearing only the preamble and the first few articles. Similarly, although the other parlements opposed a series of 1672 fiscal edicts making notaries' and procureurs' offices hereditary (for a fee) and levying new duties on nonnoble holders of noble properties, the parlement of Burgundy registered the controversial edicts before the monarchy had even distributed them in printed form as a sign, Brulart maintained, of its "great submissiveness."[5] It is hardly a surprise, then, that after its return in 1659, the court was not exiled or placed under interdiction again during Louis' reign. Resistance to unpopular royal directives was limited to the time-honored tactics of foot dragging and obstruction, with the royal will invariably triumphing in the end.[6] Only with the events surrounding the "affaire des baguettes" in 1706–when a deputation of parlementaires ordered their huissiers not to dip their batons in salute to the duke of Bourbon–did Parlement begin to show signs of attempting to shake off its royal muzzle.[7]

The sovereign court's outward docility, however, did not prevent it from nurturing a number of influential figures who defended traditional conceptions of restrained royal authority. Many of Brulart's *harangues,* for example, continued to emphasize both the king's traditional role as the font of justice (rather than his "absolutist" quality as legislator) and the voluntary self-restraint with which he ought to employ his "absolute" power. At the *rentrée* of 1666, for example, Brulart described Louis XIV as "the image of Justice," noting that this was the source of his power and future glory, as well as the "common happiness" of the French people. Three years later, he asked the audience to "see Justice seated on the throne of the empire of the world with all the kings beneath, from whom they receive at the same time the laws and their scepters." Finally, in 1677, he observed that "supreme power, while freed from the laws, moderates itself to them and draws marvelous advantages from them. Have we ever seen a prince more powerful and more glorious than our king? Nonetheless, this redoubtable power and this glory admired by the entire world earns him no more honor than his moderation."[8]

A number of magistrates and others affiliated with the sovereign court, meanwhile, were hostile to the Sun King's policies throughout his reign. The conseiller Philibert de La Mare, for example, possessed a large collection of scandal sheets mocking the decadence of the king and his court, and also displayed considerable interest in the political theorists of the Catholic League. His manuscript *Mémoires* denounced everyone from "the avaricious Colbert," who "overturned the most august laws of the State," to Louis XIV himself, whom La Mare compared with the first king of the Israelites, the hero-turned-tyrant Saul. In his correspondence, the conseiller J.-B. Lantin denounced Reason of State theory as both ridiculous and odious, writing that "the morals and rules of those who govern a state are well opposed to those of individuals. They are most often even contrary to humanity." He also criticized what he believed was the excessive influence wielded by the king's mistresses. "If the family of the one who reigns is not at peace, then neither can be the state." Bernard de La Monnoye, a nonpracticing avocat who later purchased the office of corrector in the Chamber of Accounts, wrote and collected poetry critical of the king and his ministers. "The flock that Louis leads /" went one, "was already handsome and fat / Colbert has taken its wool / Pelletier will have its skin." Another exclaimed: "Kings, authors of our misery / Who want to pass for gods / You resemble those of Homer / *Honnêtes hommes* are worth more than you." The circulation of titles such as *La France devenue italienne avec les autres désordres de la Cour,* and poems with incendiary lines such as "What we need is a King William" and "Let us do what the English have done" in some quarters of the palais de justice provide further hints of hostility toward the king and his ministers.[9]

Many parlementaire criticisms of Louis XIV's policies were understandably based on historical, juridical, and "constitutionalist" grounds. In May 1673, for instance, Brulart protested the intendant's and lieutenant-général's demands that the court register several edicts by pointing out that parlements functioned as "agreeable and accredited mediators for the good of the state and the glory of its kings." By representing subjects' needs to the king, he continued, parlements ensured good order and obedience; should they lose their ability to remonstrate against unwise edicts, they would no longer be able to persuade ordinary men and women to obey the law. "What would become of the sage precautions of all of the ordinances of our kings," he asked, "who believed it was as much for their authority as for their justice, to listen above all to the faithful and incorruptible sentiments of their courts?" While praising Louis XIV, Brulart also reminded his agents that not all kings were up to the level of the current monarch. "Not all of the Caesars were Augustus; the state endures and its greatest security comes from the stability and vigor of its old laws, whose long execution have for centuries strengthened it and made it flourish and have always so strongly brought together kings and the love of their peoples."[10] Not surprisingly, a number of parlementaires were part of the swelling ranks of Burgundian jurists interested in studying the history and character of Burgundy's legal customs.[11] Avocats and conseillers alike, Bouchard writes, "hastened to assemble arrêts, draw up consultations, publish the summaries of their plaidoyers or their reports, each one wanting to add a stone to the singular monument, each one putting all of his efforts into enriching the slender articles of the province's primitive customs in order make of them something like a constitution for the province."[12] A few parlementaires, such as the eighteenth-century president and future academician Jean Bouhier, vigorously defended the superiority of Roman law, suggesting a legal and political temperament more in line with the absolutist theories emanating from Versailles. As Jean Bart has shown, however, these individuals were a distinct minority. Most Burgundian jurists–judges and avocats alike–clearly favored a jurisprudence rooted in a common "French customary law" or a historically grounded analysis of Burgundy's customs and their evolution.[13] Dijon's robe, Bouchard writes, "consecrated a good part of its leisure time to defining the code of Burgundian liberties, the municipal laws of the region which were its only means for combating the monarchy's total power."[14]

A number of magistrates were also well informed about the rationalist, antihistorical currents that were becoming increasingly fashionable in European philosophical circles at the close of the century. Despite a striking absence of Jansenist and Protestant influences at the palais de justice–Burgundy had a long history as a center of Catholic orthodoxy–parlementaires were quite familiar with many of the leading philosophers and theorists of the day, including those whose orthodoxy was by no means beyond reproach. Lantin, for example, was a personal acquaintance of Hobbes (whose works he translated into French), Algernon Sidney, and Leibniz. The works of these authors were well known to Dijon's judicial elite, as were those of Bayle, Gassendi, Locke, and even Spinoza. Furthermore, Dijon's location on various trade routes provided easy access to the latest national and foreign periodicals, including the *Journal de Trévoux,* the *Nouvelles* of Pierre Bayle, and numerous German and Dutch publications.[15] "Nothing which was of interest to people of the century, nothing which men produced, remained foreign [to the Dijonnais elite]," according to Bouchard. "It perceived the echo of political storms, theological quarrels, and literary disputes; it participated in all of the movements that agitated France and Europe." For this reason, he concluded, "There was no monarchical religion among the Burgundians; [they were] capable of judging the regime with liberty [and] of criticizing it when necessary."[16]

Dijon's avocats were an integral part of the cultural and intellectual world of the palais, centered as it was on the study and practice of the complex body of edicts, customs, commentaries, and jurisprudence that made up "the law" in early modern France. One of the main concerns for many participants in this culture was how to protect the boundary between "absolute" royal power–which was synonymous with and even essential to the "rule of law"–and unchecked, unregulated "tyranny," which was its antithesis. Hence the seemingly paradoxical belief that royal power, though "absolute," was also supposed to be limited. Kings were supposed to respect traditional political arrangements and to use their authority to maintain the fragile balances of France's traditional corporate polity–a polity that allowed for a considerable degree of political participation at the local level. Throughout the late seventeenth and early eighteenth centuries, Dijon's avocats repeatedly turned to the region's legal customs and historical traditions to defend this view of the monarchy, a trend that would become increasingly common across France over the course of the eighteenth century.[17]

Customary Law and Royal Authority

Like their counterparts elsewhere in France, Dijon's avocats appear to have developed a particular interest in private law, especially regional jurisprudence and custom, in the late seventeenth century.[18] This interest, of course, was not entirely new. The obscure, lacunary character of the fifteenth-century Coutumes de Bourgogne placed a premium on interpretation and commentary almost from the beginning. The coutumiers of most regions were updated in the late sixteenth century, but efforts to do so in Burgundy failed almost entirely.[19] Although some reform articles were published and became influential, they were never officially incorporated into the Coutumes. Throughout the early modern period, Burgundian jurists worked to cobble together a coherent jurisprudence out of the old coutumes and Roman law–which the 1459 patent letters designated as "droit supplémentaire." The difficult task of explicating and applying the coutume's archaic language fell primarily to avocats, and many leading members of Dijon's bar compiled commentaries, notes, recueils des arrêts, and other interpretative aides throughout the period.[20] Not until the late seventeenth century, however, did avocats, as well as other jurists, begin to undertake a systematic, critical analysis of Burgundian customs as a way of understanding the province's particular character and its unique relationship to its sovereign.[21]

The flurry of published commentaries and other related works between 1688 and 1736 included major new commentaries by Nicolas Perrier (1688), Joseph Durand (1697), Pierre Taisand (1698), President Jean Bouhier (1717), and the conseiller François Bretagne (1736). These were accompanied by the publication of important reference works such as François Perrier's *Arrêts notables du Parlement de Dijon,* which was edited and published with a commentary by Guillaume Raviot in 1735.[22] Like François Perrier's *Arrêts,* many of these works collected avocats' notes that had circulated in manuscript form. Joseph Durand's *Institutes au droit coutumier du duché de Bourgogne* (1697) was actually taken from a manuscript by his grandfather Bernard, a leading seventeenth-century avocat, which had been extensively revised and annotated by a leading avocat of the next generation, Jacques-Auguste de Chevanes.[23] The publisher A.-J.-B. Augé compiled Bretagne's *Coutume Générale* of 1736 from the late conseiller's personal notes and collated them with others by the well-known avocats Philibert de La Mare and François-Claude Jehannin and the previously published *Observations* of Nicolas Perrier.[24] Others, such as Taisand, readily acknowledged their debts to several generations of jurists and avocats.[25]

The private law treatises produced by Dijon's late-seventeenth- and early eighteenth-century avocats rarely addressed the nature of royal government directly. Nevertheless, careful examination of these works reveals that avocats' attitudes about the limited scope of the king's absolute power and the devolved nature of royal authority had changed little over the course of the century. If anything, the forced retreat from public life brought about by the 1668 reorganization of the hôtel de ville was followed by the reemergence of these older ideals. The private law writings of avocats under Louis XIV continued to blend absolutist and constitutional elements to limit the legitimate range of royal authority.

Commentators generally accepted several key elements of absolutist theory, such as the application of the doctrine "le mort saisit le vif" to the royal succession, with its implication that the royal *dignitas* inhered in the king's person and the royal dynasty rather than in a separate, immortal office.[26] They also echoed the absolutist claim that the monarch was the source of all public authority. Nicolas Perrier pointed out that "the property of public power resides in [the king] alone." "The king is sovereign in his estates," Taisand observed, "and only recognizes God as his superior."[27] The avocats also appear to have accepted the concept of royal legislative sovereignty. In a commentary on kidnapping, Jean Melenet argued that parlements could not use the threat of the death penalty to force seducers to marry their victims because such sentences usurped royal legislative power.[28]

In spite of the absolutist language, the avocats emphasized that customary laws limited the king's legislative authority, that Burgundy's relationship to the crown was contractual in nature, and that royal power was devolved to local authorities. None of the avocats went so far as René de la Bigiotière, who argued in his 1702 commentary on Breton customs that transgressions of provincial customs and privileges were criminal violations of the coronation oath. But the private law works of Dijon's avocats are consistent with Gerald Greenberger's observation that "extension of the royal authority outside of customary areas was considered to be extra-legal and thus . . . contrary to the very nature of the monarchy as a legal and moral institution."[29]

The avocats' private law writings emphasized the independent evolution and self-sufficiency of Burgundian laws. Several avocats and other jurists described the customs as the province's "Fundamental Law."[30] Taisand portrayed them as "the veritable laws of Burgundy" and asserted that they were "established by the authority of good sense and a universally approved usage, and not on the sole authority of humans." Durand and Chevanes' *Instituts au droit coutumier,* meanwhile, characterized them as "a sure law [*un droit certain*] which has been insensibly established by the approbation of the People for a great many years."[31] By 1717, the parlementaire Bouhier could describe the customs, in Marcel Bouchard's words, as "patrimonial to the province, of its own creation, and expressing the soul of the region."[32] In this regard, Burgundian jurists paralleled their colleagues in other provinces, who also portrayed customs as the product of long usage and popular consent, and who viewed them as restraints on royal power.[33]

The avocats also called attention to the limits of royal authority over Burgundian institutions and practices. Taisand pointed out that the feudal *droit d'indire,* which permitted a seigneur to levy double rents and dues in the event he was captured, received a new knighthood, undertook an overseas voyage, or was to be married, was still commonly observed in Burgundy despite three separate royal ordinances forbidding it. He also asserted that the 1567 Edict of Saint-Maur, which prevented married women from inheriting *meubles* and *conquêtes* from the paternal side of the family, "has never had force in Burgundy; it does not derogate from the disposition of our Custom, which retains its force and vigor, notwithstanding the ordinary and sovereign authority of [Royal] edicts." Burgundian custom even went so far as to restrict basic royal prerogatives such as the *droit d'aubaine,* which allowed the king to inherit the goods of all foreigners who died while in France.[34] "The province," Bouchard writes summarizing these commentaries, "was not to be confused with France, because not only did it have its own constitution, but also its own life and history."[35]

One of the most important cases in which the avocats used regional customs to limit royal authority came in 1692–93, when Louis XIV tried to assert his lordship over allodial lands across the kingdom. Free allods were lands held without any financial or symbolic obligations to a lord or superior. Desperate to raise money for his wars, Louis XIV issued an edict in August 1692 asserting his ultimate lordship, or *directe universelle,* over all French lands. Those who could not produce titles to prove allodial status were ordered to pay the equivalent of one year of their lands' revenues in return for confirmation of their titles. If the lands in question were noble, a payment of 10 percent of their value was also required to offset feudal dues owed the king. The royal edict threatened havoc in Burgundy, where all lands were presumed allodial and where most large landholders would likely have been unable to produce the required titles.[36] Several of Dijon's leading avocats and other jurists quickly produced arguments that Burgundy was exempt from the edict. The conseils des états Guillaume and Petit argued that Burgundian custom differed from that of other regions because "one finds in it neither any mark of general servitude nor *directe universelle* found in several others of this kingdom." Jehannin claimed that Burgundy's freedom dated back to the Roman empire. Burgundy was never conquered, he argued; the region joined the empire voluntarily and was exempt from all tribute payments. It maintained this freedom when it became part of the kingdom of France. The conseiller Le Belin argued that allodial lands had been established in Burgundy by long-standing practice and royal toleration. The Master of Accounts and former mayor of Dijon François Baudot appealed to regional history to show that the dukes of Burgundy never claimed the directe universelle and even admitted explicitly that they did not enjoy it. Burgundian custom, Roman law, the region's ducal and Roman past, and the principle of Burgundian "liberty" were thus all invoked to show that royal efforts to claim suzerainty over allodial lands would "destroy the fundamental laws of this province." In July 1693, the royal council issued an edict recognizing the existence of allodial lands in Burgundy and exempting the province from the August 1692 edict.[37]

The free-allods controversy highlighted another aspect of the avocats' political thought, their belief that the relationship between king and province was contractual in nature. It was a commonplace among late-seventeenth-century jurists that customs were a form of contract that could not be easily changed or violated.[38] Many of the arguments in 1692–93 referred back to the "*anciens franchises*" that Louis XI promised to respect in return for Dijon's and the duchy's voluntary recognition of his sovereignty after Charles the Bold's death. The king's justice, Baudot noted, required him to maintain the region's privileges "because these promises are accompanied by the Royal Seal and have been renewed so many times." Even Jehannin, who claimed that Burgundy had never been separated from France, believed the province's customs and liberties had the force of contract. As noted above, he simply displaced the pivotal moment from 1477 to Burgundy's voluntary association with the French kingdom after the Roman empire's fall.

Avocats often invoked the metaphor of a marriage to express their belief in the contractual nature of royal government. In his speech to Louis XIII after Lanturelu, Fevret recalled the city's "day of marriage," when Dijon presented Louis XI with "the consecrated ring" of perpetual fidelity.[39] Bréchillet's *Les nopces de bontems avec la Bourgogne* (1636) added a twist to this theme by portraying the marriage as a sort of *ménage à trois* among père Bontems, La Bourgogne, and the young Louis II de Bourbon.[40] In his design for Condé's gubernatorial *entrée* twelve years later Bréchillet depicted the young Louis XIV as Jupiter and France as Juno to illustrate that "France is joined by a tight and indissolvable knot to her king."[41]

In describing the king (or his representative) as a husband, Dijon's avocats alluded to a body of established jurisprudence equating the coronation oath with a marital vow. The main purpose of this legal fiction was to reinforce the inalienability of the royal domain.[42] It may also, as Sarah Hanley has argued, have "contractually unit[ed] king and kingdom in a political state marriage likened legally to that of husband and wife in a social civil marriage."[43] Avocats knew from experience that marriages literally involved the drawing up of contracts between two inherently unequal parties and that they did not give one spouse unfettered dominion over the other. As Durand and Chevanes explained, Burgundian custom defined marriage as a community. And although the husband was "seigneur and master of this community," his authority was limited by law and the "jurisprudence of the arrêts." His power, Taisand wrote, must be "honnête et moderée" and not "tyrannique."[44] Eschewing the unlimited patriarchical authority of the Roman *patria potestas* in favor of the husband's contractual authority implied boundaries on the king's power over the province. Royal authority in Burgundy was contractual in nature and limited by law, custom, and the good of the community. The king, like the husband, did not embody the community. Furthermore, royal interest and regional interest were not always, as absolutist theorists implied, one and the same.

The avocats' conception of royal power as contractual in nature and devolved in practice is also apparent in their repeated characterizations of the monarch as a feudal lord. Greenberger has shown that commentators in other regions portrayed the king "as essentially a feudal lord with precisely defined privileges and responsibilities. There was relatively little attention given to his special character, while the role of the king as feudal suzerain was emphasized."[45] Relying extensively on theorists such as Loyseau, Guy Coquille, and Jean Bacquet, as well as accounts of early French and Burgundian history, Dijon's avocats placed the king at the apex of a feudal hierarchy characterized by bonds of fidelity and obligation. Taisand, for instance, described the law of fiefs as one of the foundations of the French monarchy. Nicolas Perrier, Jehannin, and Philibert de La Mare similarly limited their observations on "the king" to issues surrounding the droit d'aubaine and the king's right to succeed bastards.[46] The avocats also inverted Loyseau's distinction between royal sovereignty ("public seigneury") and the privatized judicial authority usurped by feudal lords and held by right of prescription ("private seigneury"). Whereas Loyseau used the distinction to enhance the monarch's "absolute power," the Burgundian jurists focused instead on the nearly irrevocable devolution of royal power to local lords.[47] Judicial authority, Durand and Chevanes argued, was patrimonial and annexed to fiefs. Furthermore, since Burgundian fiefs were held "*de danger*" and not "*de profit,*" the king could neither require payments from fief holders nor dispossess them except under specific circumstances.[48]

Although absolutist ideas gained greater currency and influence among Dijon's avocats during the first half of the seventeenth century, the pendulum was clearly swinging back toward constitutionalist ideas of limited royal authority by the end of the century. This trajectory can be seen in the political thought of one of the period's most eminent jurists, Pierre Taisand. The son of a Bailliage conseiller, Taisand was groomed for the bar, studying law at Toulouse and Orléans. He pled his first case at the Parlement of Dijon at age eighteen and was active in the late 1660s and early 1670s. During a 1673 visit to Paris, Taisand continued his training at the Parisian bar, plead several cases at the Parlement of Paris, and participated in legal conferences at the home of First President Guillaume de Lamoignon. On returning to Dijon, Taisand reestablished himself as a leading avocat and published his first major legal work, a *Histoire du droit romain* (1678). Poor health eventually prompted him to purchase the office of treasurer general, but his interests and attitudes remained those of an avocat. Having been forced to quit the bar, Taisand wrote, "I could not think of a better way to occupy myself than by continuing an individual study of the same civil and customary laws [which I learned as an avocat], for this has always seemed to me to be preferable to all other studies." The result was Taisand's massive 1698 commentary on Burgundy's customs, the *Coutume générale des pays et duché de Bourgogne*.[49]

A comparison of the *Coutume générale* with the *Histoire du droit romain* shows how the absolutist tendencies in Taisand's earlier work gave way to a more traditional conception of royal authority. The *Histoire,* which Taisand dedicated to his cousin Bossuet, probably reflects the intellectual influences Taisand encountered in Paris. Customary laws, such as those of the Visigoths and Lombards, he wrote, were "rude" and "ignorant," whereas Roman law contained "[t]he highest maxims of Natural law and the Law of Nations."[50] Taisand also argued that Roman law was the "source of all good laws," in which "everyone finds the rules of his duty: subjects learn how to obey with submission and sovereigns to command with justice." He observed that Louis XIV "has arrived at such a high degree of authority that our imaginations can scarcely comprehend," and urged the dauphin to study the history of Roman law in order to emulate his father. In the remainder of his work, Taisand traced the evolution of Roman law back to Romulus–the original example of legislative sovereignty. Though noting that these original laws had been made "in a general assembly and with the consent of the people," Taisand's reading of the *lex regia* was decidedly absolutist. He noted that the Romans eventually transferred their legislative power to the emperors to end to the factional conflicts that threatened to destroy them.[51]

Taisand's *Coutume générale,* in contrast, was dedicated to a figure more commonly associated with Burgundian political life–the prince of Condé.[52] The influences of Paris and the court, so prominent in the *Histoire,* were replaced by those of two prominent Dijonnais avocats, Jehannin and Gabriel-Guillaume Morisot, with whom Taisand consulted extensively. Taisand also acknowledged his debt to the works of more than a dozen prominent local avocats and jurists.[53] Taisand's primary goal, Jean Bart has noted, was to show how Burgundian custom conformed to other regional customs while calling attention to the particularities that made it suited for Burgundy.[54] Consequently, Taisand abandoned his earlier views on the superiority of Roman law, despite its special status in the province, and praised customary law as a form of universally accepted natural law, "more natural than positive."[55] This resulted in a more reciprocal view of the relationship between king and province. Instead of portraying the monarch as the sole source of order, Taisand now pointed to historical and customary structures that regulated interactions between sovereign and subject. In place of Roman law, with its emphasis on the royal will, legislative sovereignty, and a rationalist political order, Taisand substituted the wisdom of venerable local traditions, concepts of feudal monarchy, and the "natural" merits of Burgundy's particular laws and institutions.

The traditionalist elements in the political thought of Dijon's avocats, which had become increasingly muted during the first half of the seventeenth century, reasserted themselves with greater frequency in the latter stages of Louis XIV's reign and would continue to do so into the eighteenth century. In a series of "letters" on the customary law of Burgundy written in the late 1720s, for instance, an anonymous avocat repeated his predecessors' arguments that Burgundian customary law–which he described as a product of the customs of the Burgundians who conquered the region from the Romans, tempered by the "civility" of Roman law–was the region's "natural law." Echoing Jehannin's claim that Burgundy had never been conquered, the author of the "letters" conceded that although the Frankish king Clovis had defeated the Burgundian king Gondembaut, "he never abolished this nation," which had been established some seventy years before the Frankish kingdom. Indeed, in a clever reversal, the anonymous avocat went on to point out that Gondembaut's niece converted Clovis. Thus France owed its first Christian king to Burgundy, an argument that echoed those of sixteenth-century Burgundian writers who invoked the "foi de Bourgogne" to posit Burgundy as a model for France, rather than vice versa.[56]

Avocats' private law works and commentaries on Burgundian customs, while accepting some absolutist principles, then, reflected the persistence of older ideas of limited royal authority. In contrast with the prevailing absolutist theories of Bossuet, Domat, and others, the avocats argued that the king's authority over Burgundian laws and institutions was limited by both regional customs and the province's contractual relationship with the crown. In their eyes, the king was not the image of God whose will was the sole source of public order, but a feudal monarch whose job was to oversee the complex network of devolved authorities that made up the French state. Underlying this conception of royal power was the avocats' persistent belief that the monarchy's laws, customs, and traditional arrangements ensured the right of elites (such as themselves) to participate actively in local governance through corporations such as the Mairie de Dijon.[57]

The Right to Participate

One of the most contested concepts in ancien régime political thought was privilege. One of the greatest successes of seventeenth-century absolutist ideology was the transformation of privilege from something approaching a contract conditioning the relationship between king and subject into a royal gift that could be revoked at will.[58] Absolutist theorists thus reduced the political privileges of the king's subjects and their right to participate in local governance to mere grants of royal favor. This view was at odds with the avocats' persistent conception of the king as a judicial monarch whose function was to preserve and maintain the traditional arrangement of institutions, jurisdictions, and authorities. In the avocats' understanding of the French state, the king, though "absolute," was supposed to respect the existing political order, allowing intermediate corporations and members of certain social orders to participate in governance and to share in the legitimate exercise of public authority.[59] In the avocats' eyes, the ideal subject did not withdraw from public life, as many absolutist theorists held, he sought to take part in it.

The avocats believed that their rights to participate in the local workings of the French state were rooted in the city's and province's contractual and historical relationship with the king. Souvert's *Avis,* for instance, blamed the king's "wicked advisors" for the decline of Estates in other provinces and argued that existing political arrangements could not be unilaterally or arbitrarily changed. "Innovations," Souvert wrote, "are harmful to all bodies, human and celestial. . . . I do not know if I should dare to say that the one thing a *corps politique* must do, and must avoid, is to abstain from all innovations."[60] Fevret described parlements as "the most solid bases" of the state and proclaimed that a wise prince respects their authority. He also wrote that the coronation oath and the king's symbols of office were "sacred symbols of a solemn pact" by which successive French monarchs limited their authority. The second archway of Bréchillet's design for the Grand Condé's 1648 *entrée* located the exercise of justice and *la police*–La Politique–in the Third Estate. Well into the second half of the century, avocats continued to argue that privileges could create a contract between the king and those who governed on his behalf. Fevret and Nicholas Perrier, for example, cited Loyseau to distinguish "*privileges à titre onéreux,*" which could not be revoked, from ordinary, revocable privileges. *Privileges à titre onéreux,* such as those conceded to Dijon's mairie, were granted in return for services rendered or for a sum of money and were thus beyond the king's power to revoke at will.[61]

The avocats, then, accepted that the king was the sole source of authority, but this did not preclude them from arguing that royal power was by necessity devolved to intermediate authorities who shared in the governance of the realm. Pierre Monin argued that kings needed magistrates to enforce laws, provide justice, and preserve the sovereign's authority. Nicolas Perrier meanwhile, emphasized that *police* power belonged exclusively to municipal and/or seigneurial authorities, whose powers superseded even those of royal officers when it came to regulating local life. "City officers, that is mayors, échevins, consuls, and capitouls," he wrote, "still have the power of government over their cities, [as well as] the force and command of arms in the governor's absence."[62]

The avocats' belief in the necessity and importance of participation in local governance can be seen the June 1679 farewell speech of Pierre Monin, the last avocat to serve as mayor during the reign of Louis XIV. Referring to the municipal elite's declining political participation in wake of the 1668 reorganization of the hôtel de ville, Monin began his speech by lamenting, "[w]e encounter few men who are inclined to undertake the government of public affairs," especially without the motivation of "honor and monuments to a justly regulated ambition."[63] In the first half of his speech, Monin recalled Seneca's comparison of "tranquil and peaceful" Athens with "turbulent and unstable" Carthage. He noted the Roman philosopher's conclusion that the perfect citizen is more useful to the state as a moral exemplar and a voice of wisdom than he would be if constantly occupied with public affairs.[64] At first glance, then, Monin's speech would appear to fit into a Neostoic tradition that gave the prince a monopoly on public authority so that private individuals could avoid the corrupting influence of politics in order to cultivate personal morality and bring order to their souls.[65]

Monin's views, however, more closely resembled another early modern variant of Stoic philosophy–Christian Stoicism. In the remainder of his speech, Monin reflected on the traditional Stoic ideal of withdrawal from political life, ultimately rejecting it in favor of a Christian Stoic tradition that encouraged participation in the tasks of governance and public life.

Proponents of Christian Stoicism, such as Guillaume Du Vair, insisted that the virtuous could not allow their desire for personal tranquility to supersede the needs of others.[66] For Monin, the moral perils of public life necessitated, rather than excused, the virtuous person's political participation. "If all subjects of all estates entered into the spirit of Seneca's philosophy," Monin told his audience, "they would fall into anarchy and confusion, in which case the counsels of the worldly sage and the model of a perfect citizen would be useless, because there would be no ministers, officers, or magistrates for him to serve." The rest of his speech argued that virtuous men, such avocats and other members of Dijon's municipal elite, needed to participate in public life in order to demonstrate their virtue and promote the well-being of their fellow citizens. Political "experience and practice," Monin concluded, actually made one a better moral example and advisor than one who followed Seneca's advice.[67]

Although Monin's message was couched in the language of Stoicism, its meaning could not have been lost on his audience in the aftermath of 1668. By closing the hôtel de ville, Louis had deprived Dijon's best inhabitants of valuable opportunities to cultivate their virtues and gain the political experience that would make them better, wiser citizens. With fewer opportunities to obtain honor and to satisfy their "justly regulated ambition," fewer men would seek to occupy themselves with public affairs, leading to disastrous consequences. "Not only would the laws be useless without the aid of magistrates, but even worse, the power and authority of sovereigns would destroy itself."[68]

A Lawyer's Paradise: Claude Gilbert's *Histoire de Caléjava* (1700)

Throughout the late seventeenth and early eighteenth centuries, most of Dijon's avocats remained conservative in their political outlook. They turned to the highly technical and particularist language of private law and to learned humanistic references to articulate a view of royal authority that was more circumscribed and that allowed for greater levels of political participation. Most avocats did not challenge the monarchy's ultimate authority but did question the monarchy's interpretation of certain legal and cultural principles, which it used to legitimize its expansion during this period. The avocats offered "constitutionalist" alternatives to the "absolutist" rhetoric emanating from Versailles. At least one avocat, however, clearly found these traditional languages and ideas inadequate for expressing his frustrations with Louis XIV's policies. Claude Gilbert's *Histoire de Caléjava, ou l'île des hommes raisonnables* merged legal and humanistic ideas widespread among Dijonnais avocats with more recent trends in philosophical and religious thought to challenge not only Louis XIV's policies but also the very principles underlying the monarchy and ancien régime society as a whole.

Other than a short biographical sketch by the learned eighteenth-century abbé Philibert Papillon and some information gleaned from a variety of scattered documents, we know relatively little about Gilbert's life and career.[69] The son of Philippe Gilbert and Marguerite Pain, Claude Gilbert was born in Dijon on 7 June 1652. Although he was not formally received at the bar until his late thirties (c. 1690) and was nearly fifty when he married, he otherwise appears to have been a fairly typical avocat. Like many of his colleagues, he lived in Nôtre-Dame parish at the center of the city and enjoyed a comfortable but hardly luxurious lifestyle, paying tailles slightly below the average for taillable avocats.[70] Gilbert also appeared on the tableau of 1710, which strongly suggests that he was an active avocat, at least until the day he suffered a stroke that left half his body paralyzed. Gilbert died in Dijon on 18 February 1720 at the age of sixty-seven. In spite of his deist beliefs (expressed in his brief manuscript *Projet d'un religion raisonnable*), he was buried in Nôtre-Dame Church.[71]

Much like Gilbert himself, the exact circumstances around the composition and circulation of the *Historie de Caléjava* remain obscure. The book was published anonymously in 1700, probably by the bookseller Jean Ressayre in Dijon. Despite his anonymity, Gilbert was clearly concerned about the potential risks he faced for expressing such radical ideas. Either Gilbert or Ressayre, for instance, excised two chapters on Christianity and Judaism prior to the work's publication.[72] According to Papillon, a fearful Gilbert quickly burned all but one copy of *Caléjava*–which Papillon claimed he received from Gilbert's widow after his death–shortly after its publication. More recent scholarship indicates that at least one other printed copy escaped the flames. Moreover, it appears that *Caléjava* circulated in manuscript form and was known in intellectual circles around Europe.[73]

Despite the absence of specific information about Gilbert's educational background, professional experience, or intellectual influences, we can infer a great deal from the *Histoire de Caléjava*. Gilbert appears to have been far more familiar with, and much more heavily influenced by, contemporary intellectual currents than many of his colleagues. In contrast to avocats such as Taisand, the Perriers, and Melenet, who remained squarely on the side of the "ancients" while continuing to produce traditional juridical works punctuated with classical references and lengthy Latin citations, Gilbert wholeheartedly embraced Cartesian philosophy. The *hommes raisonnables* of Caléjava, according to Gilbert, deduce their conclusions from "clear and evident principles"; describe people as unextended, thinking souls united to inanimate, extended bodies; and prove God's existence along the lines of Descartes' proof in the fourth book of the *Discourse on Method*.[74] The methodical doubt and pyrrhonism of Gilbert's Caléjavans was directly inspired by the writings of Pierre Bayle, particularly his *Pensées diverses sur la comète* (1682) and the *Dictionnaire historique et critique* (1686–87).[75] Gilbert's views on human nature and society owed a considerable debt to Thomas Hobbes (whose *De Cive* he cites in Books VI and XI); his views on natural law bear a strong resemblance to those of Hugo Grotius and Samuel Pufendorf.[76] Other seventeenth-century thinkers, such as Malebranche, Spinoza, Fontenelle, Locke, and Gassendi (to name only a few) also influenced Gilbert's thinking, as did, in all likelihood, a number of English deists.[77]

Although some literary scholars have portrayed Gilbert as a forerunner of the eighteenth-century *philosophes,* his adherence to the cause of the "moderns" was tempered considerably by the humanist education and legal training he received as an avocat.[78] Throughout the *Histoire de Caléjava,* Gilbert is as comfortable citing the authority of the "ancients" as he is in drawing on the insights of the "moderns." The book opens and closes with an epigram from Book I of Lucretius's *De rerum natura* while drawing frequently throughout from Plato's *Republic*.[79] Like any good avocat, Gilbert sprinkles his text liberally with references to Cicero, Tacitus, Seneca, Juvenal, and even Homer.[80] At the same time, he also shows a marked predilection for historical works, citing histories of the reign of Charles V and a rare work on *L'histoire de l'état présent de l'Empire Ottoman*.[81] References to the New Testament and even such decidedly un-modern thinkers as Saint Thomas Aquinas and the Council of Trent abound, and the philosophy of the Caléjavans is compared favorably with both Stoicism and milder forms of Epicurianism.[82] Indeed, Gilbert's debt to the humanist culture shared by most avocats was so deep that he has the Caléjavans conduct most of their affairs in Latin rather than in their own vernacular.[83]

Gilbert's professional experience as an avocat also explains why he devotes so much attention to issues of law and the preservation of order.[84] Laws, according to Gilbert, are the very foundation of human society. "If there were no laws," he writes,

> [n]o one would be able to possess anything without perpetual fear that an infinite number of people would steal it, [or] without fearing loss of life at every moment. If we did not establish laws that were the base and foundation of civil society, or even if we did not have some reciprocal confidence that these laws would be observed in good faith, we would be right to complain about having to constantly mistrust each other.[85]

Gilbert also addresses a preoccupation shared by many of his colleagues: the qualities of a good magistrate. Neither lax nor overbearing, a good judge, Gilbert writes, does not seek wealth or flattery from those under his jurisdiction. Rather, he exists only "to defend and uphold the laws, and, with [his] wisdom, to serve their repose and happiness."[86] Gilbert's overriding concern for the preservation of social order even leads to a somewhat self-contradictory apology for custom, tradition, and legal formalism in the name of Reason. According to one commentator, even Gilbert's deism—a "legal universe directed by general laws"—reflects an avocat's worldview.[87]

The *Histoire de Caléjava* purported to be the publication of recently discovered papers relating the flight of the Protestant Abraham Christofile and his family from France shortly before the revocation of Edict of Nantes (1685).[88] Although Christofile was himself a devout Protestant, the rest of his family and traveling party were an extraordinary religious mix. Eudoxe (Greek for "good faith"), Christofile's daughter by his late Catholic wife, had created her own system of Christianity after having been raised "eight days in the religion of her father, four in that of her mother, and superstitious otherwise." Her husband, Alatre (Greek for "against adoration"), though nominally Catholic, was "a good philosopher, a good mathematician, and a good jurisconsult with an extreme mistrust of scholastic theology." A rationalist and a deist by inclination, Alatre frequently serves as Gilbert's spokesman throughout *Caléjava*.[89] The story opens with the three voyaging through Lithuania in the middle of the winter with Samieski, a Muslim Turkish horse driver. A sudden and unexpected thaw leaves the four marooned on a drifting iceberg for several days before they are rescued by a ship returning to the distant island of Caléjava, where society is based exclusively on the principles of natural reason.[90] Once rescued, they are befriended by a character known as the Avaïte, who convinces them to undertake the two-month journey to his island to learn more about the virtues of Caléjavan society.

The word *Caléjava,* according to Gilbert, means "land of humanity" in the language of these unknown people. "In their minds," Gilbert writes, "they believe that they are the only reasonable people on earth; they find the sentiments of other peoples so extravagant [and] their customs so ridiculous, that they have no difficulty in denying them the quality of being human." The Caléjavans, he continues, prefer to be called Avaïtes in honor of the doctor Ava, their society's founder. More than nine hundred years earlier, we learn, Ava was forced to flee his homeland with more than one hundred of his followers after failing to persuade his prince to adopt a code of laws based solely on reason. When Ava settled on Caléjava (then called Marothi), his reputation as a supremely skilled doctor capable of indefinitely prolonging human life attracted the populace in droves, even catching the attention of the island's king, Cacoumison, whom Ava later cured of a life-threatening illness. Eventually, Ava convinced Cacoumison to abolish the monarchy and replace it with the very system that his own prince rejected–a republic based on universal equality and new laws "better than those Theseus made for Athens."[91]

Over the course of their two-month voyage and eventual stay on Caléjava, the four Europeans learn all about the island's economy, social structure, culture, religion, and even its military capabilities. As in many utopian societies, both private property and privilege are entirely unknown. Everyone, including the island's chief legislators and magistrates, works the land five hours a day during the growing seasons in addition to exercising another useful trade or craft. All goods, both manufactured and agricultural, are then stored in collective warehouses and distributed "to each according to his needs."[92] Money has no meaning on the island; when Alatre gives his guide a purse full of gold pieces as a reward for saving him and his party, the Avaïte promptly attempts to plant it, "saying that we must see what fruit this plant, useless in itself, can produce."[93]

Although profoundly religious, the Caléjavans are also remarkably tolerant. Those who would live among them are required only to believe in the existence of God, the immortality of the soul, and the certitude of punishments and rewards for earthly behavior in the afterlife, provided that "they are convinced of these truths by solid and natural reasons, and not by authority."[94] Much of the *Histoire de Caléjava,* in fact, consists of a series of dialogues in which the Avaïte and the *philosophe* Alatre attempt to persuade Eudoxe and Christofile of Reason's superiority to all forms of authority, custom, and tradition, with the free-thinking daughter proving far more receptive than her dogmatic father. In the course of these dialogues, we learn that the Caléjavans are essentially deists who believe in a benevolent but remote God while placing considerable emphasis on earthly pleasure and utility.

Following the explication of the Avaïtes' religion, the Europeans begin to debate the merits of their own creeds. Although Samieski skillfully defends Mohammed's teachings, Islam is still thoroughly criticized for its reliance on authority and miracles. This is followed by an extended comparison of

Christianity with the religion of the Avaïtes. True to his beliefs, Christofile denounces the Caléjavans as "infidels" and declares that their morals and sentiments demonstrate an "extreme repugnance" for Christianity. Eudoxe replies that the similarities between their two faiths far outweigh the differences. The Caléjavans' emphasis on equality, their communal style of living, and their beliefs about the afterlife, she points out, resemble those of the early Christians. The main tenets of the Avaïte faith, she continues, are entirely compatible with the teachings of the Gospels, which are nothing more than the laws of reason and nature.[95]

Although much of the *Histoire de Caléjava* is devoted to religious issues, Gilbert also describes the Avaïtes' ideal sociopolitical order in detail. The prosperous and harmonious society that the four Europeans encounter differs in almost every imaginable way from the France of Louis XIV. Although the Caléjavans possess an early-eighteenth century version of the "ultimate weapon"–a lethal poison developed by Ava that can be projected up to 5 miles–they have no expansionist desires and use it only for defensive purposes.[96] Laws are made by the one hundred *Glebirs,* or counselors, who live in a large dwelling at the island's center and devote their lives to the study of law. The Glebirs, however, do not simply dictate new laws. Rather, they

> [p]ropose them to the two Calaudes, or intendants, of each residence, who then discuss them with the individual inhabitants who, after conferring among themselves, express their sentiments and their reasons at the third full moon [after the law is proposed]. One Calaude from each residence then reports to the Glebirs, who then decide whether or not to ratify the proposed law, which must pass unanimously, or else remain undecided.[97]

Such unanimity, Gilbert continues, rarely eludes the Glebirs, because every one of them is motivated solely by reason and unaffected by the desire to obtain riches, amass honors, or flatter themselves with vain ceremonies. Once a law has been approved, Gilbert says,

> the Calaudes announce it to the inhabitants of each residence one month before it goes into effect, during which time, each person attempts to convince the others of the new law's goodness. No one believes that [in obeying the law] they obey the Glebirs, who say in turn that they have the same master as everyone–Reason.[98]

Calejavan government thus represents a complete inversion of the model advocated by absolutist theorists such as Bénigne Bossuet and Jean Domat. For Bossuet, the king was the only "public personage," and he alone was capable of knowing and willing the good of the entire kingdom. In a similar vein, Domat equated the critical examination of royal orders with sedition. Law emanated from the commands of the unitary royal will, which was the sole source of peace and social stability. Subjects must be "submissive and obedient" to the king's orders, even when these are unjust, Domat argued, "for otherwise they would resist God, and the government which would be the source of the peace and unity that make possible the public good would suffer from dissention [*sic*] and trouble that would destroy it." For Bossuet, "royal power acts simultaneously throughout the kingdom. It holds the whole kingdom in position just as God holds the whole world. If God were to withdraw his hand, the entire world would return to nothing: if authority ceases in the kingdom, all lapses into confusion."[99] On Caléjava, in contrast, political authority is vested in one hundred men who merely "propose" laws to the island's inhabitants. Far from being the "secret du roi," Caléjavan governance involves all Avaïtes, who debate the wisdom of potential laws, advise the Glebirs through the Calaudes, and work to convince their fellow citizens to obey new laws. These laws, in turn, are the product not of a monarch's potentially irrational and self-interested will, but rather the unanimous consent of one hundred rational and disinterested "philosopher-jurists" in consultation with the island's population.[100]

The island's egalitarian social structure presents an equally thorough critique of ancien régime society. As historians have noted, Louis XIV consolidated power, in part, by stabilizing traditional hierarchies and reinforcing the status distinctions of France's aristocratic society.[101] In a similar vein, the increasingly elaborate etiquette and ceremonial of courtly life at Versailles created and maintained finely shaded distinctions of prestige, influence, and status.[102] In contrast, Caléjava is marked by a complete absence of social distinctions or privileges of any sort; everyone wears the same, simple outfits and is known only by a numeric code indicating his or her place and order of birth. All Avaïtes live like monks in large, collective houses and eschew private property and individual wealth. Leisure time is given to the pursuit of philosophy and other simple, contemplative pleasures. Celibacy is unknown and the Calaudes arrange all marriages with an eye toward procreation and the compatibility of the prospective spouses. Men and women enjoy complete equality, and divorce and polygamy are permitted under specific circumstances. Dynastic or familial concerns do not interfere with the common good, because all children are taken from their parents at the age of four to be raised by specially trained educators, the *Lucades y Bergli*.

The twelfth and final book of the *Histoire de Caléjava* opens with Christofile and Samieski deciding to leave Alatre and Eudoxe behind and return to Europe. When the elderly Protestant and the Muslim horse driver ask how they might adapt Caléjavan principles to their life in Europe, the Avaïte quickly responds that any attempt to transform France or Europe according to the principles of Reason would be futile. Instead, he offers a provisional morality similar to those proposed by Neostoic thinkers and figures such as Montaigne and Descartes. "Whatever the laws are," the Avaïte tells Christofile and Samieski, "they must be followed, at least on the surface, or else civil society will be ruined." In fact, he continues, Reason dictates that we must submit in thought as well as in deed rather than risk the anarchy that would follow if the generally accepted conventions of social intercourse were suddenly called into question.[103] Change, the Avaïte concludes, can occur only gradually through a process of self-reflection and moral reform. To aid in this process, Eudoxe and Alatre promise to raise their infant son as an Avaïte and send him to Europe to spread awareness of the Caléjavan way of life once he reaches adulthood.[104] The story ends with a description of Christofile's death a week after his return to Europe, Gilbert's explanation of how Christofile's papers came into his possession, and the author's concluding remarks about the parallels between the morals of the Avaïtes, Stoicism, and true (rational) Christianity.[105]

The *Histoire de Caléjava* belongs to a trend that saw utopias emerge as a significant form of protest literature in the latter years of Louis XIV's reign. At least fifteen important "extraordinary voyages" or utopian treatises, including Gilbert's, were published between 1676 and 1720. Many, such as Denis Veiras's *Histoire des Séverambes* (1677–79) and Fénélon's *Les aventures de Télémaque* (1699) enjoyed considerable success.[106] The popularity of such works was based, in part, on the French public's mounting fascination with real travel accounts, which the "extraordinary voyages consciously imitated, as well as the growing interest in Cartesian rationalism and the skeptical philosophy of Pierre Bayle, which many utopias embraced."[107] At the same time, utopian fantasies became one of the few avenues of social protest and political criticism available to writers under a regime that virtually prohibited all public political discourse of a critical nature.[108] With France suffering the ruinous effects of Louis' wars–insupportable taxation, widespread impoverishment, declining harvests, and unchecked venality of offices–individuals such as Gilbert abandoned efforts to reform society and government and instead looked to create new orders from the ground up. For Myriam Yardeni, late-seventeenth- and early eighteenth-century utopias were, by their very nature, "revolts against the state of Louis XIV, which had emptied human values of all their sense." The utopists' goal, she continues, was nothing less than "the reconstitution of these human values, even their reinvention, by shattering the frameworks that had killed them. If making happiness accessible to all could only be obtained by detriment to the glory of the king and the state, then that was of little consequence."[109]

Although all late-seventeenth- and early eighteenth-century utopias were, in Yardeni's words, "incendiary, even revolutionary," they were not equally so.[110] Fénelon's *Télémaque,* for example, criticizes Louis XIV's reign without questioning the principles of monarchy, social hierarchy, or revealed religion that supported it. Rather than abolishing social distinctions, Fénelon reinforces them by dividing the utopian society of Salente into seven orders ranked by wealth and nobility, and distinguished by housing and dress–hardly surprising for an archbishop from a noble family. His main concern, as tutor to the duke of Burgundy, was to keep the heir to the throne from repeating his grandfather's mistakes and excesses. Thus Telemachus learns during his voyages that good kings do not monopolize power; rather than the kings' being all-powerful over their people, "the laws are all-powerful over [them]." Once a monarch sacrifices the good of his people and the health of his state for his own wealth and glory, Odysseus's son learns, royal authority ceases. This point is driven home when Telemachus chooses a peaceful and wise king who loves his subjects to rule Salente over an unjust warrior-king clearly modeled on Louis XIV.[111]

Pierre de Lesconvel's *Naudely* (1703) and Veiras's *Histoire des Séverambes* are similarly hesitant in criticizing the foundations of French government and society, even as they attack the abuses of Louis XIV. Unlike in late-seventeenth-century France, life in Naudely is characterized by free trade, efficient agriculture, pleasant living conditions, a prosperous peasantry, and widespread social mobility, though not equality. Naudely's nobility, clergy, and army, unlike their French counterparts, are all chosen by merit through a series of examinations. Outward signs of wealth and luxury are reserved for the king, the princes of the blood, and a few other important nobles. Wealthy bourgeois and even bishops walk through the streets rather than ride in carriages.[112] In Veiras's utopia, the laws of the Séverambes are known as the *Code Soleil* and the country's divine-right monarch is known as the "Viceroy of the Sun." Though theoretically absolute, Veiras's monarchy limits its royal authority through a series of self-proclaimed restrictions that recalled "constitutionalist" interpretations of the Roman law principle *digna vox*. ("It is a statement worthy of the ruler's majesty for the Prince to profess himself bound by the laws.")[113] It also promoted a participatory structure of government that incorporated aristocratic and democratic elements that resembled the sixteenth-century "Renaissance monarchy" described by figures such as Claude de Seyssel, or the English monarchy in the wake of 1688.[114]

On the other side of the spectrum, utopias such as Gabriel de Foigny's *La terre australe connue* (1676) and Fontenelle's *République des philosophes* (c. 1682, pub. 1768) thoroughly rejected the very principles of French society, government, and religion. Institutionalized religion, organized government, and all social distinctions are entirely unknown among the Australians discovered by the fictional Jacques Sardeur. Because they live in primitive happiness according to reason and the laws of nature, he says, human laws and institutions are entirely superfluous. The Australians, we learn, worship their divine creator and motor of the universe in a private, personal, contemplative manner. Indeed, the *Haab* is believed to be so incomprehensible that all religious discussions are forbidden, "to the point where we can say that their religion is to not talk about religion." As hermaphrodites, he continues, the Australians have conquered their physical, sensual urges and live a temperate, rustic lifestyle that is distinguished by their universal vegetarianism and a schooling program that lasts for thirty-two years. Believing that "the essence of humanity is liberty," they live in complete equality without any traces of wealth or private property.[115] Fontenelle's Ajaoiens, meanwhile, also practice a communistic lifestyle marked by the absence of private property and by collective living patterns. Unlike Foigny's Australians, the Ajaoiens do have an organized system of government–a hierarchical series of elected councils and representatives. They do not, however, believe in the existence of a Supreme Being, even one as remote and inscrutable as the *Haab*. Nevertheless, these atheists manage to create a virtuous society from the principles of reason, much to the chagrin of their discoverer, the devout M. van Doelvelt.[116]

Previous studies of the *Historie de Caléjava* have tended, for the most part, to focus on Gilbert's hostility toward the Catholic church, his opposition to Louis XIV's persecution of French Protestants, and his distaste for the asceticism of Pascal and the Jansenists. Indeed, for a number of scholars, only Gilbert's iconoclastic religious opinions deserve serious analysis. These scholars dismiss his views on politics and society as minor asides derived from a larger utopian tradition and devoid of any original qualities.[117] Such dismissals, I would argue, greatly underestimate the significance of Gilbert's utopia as both a critique of Louis XIV's absolutism and a work of political theory.[118] Although it is true that much of the *Histoire de Caléjava* is devoted to religious concerns, the social and political ramifications of Gilbert's views on authority and morality would have been easily recognizable to his contemporaries. Furthermore, although Gilbert's depiction of Caléjavan government and society undoubtedly drew on utopian traditions dating back to Thomas More and even to Plato, the many differences between Caléjava and other utopias of the same period testify to both the originality and the seriousness of Gilbert's political ideas. Unlike Fénelon, Veiras, Lesconvel, and others, whose utopias were little more than "purified" versions of Louis XIV's France, Gilbert rejected the authority of historical precedent and local custom, even as many of colleagues were promoting them as the true basis for a just government and society.[119]

The political system of the Avaïtes, it must be emphasized, was completely antithetical to the absolutism of the *roi soleil* in both theory and practice. Gilbert replaces the royal monopoly on political authority and public discourse with a system in which all citizens participate in the legislative process, from debating proposed laws to ensuring their enforcement by convincing others of their soundness.[120] At the same time, he strips authority, custom, and tradition–all pillars of French royal authority as well as of moderate constitutionalism–of their privileged status as sources of political legitimacy. Gilbert emphasizes the Caléjavans' assertion that they obey reason rather than the Glebirs. Indeed, he even has the Avaïte espouse limited resistance to unjust laws, something the Sun King's apologists would have considered anathema.[121] In a similar fashion, Gilbert rejects divine-right theories in favor of a contractual theory of government that emphasizes reciprocal obligations between governor and governed.[122] Betraying a lawyer's preference for the law, Gilbert claims that rational laws, not the irresistible authority of the royal will, are the true source of social order and tranquility. In short, Gilbert transforms the state from an expression of the absolute royal will, embodied in the person of the monarch, into an abstract entity based on the transcendent principles of natural law, reason, and utility.

In contrast to the regime of Louis XIV, which made extensive and careful use of art, ritual, public spectacle, and even new methods of organizing space to elevate the monarch over the polity by enhancing his majesty, the rulers of Caléjava (if the Glebirs can be so called) are both accessible and virtually indistinguishable from the rest of the Avaïtes. Their duties, for example, do not excuse them from working five hours a day in the fields with the rest of the inhabitants. Furthermore, since the Glebirs are selected for their intellectual merit, probity, and commitment to public service, any claims of dynastic superiority, such as the Bourbon cult of the *sang royal,* would be inherently absurd.[123] Justifications of rulership by divine right, as noted above, are equally ridiculous. "In vain do we say that God knows [the effects of laws]," the Avaïte says, "for they are made by people, not God, who make them with complete liberty."[124] It is true that the Glebirs live in a separate residence at the center of the island, much as Louis XIV lived at the symbolic center of the kingdom in Versailles. However, their dwelling resembles other Avaïte houses and, unlike Versailles, does not glorify or exalt the Glebirs as individuals. Thus, whereas Louis carefully limited and managed access to his person, the Glebirs are easily accessible to the Avaïtes, both personally and through their intermediaries, the Calaudes.[125]

Even Gilbert's description of the Caléjavan family reflects his unyielding hostility to the principles of monarchy and absolute sovereignty. French absolutist theorists made an explicit parallel between the patriarchal family and the royal state; similarly, the Caléjavan family reflects the egalitarian and utilitarian principles of Gilbert's utopia.[126] Husbands and wives are treated as equal partners. Marriage is undertaken for procreative purposes, not to cement familial alliances or to transfer property. Unlike France, where divorce was considered a threat to patriarchal authority, the Caléjavans permit the dissolution of marriages because of sterility, mutual consent, or valid cause.[127] Children, meanwhile, are raised and educated by the state (with little regard for gender) in order to "free [them] from the paternal empire, whose weight often overwhelms them in other countries and exposes them to the caprices of a man who is almost always unreasonable." In response to Bodin, Bossuet, and others who cited the *patria potestas* to justify unquestioned royal authority, Gilbert retorts, "Being a father does not confer the slightest amount of reason. Far from it, it appears to discharge us from the painful obligation to use it with regard to those who are under our discipline."[128] Thus Gilbert subverts the absolutist parallel between paternal and royal authority by equating the irrational rule of the father with the irrational tyranny of the monarch.

Ultimately, the *Histoire de Caléjava* is as striking for the ideas it expressed as it is for the identity of the author who expressed them. A little more than three decades earlier, such wholesale rejections of ancien régime government and society would have been unthinkable among avocats such as Gilbert. Prior to 1668, Dijon's avocats were participants in the local workings of the early modern French state, sharing in the exercise of royal authority through their positions in Dijon's hôtel de ville. By the end of the seventeenth century, however, the vast majority of them had been marginalized from politics and the state by the consolidation of local political power in the hands of the monarchy's few, trusted agents. The *Histoire de Caléjava*'s critique of monarchy, its emphasis on shared reason as the sole basis of political authority, and its defense of radical social egalitarianism and the right of all rational individuals to participate in the processes of government testify to the widening split between at least some Dijonnais avocats and the monarchy in the wake of the 1668 reorganization of Dijon's city council. The *Histoire de Caléjava,* in short, shows how one modest provincial avocat could draw on his legal training and the leading intellectual currents of his day to offer an alternative to the absolutist vision of the French state emanating from Versailles, a vision that did not exclude worthy, rational individuals from rightful position as participants in the state and local governance.

Conclusion

The *Histoire de Caléjava* was a radical social and political critique, especially coming from an individual imbued in the laws and culture of late-seventeenth-century France. Gilbert's defense of rational political debate and participation, though cast in rather fantastic terms, also marked him as the kind of defender, described by Lucien Karpik, of civil society against the encroachments of the state. Eighteenth-century avocats, Karpik argues, "actively practiced 'the public usage of reason,'" which Habermas defined as the crucial component of the emerging "bourgeois public sphere." Through their writings, speeches, and activities, Karpik contends, avocats participated "in rational public discussions" that, much like those of the citizens of Caléjava, "sought to institute collective [political] judgments."[129]

Karpik's claim that the eighteenth-century French bar became politicized as avocats adopted the mantle of spokesmen for the "public" has been largely corroborated by the work of Bell and Maza. All three, however, generally concur that this politicization took place during the eighteenth century as a result of various controversies, including the quarrels over Jansenism and the papal bull *Unigenitus,* Maupeou's coup against the parlements in the early 1770s, and a number of other *causes célèbres.* I would argue, however, that Gilbert's *Histoire de Caléjava* suggests an alternative route to understanding how French avocats came to position themselves as spokesmen for and representatives of "the public" during the eighteenth century. This route had as much to do with the experiences and consequences of state formation in the seventeenth century as it did with events in the decades preceding the French Revolution. Far from being apolitical figures devoted to the pursuit of justice, as Karpik, Church, and others have implied, avocats such as those active at Dijon's hôtel de ville during the first half of the seventeenth century were politically active "insiders," legitimate participants in the local workings of the French state. By the end of the seventeenth century, however, they had essentially been excluded from any meaningful share in the processes of local governance. Although reduced to the status of political outsiders, they retained an educational and professional culture that trained them to think about the nature of power, justice, and the legitimate (and illegitimate) uses of political authority. From their new position as "participants écartés," Dijon's avocats continued to examine, discuss, and comment on the ideological foundations and political actions of the early modern state. In the process, they contributed to the transformation of the "legal public sphere" of the seventeenth century into the "bourgeois public sphere" that came to dominate the political culture of eighteenth-century France.

"Absolutism in practice," Rebecca Kingston has observed, "harbored a variety of languages."[130] Although the monarchy and its theorists promoted a vision of the king as a legislative sovereign whose will was the kingdom's only source of order, Dijon's avocats continued to see the king as a traditional judicial monarch whose function was to preserve the existing arrangement of authorities and to maintain the proper balance among intermediate governing institutions. In contrast with those who increasingly emphasized the king's person and the royal will as the sole sources of legitimate political authority, Dijon's avocats continued to believe that the king's power was absolute in its sphere, but otherwise limited by contract and custom. They believed that municipal and regional institutions and those who staffed them had a legitimate role in local governance, one that the king was supposed to ensure and respect. This view can be seen in the rapid increase in the number of commentaries by Dijon's avocats on private law and regional customs. Although Church saw this growing interest in regional customs as a consequence of the jurists' decline as political theorists, in actuality, the avocats' treatment of Burgundy's customs as a form of contract or natural law, and as the outcome of "the consent of the people and the authority of the sovereign," was a counterpoint to the ideology of *louis-quatorzien* absolutism.

Even as the French state evolved into what historians have termed an "administrative monarchy" by the late seventeenth century, most of Dijon's avocats continued to conceive of it in traditional terms as a "judicial monarchy." Their view of the king as the head of a corporate polity whose main function was to ensure the proper distribution of authority did not disappear. Instead, this view remained a latent political discourse that would reemerge during the eighteenth century in the writings of figures such as Montesquieu and Boulainvilliers, the pro-Jansenist avocats of the Parisian bar, and the increasingly assertive magistrates of the Parlement of Paris and other regional sovereign courts.

Although most of Dijon's avocats relied on traditional concepts and authorities, the experiences of the late seventeenth century radicalized others. The *Histoire de Caléjava* shows how at least one Dijonnais avocat combined his legal training with elements of late-seventeenth-century rationalist philosophy to question the very legitimacy of ancien régime monarchy and society. Although we should be careful not to read too much into the work of one avocat, Gilbert's utopia indicates how Louis XIV's transformation of the local workings of the French state, his consolidation of political authority in the hands of a narrow social and political elite, and his exclusion of many members of the kingdom's "middling sort" from local governance paved the way for profound shifts in eighteenth-century French political culture.

Middling urban notables such as the avocats of Dijon were not mere spectators to displays of absolute royal power in the seventeenth century, as Jürgen Habermas and some of those influenced by his work have suggested.[131] They used their membership in corporate bodies such as Dijon's mairie and their knowledge of the law and informal networks of influence to play an active role in local politics and governance. If the experience of Dijon's avocats is any indication, those who belonged to this "middling" social and political group were forcibly reduced to the position of passive spectators by an increasingly assertive and authoritarian monarchy, one that co-opted those who could resist its power while excluding or marginalizing the rest from their traditional roles in the French state. Those who found themselves "écartés" did not suddenly become depoliticized, however. Instead, they began to reexamine and reconceptualize the legitimate foundations of political authority as well as their own relationship to it. As they did, they became more distant from the state over the course of the following century. They also became more critical of its workings and more willing to consider alternative sources of political legitimacy and relationships of power and authority than those sanctioned by the monarchy and ruling elites.

Conclusion

Avocats, Politics, and "The Public" in Eighteenth-Century Dijon

Dijon's municipal government returned to a routine, regular pattern in the decades following the passing of the Sun King. The revocation of the 1692 sale of municipal offices, which had led to their concentration in the hands of a few, reliable clients of the Condés and their agents with the ability and willingness to finance the city's needs, led to a partial return to the system of municipal governance established by the arrêt of 20 April 1668. At the same time, further developments consolidated the mairie's transformation from a local governmental body into an arm of the "administrative monarchy." The mairie's operations, both internally and in its relationship with other local authorities, were marked by the increasingly impersonal, mechanistic procedures and greater sense of routineness and predictability that a number of historians have argued became characteristic of the French state's evolution during this period.[1] Supervision by the region's governors, intendants, and their agents became even more thorough and systematic. With the exception of relatively mundane matters, the mairie's officers rarely acted on their own initiative, looking instead for guidance from above. In this new context, it is hardly surprising that local political culture evolved in response and that the city's avocats would continue to be drawn to regional customs, local history, and the dictates of reason–embodied in the figure of "public opinion"–as alternatives to an official ideology that largely excluded them from both public life and political debate.

The early eighteenth century witnessed yet another change in the way Dijon's vicomte-mayeur and échevins were selected. The arrêt of 1668 had called for mayoral elections and the renewal of the échevinage every other year, although, as noted in chapter 4, Burgundy's governors routinely kept compliant city councils in office for an additional year. Mayors were limited to one two-year term of office (sometimes extended to a third year) and were then ineligible for office for four years, although this provision, too, was sometimes ignored.[2] A new arrêt, dated 6 June 1703, gave the mairie "permission to continue those magistrates it elects in the future in cases where it judges this to be advantageous."[3] Though less dramatic in tenor or implementation than the arrêt of 20 April 1668 or the 1692 sale of offices, the new arrêt nonetheless transformed the mechanics of municipal government in Dijon yet again. Once chosen, mayors generally held office for a decade or more, often serving until driven from their post by fatigue, death, or the displeasure of their superiors.[4] Elections, once a highlight of the municipal political calendar, were now held only on an ad hoc basis and no effort was expended to stage them on the eve of Saint John the Baptist, as had been traditional for centuries.[5] Not surprisingly, participation declined sharply, from roughly 350 at the election of Philippe Baudot in 1729 to just 168 for Claude Marlot's election in 1750.[6]

Positions on the échevinage, in contrast, became somewhat more accessible during the first half of the eighteenth century. The arrêt of 20 April 1668 called for the selection of four new échevins every other year, while two others were to be retained as anciens, provided that they did not exceed the four-year term limit. By the mid 1720s, however, this process was replaced by a rotation in which half of the city council was usually replaced on an annual basis. In typical year, such as 1737, the three senior échevins would retire from the city council; the three junior échevins, who had entered the council the year before, would become the new senior échevins; and three new individuals would be named to the city council.[7] Moreover, positions on the échevinage appear to have been divided up by profession, with two seats generally going to avocats; two to procureurs, notaries, or other minor legal professionals; and two to merchants, bourgeois, or other liberal professionals.[8] Although there was some variation in the overall pattern, with some years seeing four, two, or, in rare cases, one or even no échevins replaced according to the governor's or intendant's instructions, Dijon's échevinage turned over with almost metronymic regularity throughout the first half of the eighteenth century.[9] The result was a limited, but noticeable increase in the number of seats available at the échevinage, from an average of two per year (in theory) after 1668 to three per year in the early eighteenth century. Though undoubtedly an improvement, however, this was still a far cry from the number of seats available on the city council prior to 1668.

As was the case after 1668, the workings of this machine were carefully monitored by Burgundy's governors and royal intendants, and their agents. If anything, their surveillance of the mairie and its officials appears to have become even more detailed and systematic with the passage of time. Not only did they name all but minor officials (such as the lieutenants de la mairie), they also began to keep records on potential candidates for municipal offices. A circular letter from Chartraire de Montigny, Louis-Henri de Bourbon's personal intendant, to the mayors of all Burgundian towns reveals just how thorough this surveillance had become by the 1730s. Noting Louis-Henri's dissatisfaction with the annual lists of candidates he had been receiving from the various towns, Montigny instructed the mayors to compile "an exact and faithful list of all the inhabitants of [your] city capable of occupying places as échevins, syndics, and secretaries." In addition, Montigny emphasized that mayors had to provide "exact reasons" that échevins, syndics, and other officers should be continued in office. The mayor's "satisfaction," he noted, was itself insufficient and even created suspicion that those recommended were more devoted to the mayor than the public good.[10] The resulting *registre du diable* provides a detailed snapshot of the *bons sujets* deemed capable of holding municipal offices. From his bureau at Chantilly, Louis-Henri could know that Nicolas Le Gros of Auxonne was a skilled procureur but also that he "liked to drink a little," or that the avocat Nicolas Singet, conseil de la ville and a second-time échevin at Châtillon-sur-Seine, was "not rich, but has spirit, rectitude, and capacity."[11]

A few weeks prior to the annual renewal of Dijon's échevinage in late June, the prince would send his local intendant a letter addressed to the mairie with a list of individuals to be elected and retained on the échevinage. Condé's agent, in turn, would forward the prince's instructions shortly before the election with admonishments such as "I do not doubt, messieurs, that you will execute His Serene Highness's wishes as marked in this letter." To ensure that Condé's orders were promptly carried out, the mairie was also instructed to acknowledge receipt of the prince's letter in writing and to forward an account of the election so that the prince's intendant could "inform His Serene Highness Monseigneur the Duke that his orders have been executed."[12] In contrast with the Grand Condé and Henri-Jules de Bourbon, who cast their nominations as "recommendations" to the city council, Burgundy's eighteenth-century governors did not hide the fact that it was they who dictated the composition of Dijon's mairie. And although the mairie might occasionally raise objections, as it did in one case when it feared that a nominee for municipal receiver lacked the personal wealth necessary to fulfill his obligations, it always adhered to the wishes of Burgundy's governors and intendants in personnel matters.[13]

The surveillance of the mairie was reflected not only in the naming of municipal officials but in the removal of those who failed to perform their duties as well. As noted in chapter 2, Dijon's mairie fought throughout the first half of the seventeenth century to maintain its authority to supervise and discipline its officials. By the early eighteenth century, however, this had become a prerogative of Burgundy's governors. In September 1717, for example, Condé ordered the conseil de la ville Grozelier removed for "comport[ing] himself contrary to what he owed to the magistrature." In May 1730, the prince ordered the captain of St.-Jean Parish, removed for bad conduct. Seven years later, Condé stripped the major of St.-Michel Parish of his post when he failed to fulfill his functions properly during the arrival of the queen of Sardinia.[14] Municipal officials who shirked their duties faced the possibility that reports of their behavior could reach the prince's ears, as in the case of the substitut du procureur-général

Montchinet, whom Louis-Henri de Bourbon ordered removed from office after receiving several complaints about his behavior.[15] Like those outside the hôtel de ville, the mairie could only report misconduct to the prince, who then decided how to deal with the offending individuals.[16] Governors also made wholesale changes in certain offices, especially those of the milice bourgeoise, from time to time, even in the absence of any sign of misconduct.[17]

The numbers of avocats entering the échevinage, meanwhile, returned to roughly the level they had achieved between 1668 and 1692. Five new avocats entered the city council during the 1720s and 1740s, and six during the 1730s. One tour of two to three years appears to have been the norm, though a few, such as Jean-Baptise Arnoult, did return to the échevinage later in their careers. Other municipal posts, meanwhile, seem to have become harder to obtain. For instance, although the mairie continued to employ anywhere from twelve to eighteen lieutenants, as it had in the late seventeenth century, it no longer appointed them annually. Instead, lieutenants could hold their posts for more than a decade, and new lieutenants were only appointed when a position opened up.[18] Many slots in the ranks of the parish officers and conseils de la ville appear to have circulated within a small group of families, undoubtedly those with the best connections to the Condés and their agents.[19] Until Claude Marlot was named mayor in 1750, the city's highest post, that of vicomte-mayeur, had not been held by an avocat for more than seventy years. All of these developments, meanwhile, took place at a time when membership in the bar of Dijon literally doubled from a low of forty-five avocats in 1699 to ninety-one in 1746. Overall, then, the vast majority of Dijonnais avocats during the first half of the eighteenth century never entered the hôtel de ville in any official capacity whatever.

Many of the mairie's concerns during the first half of the eighteenth century remained largely unchanged from the late seventeenth century. Jurisdiction conflicts with the Présidial and other local tribunals over the affixing of seals and other matters continued to occur, although they appear to have been less intense and more quickly resolved than in the past. When Présidial officers affixed seals in the home of the late conseiller Espiard de Vernot, for instance, the mairie quickly protested to the intendant. But the mairie dropped its complaint six weeks later when papers were produced showing that Espiard was, in fact, a nobleman and thus under the royal court's jurisdiction. When the sieur Goujet Duval passed away in 1737, the Présidial's officers affixed their seals in his home and forwarded an account to the mairie, which acknowledged it without incident.[20] The mairie also sought to defend its interests and status when possible. In 1727, both Louis-Henri and Cardinal Fleury, the first minister, asked the city council to pay for the lodgings of Burgundy's lieutenant-général, the count of Tavannes. Although the mairie conceded that Tavannes was worthy of such an honor, it voted unanimously to refuse the request, citing both its lack of funds and the unprecedented nature of the request. When the intendant, La Briffe, renewed the request a few months later, the mairie once again refused, noting that it had housed Burgundy's lieutenants-général only in "exceptional circumstances."[21] A few years later, a running dispute developed when Mayor Baudot refused to address Tavannes as "monseigneur," citing "the preeminence and the prerogatives attached to [the mayor's] position, which are above those of the other mayors of the kingdom." His successor, Jean-Pierre Bureteur, persisted following his election two years later, noting that Dijon's mayors were *presidents-nés* of the Third Estate of Burgundy and *élus perpetuels*.[22] With the exception of its run-ins with Tavannes, which may have been a product of the personalities involved as much as any larger issue, however, the early eighteenth-century mairie continued to be much more conciliatory in its dealings with other authorities and less tenacious in defense of its rights than it had been a century earlier. When a *traitant* claimed that the mairie was required to pay the *droit de petite scelle,* a fee on judicial acts produced by the mayoral court, the city council, citing a 1715 ruling by the intendant, objected that the city's judicial powers were patrimonial and therefore exempt from the relevant royal edicts. Nonetheless, the mairie soon decided that it would pay the fees in question while its case was pending at the royal council, "out of the respect and obedience which are due to the king's orders and under protest that [the monies] will be recovered when the case is decided."[23] A decade later, the mairie became embroiled in a precedence conflict with the city's sovereign courts, which claimed that the city council should not sit alongside them for the singing of a *Te Deum* in the choir of the city's new cathedral. After Tavannes' intervention, the Mairie compromised, agreeing to seats in the choir that were two steps lower than those of the sovereign courts.[24]

The mairie's occasionally spirited defense of its status and interests should not obscure the fact that its activities remained under the careful supervision of Burgundy's governors and intendants, and their agents. Despite their occasional pretensions, Dijon's mayors and échevins continued to be little more than administrative agents executing orders that came from above. This can be seen in the ambitious plan by the intendant La Briffe and the Parlement of Burgundy to stockpile food and medicine in 1720 following the outbreak of plague in Marseille. After consulting with leading inhabitants and local apothecaries, La Briffe asked Secretary of State Phélypeaux de La Vrillière and Controller General Le Pelletier de La Houssaye to authorize the city to borrow 60,000 livres to procure the necessary supplies. In mid-August, Le Pelletier de La Houssaye replied that the royal council could permit such a loan only at the mairie's request. On 27 August, the city council, which does not appear to have discussed the intendant's plan previously, dutifully requested the loan. Three days later, La Briffe forwarded the mairie's deliberation to

Versailles. Two weeks later, the intendant received the royal council's arrêt approving the loan and immediately forwarded it to the vicomte-mayeur to be executed.[25] In the past, the mairie would have insisted on playing an active, central role in a matter that so clearly affected the health and well-being of the urban population. Now it was virtually an afterthought whose only action seems to have been a pro forma deliberation taken at the intendant's behest to satisfy a procedural requirement imposed by the royal council.

The mairie was subjected to extensive supervision in other areas as well. At least four times between 1731 and 1748, Burgundy's governors and intendants ordered the mairie to present them with detailed accounts of the city's revenues, expenses, and debts, indicating careful surveillance of the city council's activities.[26] The mairie also needed permission to pursue lawsuits, send deputies to Paris, and undertake a number of other routine actions.[27] Indeed, the mairie actually made a point of seeking instructions from governors or intendants in matters that had long been its unquestioned prerogative. After Mayor Baudot's death in February 1731, for instance, the city council decided not to name first échevin Jean-François Joly commis à la magistrat until it had first consulted the prince. When the time came to plan the bicentennial of the city's vows to Saint Anne, the mairie wrote to Condé, seeking his instructions for the planned procession. It also asked Condé to issue a new ordinance to improve the organization and discipline of the nocturnal watch.[28] The mairie's ability to act on its own was limited to more mundane matters, such as ensuring the uniformity of buildings on the new rue Condé (which was to link the newly created place Royale with the coin de la miroir), bringing an equestrian statue of Louis XIV from a village outside of Auxerre where it had been stored for twenty-eight years, and issuing regulations against bringing dogs to mass or raising sheep within the city walls.[29]

Some historians have highlighted the stability of the "ministerial state" and its growing bureaucracy as one of the most important developments in early modern French state formation. In contrast with the reigns of Henri IV and Louis XIII, during the reign of Louis XIV, the removal of individual ministers had little impact on royal administration, which maintained its routines despite changes at the top.[30] The same pattern held for municipal government in mid-eighteenth-century Dijon as well. The mairie's workings had become so routinized and so well integrated into the larger structures of the administrative monarchy that even the absence of the Condés from the governorship had little impact on the city council's operations. The stability in Dijon after Louis-Henri de Bourbon died in early 1740 with only a small child as his heir stands in marked contrast with the 1650s. At that time, the Grand Condé's arrest and eventual self-imposed exile to Spain created a power vacuum and a decade of crises that ultimately doomed the local political system that had evolved over the preceding half century. Shortly after Henri-Jules's death, by contrast, Tavannes informed the mairie of the king's order that the count of St.-Florentin, a member of the Phélypeaux clan and one of the secretaries of state, would take over the prince's functions. All matters previously referred to the Condés would now be handled by St.-Florentin instead.[31] Judging from the city council records, the transfer took place with no discernible complications. In the years that followed, St.-Florentin simply replaced the princes in overseeing local government, at least until Condé's heir, the young Louis-Joseph de Bourbon, became old enough to exercise the governorship of Burgundy himself.[32] Burgundy's interim governor, Paul-Hippolyte de Beauvilliers, the duke of Saint-Aignan, appears to have played little role in overseeing the mairie, with the exception of the urban militia.

If anything, the transfer of authority to St.-Florentin resulted in increased surveillance of the hôtel de ville. The mairie, for instance, was now instructed to provide him with a list of three candidates every time a municipal office became vacant.[33] The way new municipal officers were named also implied even closer royal surveillance. The Condés had always made selections themselves when the time came to name new échevins or fill other vacant posts. In contrast, when a position as conseil de la ville came open in 1744, St.-Florentin wrote to the mairie, "I have given the king an account of the presentation that you have made of sieurs Disson, Arnoult, Roche, and Colin, avocats, to fill the post of conseil de la ville de Dijon. . . . His Majesty has decided that it is appropriate to choose sieur Disson. I inform you of this so you can have him swear the customary oath and install him in this position."[34] Similarly, échevins and mayors were now named by the monarch (at least rhetorically) and accountable directly to him and his ministers.[35] St.-Florentin also invoked the king's authority to intervene in Dijonnais affairs, as in May 1742 when he informed the mairie of the king's orders that the civic militia would no longer make its customary visits under arms after the Sainte Hostie procession and that it would henceforth beat its tocsin only in honor of God, the king, "and those who deserve this honor according to the laws of war." The "sovereign's gaze," which had been mediated for decades through the familiar figures of the princes of Condé, now looked directly on the actions of Dijon's mairie and its magistrates.[36]

As the transformation of local governance initiated during the second half of the seventeenth century became consolidated during the first half of Louis XV's reign, local political culture and practice changed in response to the new realities. An incident from the middle of the century illustrates how some avocats adapted to the new political situation in Dijon and how their ideas about the city and its place in the larger structure of the state had changed from the previous century. In adapting to these new realities, avocats drew on a combination of references to custom and history as well as appeals to the authority of "the public," as they had in the latter years of the seventeenth century. If anything, these two strands of thought, largely separate around 1700, drew closer together and became mutually reinforcing by the mid-eighteenth century.

These developments can be seen in the mairie's resistance to efforts by the Parlement's first president to obtain the seigneurial justice rights over his lands at Montmuzard, just outside the city walls, from the hôtel de ville in 1749–50. Some aspects of the mairie's opposition echoed past episodes of municipal resistance to "encroachments" on its privileges. In spite of this fact, however, the manner in which François-Bernard Cocquard and Jean-Baptiste Petitot–the two avocats who formulated the city council's objections–and their allies pursued their opposition reveal how completely the practice and culture of municipal politics had changed in the eight decades after 1668. At the same time, they also show how the politics of the "legal public sphere" of the past were evolving into that of the "bourgeois public sphere" that would dominate the last decades of the ancien régime.

At first glance, it seems difficult to understand why the Montmuzard affair would become a cause célèbre. Sometime in April 1749, First President Fyot de la Marche, who seems to have generally enjoyed good relations with the hôtel de ville, asked the mairie to grant him the high, medium, and low justice rights over his lands at Montmuzard.[37] To accomplish this, he proposed that the mairie convert Montmuzard into a subfief, which the first president would then hold from the city in return for the customary homage and an annual donation of grain to the poor in the municipal hospital. Fyot de la Marche's exact motives for requesting the transfer are unclear.[38] At first, he told the mairie that he wanted to ensure the success of his new estate and promenade, but later he claimed that he needed the authority to repress the "coureurs de nuit" and other "enemies of public pleasure and tranquility" who had taken to congregating there. The exact size and scope of the territory in question is also somewhat unclear. According to Fyot de la Marche, only a few gardeners and domestics would be removed from city's jurisdiction, though he agreed that they would remain liable for tailles and service in the urban watch. The mairie, however, challenged this assertion, as well as the first president's claim that the city would lose only a negligible amount of revenue by conceding the judicial rights over Montmuzard.[39]

Whatever Fyot de la Marche's motives or the potential consequences of his plan, it is clear that he did not consider the matter to be a potentially contentious one. He had already obtained the support of the procureur-syndic and one of the échevins, the avocat Antoine Guyton. Indeed, although Fyot de la Marche's initial request respected municipal sensitivities, it also included instructions on how to get the subfief's creation approved by the intendant without any problems.[40] According to a later version of events by the mairie, the procureur-syndic presented Fyot's proposal at the very end of a council session, which perhaps suggested that he expected no opposition

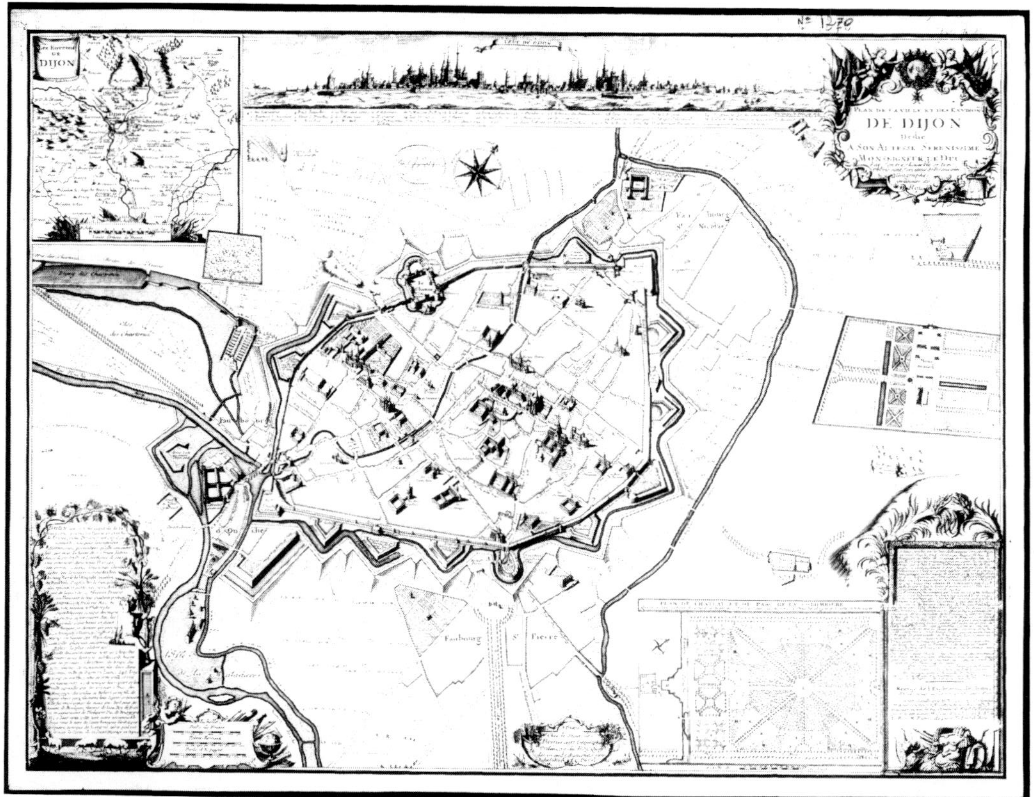

Figure 8. Map of Dijon and its environs, ca. 1750, by Denoinville. First President Fyot de la Marche's Montmuzard estate is on the right. Photo: Bibliothèque Nationale de France.

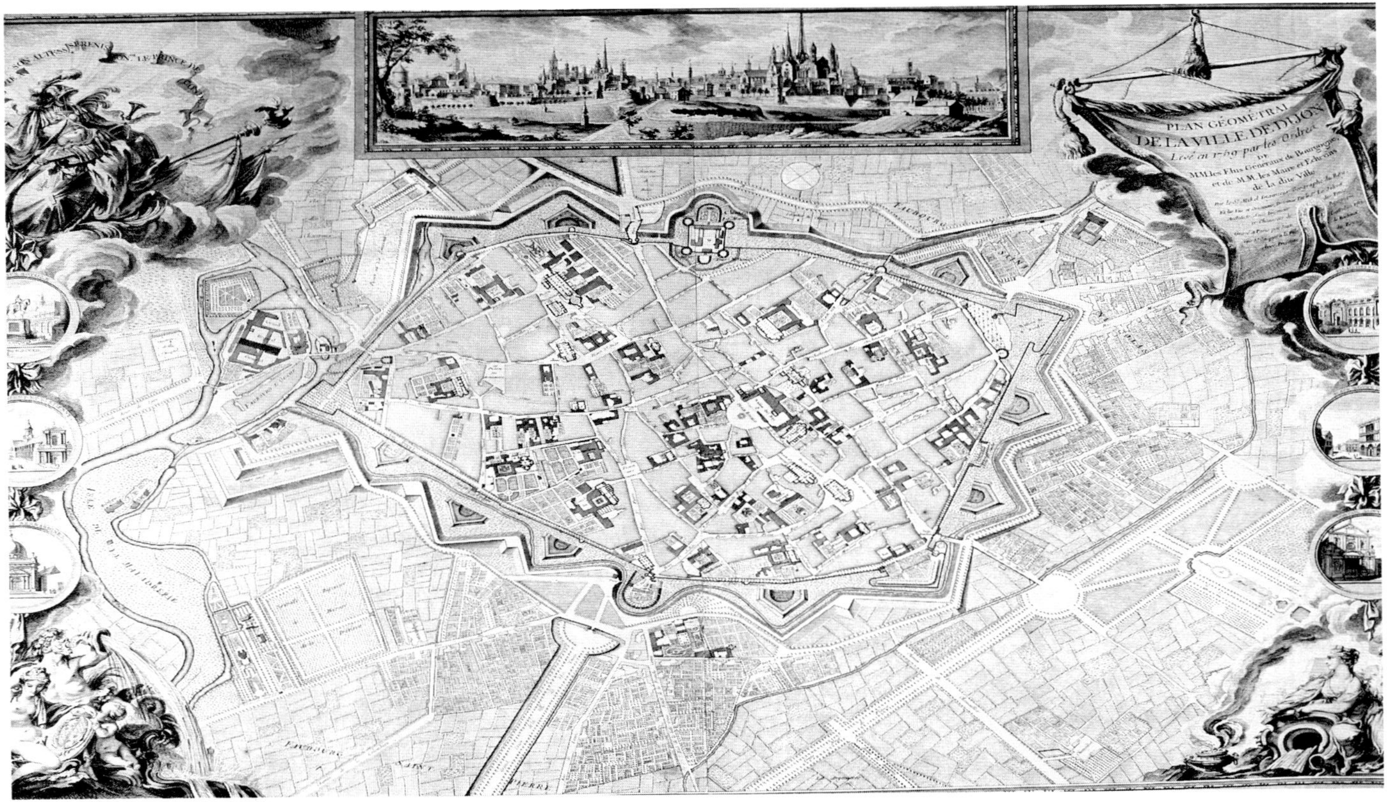

Figure 9. The Plan Mikel. Dijon and its surroundings, 1759. First President Fyot de la Marche's Montmuzard estate is at the lower right. Photo: Bibliothèque Municipale de Dijon.

to it.[41] When the mairie sent a deputation to inform Fyot that it would need to study the matter further, the first president only asked them to resolve the matter in time for one of his in-laws, who would be passing through the city, to take the necessary documents to the intendant in Paris.[42] Fyot de la Marche's later mémoires repeatedly claim that the mairie had agreed to his proposal, only to suddenly change its mind as the result of a "plot" and a "cabal."[43] Although the first president's version of events is certainly questionable, his sense of shock and outrage seems to have been genuine and undoubtedly helps to explain why the conflict between him and the mairie escalated in the months that followed.

Several other factors might also explain the mairie's unexpected opposition. Mayor Bureteur, a parlementaire, may have been upset that his relative Fyot de la Marche had not consulted him in advance, though Bureteur ultimately seems to have been a passive bystander.[44] The other échevins, most notably the procureur Genot, who was a frequent target of Fyot's wrath, may have objected to what they perceived as Guyton and the syndic's high-handed efforts to force the plan's ratification.[45] Mounting public opposition as rumors of the plan spread also appears to have been a motivating factor. St.-Florentin, for instance, reported receiving several mémoires against the proposal.[46] Regardless of the exact cause, the mairie informed Fyot that it needed to consider his request further and raised several questions about the plan's consequences for the city. It also began to raise an issue that would become central to its opposition to Fyot, namely, whether the mayor and échevins, as "simple administrators of the city's patrimony," could approve or deny La Marche's request without the king's permission.[47]

By all accounts, the real turning point in the affair appears to have been the circulation of a mémoire entitled "Observations anonymes sur la proposition de M. le Premier Président de Dijon." The "Observations anonymes" were almost certainly written by François-Bernard Cocquard, an échevin and leading member of the bar who enjoyed a prominent place in Dijonnais literary and intellectual circles.[48] The "Observations anonymes" were given to one of the échevins by the daughter of one of the mairie's *sergeants,* who ostensibly had found it while sweeping up the council chamber. Its contents were read at an audience of the city council, but what happened next remains in dispute. The mairie claimed it sent copies of the "Observations anonymes" to Fyot de la Marche and St.-Florentin and then kept the text under seal. The first president, by contrast, accused the Mairie of circulating the document and publicizing its contents. Whatever the case, word of the "Observations anonymes" and its arguments spread throughout the city, mobilizing opposition to the first president's plan.[49]

With Cocquard scheduled to leave the city council in June, Bureteur and the other échevins asked St.-Florentin to keep the échevinage intact, citing its familiarity with the Montmuzard affair among other reasons.

St.-Florentin, however, refused, citing the disorder it would cause in the échevinage and saying that the outgoing échevins could instruct their successors on the matter.[50] Cocquard was replaced by Jean-Baptiste Petitot, another highly respected avocat whom Fyot de la Marche had recently praised in an audience at Parlement. Shortly after the installation of the new échevins, the first president again started to pursue the matter, sending his secretary, along with Guyton, to search the municipal registers for precedents that would bolster his case. Outraged at this violation of the secrecy of its deliberations, the mairie sought and obtained a royal arrêt establishing guidelines to ensure the registers' protection and to prevent unauthorized access to them in the future.[51]

In the months that followed, the Montmuzard affair escalated into a pamphlet war between Fyot de la Marche and the mairie. Claiming to speak on behalf of "public opinion" and as "a good citizen in service of the public and individuals, whose rights and privileges are inviolable," the author of the "Observations anonymes" had laid out the historical and legal arguments against Fyot's plan while enumerating the many ways it would harm the city's interests. The "Observations" traced the mairie's judicial powers back to the commune's establishment by Eudes III in 1187 and the city's subsequent acquisition of the ducal viscounty a century later. Both of these rights, Cocquard noted, had been granted "à titre onéreux" and confirmed by subsequent dukes and kings. To grant Fyot de la Marche's request, he argued, would violate the oaths that the commune's founders swore to Eudes III, that Dijon's inhabitants would always defend the city's rights and not suffer them to be diminished. Moreover, Cocquard noted, the mairie lacked the authority to grant the first president's request. Unlike an ordinary vassal, who could divide his territories into subfiefs, Dijon "enjoys the privilege of being a minor" and is thus incapable of doing so. Without the unanimous consent of the mairie, the entire population of the city and its banlieues, the intendant, the élus, and the Parlement–all of whom had an interest in the maintenance of the city's jurisdiction over Montmuzard, Cocquard continued–the mairie was powerless to act. In addition, he noted, granting Fyot's request would not only be an unprecedented diminution of the city's judicial authority, it would also result in lost revenues, create unnecessary litigation between the mairie and the new jurisdiction, and turn Montmuzard into an asylum for those fleeing municipal justice. It would also create a dangerous precedent that would lead to the eventual dismemberment of the city's jurisdiction over its suburbs.[52]

Fyot's "Troisième and Quatrième Mémoires," in response to the "Observations anonymes," heightened the tone of the conflict even further. The author of the first president's mémoires denounced the "Observations anonymes" as false and slanderous and derided as "absurd" its claims that the mairie lacked the necessary authority. He compared the "Observations'" claim that the proposal required unanimous approval from multiple authorities and an assembly of inhabitants with the Polish Diet and cited multiple precedents from the city's history to show that it had ceded judicial rights over its suburbs in the past. The "Mémoires" also claimed that the city would suffer no harm from the agreement; any rights that it wanted to protect could be enshrined in the contract establishing the subfief. Moreover, in return for the loss of jurisdiction over "two or three laborers and a gardener" and a few sous of annual revenue, the city would benefit by gaining the first president as a vassal and an annual gift of wheat worth 40 to 50 francs. In addition, Fyot noted, he was only seeking judicial rights over his lands because the mairie had failed in its obligations to pursue the wrongdoers who congregated there in the first place.[53]

In October 1749, the mairie decided to draw up a response to Fyot's latest mémoires. Several weeks later, however, the intendant ordered it not to publish them without his prior approval.[54] The dispute, after all, was being considered by the royal council, the controller general, and the secretary of state in charge of Burgundy. It concerned the distribution of power within the state and the interests of a prominent regional figure, the first president of Burgundy's highest royal tribunal. As such, it was hardly a matter for public debate or consideration. Just as Parisian avocats were breaching judicial secrecy by publishing mémoires judiciaries that appealed to the "tribunal of public opinion" as an alternative to the royal law courts, the mairie decided to breach the secrecy that ordinarily governed the relationship between the royal administration and local institutions.[55] Sometime in December 1749, the mairie published the *Réponse* and *Moyens* without the intendant's approval.

Although the mayor and all the échevins save for Guyton signed the *Réponse* and *Moyens,* the mairie's deliberations identify Jean-Baptiste Petitot as their author.[56] In the *Réponse,* Petitot contested almost every element of Fyot's account, in particular his claim that the mairie had consented to his proposal before changing its mind. He reiterated Cocquard's claims that the mayor and échevins were "only faithful administrators of the city's patrimony" who opposed the first president's plan, not out of any malice, but because of their obligations to the king.[57] He accused Joly, the procureur-syndic, and Guyton of violating their duties to the hôtel de ville and acting either out of personal ambition or fear of the first president's *grand crédit.* He also denied Fyot's accusations that the mairie had circulated the "Observations anonymes" to turn public sentiment against the proposal. Building on the arguments of the "Observations anonymes,"[58] Petitot reemphasized the mairie's inability to grant Fyot's request. "Does it make any sense," he wrote, "that the vicomte-mayeur and échevins, the entire body of the magistrature of a capital city, would be capable of imposing themselves on the king, on Monseigneur the Count of St.-Florentin, and on Monseigneur le Controlleur-Général?" Citing the advice of the conseils de la ville, he repeated Cocquard's claim that the city enjoyed the "privilege" of being a minor and argued that the mairie, as a mere administrator, could not make such an important decision without the agreement of the city's inhabitants, especially in the face of public opposition.[59]

The *Moyens,* meanwhile, elaborated on the historical, legal, and practical arguments that Cocquard had made in the "Observations anonymes." Rejecting the validity of the first president's claims, Petitot argued that the project had no utility for the city and that it would violate the original oath between the dukes of Burgundy and the inhabitants and municipality of Dijon, as well as various royal patent letters. He also noted that "according to public opinion, it will be very prejudicial to the city."[60] In response to Fyot's claim that the transfer was justified by the promenade of linden trees that he had planted for the public's benefit, Petitot responded that "the Public is not persuaded that the rows of linden trees planted between the city and Montmuzard are meant for it" rather than for Fyot's enjoyment in his "maison de plaisance."[61] Neither the supposed public utility nor the city's respect for Fyot required the mairie to surrender a privilege that had been obtained by the "great efforts" of the city's ancestors and held for so many centuries, Petitot argued.[62] The rest of the *Moyens* went on to refute the first president's claims that the creation of a subfief at Montmuzard would not harm the city's interests and reiterated the historical and legal objections developed in the "Observations anonymes."

Shortly after the publication of the *Réponse* and the *Moyens,* Fyot abandoned any attempt to reach an agreement with the mairie, opting instead to present his case personally at Versailles and to draw on the influence of his allies there. In late January 1750, he obtained an arrêt from the royal council suppressing the mairie's deliberations against his proposals and ordering them struck from the city council's registers. Burgundy's new intendant, Joly de Fleury, appointed the avocat and substitut du procureur-général Claude Marlot to execute the council's arrêt. Genot and Petitot, meanwhile, were summoned to Versailles to explain their actions, but were left to cool their heels for two months before the controlleur-général and St.-Florentin would agree to see them. In May, Fyot obtained two more arrêts from the royal council. The first ordered Bureteur's immediate removal as mayor despite his nearly twenty years of service. The second summarily ordered the replacement of the échevins Genot and the merchant Navier the elder, even though both were scheduled to leave the hôtel de ville the following month. The mairie's chastisement was completed when Marlot, who had supervised the removal of the offending deliberations, was named as Bureteur's successor. Genot, Navier, and Cocquard, meanwhile, were all exiled by lettres de cachet.[63]

Despite the mairie's insistence that it lacked the authority to approve Fyot de la Marche's request, St.-Florentin, the intendants St.-Contest and Joly de Fleury, and even the royal council had little interest in getting caught up in the matter. In early May, St.-Florentin informed the mairie that since the proposal involved the city's seigneurial rights, it would have to learn the king's will from the controller general rather than himself. Five months later, he wrote again, this time on behalf of Controlleur-Général Machault d'Arnouville to inform the mairie that it could proceed as it wished with regard to the first president's request. "It is up to you to consent to or oppose [Fyot's] request as you consider the city's interests to require." He added that the city needed no permission from the king to proceed and that "all paths are open to you, it is up to you to follow them."[64] After Fyot de la Marche sent his "Quatrième mémoire" to the controller general in the summer of 1749, St.-Contest forwarded the mémoire to the mairie and asked for the city to respond.[65] The following year, Joly de Fleury, the new intendant, insisted that the mairie decide the matter after the new mayor and échevins were named in May 1750. Although Fyot may have expected the new mayor and échevins to approve the proposal, the opposite happened. In spite of St.-Florentin's letter affirming that the mairie could act as it saw fit in the matter, the mayor and échevins reiterated their predecessors' position that as "simple administrators," they lacked the power to do so and referred the matter back to the royal council with a request that several conditions and limitations be imposed on Fyot and his heirs should the council approve his request. Accompanied by the intendant, Petitot and another échevin presented Fyot with the city council's decision at his home. Shortly thereafter, the first president dropped the matter. Genot, Navier, and Cocquard were eventually recalled from exile. The mairie had publicly challenged the first president of Burgundy's Parlement and had won.[66]

The mairie's opposition to Fyot de la Marche's plan would, on the surface, suggest a return to the municipal political culture of the first half of the seventeenth century, when the mairie vigorously defended itself and its privileges from external "encroachments." As in the decades prior to 1668, several avocats at the hôtel de ville, in this case Cocquard and Petitot, along with the procureur Genot, led the city council's opposition to a proposal that threatened to diminish the mairie's power and prestige. They were bolstered, moreover, by the arguments and support of the conseils de la ville. Even in the face of the first president's retribution, the mairie kept a (nearly) united front and in the end thwarted Fyot de la Marche's plan to wrest the seigneurial justice rights over Montmuzard from the hôtel de ville.

Despite these apparent similarities, however, the Montmuzard affair reminds us how much local political culture and practice in Dijon had changed in the decades after 1668. First of all, the city's avocats were far from united in defense of municipal privilege. Whereas Cocquard, Petitot, and the conseils sought to defend what they saw as the city's prerogatives, Guyton actively promoted the first president's plan and may have even violated his oath to keep municipal deliberations secret in order to do so.[67] Marlot, meanwhile, acted as an agent of the intendant, not the city, and was soon rewarded with the post of vicomte-mayeur as a result.

The more important difference, however, is to be found in the kinds of arguments Cocquard, Petitot, and the mairie offered in opposition to Fyot de la Marche's plans, arguments that differed widely from those their predecessors invoked a century earlier. For the avocats who dominated the mairie prior to the reign of Louis XIV, the ducal privileges were a contract between the city and the crown, one that defined the rights and jurisdictions of a municipality that governed the city in its own right. The privileges were not simply an inheritance to be protected, but an agreement that defined the reciprocal relationship between the city and the crown–hence the mairie's obligation to defend them, as Bernard Coussin put it, "even against the king and his officers." In the Montmuzard dispute, in contrast, the mairie repeatedly invoked its weakness to justify its opposition to the first president's plan. The city's privileges were no longer part of the foundation of local political order that could not or should not be changed. Rather, they were the product of a venerable oath and an inheritance from past generations that could be undone only by the king and his council, not by the "simple administrators" of the municipality. Whereas during the first half of the seventeenth century the mairie's avocats defended the municipality's (and by extension their own) place in the local workings of the state, a century later, Cocquard, Petitot, and the mairie could only highlight their own lack of authority and agency. When they repeatedly invoked the city's "privilege" of being a minor, they revealed an understanding of the notion of privilege that was the inverse of its usage among their predecessors a century earlier.

The other main difference between the seventeenth and eighteenth centuries is evident in Cocquard and Petitot's invocations of the "public." The "Observations anonymes," the *Réponse,* and the *Moyens* all claimed to be speaking on behalf not just of the mairie, but of the "public" as well. Cocquard and Petitot invoked the "public" as both a judge and a party in this seemingly obscure case about arcane feudal rights and a parlementaire's country estate. Public hostility to Fyot's plan, Petitot noted, was manifested both in the widespread rumblings of discontent against the plan and in the many mémoires opposing it that St.-Florentin had received. According to Petitot, it was "the public" that doubted that the linden trees at Montmuzard were really being planted for its benefit. It was the public's interest that was at stake in Fyot's proposal to create a subfief at Montmuzard. As a group of "simple administrators," Cocquard and Petitot argued, the mairie lacked authority to contravene the Dijonnais public's will. Only the assembled populace of the city and its surrounding suburbs could do that.

This "public," it should be emphasized, was not necessarily at odds with royal authority; indeed, Cocquard, Petitot, and the Mairie clearly hoped that the monarchy would side with "public opinion." At the same time, however, the city council also made it clear that it was willing to obey the king's orders, especially if its conditions on Fyot and his descendants were met. Nonetheless, I would argue, the *Réponse* and the *Moyens* reflect a transition to the "politics of public opinion" in mid-eighteenth century Dijon. Not only did these documents claim to speak for the "public," they also claimed that their opposition to Fyot's plan was motivated by an adherence to "public opinion." And although the summary dismissal of the mayor and two échevins in May 1750 demonstrated that the monarchy was hardly cowed by "public opinion" in Burgundy's capital, the language of the "Observations anonymes," the *Réponse,* and the *Moyens* showed that Dijonnais political culture was moving in a different direction, one that would grow in strength during the final decades of the ancien régime. As noted above, the mairie had published the *Réponse* and *Moyens* at least in part to strip away the veil of secrecy from its dealings with Fyot de la Marche, St.-Florentin, and the royal council. The mairie also wanted to show the Dijonnais public that it was acting on the latter's behalf, so much so that it published the two documents over the intendant's explicit prohibition, a decision that ultimately cost the mayor and two échevins their posts.

This episode, like the case of Gilbert's *Caléjava* and the other works of Dijon's avocats, brings us back to one of the larger questions raised by this book: how did changes in the workings of the state and the nature of political experience at the local level contribute to the transformation of early modern political culture? Revisionist studies of the French monarchy during the past two decades have stressed the traditional nature of Louis XIV's reign and its continuity with the past. They have also highlighted the cooperative and mutually beneficial relationship between the king and the governing elites during this period. The experience of Dijon's avocats, however, reveals the profound transformation of political practice, participation, and culture at the local level as the monarchy strengthened its ability to supervise and regulate provincial life. The avocats and the other notables of Burgundy's capital did not experience Louis XIV's reign as a time of mutually beneficial cooperation. Regardless of whether or not historians care to describe the monarchy from the second half of the seventeenth century onward as "absolutist," and regardless of how they choose to define the term, the period saw profound political transformation and dislocation at the local level–changes that are too easily obscured when we focus primarily on the experiences of France's nobles, parlements, Estates, and other national and regional elites and institutions. For the avocats of Dijon, as for their fellow urban notables, the growth of royal power and the elaboration of the "administrative monarchy" did not preserve their status or protect their jurisdictions. Rather, it entailed their exclusion from the governmental roles that they and their predecessors had long dominated. They were reduced to a marginal role in the administrative framework of the state and subjected to increasingly careful surveillance and impersonal, bureaucratic regulation. The result, for many, was an ever increasing gap between the "judicial monarchy," as they conceived of it, and the "administrative monarchy" that they now experienced.

The political exclusion and marginalization of Dijon's avocats and other notables, in turn, helped foster a new political culture, one that responded to the new political exigencies. Except for figures such as Claude Gilbert, the development of these new relationships toward the networks of power that the ancien régime state comprised did not lead to an immediate or widespread rejection of royal authority. But although Dijonnais avocats and notables continued to accept the king's ultimate authority, they also reexamined its foundations and its proper limits. They harked back to regional customs and local history as sources of legitimacy. At the same time, they also looked to the rationalist philosophy of the *lumières* and the nascent authority of "the public" as alternative sources of legitimacy that could coincide with royal authority, but need not do so. If the experience of Dijon's avocats is any guide, these cultural developments were themselves the product of a new and growing social divide between ruler and ruled that developed from the late seventeenth century onward. For centuries, urban notables such as the avocats of Dijon had been important intermediaries between elites and masses, a role they could no longer fulfill once they had been excluded from participation in local governance and marginalized from the workings of the state. Indeed, from Laverdy's proposed municipal reforms in the 1760s to attempts to create new provincial assemblies in the 1780s, the monarchy tried and failed to undo the consequences of these late-seventeenth-century changes and expand the social basis of participation in governance that it had so sharply narrowed.

Scholars working on other countries, most notably England, have highlighted the close relationship between the "middling sort's" participation in the state and the development of the "rule of law" as a widely shared value that legitimated and conditioned the exercise of political power and authority.[68] As this study of the political activities and experiences of Dijon's avocats has shown, French notables also played an important role in local governance, especially during the first half of the seventeenth century. Whereas the English "middling sort" participated in local governance through their service on juries and their actions as vestrymen, and as unpaid local commissioners of the crown,[69] French notables staffed municipalities, served as militia leaders, and were members of the various corporations that structured local life. For them, as for their counterparts in England and elsewhere, the law was central to the way they conceived of their place in society, their relationship with other authorities, and their political culture in general. Even at the height of *louis-quatorzien* absolutism, they continued to believe that the main purpose of royal authority was to ensure justice and uphold the law. As Guillaume Davot, the first professor of French law at the newly founded University of Dijon (1723) observed in his commentaries on Loisel's *Instituts coutumiers,* the maxim "Qui veut le roi, si veut la loi" (As the king wishes, so does the law) could be interpreted in two different ways. The first was the familiar absolutist principle that "by the effect of the king's sovereign power, his will is a law for his subjects," an interpretation that would have elicited no objection from the Bourbon kings and their apologists. According to Davot, however, the second interpretation–that "the law is the will of the king, that is to say, that the king's will conforms to the law and the rules of justice"–"is more noble and worthy of the Justice of our kings."[70] The law, in other words, did not emanate from the monarch's sovereign will; on the contrary, it constrained it.

For the avocats of early modern Dijon, a monarchy that governed in accordance with law was one that allowed notables such as themselves to participate in the state's workings. It respected the rights and jurisdictions of local corporations such as the Mairie de Dijon, which enabled avocats and other urban notables to affirm their status and utilize their talents (and, to be sure, pursue their interests) in the governance of their communities. For much of seventeenth century, Dijon's avocats successfully utilized their mastery of law and rhetoric to defend the mairie's privileges and their own ability to participate in the local workings of the early modern French state. Internal divisions were exacerbated by the removal of the Grand Condé as royal governor in 1650 and the decade of upheaval that followed; the presence and growing activity of royal intendants capable of supervising the municipality's actions and coordinating various local authorities; and the growing assertiveness and authoritarian tendencies of an increasingly bureaucratic, impersonal "administrative" monarchy devoted to financing France's military machine rather than maintaining the intricate (and quite possibly unworkable) balances of the "judicial monarchy." The combination of all of these factors undermined the mairie's ability to defend its authority and resulted in its transformation from an active member of the local state to a passive, subordinate agent of municipal administration in the years following its dramatic reorganization in 1668. The city's avocats and other notables, who had long played an important role in local governance, now found themselves largely excluded from public life as the monarchy progressively narrowed the ranks of those who could legitimately share in the exercise of public power. One of the consequences of this exclusion was the progressive alienation of Dijon's avocats from the monarchy over the course of the late seventeenth and eighteenth centuries. In the decades after the Wars of Religion, the avocats of Burgundy's capital supported a strong monarchy as a bulwark against faction and the "tyranny" of other local authorities and corporations. Although they believed the king's power was "absolute," they also believed that its purpose was to protect their political rights and privileges. In the aftermath of 1668, however, Dijon's avocats began to examine alternatives to the "absolute" royal power that had deprived them of their place in the municipality and had even attempted to sell off the mairie's venerable offices during the last decade of the seventeenth century. They turned on the one hand to regional customs and local history to discover elements of Burgundy's "natural law" that were beyond the scope of legitimate royal authority. At the same time, they also began to view the dictates of reason and the nascent authority of "public opinion" as legitimate alternatives to the supposedly unquestionable authority of the king. The transformation of French political culture in the eighteenth century, in other words, was as least partly the result of the radical transformation of politics and governance at the local level over the course of the seventeenth century.

Dijon's avocats, along with other educated, well-to-do urban notables may have made up only a small portion of early modern France's population, and their experiences were certainly not typical. Nonetheless, they occupied an important and revealing place in the social, cultural, and political order of early modern France and Europe. More important, the experiences of Dijon's avocats and others like them were hardly unique in the history of early modern France. During the late seventeenth and eighteenth centuries, other groups in French society began to encounter fates similar to those whose experiences we have analyzed in detail here as an increasingly authoritarian and administrative crown brought the kingdom's parlements, military, and provincial estates to heel and even, for the first time, breached the nobility's privileges against direct royal taxation. As the eighteenth century progressed, a series of crises–ranging from the controversy over the papal bull *Unigenitus,* to the Maupeou coup against the parlements, to the monarchy's increasingly desperate and aggressive search for revenue to stave off impending bankruptcy–narrowed the social bases of its power and the ideological foundations of its legitimacy, until they finally crumbled in the years leading up to the revolution of 1789. And when royal authority ultimately collapsed, it was hardly a coincidence that the kingdom's avocats, most of whom had been staunch supporters of strong royal power during the late sixteenth and early seventeenth centuries, emerged as the monarchy's leading critics and the dominant figures in the Revolutionary regimes that sought first to reform, and then abolish, the monarchy itself.

Notes

Introduction

1. City council deliberations, 2 Aug. 1627, AMD B-265, fol. 74r–v.
2. City council deliberations, 8 Oct. 1627, Ibid., fols. 115v–17r.
3. City council deliberations, 12–14 Oct. 1627, Ibid., fols. 118r–20v, 124.
4. City council deliberations, 25–27 Oct. 1627, 22 Dec. 1627, Ibid., fols. 128v–29v, 162r–v; De Pontoux and Pérard to Mairie (10 Nov. 1627); De Pontoux, Pérard, Bréchillet, and Lyvet to Mairie (16 Nov. 1627); Bellegarde to Mairie (22 Nov. 1627), in Garnier, 171–75.
5. Parlement deliberations, 10 Jan. 1629, BMD Ms. 774, 572–73.
6. David A. Bell, *Lawyers and Citizens: The Making of a Political Elite in Old Regime France* (Oxford: Oxford University Press, 1994), 8.
7. Philip Benedict observes that in 1789, after a sustained period of growth in the urban population, only about 20 percent of France's population lived in communities with two thousand or more inhabitants. See "French Cities from the Sixteenth Century to the Revolution: An Overview," in *Cities and Social Change in Early Modern France*, ed. Philip Benedict (London: Unwin Hyman, 1989), 7.
8. William Beik, *Absolutism and Society in Seventeenth-Century France: State Power and Provincial Authority in Languedoc* (Cambridge: Cambridge University Press, 1986), 59.
9. Richard Bonney, *Political Change in France Under Richelieu and Mazarin, 1624–1661* (Oxford: Oxford University Press, 1978); Michel Antoine, *Le conseil du roi sous Louis XV* (Geneva: Droz, 1970); Antoine, *Le dûr métier du roi: Études sur la civilization politique de la France d'ancien régime* (Paris: Presses Universitaires de France, 1986); James B. Collins, *The Fiscal Limits of Absolutism: Direct Taxation in Early Seventeenth-Century France* (Berkeley: University of California Press, 1987); Daniel Dessert, *Argent, pouvoir et société au grand siècle* (Paris: Fayard, 1984); David D. Bien, "Offices, Corps and a System of State Credit: The Uses of Privilege Under the *Ancien Régime*," in *The Political Culture of the Old Regime*, ed. Keith Michael Baker (Oxford: Pergamon Press, 1987), 89–114; Mark Potter, *Corps and Clienteles: Public Finance and Political Change in France, 1688–1715* (Aldershot: Ashgate, 2003); Jean-François Solnon, *La Cour de France* (Paris: Fayard, 1987); John A. Lynn, *Giant of the Grand Siècle: The French Army, 1610–1715* (Cambridge: Cambridge University Press, 1997); Guy Rowlands, *The Dynastic State and the Army Under Louis XIV: Royal Service and Private Interest, 1661–1715* (Cambridge: Cambridge University Press, 2002); David Parrott, *Richelieu's Army: War, Government and Society in France, 1624–1642* (Cambridge: Cambridge University Press, 2001).
10. Beik, *Absolutism and Society*; James B. Collins, *Classes, Estates and Order in Early Modern Brittany* (Cambridge: Cambridge University Press, 1994); Sharon Kettering, *Patrons, Brokers and Clients in Seventeenth-Century France* (Oxford: Oxford University

Press, 1986); Katia Béguin, *Les princes de Condé: Rebelles, courtisans, et mécènes dans la France du Grand Siècle* (Seyssel: Champ Vallon, 1999); Jay M. Smith, *The Culture of Merit: Nobility, Royal Service, and the Making of Absolute Monarchy in France, 1600–1789* (Ann Arbor: University of Michigan Press, 1996); Sara E. Chapman, *Private Ambition and Political Alliances: The Phélypeaux de Pontchartrain Family and Louis XIV's Government, 1650–1715* (Rochester, NY: University of Rochester Press, 2004); Robert Descimon, "Power Elites and the Prince: The State as Enterprise," in *Power Elites and State Building*, ed. Wolfgang Reinhard (Oxford: Clarendon, 1996): 100–121.

11. John J. Hurt, *Louis XIV and the Parlements: The Assertion of Royal Authority* (Manchester: Manchester University Press, 2002); Julian Swann, *Provincial Power and Absolute Monarchy: The Estates-General of Burgundy, 1661–1790* (Cambridge: Cambridge University Press, 2003); J. Russell Major, *Representative Government in Early Modern France* (New Haven, CT: Yale University Press, 1980); Major, *From Renaissance Monarchy to Absolute Monarchy: French Kings, Nobles and Estates* (Baltimore: Johns Hopkins University Press, 1994); Joseph Bergin, *The Making of the French Episcopate, 1589–1661* (New Haven, CT: Yale University Press, 1996); Bergin, *Crown, Church and Episcopate Under Louis XIV* (New Haven, CT: Yale University Press, 2004); Albert Hamscher, *The Parlement of Paris After the Fronde* (Pittsburgh: University of Pittsburgh Press, 1976); Hamscher, *The Conseil Privé and the Parlements in the Age of Louis XIV: A Study in French Absolutism* (Philadelphia: Transactions of the American Philosophical Society, 1987); Daniel Hickey, *The Coming of French Absolutism: The Struggle for Tax Reform in the Province of Dauphiné, 1560–1640* (Toronto: University of Toronto Press, 1986); Marie-Laure Legay, *Les États Provinciaux dans la construction de l'état moderne aux XVIIe et XVIIIe siècles* (Geneva: Droz, 2001).

12. Hilary J. Bernstein, *Between Crown and Community: Politics and Civic Culture in Sixteenth-Century Poitiers* (Ithaca, NY: Cornell University Press, 2004), 274–75.

13. Alexis de Tocqueville, *The Old Regime and the Revolution*, ed. François Furet and Françoise Melonio, trans. Alan S. Kahan (Chicago: University of Chicago Press, 1998), 125–27.

14. Bernard Chevalier, *Les bonnes villes de France du XIVème au XVIème siècles* (Paris: Aubier Montaigne, 1982); Nora Temple, "The Control and Exploitation of French Towns During the Ancien Régime," *History* 51 (1966): 16–34; Temple, "Municipal Elections and Municipal Oligarchies in Eighteenth-Century France," in *French Government and Society*, ed. J. F. Bosher (London: Athlone Press, 1973), 70–91. Roland Mousnier, "La participation des gouvernés à l'activité des gouvernants dans la France des XVIIe et XVIIIe siècles," in *La plume, la faucille et le marteau* (Paris: Presses Universitaires de France, 1970), 252.

15. Bernstein, *Between Crown and Community*, 273; Yann Lignereux, *Lyon et le roi: de la «bonne ville» à l'absolutisme municipal (1594–1654)* (Seyssel: Champ Vallon, 2003).

16. S. Annette Finley-Croswhite, *Henry IV and the Towns: The Pursuit of Legitimacy in French Urban Society, 1589–1610* (Cambridge: Cambridge University Press, 1999); Robert Descimon, "L'échevinage parisien sous Henri IV (1594–1610): Autonomie urbaine, conflits politiques, et exclusives sociales," in *La ville, la bourgeoisie, et la genèse de l'état moderne (XIIe–XVIIIe siècle)*, ed. Neithard Bust and Jean-Philippe Genet (Paris: Editions du C.N.R.S., 1988), 113–50; Robert A. Schneider, *Public Life in Toulouse, 1463–1789: From Municipal Republic to Cosmopolitan City* (Ithaca, NY:

Cornell University Press, 1989); Schneider, "Crown and Capitoulat: Municipal Government in Toulouse, 1500–1789," in *Cities and Social Change in Early Modern France*, ed. Philip Benedict. (London: Unwin Hyman, 1989), 195–220; Guy Saupin, *Nantes au XVIIe siècle: Vie politique et société urbaine* (Rennes: Presses Universitaires de Rennes, 1996); Louis Ternard, "D'une culture regionale à une culture française: Lille de 1667 à 1715" in *Pouvoir, ville, et société en Europe, 1650–1750*, ed. Georges Livet and Bernard Vogler (Paris: Editions Ophrys, 1983), 381–91; Peter C. Wallace, "Civic Politics and Civic Values in Colmar, 1648–1715," *French Historical Studies* 18 (1994): 907–37; Wallace, *Communities and Conflict in Early Modern Colmar, 1575–1730* (Atlantic Highlands, NJ: Humanities Press, 1994), 227.

17. Beik, *Absolutism and Society*, 312–14; Beik, "Louis XIV and the Cities," in *Edo and Paris: Urban Life and the State in the Early Modern Era*, ed. James L. McClain, John M. Merriman, and Ugawa Kaoru (Ithaca, NY: Cornell University Press, 1994), 72–76, 83–84.

18. Major, *From Renaissance Monarchy*, 24; Mousnier, "Participation des gouvernés," 231.

19. Michel Antoine, "La monarchie absolue," in *The Political Culture of the Old Regime*, ed. Keith Michael Baker (Oxford: Pergamon Press, 1987); Antoine, *Le conseil du roi.* Collins offers a variation on Antoine's model, arguing for a three-stage evolution from a "judicial" monarchy (up to the end of the fifteenth century), to a "legislative" monarchy in which the king's primary function was to make law (sixteenth and early seventeenth centuries), to an "administrative" monarchy (late seventeenth and eighteenth centuries). See his *State in Early Modern France* (Cambridge: Cambridge University Press, 1995), 3. Joël Cornette, meanwhile, has referred to the monarchy during the first half of the seventeenth century as an "executive monarchy." See "Figures politiques du Grand Siècle: Roi-État ou État-Roi," in *La monarchie entre Renaissance et Révolution, 1515–1792*, ed. Joël Cornette (Paris: Seuil, 2000), 151–215. For a summary of the relevant literature, see Fanny Cosandey and Robert Descimon, *L'absolutisme en France: Histoire et historiographie* (Paris: Seuil, 2002), 147–54.

20. Collins, *State*, 3–4; Michael Kwass, *Privilege and the Politics of Taxation in Eighteenth-Century France: Liberté, Egalité, Fiscalité* (Cambridge: Cambridge University Press, 2000), 48; J. Smith, *Culture of Merit*, 9, 263–67; Antoine, *Dûr métier*, 168–69.

21. Collins, *State*, 144–45; Jay M. Smith, "'Our Sovereign's Gaze': Kings, Nobles and State Formation in Seventeenth-Century France," *French Historical Studies* 18 (1993): 413–14; Jean-Louis Thireau, "L'absolutisme monarchique, a-t-il existé?" *Revue française d'histoire des idées politiques* 6 (1997): 309. Jean-Marie Apostolides has traced the increasing abstraction and mechanization of the king in symbolic representations of the monarchy during this period in *Le roi-machine: Spectacle et politique au temps de Louis XIV* (Paris: Éditions de Minuit, 1981).

22. Denis Richet, *La France moderne: L'esprit des institutions* (Paris: Flammarion, 1973), 120.

23. Jonathan Barry and Christopher Brooks, eds., The *Middling Sort of People: Culture, Society and Politics in England, 1550–1800* (New York: St. Martin's Press, 1994), 130–31; Steve Hindle, *The State and Social Change in Early Modern England, c. 1550–1640* (Houndmills: Palgrave, 2000); Michael J. Braddick, *State-Formation in Early Modern England, c. 1550–1700* (Cambridge: Cambridge University Press, 2000).

24. Eric R. Wolf, "Facing Power–Old Insights, New Questions," *American Anthropologist* 92 (1990): 586–87.

25. Frederick M. Irvine, "From Renaissance City to Ancien Régime Capital: Montpellier, c. 1500–c. 1600," in *Cities and Social Change in Early Modern France*, ed. Philip Benedict (London: Unwin Hyman, 1989), 125; Barbara Diefendorf, *Paris City Councilors in the Sixteenth Century* (Princeton, NJ: Princeton University Press, 1983), 44; Bernstein, *Between Crown and Community*, 69–70.

26. Aldo Mazzacane, "Law and Jurists in the Formation of the Modern State in Italy," in *The Origins of the State in Italy, 1300–1600*, ed. Julius Kirshner (Chicago: University of Chicago Press, 1995), 62–63; Peter Stein, *Roman Law in European History* (Cambridge: Cambridge University Press, 1999), chap. 3; Gerald Strauss, *Law, Resistance and the State: The Opposition to Roman Law in Reformation Germany* (Princeton, NJ: Princeton University Press, 1986); Donald R. Kelley *The Beginning of Ideology: Consciousness and Society in the French Reformation* (Cambridge: Cambridge University Press, 1981), chap. 5; Kenneth Pennington, *The Prince and the Law, 1200–1600: Sovereignty and Rights in the Western Tradition* (Berkeley: University of California Press, 1993).

27. Lauro Martines, *Lawyers and Statecraft in Renaissance Florence* (Princeton, NJ: Princeton University Press, 1968), 3, 146, 466.

28. Hindle, *State and Social Change*, 89; Braddick, *State-Formation*, 26–27, 39; Beik, *Absolutism and Society*, 225–26.

29. David A. Bell, "The 'Public Sphere,' the State and the World of the Law in Eighteenth-Century France," *French Historical Studies* 17 (1992): 933.

30. This was perhaps best expressed by the oft-cited Roman Law principle *digna vox maiestate regnantis legis alligatum se principem profiteri.* ("It is a statement worthy of the ruler's majesty for the Prince to profess himself bound by the laws.") *Codex* 1.14(17). 4. For a further discussion, see Pennington, *Prince and the Law*, 78–83.

31. Jean Bodin, *The Six Books of a Commonweale*, ed. Kenneth Douglas McRae, trans. Richard Knolles (Cambridge, MA: Harvard University Press, 1962), IV.6; David Parker, "Law, Society and the State in the Thought of Jean Bodin," *History of Political Thought* 2 (1981), 273–75.

32. Keith Michael Baker, *Inventing the French Revolution: Essays on French Political Culture in the Eighteenth Century* (Cambridge: Cambridge University Press, 1990), 4–5.

33. Gabriel Davot, *Traités sur diverses matiéres de droit françois à l'usage du Duché de Bourgogne & des autres Pays qui ressortissent au Parlement de Dijon . . . avec des notes de Me. Jean Bannelier, ancien bâtonnier des Avocats du Parlement & Doyen de la même Université* (Dijon, 1751).

34. Thomas Kuehn, *Law, Family and Women: Toward a Legal Anthropology of Renaissance Italy* (Chicago: University of Chicago Press, 1991), 122–26, 190–93; Roberto Bizzocchi, "Church, Religion and the State in the Early Modern Period," in *The Origins of the State in Italy, 1300–1600*, ed. Julius Kirshner (Chicago: University of Chicago Press, 1995), 159. On problems of legal interpretation during this period, see Ian Maclean, *Interpretation and Meaning in the Renaissance: The Case of Law* (Cambridge: Cambridge University Press, 1992).

35. Kuehn, *Law, Family and Women*, 9.

36. Kuehn, *Law, Family and Women*, 9–10; Pierre Bourdieu, "La Force du droit: éléments pour une sociologie du champ juridique," *Actes de la recherche en sciences sociales* 64 (1986): 3–19.

37. J. A. Crook, *Legal Advocacy in the Roman World* (Ithaca, NY: Cornell University Press, 1995), 5.

38. J. B. White, cited in Crook, *Legal Advocacy*, 26.

39. Tocqueville, *Old Regime*, 176–77.

40. According to Max Weber, "every body of law consists essentially in a consistent system of abstract rules which have normally been intentionally established. Furthermore, administration of law is held to consist in the application of these rules to particular cases; the administrative process in the rational pursuit of the interests which are specified in the order governing the corporate group within the limits laid down by legal precepts and following principles which are capable of generalized formulation and are approved in the order governing the group, or at least are not disapproved in it." In *The Theory of Social and Economic Organization*, ed. Talcott Parsons, trans. A. M. Henderson (New York: Free Press, 1947), 330.

41. Beik, *Absolutism and Society*, 225; David Parker, "Sovereignty, Absolutism, and the Function of the Law in Seventeenth-Century France," *Past and Present* 122 (1989): 43–47.

42. David Parker, *La Rochelle and the French Monarchy: Conflict and Order in Seventeenth-Century France* (London: Royal Historical Society, 1980), 19.

43. Simon Roberts, "The Study of Dispute: Anthropological Perspectives," in *Disputes and Settlements: Law and Human Relations in the West*, ed. John Bossy (Cambridge: Cambridge University Press, 1983), 1–24; Sally Falk Moore, *Law as Process: An Anthropological Approach* (London: Routledge and Kegan Paul, 1978); Moore, "Certainties Undone: Fifty Turbulent Years of Legal Anthropology, 1949–1999," *Journal of the Royal Anthropological Institute* 7 (2001): 95–116; Jacek Kurczewski, "Dispute and its Settlement," in *Disputes and the Law*, ed. Maureen Cain and Kálmán Kulcsár (Budapest: Akadémai Kiadó, 1983), 223–45; Steven G. Reinhardt, *Justice in the Sarladais, 1770–1790* (Baton Rouge: Louisiana State University Press, 1991), chaps. 3–5; Kuehn, *Law, Family and Women*, 19–100.

44. Kuehn, *Law, Family and Women*, 87.

45. Kuehn, *Law, Family and Women*, 95, 97.

46. See below, chap. 1.

47. Nicolas Perrier, "Recueil des arrêts du parlement de Dijon," 3 vols, BMD Mss. 944–45 and 1138, I, 60; Lenard Berlanstein, *The Barristers of Toulouse in the Eighteenth Century (1740–1793)* (Baltimore: Johns Hopkins University Press, 1975), 28–31; Maurice Gresset, *Gens de justice à Besançon: De la conquête par Louis XIV à la Revolution Française* (Paris: Bibliothèque Nationale, 1978), 1:101; Bell, *Lawyers and Citizens*, 37–38.

48. James R. Farr, *Hands of Honor: Artisans and Their World in Dijon, 1550–1650* (Ithaca, NY: Cornell University Press, 1988), 122–23.

49. Lucien Karpik, *Les Avocats: Entre l'état, le public, et le marché (XIIIe–XXe siècles)* (Paris: Gallimard, 1995), 45–56; Marc Fumaroli, *L'âge de l'éloquence: Rhétorique et "res litteraria" de la Renaissance au seuil de l'époque classique* (Geneva: Droz, 1980), 586–90.

50. William J. Bouwsma, "Lawyers and Early Modern Culture," *American Historical Review* 78 (1973): 309.

51. Donald Kelley, "Jurisconsultus Perfectus: The Lawyer as Renaissance Man," *Journal of the Warburg and Courtald Institutes* 51 (1988): 89–90.

52. Jacques-Bénigne Bossuet, *Politics Drawn From the Very Words of Holy Scripture*, trans. and ed. Patrick Riley (Cambridge: Cambridge University Press, 1990), V.4.1.

53. See, for instance, Vivian B. Gruder, *The Royal Provincial Intendants* (Ithaca, NY: Cornell University Press, 1968); Robert Mandrou, *L'Europe «absolutiste»: Raison et raison d'état, 1649–1775* (Paris: Fayard, 1977), 42–59; and the essays in John C. Rule, ed., *Louis XIV and the Craft of Kingship* (Columbus: Ohio State University Press, 1969), especially Rule's "Louis XIV, Roi-Bureaucrate." The persistence of the linkage between absolutism and sweeping political change can be seen in the title of Yves-Marie Bercé's *Naissance dramatique de l'absolutisme* (Paris: Seuil, 1992).

54. William Beik, "The Absolutism of Louis XIV as Social Collaboration," *Past and Present* 188 (2005): 195.

55. Beik, "Absolutism of Louis XIV," 223–24.

56. Perry Anderson, *Lineages of the Absolutist State* (London: NLB, 1974).

57. Beik, *Absolutism and Society*, 339.

58. David Parker, *Class and State in Ancien Régime France: The Road to Modernity?* (London: Routledge, 1996), 26–27.

59. Collins, *Classes, Estates and Order.*

60. Roger Mettam, *Power and Faction in Louis XIV's France* (London: Basil Blackwell, 1988), 188; Kettering, *Patrons, Brokers and Clients*; Kettering, "The Decline of Great Noble Clientage during the reign of Louis XIV," *Canadian Journal of History* 24 (1989): 157–77. See also Robert R. Harding, *Anatomy of a Power Elite: The Provincial Governors of Early Modern France* (New Haven, CT: Yale University Press, 1978); J. Smith, *Culture of Merit.*

61. Beik, *Absolutism and Society*, 318.

62. Parker, *Class and State*, 206.

63. Hamscher, *Parlement of Paris*; Hamscher, *The Conseil Privé*; Beik, *Absolutism and Society*, 303–28; Collins, *Classes, Estates and Order*, 285; Potter, *Corps and Clienteles*; Swann, *Provincial Power.*

64. Parker, *Class and State*, 167–68, 180–81; Beik, *Absolutism and Society*, 338–39. On the Intendants, see Bonney, *Political Change* and Anette Smedley-Weill, *Les intendants de Louis XIV* (Paris: Fayard, 1995).

65. Parker, *Class and State*, 159.

66. Jean-François Dubost, "Absolutisme et centralisation en Languedoc au XVIIe siècle (1620–1690)," *Revue d'histoire moderne et contemporaine* 37 (1990): 369–97; Mettam, *Power and Faction*, 7–8; Collins, *Classes, Estates and Order*, 286.

67. Cosandey and Descimon, *L'absolutisme en France*, 296.

68. Nicholas Henshall, *The Myth of Absolutism: Change and Continuity in Early Modern European Monarchy* (Harlow: Longman, 1992). Collins has declared, "I believe the prevailing historiographical concept of 'absolute monarchy' is a myth, promulgated by the royal government and legitimated by historians." *State*, 1.

69. Hurt, *Louis XIV and the Parlements*, 12, 195; Kwass, *Politics of Taxation*, 60–61.

70. Lynn, *Giant*, 599; Rowlands, *Dynastic State*, 11.

71. Cosandey and Descimon, *L'absolutisme en France*, 112.

72. Geoffrey Parker, *The Military Revolution: Military Innovation and the Rise of the West, 1500–1800* (Cambridge: Cambridge University Press, 1988). Charles Tilly, *Coercion, Capital and European States, A.D. 990–1992* (Oxford: Blackwell, 1992). See also Brian M. Downing, *The Military Revolution and Political Change: Origins of Democracy and Autocracy in Early Modern Europe* (Princeton, NJ: Princeton University Press,

1992); and Jeremy Black, *A Military Revolution? Military Change and European Society, 1550–1800* (Atlantic Highlands, NJ: Humanities Press, 1991).

73. Gerhard Oestreich, *Neostoicism and the Early Modern State*, trans. David McLintock (Cambridge: Cambridge University Press, 1982), 265–68.

74. Oestreich, *Neostoicism*, 186.

75. Braddick, *State-Formation*, 6. See also Elena Fasano Guarini, "Center and Periphery," in *The Origins of the State in Italy, 1300–1600*, ed. Julius Kirshner (Chicago: University of Chicago Press, 1995), 95–96; Giorgio Chittolini, "The 'Private,' the 'Public,' and the State," in *Origins of the State*, ed. Kirshner, 46, 47, 54.

76. Hindle, *State and Social Change*, 19; Michael Mann, *The Sources of Social Power*. vol. 1, *A History of Power From the Beginning to A.D. 1760* (Cambridge: Cambridge University Press, 1986), 481; Braddick, *State-Formation*, 16.

77. Hindle, *State and Social Change*, 23. See also George Steinmetz, "Introduction: Culture and the State," in Hindle, *State/Culture: State Formation After the Cultural Turn* (Ithaca, NY: Cornell University Press, 1999), 9; Wolf, "Facing Power," 591.

78. Pierangelo Schiera, "Legitimacy, Discipline, and Institutions: Three Necessary Conditions for the Birth of the Modern State," in *The Origins of the State in Italy, 1300–1600*, ed. Julius Kirshner (Chicago: University of Chicago Press, 1995), 33; Steinmetz, Introduction, 8; Hindle, *State and Social Change*, 23.

79. Chittolini, "Private, Public, and State," 46, 47, 54.

80. Schiera, "Legitimacy, Discipline and Institutions," 14; Hindle, *State and Social Change*, 236 (author's emphasis); Braddick, 9, 428. Also see Eric R. Wolf, *Envisioning Power: Ideologies of Dominance and Crisis* (Berkeley: University of California Press, 1999): 285.

81. Hindle, *State and Social Change*, ix.

82. Finley-Croswhite, *Henry IV and the Towns*. On legitimacy and its constraining effects, see Braddick, 68–69, 428; and Simon Roberts, *Order and Dispute: An Introduction to Legal Anthropology* (New York: St. Martin's Press, 1973), 141.

83. Beat Kumin and Andreas Wurgler, "Gravamina, Petitions, and Early Modern Legislation in England and Hesse-Kassel," *Parlements, Estates, and Representations*, 17 1997, 40, quoted in Hindle, *State and Social Change*, 16; Braddick, *State-Formation*, 1–8.

84. Pierre Bourdieu, "Rethinking the State: Genesis and Structure of the Bureaucratic Field," in Steinmetz, *State/Culture*, 53–75; Hindle, *State and Social Change*, 16–17; Chittolini, "Private, Public and State," 50–55.

85. Braddick, *State-Formation*, 77, 428. This point is largely echoed by Chittoloini, "Private, Public, and State," 54.

86. Hindle, *State and Social Change*, 16, ix; Braddick, *State-Formation*, 28, 433.

87. Hindle, *State and Social Change*, 237, 12.

88. Jürgen Habermas, *The Structural Transformation of the Public Sphere: An Inquiry into a Category of Bourgeois Society*, trans. Thomas Berger and Frederick Lawrence (Cambridge, MA: MIT Press, 1989). On the applicability of Habermas's ideas for France, see Mona Ozouf, "L'opinion publique," in *The Political Culture of the Old Regime,* ed. Keith Michael Baker (Oxford: Pergamon Press, 1987), 419–34; Keith Michael Baker, "Defining the Public Sphere in Eighteenth-Century France: Some Variations on a Theme by Habermas," in *Habermas and the Public Sphere*, ed. Craig Calhoun (Cambridge, MA: MIT Press, 1992), 181–211; and Benjamin Nathans,

"Habermas's 'Public Sphere' in the Era of the French Revolution," *French Historical Studies* 16 (1990): 620–44.

89. Karpik, *Les Avocats*; Bell, *Lawyers and Citizens*; Sara Maza, *Private Lives and Public Affairs: The* Causes Célèbres *of Pre-Revolutionary France* (Berkeley: University of California Press, 1993).

90. The lack of attention given to French avocats is even more striking when compared with the work on English barristers during this period. See, for example, David Lemmings, *Gentlemen and Barristers: The Inns of Court and the English Bar, 1680–1730* (Oxford: Oxford University Press 1990); Lemmings, *Professors of the Law: Barristers and English Legal Culture in the Eighteenth Century* (Oxford: Oxford University Press, 2000); Brian P. Levack, *The Civil Lawyers in England 1603–1641: A Political Study* (Oxford: Clarendon, 1973); Wilfrid Prest, ed., *Lawyers in Early Modern Europe and America* (New York: Holmes and Meyer, 1981); Prest, *The Rise of the Barristers: A Social History of the Bar in Early Modern England* (Oxford, 1986). Hilton L. Root, *Peasants and King in Burgundy: Agrarian Foundations of French Absolutism* (Berkeley: University of California Press, 1987); Berlanstein, *Barristers of Toulouse*; and Gresset, *Gens de justice,* provide some insights into the political activities of provincial avocats.

91. Hindle, *State and Social Change*, 235.

92. Peter Campbell, *Power and Politics in Old Régime France, 1720–1745* (London: Routledge, 1996), 11.

93. Baker, *Inventing*, 24–25.

94. Kwass, *Politics of Taxation*, 312. Beik has recently made a preliminary attempt to address this difficult question. See "Absolutism of Louis XIV," 221–24.

95. Campbell, *Power and Politics*, 303.

96. Cited in Kwass, *Politics of Taxation*, 38.

97. J. A. W. Gunn, *Queen of the World: Opinion in the Public Life of France from the Renaissance to the Revolution* (Oxford: Voltaire Foundation, 1995), 5; see also 2–12, 123–24. See also Colin Jones, *The Great Nation: France from Louis XV to Napoleon* (London: Penguin, 2002), xxii.

98. Jeffrey K. Sawyer, *Printed Poison: Pamphlet Propaganda, Faction Politics, and the Public Sphere in Early Seventeenth-Century France* (Berkeley: University of California Press, 1990). The early modern "public," some of these studies argue, was not restricted to literate, middle-class individuals engaged in the private use of reason. Arlette Farge, *Subversive Words: Public Opinion in Eighteenth-Century France*, trans. Rosemary Morris (University Park: Pennsylvania State University Press, 1994), 152, 197–99; Mack P. Holt, "Culture populaire et culture politique au XVIIe siècle: L'émeute de lanturelu à Dijon en février 1630," *Historie, économie, et société* 16 (1997): 597–615.

99. Sarah Hanley, "'The Jurisprudence of the *Arrêts*': Marital Union, Civil Society, and State Formation in France, 1550–1650,' in *Law and History Review* 21 (2003): 28, 34–35; Hanley, "The Transmission of Legal Knowledge and the Genesis of Civil Society in Early Modern France," in *Historians and Ideologues*, eds. Anthony Grafton and J. H. M. Salmon (Rochester, NY: University of Rochester Press, 2001), 71–86; "Social Sites of Political Practice in France: Lawsuits, Civil Rights, and the Separation of Powers in Domestic and State Government, 1500–1800," *American Historical Review* 102 (1997): 27–52.

100. Karpik, *Les avocats*, 13, 446–48.

101. Habermas, *Structural Transformation*, 24.

Chapter 1

1. Henri Drouot, *Mayenne et la Bourgogne: Étude sur la Ligue* (Paris: Picard, 1937), 2 vols.; Finley-Croswhite, *Henry IV and the Towns*, chap. 4.

2. Benedict, "French Cities," Table 1.2.

3. James R. Farr, "Consumers, Commerce, and the Craftsmen of Dijon: The Changing Social and Economic Structure of a Provincial Capital, 1450–1750," in *Cities and Social Change in Early Modern France*, ed. Philip Benedict (London: Unwin Hyman, 1989), 142–43.

4. Jean Richard, "Dijon au début des temps modernes (1515–1659)," in *Histoire de Dijon*, ed. Pierre Gras (Toulouse: Privat, 1987), 109–19; Kathryn A. Edwards, *Families and Frontiers: Re-creating Communities and Boundaries in the Early Modern Burgundies* (Leiden: Brill, 2002).

5. Richard Vaughn, *Valois Burgundy* (London: Penguin Books, 1975); André Kleinclauz, *Histoire de Bourgogne* (Paris: Hachette, 1924), 137–209; Bertrand Scherb. *L'état bourguignon, 1363–1477* (Paris: Perrin, 1999).

6. Kleinclauz, *Bourgogne*, 205–9; Vaughn, *Valois*, 25–28, 95–112, 163–82; Schnerb, *L'état bourguignon*; Johan Huizinga, *The Autumn of the Middle Ages*, trans. Rodney J. Payton and Ulrich Mammitzsch (Chicago: University of Chicago Press, 1996), 294–328. On the Chartreuse de Champmol as a Burgundian Saint-Denis, see Pierre Quarré, Introduction to *La Chartreuse de Champmol, foyer d'art au temps des ducs Valois* (Dijon: Musée des Beaux-Arts, 1960), 9–17.

7. "Sermens solemnels et lettres patentes portant confirmation des droits, privileges, exemptions, francishes, permissions, libertés, coutumes, usages, droitures, immunités, charters, dons, concessions, octrois, &c accordés aux Maire, Echevins, Bourgeois, Manans & Habitans de la Ville de Dijon, à eux concedes par les Ducs de Bourgogne, & depuis la reunion du Duché à la Couronne de France, successivement maintenus & confirmés par les Rois," AMD B-119,

8. Edwards, *Families and Frontiers*, 6–14.

9. Cited in Myriam Yardeni, *La conscience nationale en France pendant les guerres de religion (1559–1598)* (Louvain and Paris: Editions Nauwelaerts, 1971), 105–6.

10. Drouot, *Mayenne*; Mack P. Holt, *The French Wars of Religion, 1562–1629* (Cambridge: Cambridge University Press, 1995), 145–47.

11. Heide Gronau-Chenillet, "Le Parlement de Dijon et La Fronde: Un corps face à la crise." (Thèse de doctorat, Université de Bourgogne, 1991) shows how close the Parlement of Burgundy came to openly supporting Condé after his arrest in 1650.

12. There is no modern history of the Parlement of Burgundy. The most complete study remains Elisabeth-François de La Cuisine, *Le Parlement de Bourgogne depuis son origine jusqu'à son chute* (Dijon: J.-E. Rabutot, 1864), 3 vols. See also Richard, "Dijon au début," 120–21; Richard, "Quelques aspects de l'histoire du Parlement de Dijon," *Mémoires de l'académie des sciences, arts et belles-lettres de Dijon* 123 (1976): 133–146.

13. Richard, "Dijon au début," 121, 124–25; Daniel Ligou, "De Louis XIV à la Revolution," in *Histoire de Dijon*, ed. Pierre Gras (Toulouse: Privat, 1987), 153. City council deliberations, 2 Aug. 1627, 8–27 Oct. 1627, and 15 Jan. 1628, AMD B-265, fols. 74r–v 115v–17r, 124r, 128v–29v, 181v–82r.

14. Richard, "Dijon au début," 122; Ligou, "De Louis XIV," 154.

15. André Bourée, *La Chancellerie près le Parlement de Bourgogne de 1476 à 1790* (Dijon: Alfred Bellais, 1927), 31–57.

16. Farr, *Hands of Honor,* 3–4; Charles Bertucat, *La juridiction municipale de Dijon: Son étendue* (Dijon: J. Nourry, 1911).

17. On the workings of Burgundy's Estates, see Swann, *Provincial Power,* and Potter, *Corps and Clienteles.*

18. Farr, "Consumers," 154; Gaston Roupnel, *La ville et la campagne au XVIIe siècle: étude sur les populations Dijonnais,* 2d ed. (Paris: Armand Colin, 1955), esp. 103 and Pt. III.

19. Farr, "Consumers," 140–41 and table 4.1.

20. Martine Acerra, "Les avocats du parlement de Paris (1661–1715)," *Histoire, économie, et société* 1 (1982): 215; Berlanstein, *Barristers,* 11–12.

21. Theoretically, practicing avocats were "avocats au parlement," whereas others were "avocats en parlement." In reality, however, these terms were interchangeable and cannot be used to distinguish practicing and nonpracticing avocats. Bell, *Lawyers and Citizens,* 28.

22. Richard Kagan, "Law students and Legal Careers in Eighteenth-Century France," *Past and Present* 68 (1975): 40–43; Dominique Julia and Jacques Revel, "Les étudiants et leurs études dans la France moderne," in *Histoire des Universités,* ed. Dominique Julia and Jacques Revel (Paris: Éditions de l'E.H.E.S.S, 1989), II, 119–28. Some universities, such as Rennes and later Dijon, did have reputations for being serious centers of legal scholarship. See Francis Delbelke, *L'action politique et sociale des avocats au XVIIIe siècle: Leur part dans la préparation de la Révolution française* (Louvain: Uystpruyst, 1927), 63.

23. A parlementary arrêt dated 3 Dec. 1652 mentions a three-year stage. A 1731 *reglement* by the bar and Parlement fixed the stage at two years. See Deliberations of the Compagnie de St. Yves, 19 May 1676, BMD Ms. 2324, fol. 6v; [Bouhier], "Livre IV: Des Avocats," ADCO 1F 239, 18, 23–25.

24. Karpik, *Les avocats,* 448.

25. Jean-Jacques Ninon, "L'avocat français au XVIe siècle" Revue de la société internationale pour l'histoire de la profession d'avocat 1 (1989): 39; Fumaroli, *L'âge de l'éloquence,* 435–44; Catherine E. Holmès, *L'éloquence judiciaire de 1620 à 1660: Réflet des problémes sociaux, religieux, et politiques de l'époque* (Paris: A. G. Nizet, 1967), 37–40, 205–6, 270–77. On the persuasive virtues associated with eloquence, see Sawyer, *Printed Poison,* 19–20 and Jerrold E. Seigel, *Rhetoric and Philosophy in Renaissance Humanism: The Union of Eloquence and Wisdom, Petrarch to Valla* (Princeton, NJ: Princeton University Press, 1968), viii, xiii–xiv.

26. Ninon, "L'avocat français," 38; Perrier, "Recueil des arrêts," I, 46, BMD Ms. 944.

27. Berlanstein, *Barristers,* 14–15; Bell, *Lawyers and Citizens,* 30–31; Charles Fevret, *De claris fori Burgundici oratoribus dialogus* (Dijon, 1654), 78–83; Jean Bouhier, "Histoire des commentateurs de la Coûtume du Duché de Bourgogne," in *Oeuvres de jurisprudence,* ed. Joly de Bevy (Dijon, 1787–88), I, xxxv, xxxix.

28. Françoise Vignier, "La justice de Magny-sur-Tille (XVe au XVIIIe siècles)," *Mémoires de la société pour l'histoire du droit et des institutions des anciens pays bourguignons, comtois et romands* 19 (1962): 279, 283; Midan was both a lieutenant de la mairie and the *bailli* of Magny-sur-Tille in the late 1670s and early 1680s.

29. Pierre Lefebvre, "Aspects de la «fidélité» en France au XVIIe siècle: Le cas des agents des princes de Condé," *Revue historique* 250 (1973): 63. Jean Guillaume, Charles Fevret, and Pierre Guillaume all served as the Condé's counselors in Burgundy. On the tendency of aristocratic families to employ avocats on their family councils, see Robert R. Harding, "Aristocrats and Lawyers in French Provincial Government, 1559–1648: From Governors to Commissars," in *After the Reformation: Essays in Honor of J. H. Hexter*, ed. Barbara C. Malament (Philadelphia: University of Pennsylvania Press, 1980), 95–127. According to Jean de Souvert, the annual salary for a conseil des états in 1610 was 1,500 livres. See *Remonstrance à MM. des Trois Estats du pays et duché de Bourgogne* (n.p., 1611): 75.

30. Delbelke, *L'action politique*, 85–86; Bouhier, "Commentateurs," xxxv; Bourée, *Chancellerie*, 77, 100; J. Simonnet, *Les avocats au Parlement de Bourgogne (1554–1654)* (Dijon: J.-E. Rabutot, 1886), 33.

31. "Extraits des registres de la Compagnie des Avocats," ADCO 1F 250, 9–10; Ptolomée de Dijon, *Almanach de Dijon, ou la conoissance des temps ou des saisons* (Dijon, 1683–1722). Various other almanacs, such as Aiba de Dijon's *Almanach Chronologique* (Dijon, 1723–68) and the *Almanach de la province de Bourgogne, et particulièrement de la ville de Dijon* (Dijon, 1773–88), continued to publish tableaux throughout the eighteenth century.

32. Michael P. Breen, "Legal Culture, Municipal Politics and Royal Absolutism in Seventeenth-Century France: The *avocats* of Dijon (1595–1715)" (Ph.D. dissertation, Brown University, 2000), charts 1.1 and 1.2 and 382–84. La Cuisine, *Parlement de Bourgogne*, I, 128; These figures correspond roughly with the testimony of contemporaries and estimates of similar provincial bars. See Gresset, *Gens de justice*, I, 93; Berlanstein, *Barristers*, chap. 1.

33. Berlanstein, *Barristers*, 14–16. See also Bell, *Lawyers and Citizens*, 30–31; Gresset, *Gens de Justice*, I, 97–99.

34. Bell, *Lawyers and Citizens*, 32.

35. George Huppert, *Public Schools in Renaissance France* (Urbana: University of Illinois Press, 1984), esp. chaps. 1–6. See also Roger Chartier, Marie-Madeleine Compère, and Dominique Julia, *L'éducation en France du XVIe au XVIIIe siècle* (Paris: S.E.D.E.S., 1976), chaps. 5–6; Marie-Madeleine Compère, *Du collège au lycée (1500–1850)* (Paris: Gallimard-Julliard, 1985); and François de Dainville, *La naissance de l'humanisme moderne: Les jésuites et l'éducation de la société française* (Paris: Beauchesne et fils, 1940).

36. Huppert, *Public Schools*, 52–53; L. W. B. Brockliss, *French Higher Education in the Seventeenth and Eighteenth Centuries: A Cultural History* (Oxford: Clarendon Press, 1987), 178; Eugenio Garin, *L'éducation de l'homme moderne* (Paris: Fayard, 1968). This tendency changed somewhat in the latter part of the seventeenth century, when some professors began to incorporate Cartesian science into their curricula. Chartier, Compère, and Julia, *L'éducation*, 201–2.

37. Compère, *Collège au lycée*, 71–78 and 107; Chartier, Compère, and Julia, *L'éducation*, 147–60, 196–202.

38. Huppert, *Public Schools*, 75, 85.

39. Fumaroli, *L'âge de l'éloquence*, 663–71, 689–90; Nannerl O. Keohane, *Philosophy and the State in France: The Renaissance to the Enlightenment* (Princeton, NJ: Princeton University Press, 1980), 83–84; Kelley, "Jurisconsultus Perfectus."

40. Bouwsma, "Lawyers," 311–14, 317.

41. Bouwsma, "Lawyers," 322.

42. James R. Farr, *A Tale of Two Murders: Passion and Power in Seventeenth-Century France* (Durham, NC: Duke University Press, 2005), 201.

43. Farr, *A Tale of Two Murders*, ix, 201–2. See also Farr, *Authority and Sexuality in Early Modern Burgundy (1550–1730)* (Oxford: Oxford University Press, 1995), 13–32.

44. Jonathan Dewald, *The Formation of a Provincial Nobility: The Magistrates of the Parlement of Rouen (1499–1610)* (Princeton, NJ: Princeton University Press, 1980), 31–33.

45. Dewald, *Formation*, 39–42, 112.

46. Marcel Bouchard, *De l'humanisme à l'encyclopédie: l'ésprit public en Bourgogne sous l'ancien régime* (Paris: Hachette, 1930), 104.

47. Nicolas Brulart, "De la moderation et de la douceur" (1677), in La Cuisine, *Parlement de Bourgogne*, I, 209.

48. Bouchard, *De l'humanisme*, 34.

49. Bell, *Lawyers and Citizens*, 33; Brockliss, *French Higher Education*, 278–79.

50. Brockliss, *French Higher Education*, 279; Delbelke, *L'action politique*, 58.

51. According to the eighteenth-century parlementaire Bouhier, the two groups split after a dispute over the location of religious services for St. Yves's Day. See ADCO 1F 239, 13–14.

52. In March 1679, the société agreed to pay 54 livres to André Poivre's creditors. In 1656, the avocats threatened a judicial strike after one of Parlement's présidents interrupted and berated two avocats. In 1659, the société protested First President Brulart's "innovation" requiring avocats to remove their hats when presenting remonstrances or lettres de grâce. The société also provided financial support for several precedence lawsuits involving avocats. See BMD Ms. 767, fols. 290r–91r; BMD Ms. 2324, fols. 2r–3v.

53. Society of St. Yves deliberations, 25 Apr. 1680, 28 Feb. 1716, ADCO 1F 250, fols. 2r, 13r.

54. Society of St. Yves deliberations, 12 May 1692, Ibid, fols. 4v–5r.

55. Bouhier, "Livre IV: Des avocats," ADCO 1F 239, 3–4.

56. Bouhier, "Livre IV," 18–19.

57. Society of St. Yves deliberations, 19 May 1703, 8 May 1706, ADCO 1F 250, fols. 7v–9v, 11v–12r.

58. Bouhier, "Livre IV," ADCO 1F 239, 12–13; Jean Melenet, "Recueil des arrêts du Parlement de Dijon," BMD Ms. 311, fol. 24v.

59. Paul Parisot, *Essai sur les procureurs au parlement de Bourgogne* (Dijon: Jobard, 1906); Bell, *Lawyers and Citizens*, 38–40.

60. Bell, *Lawyers and Citizens*, chaps. 2, 3, 5; Karpik, *Les avocats*, 60–150.

61. Berlanstein, *Barristers*, 10; See also Delbelke, *L'action politique*, 100–102, and Bell, *Lawyers and Citizens*, 8.

62. [François-Bernard Cocquard], *Lettres ou dissertations où l'on fait voir que la profession d'avocat est la plus belle de toutes les professions, Et où l'on examine si les juges qui président aux audiences peuvent legitement interrompre les avocats lorsqu'ils plaident* (London [Dijon], 1733), 21–22.

63. Perrier, "Recueil d'arrêts," I, 60, 64–65.

64. Cocquard, *Lettres*, 54–55.

65. Jean Gaudelet, "Journal des choses arrivées à Dijon depuis l'année 1650 jusqu'en l'année 1669," BMD Ms. 748, 66.

66. Brulart, "Le règne de la justice" (1666), in La Cuisine, *Parlement de Bourgogne*, I, 175–76.

67. Bouchard, *De l'humanisme*, 32.

68. See, for example, the many late-seventeenth-century harangues by the avocat-général and former avocat Joseph Durand in BMD Ms. 2324.

69. Cited in René Roland, *Charles Fevret, Avocat au parlement de Bourgogne: sa vie et ses œuvres (discours prononcé à l'ouverture de la conférence des avocats, le 13 décembre 1879)* (Dijon: Eugène Jobard, 1880), 40.

70. Joseph Durand, "La négligence de l'étude de droit" (1693) and "Éloge de la profession des avocats," BMD Ms. 2324, fols. 67v, 150v–53v.

71. Cocquard, *Lettres*, 8–9.

72. Perrier, "Recueil des arrêts," I, 50–51, 64–65; Durand, "Untitled harangue," BMD Ms. 2324, fol. 96v; Cocquard, *Lettres*, 30–33.

73. Brulart, "L'administration de la justice est supérieure à la profession des armes," in La Cuisine, *Parlement de Bourgogne*, I, 168–69; Cocquard, *Lettres*, 8.

74. Karpik, *Les avocats*, 9 and Fumaroli, *L'âge de l'éloquence*, 585–622; Fevret, *De claris*, 134–64.

75. Joseph Durand, "De la negligence de l'éloquence dans le barreau," BMD Ms. 2324, fols. 111r–v.

76. Society of St. Yves deliberations, 19 May 1703, 16 Mar. 1704, 3 Aug. 1704, 19 May 1706, ADCO 1F 250, fols. 7v–10v, 11v–12r.

77. This information was gathered from a wide range of sources, including family papers, marriage contracts, and *inventaires après décès* preserved at the ADCO, taille rolls and city records located at the AMD, genealogical records found at the ADCO and BMD, Papillon's *Bibliothèque*, and the extensive genealogical materials collected in Bourée, *Chancellerie*. For a detailed breakdown, see Breen, "Legal Culture," charts 6.3 and 6.4. My findings are consistent with those of other bars. See Bell, *Lawyers and Citizens*, 28–30.

78. Karpik, *Les avocats*, 53–58.

79. Breen, "Legal Culture," charts 6.5 and 6.6.

80. Albert Poirot, "Le milieu socio-professionnel des avocats au Parlement de Paris à la veille de la Révolution (1760–1790)" (Thèse de doctorat, École des chartes, 1977), II, 131–34; Berlanstein, *Barristers*, 49.

81. Taille rolls (1683), AMD L-248.

82. Bell, *Lawyers and Citizens*, 29.

83. Farr, "Consumers," 153–54; taille rolls (1601, 1690, 1699, 1710), AMD L-213, L-255, L-261, L-271.

84. Berlanstein, *Barristers*, 57. See also Berlanstein, "Lawyers in Pre-Revolutionary France," in *Lawyers in Early Modern Europe and America*, ed. Wilfrid Prest (New York: Holmes and Meyer, 1981), 169.

85. Guillaume's mansion, the Hôtel De Frasans (named for his wife, Michelle Defrasans), still stands today across from the former hôtel de ville (currently the Archives Départementales de la Côte-d'Or) on the rue Jeannin.

86. ADCO BII 356/33 no. 3, BII 356/37, BII 356/26, no. 8.

87. ADCO BII 356/26, no. 8; BII 356/37, no. 1.

88. ADCO BII 356/26, B356/33, no. 3, no. 11.

89. John A. Dickinson, "L'activité judiciaire d'après la procédure civile: le bailliage de Falaise, 1668–1790," *Revue d'histoire économique et sociale* 84 (1976), 152–53; Colin Kaiser, "The Deflation in the Volume of Litigation at Paris in the Eighteenth Century and the Waning of the Old Judicial Order," *European Studies Review* 10 (1980): 309–36.

90. Berlanstein, *Barristers*, 25–28. Although avocats were prohibited from suing to recover unpaid honoraria (see ADCO 1F 239, 18) this did not stop Jean Melenet from doing so in an unsuccessful bid to recover 4,000 livres owed him by a client. Bouhier, "Livre IV: Des avocats," ADCO 1F 239, 33–34.

91. According to Berlanstein, top provincial avocats could expect to earn between 5,000 and 6,000 livres per year from their professional activities. See "Lawyers," 168. Maurice Gresset places the figure somewhat lower for Besançon, at roughly 3,000 livres per year. See *Gens de justice*, I, 339–40.

92. Marriage contract for Me. Pierre de Villers and Damoiselle Jeanne Chisseret (14 July 1603), ADCO E 2126.

93. Ibid., and marriage contract for Philibert V de La Mare and Damoiselle Marie Tisserand (24 May 1629), ADCO 32F 907.

94. Marriage contract for Me. Claude Bourrelier and Damoiselle Anne Davignon (23 Nov. 1662). ADCO 4E2 791.

95. Taille rolls, St.-Michel parish (Apr. 1643), AMD L-234, fols. 1–175v, St.-Jean parish (1669), AMD L-248.

96. Farr, "Consumers," 153–54.

97. City council deliberations, 7 Sept. 1657, 7–15 Nov. 1656, and 9 Jan. 1657, AMD B-296, fol. 117r; B-295, fols. 128v, 134, 140r, 146v, 189v. For Griguette, see the deliberations of 22 May 1669, AMD B-307, fol. 320v.

98. City council deliberations, 25 Feb. 1661, 1 July 1666, 24 Oct. 1668, and 14 Nov. 1668, AMD B-299, fol. 311v; B-305, fols. 39r–40r; B-307, fols. 144r, 177v.

99. City council deliberations, 5 Feb. 1666, 23 July 1666, 9 Aug. 1666, 21 July 1670, 23 Jan. 1671, 29 Nov. 1678, and 26 May 1684, AMD B-304, fol. 183v; B-305, fols. 54r, 65; B-309, fols. 54r, 166; B-317, fol. 60; B-322, fols. 181v–182r.

100. City council deliberations, 5 Mar. 1666 and 6 Mar. 1674, AMD B-304, fol. 206r; B-312, fols. 112v–113r.

101. Farr, *Hands of Honor*, 122–23; Roupnel, *Ville et campagne*, 179–81.

102. Cocquard, *Lettres*, 10–11, 13.

103. Farr, *A Tale of Two Murders*, 203.

104. Jeffrey K. Sawyer, "Judicial Corruption and Legal Reform in Early Seventeenth-Century France," *Law and History Review* 6 (1988): 96–97.

105. Collins, *Classes, Estates and Order*, 288.

106. Most studies of elite values and the increased emphasis on social disciplining during this period begin with Norbert Elias, *The Civilizing Process*, trans. Edmund Jephcott (Oxford: Blackwell, 1994), 2 vols. On the growing divide between elite and popular culture during this period, see Robert Muchembled, *Culture populaire et culture des élites dans la France moderne (XVe–XVIIIe siècle)* (Paris: Flammarion, 1978). On the growing efforts of municipal elites to discipline local populations, see Chevalier, *Bonnes villes*, chaps. 6, 9; Schneider, *Public Life*, chaps. 8–10; and Lignereux, *Lyon et le Roi*, pt. II.

107. Beik, *Absolutism and Society*, 71–72; Beik, *Urban Protest*, 73–115.

108. Karpik, *Les Avocats*, 78; Bell, *Lawyers and Citizens*, 26–27.

109. Cocquard, *Lettres*, 8–11; Durand, "Discours prononcé à l'ouverture des audiences du parlement" (1699), BMD Ms. 2324, fols. 79r–88r.

110. Sawyer, *Printed Poison*, 19–20; Fumaroli, *L'âge de l'éloquence*, 227–29, 585–622, 663–72, 688–705.

111. Durand, "Untitled harangue," BMD Ms. 2324, fols 97v–98r. See also Durand, "Eloge de la profession des avocats (1698?)," BMD Ms. 2324, fols. 150r–53v.

112. Karpik, *Les Avocats*, 86.

113. Brulart, "La constance et la force de courage," and "Exhortation aux avocats" (1661), in La Cuisine, *Parlement de Bourgogne*, I, 133–34, 151.

114. Brulart, "Le règne de la justice," in La Cuisine, *Parlement de Bourgogne*, I, 175; Cocquard, *Lettres*, 6–8.

115. Antoine Loisel, *Pasquier, ou dialogue des advocats du Parlement de Paris*, ed. M. Dupin (Paris: Videcoq, 1844), 60; Karpik, *Les avocats*, 53–58.

116. Durand, "De la negligence" (1693), BMD Ms. 2324, fols. 66r–69v; Durand, "Discours" (1699), BMD Ms. 2324, fols. 85r–86r.

117. Fumaroli, *L'âge de l'éloquence*, pt. III, ch. 3.

118. See above, n. 7.

119. Finley-Croswhite, "Henry IV and the Towns," 166, 179.

120. City council deliberations, 27 Aug. 1611, AMD B-251, fols. 299v–302r. In 1618 and again in 1652, Parlement issued arrêts reiterating this requirement because it was apparently being ignored. Parlement deliberations, 19 June 1618, 7 June 1652, BMD, Ms. 774, pp. 558, 594.

121. City council deliberations, 19 June 1603, AMD B-240, fol. 314r; Parlement deliberations, 19 June 1604, 18 June 1627 BMD, Ms. 774, pp. 520–22, 574.

122. Until 1626, six "ecclessiastical échevins" selected by the city's religious communities also sat on the city council and took part in deliberations concerning Dijon's clergy. Because of their early abolition, the restricted nature of their recruitment and their relatively marginal role, they are not considered in this study. All references to "échevin(s)" refer to lay aldermen, unless otherwise noted.

123. Nôtre-Dame parish had six échevins, St.-Jean and St.-Michel parishes had three each, and the remaining four parishes (St.-Nicholas, St.-Médard, St.-Pierre and St.-Philibert) had two apiece.

124. "Serment de MM. les échevins" (after 1631), AMD, B-20/29.

125. See, for example, city council deliberations, 17 Nov. 1637 and 23 June 1644, AMD, B-275, 132v–33r; B-282, fols. 43v–49v; "Mémoire pour les échevins en chacune paroisse," AMD, B-20/29. From time to time, échevins were also charged with carrying out specific tasks, such as inspecting the structural integrity of buildings in their parishes; ensuring that hotels and cabarets obeyed abstinence laws during Lent; identifying and expelling undesirables; and identifying the poor, elderly, and invalid. City council deliberations, 1 Oct. 1610, 17 Mar. 1615, 17 Mar. 1628, 18 May 1638, and 25 June 1660, AMD B-248, fol. 120v; B-252, fol. 204r; B-265, fol. 228; B-275, fol. 270r; B-299, fol. 39v.

126. In 1622 and 1637, Parlement ordered the mairie not to replace retiring or deceased conseils until they had been reduced to "l'ancienne nombre" of four. In 1649, Condé fixed the number of conseils at six. Condé's decree specified that only the six "plus ancien" conseils were to remain in office, hinting that there were

more than the theoretical limit. See arrêts of 1 Feb. 1622 and 16 March 1637, AMD B32/60-61; city council deliberations, 19 July 1649, B-287, fol. 94v.

127. Avocats et conseils de la ville, AMD B-30 to B-37bis.

128. "Extrait des registres de la chambre de ville concernant les charges des capitaines, lieutenants et enseignes des paroisses," BMD, Ms. 1283, pp. 508, 512, 517–18, 531–32. Parish officers were treated as a separate corps. They marched after the échevins in public processions and ranked beneath them at city council meetings.

129. A sample of registers reveals that the entire city council heard 59 cases in 1602–3, 150 in 1617–18, 86 in 1632–33, and 71 in 1647–48. See AMD B-240, B-255, B-270, B-285. These cases were usually major ones, involving serious crimes, multiple defendants, or charges against an entire *corporation de métier*, such as the *boulangers* or *bouchers.*

130. Melenet, "Recueil d'arrêts," BMD Ms. 311, fol. 150v.

131. City council deliberations, 26 June 1645, AMD B-283, fol. 44r.

132. In 1612, Edme Calon and Jacques Rousseau, the nephew and son-in-law of the mayor respectively, were named lieutenants. The following year, Boussuet and Pérard, the mayor's son and nephew, respectively, were selected. Mayors' sons were also chosen lieutenants in 1628 and 1663, while sons of an échevin, a receveur au bailliage, and an auditor in the Chamber of Accounts also served as lieutenants at various times. AMD B-250, fol. 34v (1612–13); B-251, fol. 37r (1613–14), B-266, fol. 39r. (1628–29); B-292, fol. 58v. (1653–54); B-300, fol. 45v (1661–62); B-302, fol. 29r (1663–64). For the three-year restriction, see the deliberations of 26 June 1645, AMD B-283, fol. 44r.

133. "Serment des sieurs lieutenans de la mairie de Dijon," AMD C-33/9.

134. On the attempts of Parlement and the Bailliage to limit the number of lieutenants, see the deliberations of 19 Nov. 1599, 24 June 1612, AMD B-237, fol. 57v, B-250, fol. 34v.

135. Drouot, *Mayenne*, I, 421.

136. Etienne Bréchillet, *Description et interpretation des portiques erigés à l'entrée de très-hault et très-puissant prince, Louis de Bourbon, Prince de Condé . . . en la ville de Dijon, le 6 mars 1648* (Dijon, 1650); city council deliberations, 2 Oct. 1651, Muteau, II, 429–30. On factional struggles during the Fronde, see chap. 3.

137. City council deliberations, 14 Jan. 1629, 27 Mar. 1629, and 12 Oct. 1629, AMD B-266, fols. 191r–v, 276r; B-267, fol. 91r.

138. "Affaires de la ville ausquelles le soubsigné [Bréchillet] a esté employée" (30 April 1636), AMD B-31bis.

139. City council deliberations, 13 Sept. 1626, 12–14 Oct. 1627, 22 Dec. 1627, 31 Jan. 1629, 1–26 Feb. 1629, 6 Mar. 1629, 13 Mar. 1629, 15 May 1629, 7 June 1629, and 12 Oct. 1629, AMD B-264, fol. 96r; B-265, fols. 118v–20v, 124, 162r–63v; B-266, fols. 216v–25v, 227v–229v, 232r–232v, 253v–254r, fols. 262v–263r, 269v, 298v, 316v–317v; B-267, fol. 91r.

140. City council deliberations, 11 Aug. 1637, B-275, fol. 70v; Claude Malteste, *Anecdotes du parlement de Bourgogne, ou histoire secrète de cette compagnie depuis 1650*, ed. Charles Muteau (Dijon: J.-E. Rabutot, 1864), 182–83.

141. City council deliberations, 20 June 1628 and 18 Sept. 1651, AMD B-266, fols. 2v–3r; Muteau, II, 402–9.

142. Plays attributed to Bréchillet include *Le chariot des déitiés à l'honneur de M. le Prince* (Dijon, 1632); "Les nopces de bontems avec la Bourgogne," (1636); and [with Bénigne Pérard] "Le retour des bontems, dédié à M. le Prince" (1632). The last two pieces are reproduced in full in Juliette Valcke, "La société joyeuse de la Mère Folle de Dijon. Histoire (XVe–XVIIe s.) et édition du répertoire," (Thèse de doctorat, Université de Montréal, 1997), 3 vols. See also Michael P. Breen, "Addressing *la ville des dieux*: Entry Ceremonies and Urban Audiences in Early Modern Dijon," *Journal of Social History* 38 (2004): 341–64.

143. City council deliberations, 11 Apr. 1642, AMD B-279, fol. 216v.

144. City council deliberations, 2 Apr. 1658, AMD B-296, fols. 298v–299r.

145. City council deliberations, 25 June 1657, 22 Nov. 1658, and 13 Oct. 1659, AMD B-296, fols. 29v–30r; B-297, fol. 166r; B-298, fol. 182r.

146. City council deliberations, 9 July 1658, 19 July 1658, 14 Mar. 1659, 13 May 1659, 26–29 July 1659, 8 Aug. 1659, 19 Aug. 1659, 23 Sept. 1659, 13 Oct. 1659, 31 Oct. 1659, 13 Jan. 1660, 17 Feb. 1660, 21 Mar. 1660, 24 Apr. 1660, 11–12 May 1660, and 7 June 1660, AMD B-297, fols. 46r–v, 56v, 179, 217v–218r; B-298, fols. 74v–75r, 98r, 116, 156, 182r, 197v, 259r–v, 290r, 323v–324r, 351, 366v–368r, 393v–394v.

147. Of the thirty-four conseils who served between 1596 and 1667, twenty-eight had served at least one term as échevin or mayor before being named to the post. Only two appear not to have been avocats.

148. The échevinage contained ten or more avocats in 1637–39, 1650–53, 1658–59, 1662–64, and 1665–66.

149. This number includes the commis à la magistrat, who completed the term of a mayor who died in office or could not complete his term for any reason.

150. City council deliberations, 18 June to 26 Oct. 1599, AMD B-236, fols. 237v *et suiv.*; "Prétensions de la Garde des Évangiles" (24 June 1627), B-18/11; City council deliberations, 2 Aug. 1630, 20 June–21 July 1650, AMD B-267, fol. 295r; Muteau I, 308–48.

151. City council deliberations, 24–26 June 1626, 7 July 1626, 10 June 1627, 15 June 1627, 20–22 June 1654, 2–3 July 1654, and 22 June 1655, AMD B-264, fols. 25v–27r, 36v–37r, 47v, 285, 288v–292r; B-293, fols. 22v–24r, fols. 64r–66r; B-294, fol. 18v. See also parlementary deliberations, 22 June 1652, 19–27 June 1654, 15 June 1655, 21 June 1655, BMD, Ms. 774, pp. 594–99, 609–13, 619–21.

152. Parlementary deliberations, 28 June 1599, 10 Jan. 1629, BMD Ms. 774, pp. 506–7; Marc-Antoine Millotet, *Mémoires des choses qui se sont passes en Bourgogne depuis 1650 jusqu'à 1668*, ed. Charles Muteau (Dijon: J.-E. Rabutot, 1864), 112–13; Malteste, *Anecdotes secrètes*, 102–3; Arrêt of Parlement de Dijon, 26 June 1651, BMD, Ms. 766, p. 826.

153. City council deliberations, 3 June 1633, 19 July 1633, and 29 July 1633, AMD B-270, fol. 339v; B-271, fols. 85r, 93v; requête of 25 July 1633, AMD B-80/82. For a detailed analysis, see chap. 2.

154. Requête of the conseils et avocats de la ville de Dijon, AMD B-81/90; city council deliberations, 10–11 Jan. 1648, 4 Feb. 1648, 20 Mar. 1648, and 19 July 1649, AMD B-285, fols. 212v–213r, 218v–219v, 254r, 285v; B-287, fol. 94v.

155. City council deliberations, 26 July 1658 and 12 July 1661, AMD B-297, fols. 67v–68r; B-300, fol. 58v.

156. Hindle, *State and Social Change*, ix.

Chapter 2

1. Parker, *La Rochelle*, 19.
2. Parker, "Sovereignty," 43, 73 (author's emphasis).
3. Beik, *Absolutism and Society*, 64; Beik, *Urban Protest*, 144.
4. Kettering, *Judicial Politics*, 49–50.
5. Beik, *Absolutism and Society*, 255–56.
6. Parker, "Sovereignty," 73; Parker, *Class and State*, 184–86.
7. Campbell, *Power and Politics*, 312.
8. Sawyer, *Printed Poison*, 15.
9. City council deliberationss, 20 June 1607, AMD B-245, fol. 2.
10. Joseph Garnier and Ernest Champeaux, *Chartes de communes et d'affranchissements en Bourgogne* (Dijon: Darantière and Jobard, 1918), 312–30.
11. According to Chevalier, *Bonnes villes*, 204–5, by Henri IV's reign, the monarchy selected the mayors of most French cities from a list of the three top vote getters. In some cities, such as Lyon, it did not hesitate to choose mayors who were not among the three nominees. See Lignereux, *Lyon et le roi*, 548. For descriptions of municipal regimes in other cities, see Parker, *La Rochelle*, 176–80; Pierre Deyon, *Amiens, capitale provinciale. Etude sur la société au XVIIe siècle*, 2d ed. (Amiens: C.R.D.P., 1986), 427–32; Saupin, *Nantes au XVIIe siècle*, 19–46; Jacques Maillard, *Le pouvoir municipal à Angers de 1657 à 1789* (Angers: Presses de l'Université d'Angers, 1984) I, 25–27; Schneider, "Crown and Capitoulat," 196–206; Lignereux, *Lyon et le roi*, 189; Kevin C. Robbins, *City on the Ocean Sea, La Rochelle 1550–1650: Urban Society, Religion, and Politics on the French Atlantic Frontier* (Leiden: Brill, 1997), 30–37; Penny Roberts, *A City in Conflict: Troyes During the Wars of Religion* (Manchester: Manchester University Press, 1996), 15; Michel Cassan, *Le temps des guerres de religion: le cas du Limousin (vers 1530–vers 1630)* (Paris: Publisud, 1996), 298–99; Descimon, "L'échevinage parisien"; Bernstein, *Between Crown and Community*, 28–37.
12. City council deliberations, 27 Oct. 1599, AMD B-237, fols. 1r–33r.
13. Mack P. Holt, "Popular Political Culture and Mayoral Elections in Sixteenth-Century Dijon," in *Society and Institutions in Early Modern France (Essays in Honor of J. Russell Major)* (Athens: University of Georgia Press, 1991), 98–107.
14. La Cuisine, *Parlement de Bourgogne*, I, 215.
15. My account elaborates on the summary by Finley-Croswhite in her dissertation on "Henry IV and the Towns," 154–70, as well as her book of the same title, 75–77.
16. Holt, "Popular Political Culture," 106.
17. Gabriel Breunot, *Journal, 1575–1602*, ed. Joseph Garnier (Dijon: J.-E. Rabutot, 1864), III, 25–30. Colin's speech is reprinted in III, 27–28, n. 1 (henceforth all references to Breunot are to vol. III); Henri Drouot, "Henri IV et les officiers de la milice dijonnaise (1595)," *Annales de Bourgogne* 7 (1935): 259.
18. City council deliberations, 18 Nov. 1597, AMD B-235, fol. 135r; Breunot, *Journal*, 101–2.
19. Breunot, *Journal*, 116–18.
20. City council deliberations, 20 June 1598, AMD B-236, fols. 5r–41v; Parlementary deliberations, 19–20 June 1598, BMD Ms. 774, pp. 480–83.

21. City council deliberations, 13–14 May 1599, AMD B-236, fols. 217–219v; Breunot, *Journal*, 149–52; François Bourcier, "Le régime municipal à Dijon sous Henri IV," *Revue d'histoire moderne* 17 (1935), 109–10.

22. City council deliberations, 24 May 1599, AMD B-236, fols. 226r–227v; Parlementary deliberations, 28 June 1599, BMD Ms. 774, pp. 506–7; Breunot, *Journal*, 152–55.

23. City council deliberations, 13–14 May 1599, AMD B-236, fols. 217r–219v; Breunot, *Journal*, 149–52.

24. Cited in Finley-Croswhite, "Henry IV and the Towns," 166.

25. Breunot, *Journal*, 160–61; Bourcier, "Régime municipal," 110.

26. City council deliberations, 7 July 1599, AMD B-236, fol. 246r; Breunot, *Journal*, 164–80.

27. City council deliberations, 29 July 1599, AMD B-236, fols. 252r–252v; Biron to mairie (13 July 1599) in Garnier, 23–24; Parlementary deliberations, 25–28 July 1599, BMD Ms. 774, pp. 510–15.

28. Biron to Mairie (13 Oct. 1599) in Garnier, 38–39.

29. Breunot, "Journal," 153.

30. City council deliberations, 16 and 20 Jan. and 7 Feb.–5 June 1603, AMD B-240, fols. 219v–220v, 222v–223r, 231r, 233r, 234v–235r, 237r–239r, 242r, and 298v–299r; Parlementary deliberations, 23 Jan. 1603, BMD Ms. 774, pp. 519–20.

31. City council deliberations, 19 June 1603, AMD B-240, fol. 314r; Parlementary deliberations, BMD Ms. 774, p. 522.

32. Parlementary deliberations, 19 June 1606, BMD Ms. 774, pp. 525–26.

33. Parlementary deliberations, 20–23 June 1608; BMD Ms. 774, pp. 529–30.

34. City council deliberations, 20 June 1608, AMD B-246, fols. 1r–34v; Holt, "Popular Political Culture," Table 1.

35. Pieces concerning Le Masque controversy, 23–28 June 1608 AMD B-20, no. 20; Bourcier, "Régime municipal," 116.

36. City council deliberations, 23 June 1608, AMD B-246, fols. 35v–36r. Although the content of Martin's *requête* is not specified in the sources, the context makes clear that he was protesting Parlement's interference.

37. City council deliberationss, 24 June 1608, AMD B-246, fols. 44r–45r; arrêt of royal council reestablishing removed échevins, 28 Feb. 1609, AMD B-20, no. 21.

38. City council deliberationss, 8–18 July 1608, AMD B-246, fols. 58v–59r, 65r–67r.

39. Robbins, *City on the Ocean Sea*, 96, notes a similarly rare example of a traditional municipal system being restored in sixteenth-century La Rochelle.

40. Claude Sullot, *Le journal de . . . procureur au parlement de Dijon*, ed. Joachim Durandeau (Dijon: Sirodot-Carré, 1911), 108; Bourcier, *Journal*, 116–17; Henri IV to mairie, 3 and 30 June 1609; mairie to Bellegarde, 21 June 1609; Bellegarde to mairie, 2 July 1609; Louis XIII to mairie, 31 May 1610, in Garnier, 101–2, 104–8, 114; City council deliberations, 4 June 1610, AMD B-247, fols. 272v–273r.

41. City council deliberations, 18 and 21 Feb. 1611, AMD B-248, fols. 198, 200r–202v.

42. City council deliberations, 4–11 Mar. 1611, AMD B-248, fols. 207v–214v.

43. City council deliberations, 10 June and 27 Aug. 1611; AMD B-248, fols. 256v–260r, 299v–302r; Louis XIII to mairie, 28 May 1611, in Garnier, 118–19; Sullot, *Journal*, 116–17, 119; Holt, "Popular Political Culture," 109.

44. Vote totals in the 1630s and 1640s ranged from 646 to 1,275; see AMD B-269 to B-287.

45. Bonney, *Political Change*, 319.

46. Bertucat, *Juridiction*, 99–115.

47. City council deliberations, 15 June 1627, 27 June 1628, 21 July 1637, and 12 Dec. 1642, AMD B-264, fol. 289r; B-266, fol. 33r; B-275, fol. 53; B-280, fol. 179r.

48. City council deliberations, 19 Jan. 1627, AMD B-264, fol. 183r.

49. City council deliberations, 22 Aug. 1631 and 27 Jan. 1632, AMD B-269, fols. 110r, 36v–37r.

50. City council deliberationss, 22 Aug., 19 Dec. 1625, 26 Sept., and 7 Oct. 1631, AMD B-263, fols. 87v–88r, 169v–170r; B-269, fols. 141v–142r, 151v–152r.

51. "Mémoire des vacations extraordinaires faictes par M. Morizot, advocat & conseil" (1607–11), AMD B-30bis; "Mémoires des affaires que l'advocat Malpoy a faittes pour la ville" (1616–44) AMD B-31bis.

52. Brigitte Bedos-Rezak, "Civic Liturgies and Urban Records in Northern France, 1100–1400," in *City and Spectacle in Medieval Europe*, ed. Barbara A. Hanawalt and Kathryn L. Reyerson (Minneapolis: University of Minnesota Press, 1994), 34–55.

53. City council deliberations, 16 Jan., 25–30 Jan., 6–13 Mar., 15 May, and 10 July 1629, AMD B-266, fols. 194r–198r, 206r–216v, 262v–269v, 298v; B-267, fol. 55r.

54. City council deliberations, 5 Jan. and 9 Jan. 1629, and 7 Jan. 1650, AMD B-266, fols. 179, 181; B-287, fol. 244r. The last deliberation notes parallel cases in 1608, 1629, 1630, and 1634.

55. Farr, *Hands of Honor*, 177–95; Reinhardt, *Justice in the Sardalais,* chap. 5; J. A. Sharpe, "'Such Disagreement betwyx Neighbours': Litigation and Human Relations in Early Modern England," in *Disputes and Settlements: Law and Human Relations in the West*, ed. John Bossy (Cambridge: Cambridge University Press), 167–87.

56. City council deliberations, 24 June, 26 June, and 7 July 1626, AMD B-264, fols. 25v–27r, 36v–37r, 48v.

57. City council deliberations, 10 and 15 June 1627, AMD B-264, fols. 285, 288v–292r.

58. Michael P. Breen, "Law, Patronage, and Municipal Authority in Seventeenth-Century France: The Aftermath of the Lanturelu Revolt in Dijon," *French History* 20 (2006): 138–60.

59. Henri IV to mairie, 12 June 1596, in Garnier, 8; city council deliberations, 25 June 1641 and 27 May 1642, AMD B-279, fols. 41v, 246r.

60. See below, p. 98.

61. City council deliberations, 14 June 1641 and 23 June 1643, AMD B-278, fols. 265r–267r; B-281, fols. 39v–59v.

62. City council deliberations, 23 June 1637, 24 May 1647, and 14 June 1647, AMD B-275, fol. 17; B-284, fols. 288v–289r, 307r–308r.

63. City council deliberations, 24 June, 3 July, and 10 July 1635, AMD B-273, fols. 28r, 43r, 49v–50r.

64. Arrêts of Parlement de Dijon, 28 June 1619 and 27 June 1629, AMD B-20, no. 23 and no. 25.

65. City council deliberations, 2 Aug. 1641, 29 May 1646, and 18 and 24 July 1636, AMD B-279, fol. 167v; B-283, fols. 242v–243r; B-274, fols. 77v, 85v–86r.

66. City council deliberations, 30 Apr. 1615, 20 and 24 Nov. 1626, 23 June 1628, 9 Apr. 1630, 17 Oct. 1631, 30 Apr. 1632, and 6 Nov. 1646, AMD B-252, fol. 130r; B-264, fols. 126r, 129; B-266, fol. 21; B-267, fols. 196v–197r; B-269, fols. 158v, 298r; B-284, fols. 129v–130r. For the second half of the century, see Beth Nachison, "Provincial Government in the Ancien Régime: The Princes of Condé in Burgundy, 1660–1730" (Ph.D. dissertation, University of Iowa, 1992), 131–94.

67. City council deliberations, 23 June and 3 July 1643, AMD B-281, fols. 39r–48r, 57v–59v; *cassation* of elections of échevins Boulier, De Mouhy, Clemandot and Chiporee, 3 July 1643, AMD B-20, no. 30.

68. City council deliberations, 29 May and 5 June 1646, AMD B-283, fols. 242v–243r, 245. A few weeks later, Soyrot was unanimously elected garde des évangiles. See the deliberation of 15 June 1646, AMD B-283, fols. 254v–255v.

69. City council deliberations, 9, 12, 18 Mar. and 1 Apr. 1649, AMD B-286, fols. 244v–246r, 251v–253r, 259v–260r, 259.

70. City council deliberations, 29 Apr. 1650, AMD B-287, fol. 358. On Baudot's subsequent career, see AMD H-9, fols. 87r–100r.

71. Chevalier, *Bonnes villes*, 303–6; Roger Chartier and Hughes Neveux, "La ville dominante et soumise," in *Histoire de la France urbaine*, vol. 3, *La ville classique de la Renaissance aux Révolutions*, ed. Emmanuel Le Roy Ladurie (Paris: Presses Universitaires de France, 1980), 16–285. Yann Lignereux's *Lyon et le roi* has recently offered a more nuanced interpretation in its analysis of the political imaginary of Lyon's municipal elite and its transformation from "bonne ville" to "absolutisme municipale."

72. Bernstein, *Crown and Community*, 65–67.

73. Municipal Accounts, 1629–30 to 1648–49, AMD M-184–221; city council deliberations, 13 May 1633 and 5 May 1634, AMD B-270, fol. 319; B-271 fols. 339v–340r.

74. Edwards, *Families and Frontiers*, 154–55.

75. City council deliberations, 28 June 1633, AMD B-271, fol. 53.

76. City council deliberations, 24 Mar. 1626, 13 Dec. 1628, 5 Apr. 1632, 20 Jan. 1648, and 18 July 1636, AMD B-263, fol. 231; B-266 fols. 164r–165v; B-269, fol. 286; B-285, fol. 232v; B-274 fols. 75v–77r.

77. City council deliberations, 15 May, 24 July, 18 Aug., 18 Sept., and 13 Nov. 1626, AMD B-263, fol. 263v; B-264, fols. 61r, 80, 97, 121v–122r.

78. Breen, "Law, Patronage, and Municipal Authority," 154.

79. Breen, "Law, Patronage, and Municipal Authority," 158.

80. Collot, échevin, to mairie, 26 July 1623, in Garnier, 155–56.

81. See above, Introduction.

82. City council deliberations, 20 Apr. 1638, 4 Jan. 1641, 28 Nov. 1642, and 2 June 1643, AMD B-275, fol. 255; B-278 fol. 149r; B-280, fols. 168r, 306r.

83. City council deliberations, 30 Jan., 1 and 12 Feb., and 12 Mar. 1638, AMD B-275, fols. 202r–204r, 210v–213v, 232v.

84. Breen, "Law, Patronage, and Municipal Authority," 149.

85. Mairie to Condé, 28 Jan. 1636; First President Legoux de La Berchère to Condé, 22 July 1636; Parlement of Burgundy to Condé, 29 July 1636; mairie to Condé, 16 Aug. 1636; mairie to Condé, 14 Oct. 1636, AC M/VII, no. 55; M/IX, no. 147, no. 188, no. 363; M/X, no. 315. City council deliberations, 28 Mar. 1637, AMD B-274, fols. 337r–345v.

86. City council deliberations, 11 May 1638, AMD B-275, fols. 266r–267r.

87. City council deliberations, 17 Apr. 1643, 22 Oct. 1644, and 22 Nov. 1647, AMD B-280, fol. 264v; B-282, fol. 142v; B-285, fol. 152r.

88. City council deliberations, 24 June 1643, AMD B-281, fol. 48r.

89. City council deliberations, 11–18, 28 July, 8 and 11 Aug., and 5 Sept. 1645, AMD B-283, fols. 62r–68r, fols. 75, 80, 85r, 96v–97r.

90. City council deliberations, 15 May 1648 and 19 July 1649, AMD B-285, fol. 285v; B-287, fol. 94v.

91. City council deliberations, 21 June 1632 and 30 July 1636, AMD B-269, fol. 338; B-274, fols. 92v–93v.

92. City council deliberationss, 8 Oct. 1646 and 29 March 1647, AMD B-284, fols. 110r-12v, 250r-51v. See also the deliberation of 28 Nov. 1642, AMD B-280, fols. 169r-71v.

93. Smith, "Our Sovereign's Gaze," 410–14; idem, *Culture of Merit*; Nachison, "Provincial Government," 297–98.

94. Nachison, "Provincial Government," 121.

95. City council deliberations, 19 Sept. 1635, AMD B-273, fols. 108v-11r.

96. Millotet, *Mémoires*, 57–58. Chevalier's destitution, while lending credence to Millotet's claims, also reveals that Bouchu had much less influence over the Mairie than the avocat-général claimed. Chevalier had been elected *ancien* in place of the mayor's nominee, the bourgeois François Arvisenet, by a vote of 15-4. Although the Mairie complied with the arrêt, it protested against the "violation of its privileges" to Parlement. See the deliberations of 19 July and 2 Aug. 1646, AMD B-284, fols. 62v–63r, 68r–69r.

97. See below, pp. 97–98.

Chapter 3

1. City council deliberations, 30 Apr. 1643, AMD B-280, fols. 269v–270.

2. City council deliberations, 4–26 Jan., 4 Feb. 1648, and 19 July 1649, AMD B-285, fols. 203v–205v, 212v–213r, 218v–219v, 233, 254r; B-287, fol. 94v.

3. City council deliberations, 5–25 Feb. 1649, AMD B-286, fols. 215, 220, 223, 229r–230r; Requête of the avocats et conseils de la ville de Dijon, AMD B-81, no. 90.

4. City council deliberations, 3 Apr. and 19 June 1649, AMD B-286, fols. 272v–273r; B-287, fol. 94v; Requête of the avocats et conseils de la ville de Dijon, B-81, no. 90.

5. Extracts of city council deliberations concerning avocats' precedence lawsuit against other échevins, 31 May to 12 Aug. 1633, AMD B-80/82.

6. City council deliberations, 20 Jan. 1648 and 15 Feb, 1649, AMD B-285, fol. 233; B-286, fol. 220.

7. Parlementary deliberations, 21 June 1633, BMD Ms. 774, pp. 573–75.

8. Millotet, *Mémoires*, 3–4.

9. City council deliberations, 3 Apr. 1649, AMD B-286, fols. 272v–273r.

10. Gronau-Chenillet, "Parlement de Dijon," 106.

11. City council deliberations, 5 Oct. 1650, Muteau I, 399.

12. City council deliberations, 23 Aug. 1652, Muteau II, 490–91. On the destitution of several parish officers, see the deliberations of 1 Sept. 1650, Muteau I, 365.

13. On Rousseau, see above, chap. 1. Chrétien Guillaume served three terms as échevin from 1647 to 1650 and then two more terms from 1653 to 1655.

14. City council deliberations, 28 Sept., 5 Oct. 1657, and 3 and 10 June 1661, AMD B-296, fols. 139v–140r, 143r–145r; B-299, fols. 387, 390v–391r.

15. Wolf, "Facing Power," 586–87.

16. See below, p. 108.

17. AN V^6/385.

18. The arrival of Condé and his son Henri-Jules in April 1660 occasioned public demonstrations of joy. Nachison, "Provincial Government, 32–33. See also, Millotet, *Mémoires*, 240–41.

19. Nachison, "Provincial Government," 69–70.

20. Gronau-Chenillet, "Parlement de Dijon," 97–105; Pierre Lenet, "Mémoires de . . . procureur-général au parlement de Dijon et conseiller d'état," in *Nouvelle collection des mémoires relatifs à l'histoire de France depuis le XIIIe siècle jusqu'à la fin du XVIIIe siècle*, ed. Michaud and Poujoulat (Paris: Didier, 1854), v. 26, 209–13.

21. M. Segaud, "La Fronde en Bourgogne. Le rôle du parlement et de la chamber de ville de Dijon (Mémoire de D.E.S., Université de Dijon, 1909), 102; Lenet, "Mémoires," 211.

22. City council deliberations, 24–25 Apr. 1650, AMD B-287, fol. 348; Lenet, "Mémoires," 209–10.

23. City council deliberations, 24 Jan., 14 Feb., and 24–25 Apr. 1650, AMD B-287, fols. 259v–265r, 294r, 348; Lenet, "Mémoires," 213.

24. Heide Gronau-Chenillet, "Le parlement de Bourgogne et l'intendant sous les ministères de Richelieu et Mazarin: du clientélisme condéean vers la fidélité au roi," in *Les parlements de province: pouvoirs, justice, société, XVe–XVIIIe siècles*, ed. Jacques Poumarède and Jack Thomas (Toulouse: FRAMESPA, 1996): 443–52; Gronau-Chenillet, "Le jeu des clienteles," Pierre Genreau, "Journal domestique d'un procureur au parlement de Dijon, 1614–1669," BMD Ms. 1011, f. 49v.

25. Gronau-Chenillet, "Parlement de Dijon," 134–39.

26. Millotet, *Mémoires*, 1–2; Gronau-Chenillet, "Jeu des clientèles," 13–18; Gronau-Chenillet, "Le parlement de Bourgogne et l'intendant," 445–48.

27. City council deliberations, 10 June 1650, AMD B-287, fols. 408v–9v.

28. Genreau, "Journal," BMD Ms. 1011, f. 49v; Millotet, *Mémoires*, 59–60.

29. Millotet, *Mémoires*, 59; city council deliberations, 24 June 1650, Muteau I, 320–25; Genreau, "Journal," BMD Ms. 1011, fols. 51v, 54r; La Vrillière to mairie, 4 July 1650, in Garnier, 349–50.

30. City council deliberations, 18 and 22 Feb. 1651, Muteau I, 418–20; Millotet, *Mémoires*, 90–97; Jean Godran des Chasans, "Réjouissance faicte en la ville de Dijon sur la desliverance de MM. les Princes de Condé, de Conty, et de Longueville," BMD Ms. 864, fols. 292r–305r; Genreau, "Journal," BMD Ms. 1011, fol. 56r.

31. Millotet, *Mémoires*, 109–10, City council deliberations, 11 May 1651, Muteau I, 385–94; Parlementary arrêt, 12 May 1651, BMD Ms. 766, pp. 803–4.

32. Epernon to mairie, 1 and 2 June 1651, in Garnier, 355–57.

33. Epernon to mairie, 1 and 2 June 1651; Millotet, *Mémoires*, 115–29.

34. Gaudelet, "Journal," BMD Ms. 748, pp. 6–7.

35. City council deliberations, 9 June 1650 and 15–16 June 1651, Muteau I, 443, 446–51; Parlementary arrêt 15 June 1651, BMD Ms. 766, 819–20; Malteste, *Anecdotes secrètes*, 96–97.

36. Malteste, *Anecdotes secrètes*, 98, 103–4; Parlementary arrêt, 20 June 1651, BMD Ms. 766, pp. 822–23.

37. Malteste, *Anecdotes secrètes*, 107–8; Parlementary arrêt, 20 June 1651, BMD Ms. 766, p. 823.

38. City council deliberations, 13 June 1659, AMD B-297, fol. 239. La Croix was a member of both the provisional Condéan échevinage of 1650 and one of the six échevins named by Epernon in 1657. See the deliberations of 23 June 1650 and 23 June 1657, AMD, B-288, fols. 34v–35r; B-296, fols. 19r–20r.

39. Gaudelet, "Journal," BMD Ms. 748, 54–56, 59; city council deliberations, 18 June 1659, AMD B-297, fols. 241v–242r.

40. City council deliberations, 20–23 June 1659, AMD B-298, fols. 1r–28r; Gaudelet, "Journal," BMD Ms. 748, pp. 57–61, 84–85; Millotet, *Mémoires*, 236–37; Parlementary deliberation, 26 June 1659, BMD Ms. 774, pp. 624–27.

41. Genreau, "Journal," BMD Ms. 1011, fol. 51.

42. City council deliberations, 23 June 1650, Muteau I, 314–16; Parlementary deliberation, 23 June 1650, BMD Ms. 774, pp. 582–93.

43. City council deliberations, 24 June 1650, Muteau I, 323.

44. City council deliberations, 1 and 21 July 1650, Muteau I, 329, 348–50; Genreau, "Journal," BMD Ms. 1011, fol. 52; Gronau-Chenillet, "Parlement de Bourgogne," 209–10.

45. City council deliberations, 27 Sept. 1651, Muteau II, 416–25; Malteste, *Anecdotes secrètes*, 108, 146–47.

46. City council deliberations, 23 June 1656, AMD B-295, fols. 17v–18v.

47. City council deliberations, 11 July 1656, AMD B-295, fols. 37r–39v.

48. City council deliberations, 2 Apr. and 23 June 1658, AMD B-296, fols. 298v–299r; B-297, fols. 16r–17r.

49. City council deliberations, 20 and 25 June 1660 and 11 Mar. and 10 June 1661, AMD B-299, fols. 1r–26v, 38, 326v–327r, 392v; Gaudelet, "Journal," BMD Ms. 748, pp. 84–85.

50. Millotet, *Mémoires*, pp. 14–15, 59–60, 64, 147–53; city council deliberations, 24 June 1650, Muteau I, 320–25.

51. City council deliberations, 16 Feb., 9 Nov., 3 Dec. 1655, 15 June 1656, and 9 Jan. 1657, AMD B-293, fols. 284v–285r; B-294, fols. 132v, 150v, 253r; B-295, fol. 188v.

52. City council deliberations, 28 Sept. and 5 Oct. 1657, 1 Feb. 1658, AMD B-296, fols. 139v–140r, 143r–145r, fol. 253v.

53. City council deliberations, 15–17 Nov. 1656, 5 Dec. 1658, and 7 Mar. 1659, AMD B-295, fols. 146, 149r; B-297, fols. 131r–132, 176v.

54. City council deliberations, 26–27 Jan. 1651, Muteau 1, 408–10.

55. "Raisons pour justifier les demandes des maire et échevins de la ville de Dijon et qu'elles sont de justice contre MM du Parlement (1652)," BMD Ms. 3213, fols. 733–751; Parlementary deliberations, 22 June 1652, 27 June, 1653, 19 June 1654, and 15 June 1655, BMD Ms. 774, pp. 594–99; 609–12; 619–21; city council

deliberations, 20–22 June 1654, 17–18 June 1655, and 19 June 1656, AMD B-293, fols. 22v–24r; B-293, fols. 391r, 393v–394v; B-295, fols 17v–18r.

56. City council deliberations, 17 and 23 Jan., 4 and 6 Mar., 14 and 24 Apr., 25 and 29 June, 1–12 July 1657, 26 Oct. and 21–22 Nov. 1658, AMD B-295, fols. 203r, 207, 234v, 236r, 253r, 257v–258r; B-296, fols. 29v–30r, 38v–39r, 40r, 42r–43v, 44v–45r, 46v, 52v–54v; B-297, fols. 116r, 125v–126r (1658).

57. City council deliberations, 23 June and 21 July 1650, 23 June and 27 Sept. 1651, AMD B-288, fols. 34v–35v, fols. 61r–63r; B-289, fols. 40r–41v; Muteau II, 425.

58. City council deliberations, 23 June 1650; Muteau I, 314–16; Genreau, "Journal," BMD Ms. 1011, fol. 51, Parlementary deliberations, 23 June and 28 July 1650, BMD Ms. 774, pp. 582–93.

59. City council deliberations, 25 June 1650; Muteau I, 324–28.

60. City council deliberations, 21 July 1650; Muteau I, 348–50; Genreau, "Journal," fols. 52r–53r.

61. Malteste, *Anecdotes secrètes*, 86–87.

62. City council deliberations, 11 May 1651, Muteau I, 393.

63. Millotet, *Mémoires*, 112–13; Malteste, *Anecdotes secrètes*, 102–3.

64. City council deliberations, 11 July 1656, AMD B-295, fols. 37r–38v.

65. City council deliberations, 23 June 1659, AMD B-298, fols. 26v–29v; Parlementary deliberation, 26 June 1659, BMD Ms. 774, pp. 624–27.

66. City council deliberations, 23 June 1651, 4 July 1651, 13 Dec. 1651, and 27 Feb. 1652, AMD B-290, fols. 40r–41v; Muteau II, 371–73, 458–70.

67. City council deliberations, 14 July 1653, 11 Aug. 1654, 9 Sept. 1658, and 22 Feb. 1659, Muteau II, 543–45; AMD B-293, fol. 123v; B-297, fols. 103, 172r–173v.

68. City council deliberations, 24 June 1655, 27 June 1656, 13 May 1659, and 26–29 July 1659, AMD B-294, fol. 23; B-295, fols. 24r–25r; B-297, fols. 217v–218r; B-298, fols. 74v–75r.

69. City council deliberations, 27 June 1656, AMD B-295, fols. 24r–25r.

70. City council deliberations, 25 June and 19 July 1655, AMD B-294, fols. 29v–30r, 59r–60r.

71. City council deliberations, 16 Mar., 14 and 24 Apr., 25 June, and 11 July 1657, 20 Jan. 1659, AMD B-295, fols. 236r, 253r, 257v–258r; B-296, fols. 29v–30r, 52v–53r; B-297, fol. 155r.

72. City council deliberations, 11 Mar. 1661, AMD B-299, fol. 326r–327r.

73. City council deliberations, 27 May 1664, 20 May 1667, and 12 June 1668, AMD B-302, fol. 202r; B-305, fols. 253v–254r; B-306, fol. 197r.

74. Mairie to Louis II de Bourbon, 17 May 1662, AC P/XXVII, no. 20.

75. City council deliberations, 17 and 24 Apr., 11–12 May, 7 June and 5 Nov. 1660, and 6 Mar. 1663, AMD B-298, fols. 345, 351, 366v–367r, 393v–394r; B-299, fol. 205; B-301, fol. 213r; mairie to Louis II de Bourbon, 4 and 21 July 1660, AC P/XXIII, no. 233, no. 242; mairie to Louis II de Bourbon, 6 and 20 Feb. 1661, AC P/XXIV, no. 45, no. 69.

76. Harding, *Anatomy*, 212.

77. Richard, "Parlement de Dijon et monarchie," 111; Bonney, *Political Change*, 60, 250, 342.

78. François-Xavier Emmanuelli, *Un mythe de l'absolutisme bourbonien: L'intendance, du milieu du XIIème siècle à la fin du XVIIIème siècle (France, Espagne, Amerique)* (Aix-en-Provence: Université de Provence, 1981), 35–60; Smedley-Weill, *Les Intendants*, 101–20.

79. Bonney, *Political Change*, 362–63; Gronau-Chenillet, "Parlement de Bourgogne," 308.

80. Gaudelet, "Journal" BMD Ms. 748, p. 72; élus to Condé, 16 Feb. 1661, AC P/XXIV, no. 61.

81. See, for example, city council deliberations, 21 Jan. 1659 and 10 Apr. 1660, AMD B-297, fol. 155r, B-298, fol. 338.

82. City council deliberations, 10 Mar. 1653, 24 June and 29 Nov. 1655, Muteau II, 505–10; AMD B-294, fols. 23, 147.

83. Arrêt of the royal council (1663), AMD B-120; Bertucat, *Finances*, 40–42.

84. City council deliberations, 11 July 1656 and 23 June 1659, AMD B-295, fols 40r–41v; B-298, fols. 27r–28v. Bonney, *Political Change*, 336.

85. City council deliberations, 10–11 Sept., 13–17 Oct., and 18 Nov. 1659 and 14 Apr. 1665, AMD B-298, fols. 151r–152v, 181v–183r, 220r; B-303, fol. 151v.

86. City council deliberations, 11 July 1662, AMD B-301, fol. 50; Bertucat, *Finances*, 19–22.

87. City council deliberations, 12, 15, 19, and 20 June 1668, AMD B-306, fols. 197r, 198v, 200r; B-307, fols. 1r–20v.

88. City council deliberations, 23 June 1668, AMD B-307, fols. 24v–30r; Gaudelet, "Journal," BMD Ms. 748, p. 144; Alexandre Thomas, *Une province sous Louis XIV: Situation politique et administrative de la Bourgogne de 1661 à 1715 d'après les manuscripts et documents inédits du temps* (Paris: Joubert, 1844), 286–89.

89. City council deliberations, 23 June 1668, AMD B-307, fols. 26r, 30v; Charles Arbassier, *L'absolutisme en Bourgogne: l'intendant Bouchu et son action financière d'après sa correspondence inédit (1667–71)* (Paris: Picard, 1921), 164–65.

90. City council deliberations, 23 June 1668, AMD B-307, fols. 26v–27r.

91. Mémoire by Claude Dupelu, marchand bourgeois, to intendant de Harlay, 30 June 1687, AN G^7 157, no. 60.

92. City council deliberations, 23 June 1668, AMD B-307, fol. 25v. In a letter to Condé the day after the event, Bouchu claimed that Calon's procuration was signed by "only fifteen or twenty inhabitants, most of very modest status." Cited in Arbassier, *L'absolutisme*, 164–65.

93. City council deliberations, 23 June and 28 Nov. 1668 AMD B-307, fols. 25v–26r, 28v–30v, 189. Arbassier, *L'absolutisme*, 164–65.

94. City council deliberations, 9 Dec. 1668, AMD B-307, fols. 200v–201r. The text of the *monitoire* can be found in AMD I-119.

95. City council deliberations, 17 Dec. 1668, 6 Feb. 1669, AMD B-307, fols. 211r, 244.

96. Garnier and Champeaux, *Chartes*, 328; city council deliberations, 6 Feb. 1669, AMD B-307, fol. 244.

97. City council deliberations, 3 Oct. 1668, AMD B-307, fol. 116.

98. Parker, *La Rochelle*, 183.

99. City council deliberations, 28 July 1668, AMD B-307, fol. 71; Arbassier, *L'absolutisme*, 162.

100. Bertucat, *Finances*, 7–69.

101. Thomas, *Province sous Louis XIV*, 243–46; Arbassier, *L'absolutisme*, chap. 3; Bertucat, *Finances*, 70–83.

102. Dijon's experience thus seems to greatly resemble those of Toulouse and Montpellier. See Beik, *Absolutism and Society*, 67–69.

103. Beik, "Louis XIV and the Cities," 76.

104. City council deliberations, 14 and 24 July 1668, AMD B-307, fols. 57r, 66v–67v. Gaudelet described the new outfits as follows: "M. Joly, Mayor, wore a robe of violet satin lined with red satin, with a cornet or chaperon on the shoulder also made of violet satin lined with ermine. The six échevins, with the city's syndic, secretary, receiver and controller, wore violet robes lined with red satin and a cornet on the shoulder, the same as M. the Mayor. The Mayor . . . also had his train carried by a lackey." "Journal," BMD Ms. 748, pp. 148–49.

Chapter 4

1. Temple, "Control and Exploitation"; Mousnier, "Participation des gouvernés," 252.

2. Harding, *Anatomy*, 212; Beik, *Absolutism and Society*, 312–14; Wallace, *Communities and Conflict*, 226–27.

3. City council deliberations, 23 and 26 June, 10 July 1670, AMD B-309, fols. 21r–22r, 28r, 41r–42r; AMD B-20, no. 34.

4. Arrêt of royal council, 26 Sept. 1670, AMD B-20, no. 34; city council deliberations, 5 and 7 Jan., 14 Mar. 1671, AMD B-309, fols 155v–156r, 189.

5. City council deliberations, 14, 17, and 25 Apr., 6 May 1671, AMD B-309, fols. 204v, 208r, 218, 222r.

6. See above, pp. 84–86 and 95–96.

7. City council deliberations, 1 Apr. 1672 and 9 Mar. 1677, AMD B-310, fol. 113v; B-315, fol. 97; letters of 19 May 1679, B-469. Additional letters naming mayors, syndics, échevins, and conseils can be found in AMD B-469.

8. Nachison, "Provincial Government," 220–22; city council deliberation, 27 Apr. 1689, AMD B-328, fols. 203v–204v.

9. Nachison, "Provincial Government," 121.

10. Nachison, "Provincial Government," 96; city council deliberations, 12 June 1676, 9 Apr. 1683, 21 June 1686, 10 and 28 June 1689, AMD B-314, fols. 216r–218r; B-321, fols. 140r–141r; B-325, fols. 1v–3v; B-328, fols. 234v–235r, 243v–246v.

11. City council deliberations, 30 June and 13 July 1687, AMD B-325, fols. 188v–189v; B-326, fols. 1r–5r.

12. City council deliberations, 7 Nov. 1668, AMD B-307, fols. 168r–170v; Bouchu to mairie, 3 May 1678, AMD B-465; Argouges to mairie, 9 Dec. 1689, AMD B-467.

13. City council deliberations, 22 Apr. 1688, AMD B-328, fols. 3v–4v; Argouges to mairie, 28 July 1691 and 14 Dec. 1689, AMD B-467.

14. Nachison, "Provincial Government," chap. 5; Bouchu to controlleur-général, 16 June 1678, AN G^7 156, no. 9; Rigoley to mairie, 4 and 18 Aug. 1681, AMD B-467;

Henri-Jules de Bourbon to Rigoley, 15 Mar., 19 June, and 15 July 1682, 26 Jan. 1684, 29 Aug. 1689, BMD Ms. 2239, no. 39, no. 45, no. 52, no. 110, no. 258.

15. City council deliberations, 9 Dec. 1670, AMD B-309, fol. 144v.

16. See, for example, Bouchu to mairie, 16 Oct. 1677, 17 Mar. 1679, and 31 Oct. 1682, and élus of Burgundy to mairie, 11 Mar. 1680, AMD B-467.

17. City council deliberations, 8 Oct. 1675 and 10 May 1678, AMD B-314, fol. 83v; B-316, fol 217r; on Florent d'Argouges, see the deliberation of 20 Aug. 1693, AMD B-333, fol. 63.

18. Bouchu to controlleur-général, 16 June 1678, AN G^7 156, no. 9; Henri-Jules de Bourbon to Rigoley, 26 Jan. and 8 Aug. 1684, 31 Jan. 1687, BMD Ms. 2239, no. 110, no. 116, no. 194.

19. Bertucat, *Juridiction*, 102–7; city council deliberations, 13 Sept. 1671, 11 Dec. 1682, 14 June and 23 Aug. 1683, 26 June 1688, AMD B-310, fol. 40; B-321, fols. 81r–82r, 168r; B-322, fols. 44v–45r; B-328, fols. 29v–30r.

20. City council deliberations, 5 June 1676, 21 Apr. 1679, 21 Aug. 1697, and 15 Feb. 1698, AMD B-314, fol. 209r; B-317, fols. 126v–127v; B-336, fols. 324v–325r; B-338, fol. 25.

21. City council deliberations, 27 June 1699, AMD B-338, fol. 285; Bertucat, *Juridiction*, 107–20, 144–45; M. Chaume, "Histoire d'un banlieue: Récherches sur la consistence première et les limites successives du ban territoriale de la justice municipale de Dijon," *Mémoires de la société pour l'histoire du droit et des institutions des anciens pays bourguignons, comtois et romands* (1942) 8:57.

22. City council deliberations, 6 July 1689, AMD B-328, fol. 252. The mairie had similarly accused the bailli of St. Bénigne of removing its seals from the belongings of a widow living in a house at the Moulin du chevre-morte in 1678. See the deliberations of 7 June 1678, AMD B-316, fol. 232r.

23. City council deliberations, 21 July and 22 Nov. 1672, 21 Apr. 1688, and 13 Sept. 1689, AMD B-311, fols. 64r, 171v; B-326, fol. 131r; B-328, fol. 301r. Chaume, "Histoire d'un banlieue," 58–59.

24. City council deliberations, 2 Oct. 1676 and 15 July 1678, AMD B-315, fol. 53v; B-317, fol. 12.

25. Gaudelet, "Journal," BMD Ms. 748, p. 148; city council deliberations, 6 Apr. 1679 and 13–17 March 1688, AMD B-317, fol. 123r; B-326, fols. 111v–112r, 113r–117r.

26. City council deliberations, 16–21 June 1679, AMD B-317, fols. 86r–87r, 89v–90r.

27. City council deliberations, 11 Dec. 1682 and 26 June 1688, AMD B-321, fols. 81r–82r; B-328, fols. 29v–30r.

28. City council deliberations, 28 July 1688, AMD B-328, fols. 58r–59r.

29. City council deliberations, 13 July 1675, 27 Oct. 1672, and 16 Jan. 1693, AMD B-314, fols. 28r–30r; B-311, fols. 152v–153r; B-332, fol. 258v.

30. City council deliberations, 21 Apr. 1688, AMD B-326, fols. 130v–131v. The six cases pending before the intendant were: the aforementioned suit against the officiers de la monnoye; unspecified cases against the chassiers de la Sainte-Chapelle and M. le Sieur Soucelier; trésorier des morts payés; and three separate suits concerning claims of nobility and/or tax exemption. The other two suits, both over disputed jurisdictions, were pursued at Parlement.

31. City council deliberations, 18–28 Nov. 1670, AMD B-309, fols. 131, 134, 138r.

32. City council deliberations, 21 Oct. 1678, AMD B-317, fol. 47.

33. Mairie to Harlay, 1 May 1686; Harlay to controlleur-général, 12 June 1686, AN G^7 157, no. 14; Bertucat, *Juridiction*, 106.

34. See above, p. 80. Harlay's settlement does not appear to have been a lasting one. In 1708, the mairie complained to the intendant that the Bailliage had violated the arrêt of 11 March 1688 by affixing seals in the home of a nonnoble officer of the queen's regiment. See the city council deliberations of 13 Apr. 1708, AMD B-346, fol. 257r.

35. City council deliberations, 11 and 28 Dec. 1669, AMD B-308, fols. 144v, 156.

36. City council deliberations, 22 Sept. 1682 and 22 Mar. 1683, AMD B-321, fols. 51r, 129v–130v.

37. Jacot, president of Chambre de la Tournelle to controlleur-général, 23 Dec. 1694, AN G^7 158, no. 490.

38. Claude Dupelu, merchant bourgeois to Intendant de Harlay, 30 June 1687, AN G^7 157, no. 60.

39. City council deliberations, 30 June and 13 July 1687, AMD B-325, fols. 188v–189v; B-326, fols. 1r–5r.

40. Controlleur-général's proposal (undated), AN G^7 157, no. 88.

41. Harlay's response, 8 Dec. 1689, AN G^7 157, no. 88.

42. Brulart's mémoire, 8 Dec. 1689, AN G^7 157, no. 88.

43. Beik, "Louis XIV and the Cities," 76.

44. City council deliberation, 2 Oct. 1669, AMD B-308, fols. 86v–87r.

45. Hurt, *Louis XIV and the Parlements*, chaps. 3, 4.

46. Schneider, "Crown and Capitoulat," 209; Bossenga, *Politics of Privilege*, 36–40.

47. Brulart's mémoire, 8 Dec. 1689, AN G^7 157, no. 88.

48. Maurice Bordes, *L'administration provinciale et municipale en France au XVIIIe siècle* (Paris: Société d'éditions d'enseignment, 1972), 232–36; Benedict, "French Cities," 34–36.

49. Deyon, *Amiens*, 467; Maillard, *Pouvoir muncipale* I, 28–31; Bordes, *L'administration provinciale*, 232–36; Benedict, "French Cities," 34–35.

50. Bordes, *L'administration provinciale*, 234–36; Benedict, "French Cities," 34–35; Bossenga, *Politics of Privilege*, 23; Schneider, "Crown and Capitoulat"; Nachison, "Provincial Government," 97–98.

51. *Edit du Roy, Portant creation de maires perpetuels et d'assesseurs dans les hôtels de villes et communautés du royaume* (Dijon, n.d. [prob. 1693]), 1–6. Additional information pertaining to the sale of municipal offices can be found in AMD B-6.

52. Purchasers of municipal offices, AMD B-6; city council deliberations, 20 Dec. 1692 and 24–28 Jan. 1693, B-332, fols. 236v–37v, 272r–285r; *Edit du Roy*, 17–48.

53. Purchasers of municipal offices, AMD B-6.

54. Bertucat, *Finances*, 118–42, 148–52.

55. The city council was able to sell only a few offices on its own initiative. See, for instance, the deliberations of 6 Mar. 1694, AMD B-333, fols. 187v–188v.

56. City council deliberations, 11 May 1693, AMD B-332, fols. 373v–374r; Henri-Jules de Bourbon to mairie, 19 Dec. 1693, AMD B-466; Henri-Jules de Bourbon to Rigoley, 20 Nov. 1699, BMD Ms. 2240, no. 110.

57. *Edit du Roi*, 18; city council deliberations, 23 June 1711, AMD B-348, fols. 330v–331r. The three new lieutenants named in June 1713 were subjected to the same conditions. See the city council deliberations of 12 Aug. 1713, AMD B-351, unnumbered folios.

58. City council deliberations, 30 Dec. 1692, AMD B-333, fols. 243r–246v.

59. Henri-Jules de Bourbon to Rigoley, 18 April 1696, 3 May 1697, BMD Ms. 2239, no. 336, no. 412.

60. Nachison, "Provincial Government," 120; city council deliberations, 18 Aug. 1703, 20 June 1711, and 12 Aug. 1713 AMD B-343, fol. 28; B-345, fol.1; B-351, unnumbered folios.

61. City council deliberations, 7 and 11 Oct. 1694, 16 June 1703, and 24–28 Aug. 1714, AMD B-334, fols. 297v–301v; B-335, fols. 1r–15r; B-341, fol. 232r; B-349, fols. 539v–541v.

62. City council deliberations, 18 Aug. 1703, AMD B-343, fol. 28 (emphasis added).

63. City council deliberations, 23 June and 8 July 1710, AMD B-347, fols. 331r–332r; B-349, fol. 32v.

64. City council deliberations, 20 Aug. 1693, 9 Sept. 1694, 6 July 1695, 9 Apr. 1705, and 29 Jan. 1710, AMD B-333, fols. 63, 285r–290r; B-335, fols. 177r–179r; B-344, fols. 251r–252v; B-347, fol. 220.

65. Henri-Jules de Bourbon to Rigoley, 3 May 1697 and 20 Nov. 1699, BMD Ms. 2239, no. 414; Ms. 2240, no. 110.

66. City council deliberations, 18 June 1698, 13 June 1699, and 15 May 1700, AMD B-334, fol. 554r; B-338, fol. 277; B-339, fol. 64v.

67. City council deliberations, 23 June 1705, AMD B-345, fol. 7.

68. Nachison, "Provincial Government," 119–26, 232; city council deliberations, 9 Aug. 1714, AMD B-349, fol. 529r; Louis-Henri de Bourbon to mairie, 17 Sept. 1717, AMD B-469.

69. Mairie to Henri-Jules de Bourbon, 15 Apr. 1694 and 19 Feb. 1705; mairie to Louis-Henri de Bourbon, 27 Feb. 1714, AMD B-469.

70. Wallace, *Community and Conflict*, 197–98.

71. City council deliberations, 5 March 1694, AMD B-333, fol. 186.

72. See chap. 2. For the sake of consistency, post-1668 mayorships have been converted to annual terms.

73. City council deliberation, 14 June 1670, AMD B-308, fol. 205r; Chesne's records as conseil de la ville, AMD B-34 and B-34bis.

74. Taille rolls (1669), AMD L-248.

75. City council deliberations, 30 Dec. 1692 and 20 May 1693, AMD B-332, fols. 243r–246v, 384r–385v; *Edit du Roy*, 17–18; purchasers of municipal offices, AMD B-6bis (1694 and June 1696).

76. City council deliberations, 9 Sept. and 7 Oct. 1694, AMD B-333, fols. 285r–290r, 297v–301v.

77. Bourée, *Chancellerie*, 106–7.

78. The median for 1670–81 was 24 per year. The average for 1681–90 was 19.2, with a median of 21.

79. City council deliberations, 26 June 1669, 8 July 1672, and 26 June 1684, AMD B-308, fol. 6v; B-311, fol. 47r; B-323, fol. 23r.

80. City council deliberations, 2 Aug. 1687, AMD B-326, fol. 29.

81. Ptolomée de Dijon, *Almanach de Dijon*, 1694–1715.

82. City council deliberations, 26 June 1645, AMD B-283, fol. 44r.

83. The average term was 7.9 years, with a mean of 5 years. Prior to 1668, these figures were 3.14 and 3 years, respectively.

84. Nachison, "Provincial Government," 135, n. 7. It should be noted that the Société des Avocats tried to prevent Ravey from joining the bar in 1692, citing his unscrupulous activities as a procureur. This reputation may have been a factor in Ravey's failure to obtain a seat on the échevinage.

85. "Municipal office" refers to the posts of vicomte-mayeur, garde des évangiles, échevin, parish officer, and avocats et conseils de la ville. "Royal office" refers to positions at one of the royal law courts or fiscal offices, various permanent positions at the chambre des élus of the Estates of Burgundy, positions in the households of the royal family or governor, and the position of subdelegate of the regional intendant.

86. Bien, "Offices, Corps, and System," 95.

87. Henri Moreau, "Les subdélégues dans la generalité de Bourgogne sous l'intendant Bouchu et ses premieres successeurs," *Annales de Bourgogne* 20 (1948): 168, 184–88; Root, *Peasants and King*, 166–67.

88. Moreau, "Les subdélégues," 173.

89. Joseph Durand, "Discours prononcé à l'ouverture des audiences du Parlement de Dijon en l'année 1699," BMD Ms. 2324, fols. 84v–85r.

90. See Benedict, "French Cities," 55, n. 91; Finley-Croswhite, "Henry IV and the Towns," 141–45; Finley-Croswhite, "Absolutism and Municipal Autonomy: Henry IV and the 1602 Pancarte Revolt in Limoges," in *Society and Institutions in Early Modern France (Essays in Honor of J. Russell Major)*, ed. Mack P. Holt (Athens: University of Georgia Press, 1991), 83–92; Cassan, *Le temps*, 298–301; Parker, *La Rochelle*; Schneider, "Crown and Capitoulat," 203–8; Beik, *Absolutism and Society*, 67–68; Beik, "Louis XIV and the Cities," 75–76; Maillard, *Pouvoir municipale*, II, 157–60; Saupin, *Nantes*, 64–73; Wallace, *Communities and Conflict*, 138–41, 188; Wallace, "Civic Politics and Civic Values"; Bossenga, *The Politics of Privilege*, 20–24, 203–4; Trenard, "D'une culture régionale"; Georges Livet, "Finances municipales et souveraineté royale: le cas de la ville de Strasbourg," in *Pouvoir, ville, et société en Europe, 1650–750*, ed. Georges Vogler and Bernard Livet (Paris: Editions Ophrys, 1983), 105–23.

91. Chevalier, *Bonnes villes*, 312.

Chapter 5

1. Cited in Kelley, *Beginning of Ideology*, 203.

2. Habermas, *Structural Transformation*, 5–56, 67–73; Baker, "Defining the Public Sphere."

3. Farge, *Subversive Words*; Holt, "Culture populaire"; Beik, *Urban Protest*; Sawyer, *Printed Poison.*

4. Hanley, "Social Sites; Hanley, "The Transmission of Legal Knowledge"; Hanley, "The 'Jurisprudence of the Arrêts'"; Julie Hardwick, "Seeking Separations: Gender, Marriages and Household Economies in Early Modern France," *French Historical*

Studies 21 (1998): 157–80; Zöe Schneider, "The Village and the State: Justice and the Local Courts in Normandy, 1670–1740" (Ph.D. dissertation, Georgetown University, 1997).

5. Bouwsma, "Lawyers"; Karpik, *Les avocats*, 29–131; Kelley, "Jurisconsultus Perfectus"; Kelley, "Vera Philosophia: The Philosophical Significance of Renaissance Jurisprudence," *Journal of the History of Philosophy* 14 (1976): 267–79; Kelley, *The Foundations of Modern Historical Scholarship: Language, Law and History in the French Renaissance* (New York: Columbia University Press, 1970); Gerald Alan Greenberger, "Political Thought Under Louis XIV: The Apogee and Decline of Royal Absolutism" (Ph.D. dissertation, Brown University, 1973), chap. 5.

6. Bell, *Lawyers and Citizens*; Maza, *Private Lives*; Berlanstein, *Barristers*; Michael P. Fitzsimmons, *The Parisian Order of Barristers and the French Revolution* (Cambridge, MA: Harvard University Press, 1987).

7. Skinner, *Foundations*, vol. 2; William Church, *Constitutional Thought in Sixteenth-Century France* (Cambridge, MA: Harvard University Press, 1941); Church, *Richelieu and Reason of State* (Princeton, NJ: Princeton University Press, 1972); Etienne Thuau, *Raison d'état et pensée politique à l'époque de Richelieu* (Paris: Armand Colin, 1966); Keohane, *Philosophy and the State*, 25–82, 119–29, 220–23, 241–61, 303–7; Greenberger, "Political Thought," chaps. 2–5; Howell A. Lloyd, "Constitutionalism"; Julian H. Franklin, "Sovereignty and the Mixed Constitution: Bodin and his Critics," and J. P. Sommerville, "Absolutism and Royalism," in *The Cambridge History of Political Thought, 1450–1700*, ed. J. H. Burns and Mark Goldie (Cambridge: Cambridge University Press, 1991), 254–97, 298–328, 347–73; Adrianna E. Bakos, *Images of Kingship in Early Modern France: Louis XI in Political Thought (1560–1789)* (London: Routledge, 1997); Cosandey and Descimon, *L'absolutisme en France*, 25–105.

8. Bakos, *Images of Kingship*, 3, 178–79; Church, *Richelieu*, 32–34; Church, *Constitutional Thought*, 179, 323–24; Keohane, *Philosophy and State*, 4.

9. Bernard du Haillan, *De l'estat et succez des affaires de France* (Paris, 1571), fols. 10b, 170a. Cited in Skinner, *Foundations*, II, 272–73. See also Lloyd, "Constitutionalism," 255.

10. Pierre de Lancre, *Le livre des princes* (Paris, 1617), 423; Bernard de La Roche-Flavin, *Treze livres des parlemens de France* (Bordeaux, 1617), XIII, chap. 17, secs. 3, 9, 11–13, 23. See Church, *Richelieu*, 33, and Jacques Krynen, "A propos des *Treze livres des parlemens de France*," in *Les parlements de province: pouvoirs, justice et société (XVe–XVIIIe siècles)*, ed. Jacques Poumarède and Jack Thomas (Toulouse, FRAMESPA, 1996), 691–705; Claude Joly, True Maxims of Government," in *The Impact of Absolutism in France: National Experience Under Richelieu, Mazarin and Louis XIV*, ed. and trans. William F. Church (New York: Wiley, 1969), 47.

11. Roland Mousnier, "Comment les français voyaient la constitution au XVIIe siècle," in *La plume*, 44–46; Parker, "Sovereignty"; Cosandey and Descimon, *L'absolutisme en France*, 51–82.

12. Skinner, *Foundations*, II, 131; Jean Bacquet, *Les œuvres de Maistre Jean Bacquet . . . contenans divers traittez des droicts du domaine de la Couronne de France* (Geneva, 1625), 16.12.34, cited in Charlotte Wells, *Law and Citizenship in Early Modern France* (Baltimore: Johns Hopkins University Press, 1995), 80–81; Arlette Jouanna, *Le devoir de révolte: La noblesse française et la gestion de l'état moderne (1559–1660)* (Paris: Fayard, 1989), 9.

13. Mousnier, "Participation des gouvernés," 231.

14. Guy Coquille, *Les Oeuvres de Maistre Guy Coquille sieur de Romenay: contenant plusieurs traitez touchant les libertez de l'eglise gallicane, l'histoire de France et le droit François* (Bordeaux, 1703), I, 230.2, 277.1 and 281.2, cited in Lloyd, "Constitutionalism," 285–87.

15. Greenberger, "Lawyers," 161–62; Joly, "True Maxims," 50.

16. Bakos, *Images of Kingship*, 4; Church, *Richelieu*, 36; Church, *Constitutional Thought*, 64, 73, 334; Skinner, *Foundations*, II, 178–84, 254–67 and 284–301; Keohane, *Philosophy and the State*, chap. 2; Jean Barbey, *Être Roi: Le roi et son gouvernement en France de Clovis à Louis XVI* (Paris: Fayard, 1992), 137–52; Cosandey and Descimon, *Absolutisme en France*, chaps. 1 and 3.

17. Bodin, *Six Bookes*, I.8; Bossuet, *Politics* III.2.1–3, VI.2; Jean Domat, "The Ideal Absolute State" in Church, *The Impact of Absolutism in France*, 80–81.

18. Skinner, *Foundations*, II, 288–89; Julian Franklin, *Jean Bodin and the Rise of Absolutist Theory* (Cambridge: Cambridge University Press, 1973), 93–108; Bodin, *République*, 98, 153, 159; Bossuet, *Politics*, V, 4, 1; Domat, "Ideal Absolute State," 78.

19. Bodin, *Six Bookes*, II.2; Cardin Le Bret, *De la souveraineté du roi* (Paris, 1632), 64–65.

20. Bossuet, *Politics*, V, 4, 1.

21. Ralph E. Giesey, *The Royal Funeral Ceremony in Renaissance France* (Geneva: Droz, 1960).

22. Le Bret, *Souveraineté du roi*; Bossuet, *Politics*, III, 2; Keohane, *Philosophy and the State*, 127–28, 256.

23. Ralph E. Giesey, *The Juristic Basis of Dynastic Right to the French Throne* (Philadelphia: Transactions of the American Philosophical Association, 1961), 41–42.

24. Kelley, *Beginning of Ideology*, 182; Greenberger, "Lawyers"; Hanley, "Social Sites"; Bouwsma, "Lawyers," 309–14.

25. William F. Church, "The Decline of the French Jurists as Political Theorists, 1660–1789" *French Historical Studies* 1 (1967): 1–41.

26. Bell, *Lawyers and Citizens*; Maza, *Private Lives and Public Affairs*; Bouwsma, "Lawyers"; Hanley, "Social Sites"; Hanley, "'Jurisprudence of the Arrêts.'" The idea of avocats as "vocational intellectuals" is taken from Deyon, *Amiens*, 286.

27. Brockliss, *French Higher Education*, 292; Julia and Revel, "Étudiants et leurs études," 107–89.

28. Brockliss, *French Higher Education*, 295–96, 300–301, 320–21, 325–26.

29. Farr, "Consumers, Commerce and Craftsmen"; Bouchard, *De l'humanisme*, 104.

30. Bouchard, *De l'humanisme*, 49. See also Dewald, *Formation of a Provincial Nobility*, 39–42, 50–54.

31. Bouchard, *De l'humanisme*, 49.

32. Richard, "Quelques aspects," 144–45.

33. Malteste, *Anecdotes secrètes*, 231–32.

34. This includes several avocats received before 1595 who remained influential in the early seventeenth century.

35. Breen, "Legal Culture," chart 4.2.

36. This analysis is based on Philibert Papillon, *Bibliothèque des auteurs de Bourgogne*, 2 vols. (Dijon, 1745, reprinted Geneva: Slatkine Reprints, 1970). Compiled in

the mid-eighteenth century, Papillon's bibliography was hailed as the most complete and exhaustive work of its kind and has served as the basis for later attempts to construct systematic bibliographies of Burgundian literary production. Although I have located several works (primarily manuscripts) not mentioned in Papillon, his bibliography is largely complete, reliable, and invaluable for its information about works no longer extant. For the sake of consistency, I have not included in this sample any works not mentioned by Papillon.

37. Breen, "Legal Culture," charts 7.1 and 7.2.

38. Breen, "Legal Culture," charts 7.1 and 7.2.

39. Guillaume Raviot, *Consultation d'un avocat sur la Bulle Unigenitus; scavoir, s'il est permis d'apeller* (n.p., 1717); Papillon, *Bibliothèque*, II, 188–89. I have been unable to locate Raviot's work.

40. Rebecca Kingston has reached a similar conclusion. See her *Montesquieu and the Parlement of Bordeaux* (Geneva: Droz, 1996), 36–38.

41. Kuehn, *Law, Family, and Women*, 9, 121–26, 190–93. See also Bouwsma, "Lawyers," 316–22.

42. Giesey, *Dynastic Right*, 26.

43. Lloyd, "Constitutionalism," 257. Quentin Skinner has warned of the dangers of "the mythology of coherence," the assumption that an individual's ideas are necessarily coherent and that apparent contradictions can be resolved into a consistent system of thought. Ambiguity, inconsistency, and self-contradiction, he argues, should be treated as normal. See "Meaning and Understanding in the History of Ideas," in *Meaning and Context: Quentin Skinner and his Critics*, ed. James Tully (Princeton, NJ: Princeton University Press, 1988), 29–67.

44. André Kleinclausz, *Histoire de Bourgogne* (Paris: Hachette, 1924), 256–57; Roupnel, *Ville et campagne*, xvii–xix; Gronau-Chenillet, "Parlement de Dijon," 261–90.

45. Church, *Constitutional Thought*, 50–59, 311–23; Giesey, *Dynastic Right*, 41–42; Hanley, *Lit-de-Justice*, 331–32; Bakos, *Images of Kingship*, 116–21; Lawrence M. Bryant, "Politics, Ceremonies, and Embodiments of Majesty in Henry II's France," in *European Monarchy: Its Evolution and Practice from Roman Antiquity to Modern Times*, ed. Heinz Duchhardt, Richard A. Jackson, and David Sturdy (Stuttgart: Franz Steiner Verlag, 1992), 127–54; Cosandey and Descimon, 83–105; Michèle Fogel, *Les cérémonies de l'information dans la France du XVIe au XVIIIe siècle* (Paris: Fayard, 1989).

46. Souvert, *Avis*, 13–14.

47. AMD B-266, fols. 227v–28r (1 Feb. 1629).

48. [Pierre Malpoy], *Entrée de très haut et très puissant Prince Henry de Bourbon, Prince de Condé . . . Gouverneur et Lieutenant-Général pour Sa Majesté en Provinces de Bourgogne, Bresse et Berry, en la Ville de Dijon, le trentiesme du mois de septembre 1632* (Dijon, 1632), 10.

49. Bénigne Griguette, *Eloges des hommes illustres peints en la galerie du Palais Royal* (Dijon, 1644), 19, 43.

50. Jean Casotte, *Stances sur le progrez des armes de Monseigneur le Prince* (Dijon, 1648), 2.

51. Griguette, *Armes triomphantes*, 28–29; [Etienne Bréchillet], *Description et interpretation des portiques erigés à l'entrée de très-hault et très-puissant prince, LOUIS DE BOURBON, Prince de Condé, Premier Prince du sang, duc d'Anguien, Chasteau-Roux,*

Albret, Montmorency, &c., Gouverneur & Lieutenant General pour Sa Majesté, és Provinces de Bourgogne, Bresse, & Berry, en la Ville de Dijon le 6 Mars 1648 (Dijon, 1650), 63; Charles Fevret, *Traité de l'abus, et du vray sujet des appellations qualifiés de ce nom d'abus*, 2d ed. (Lyon, 1667), unpaginated prefatory letter.

52. Souvert, *Avis*, 39; Fevret, *Abus*, I, 102–3.

53. Souvert, *Avis*, 13–14.

54. Fevret, *Abus*, I: 58–60.

55. Griguette, *La mort de Germanic Cæsar, Tragédie* (Dijon, 1646); Jouanna, *Devoir de révolte*, 361–62.

56. Burke, "Tacitism, Scepticism and Reason of State," in *The Cambridge History of Political Thought, 1450–1700*, ed. J. H. Burns and Mark Goldie (Cambridge: Cambridge University Press, 1991), 479–98; J. H. M. Salmon, "Cicero and Tacitus in Sixteenth-Century France," in *Renaissance and Revolt: Essays in the Intellectual and Social History of Early Modern France* (Cambridge: Cambridge University Press, 1987), 27–53; Thuau, *Raison d'état*, 33–102.

57. Summing up Tiberius's reign, the second-century Roman historian Tacitus writes, "While [Tiberius] was a private citizen or holding commands under Augustus, his life was blameless; and so was his reputation. While Germanicus and Drusus still lived, he concealed his real self, cunningly affecting virtuous qualities. However, until his mother died there was good in Tiberius as well as evil. Again, as long as he favoured (or feared) Sejanus, the cruelty of Tiberius was detested, but his perversions unrevealed. Then fear vanished, and with it shame. Thereafter he expressed only his own personality–by unrestrained crime and infamy." Tacitus, *The Annals of Imperial Rome*, trans. Michael Grant (London: Penguin, 1989), 226–27.

58. Tacitus, 52–60, 104–28.

59. See, Griguette, *Germanic Caesar*, II, 1; II, 3; III, 3; IV, 1; IV, 4; V, 2.

60. Act II, scene 2, for example, opens with Sentius describing Pison as "cruel, ambitious, mercenary and insolent."

61. Griguette, *Germanic Caesar*, I, 1.

62. Griguette, *Germanic Caesar*, II, 1.

63. Griguette, *Germanic Caesar*, I, 2.

64. Griguette, *Germanic Caesar*, 1; II, 4.

65. Griguette, *Germanic Caesar*, V, 1; IV, 4.

66. Souvert, *Avis*, 25–26, 44–46; Church, *Constitutional Thought*, 313–15.

67. Pierre Guillaume, *Discours fait au Parlement de Dijon . . . le–jour du mois de May 1639. Pour Monsieur de la Mothe d'Audencourt, presenté à la charge de Lieutenant-Général pour le Roy, dans les Provinces de Bresse, Bugey, Valromey & Gex & Comté du Charrolois, sous le Gouvernement de Monseigneur le Prince* (Dijon, 1639), 1–2; Griguette, *Germanic Caesar*, IV, 1; Griguette, *Eloges des hommes illustres peints en la galerie du Palais Royal* (Dijon, 1644), 10.

68. Casotte, *Stances*, 2, 17, 25–27; Bréchillet, *Description et interpretation*, 58.

69. Defrasans's speech was reproduced in Malpoy, *Entrée*, 32; [Bénigne Pérard], *A la Bourgogne, pour l'entrée de Monseigneur le Prince dans la ville de Dijon* (np, nd), 1–3; Charles Fevret, *Harangue fait au parlement le 20 novembre 1631, sur la présentation et lecture du gouvernement de Bourgogne en faveur de Henri de Condé* (Dijon, 1631), 11–16; Griguette, *Eloges*, 7.

70. Genreau, "Journal," fols. 75r–76r.

71. Schneider, *Public Life*; Muchembled, *Culture populaire*; Benedict, "French Cities"; Lignereux, *Lyon et le roi*, 670–774. Dijonnais cultural life in the seventeenth century appears to have been conservative and relatively resistant to Parisian trends. See Bouchard, *De l'humanisme*, 316, and Augustin Jacquet, *La vie litteraire dans une ville de province sous Louis XIV* (Paris: Garnier, 1886), 227–30.

72. Pierre de Saint-Julien, *De l'origine des bourgongnons, et antiquité des estats de Bourgogne* (Paris, 1581), 642–44. Saint-Julien refers to a more detailed account by the président Desbarres. Malpoy, *Entrée*, 47–48 gave several accounts of the city's origins and ultimately endorsed the Aurelian story. Malpoy also cited a commentary by the *avocat* Jean Richard; Griguette claimed Trajan was the city's founder. See *Armes*, 5.

73. See, for example, Souvert, *Advis* (1605), 2–3; Pérard, *A la Bourgogne*, 2; Pérard, *Les voeux de la ville de Dijon à Monseigneur le Prince* (n.p., n.d.), 3; Griguette, *Armes*, 22.

74. Jean Godran des Chasans, "Mémoires sur les quatre derniers ducs de Bourgogne," BMD, Ms. 1140, fols. 8r–44r; Chassans, "Mémoires historiques concernants l'institution de l'ordre de la Toison d'Or, et la noblesse et faictes heroiques des chevaliers dudict ordre," BMD, Ms. 1140, fols. 46r–101v. Jacques-Auguste de Chevanes's "Historie de la Sainte-Chapelle de Dijon, de sa liberté, de ses prérogatives, justifiée par des titres des archives de l'église, du trésor de chartes de France et de la Chambre des Comptes de Dijon" appears to have been lost. The Sainte-Chapelle was the private chapel of the dukes of Burgundy and the original headquarters of the Order of the Golden Fleece.

75. City council deliberations, 22 Dec. 1627, AMD B-265, fols. 162r–163v.

76. Griguette, *Armes*, fol. vi r; city council deliberations, 21 and 31 Aug. 1682, AMD B-321, fols. 34v, 36r–38v. La Mare's observations are cited in Thomas, *Une Province*, 24.

77. Defrasans to mairie, 21 Apr. 1601, in Garnier, 56–57; [Etienne Bréchillet], *Dessein des arcz triomphaux erigez à l'honneur du roy, à son entrée en la ville de Dijon, le dernier de janvier, mil six cens vingt-neuf* (Dijon, 1629). City council deliberations, 18–20 Jan. 1659, AMD B-297, fols. 154r–155r.

78. Louvain Gelyot, *La brigue defaicte. A la memoire de Jean De Frasans, Escuyer, Sieur d'Orain et Terrans en partie, Advocat en Parlement, Conseiller du Roy, Vicomte Maieur de la ville et commune de Dijon . . . és années 1603 et 1604, et mort en la mesme charge le 13 du mois de janvier 1609* (Dijon, 1609), 4, 7.

79. Charles Fevret, *De la sedition arrivée en la ville de Dijon le 28 fevrier 1630, et jugement rendu par le Roy sur icelle* (Lyon, 1630), 11–12; *Harangue (1631)*, 7–8.

80. Breen, "Addressing '*La ville des dieux*,'" 354.

81. [Bréchillet], *Dessein*, 3–4.

82. [Bréchillet], *Dessein*, 6–16.

83. Kristen B. Neuschel, *Word of Honor: Interpreting Noble Culture in Sixteenth-Century France* (Ithaca, NY: Cornell University Press, 1989), 16–18, 74–102, 206–7.

84. [Malpoy], *Entrée*, 39–40, 46–50, 80.

85. [Malpoy], *Entrée*, 10–14.

86. [Malpoy], *Entrée*, 46.

87. Henri Morel, "La place de la *lex regia* dans l'histoire des idées politiques," in *Mélanges Henri Morel* (Aix-en-Provence: Presses Universitaires d'Aix-Marseille, 1989), 379–90.

88. Bréchillet, *Description et interpretation*, 15–21, 55–63, 98.

89. Bréchillet, *Description et interpretation*, 18–19, 100–105.

90. Bréchillet, *Description et interpretation*, 41–51.
91. Bréchillet, *Description et interpretation*, 44, 47.
92. Bréchillet, *Description et interpretation*, 98.
93. Griguette, *Armes*, 1–2.
94. Griguette, *Armes*, 22–23.
95. Griguette, *Armes*, 4.
96. Griguette, *Armes*.
97. Griguette, *Armes*, 45.
98. Griguette, *Armes*, 6–8, 69.
99. Clifford Geertz, "Centers, Kings, and Charisma: Reflections on the Symbolics of Power," in *Rites of Power: Symbolism, Ritual and Politics Since the Middle Ages*, ed. Sean Wilentz (Philadelphia: University of Pennsylvania Press, 1985), 13–38.
100. Neuschel, *Word of Honor*, 76–77.
101. The 1736 edition of François Bretagne's *Coutume Générale des pays et duché de Bourgogne, avec les observations de M. François Bretagne, Seigneur de Nan-sous-Thil, Conseiller au Parlement de Dijon, Celles de Me. Nicolas Perrier, Avocat, sur le premier titre, des Notes de Mes. De La Mare et Jehannin, Avocats au même Parlement, et plusieurs arrêts rendus en interpretation de quelques articles, etc.* (Dijon, 1736) opens with Philippe le Bon's preamble (pp. 1–4) and closes with his approbation (pp. 571–74) and the *procès-verbal* of the failed reformation of 1570 (pp. 575–84). Taisand reprints Philippe's approbation followed by the *procès-verbal* of 1570 at the end of his *Coutume générale*, 801–7. That Philip the Good, and not the French kings, was considered the ultimate source of the Coutume's legitimacy is evident in Jacques Baudot's dedicatory poem in Taisand's volume and A.-J.-B. Augé's dedicatory epistle at the head of Bretagne's commentary.
102. Nicholas Perrier in Bretagne, *Coutume générale*, 116–20; Pierre Taisand, *Coutume générale des pays et duché de Bourgogne avec le commentaire de Monsieur Taisand . . . dans lequel cette coutume est expliquée par le droit romain, les loix des anciens Bourgugignons, par l'Usage, le Commentaire de Monsieur de Chasseneuz, les Annotations de Monsieur Bégat, Président au Parlement de Dijon, du Sieur Avocat Despringles, & Autres. . .* (Dijon, 1698), 275, 516.
103. Saint-Julien, *De l'origine*, Introduction; Souvert, *Avis*, 9; Myriam Yardeni, "Histoire de villes, histoire des provinces et naissance d'une identité francaise au XVIe siècle," *Journal des Savants* (1993): 128–30.
104. Taisand, *Coutume générale*, 533; François Perrier, plaidoyer for the inhabitants of Boux, Salmaise, Thenissey, Bouzot, Presilly and Esbarres (9 Feb. 1679) in "Plaidoyers," no. 177, Ms., Bibliothèque du Centre Georges Chévrier; Gabriel Guillaume and Pierre Petit, *Requête* for the Estates of Burgundy, reprinted in Taisand, *Coutume générale*, 137–41.
105. Parker, "Law, Society, and State," 283.

Chapter 6

1. For a lengthier discussion, see Breen, "Legal Culture," 450–55.
2. Bouchard, *De l'humanisme*, 49.
3. La Cuisine, *Parlement de Bourgogne*, III, 86–99.

4. Richard, "Le Parlement de Bourgogne et la monarchie," 112–13; Richard, "Quelques aspects," 145–46; Hamscher, *Parlement of Paris.*

5. Hurt, *Louis XIV and the Parlements*, 23, 45–46. In contrast, the Parlement of Bordeaux was exiled for fifteen years in 1675 after a revolt over new taxes on tobacco and tin; that of Rennes was banished to Vannes for a similar duration following the Papier Timbré revolt. See Kingston, *Montesquieu*, 65, and Collins, *Classes, Estates and Order*, 227.

6. Greenberger, "Lawyers Confront Centralized Government," 165; La Cuisine, *Parlement de Bourgogne*, 121, 137; Thomas, pt. III, chap. 3. At times, such foot dragging could be moderately effective. Parlement was able to delay registration of a series of anti-Jansenist edicts first introduced by Louis in 1658 for an entire decade.

7. Richard, "Le Parlement de Bourgogne et la monarchie," 113; La Cuisine, *Parlement de Bourgogne*, III, 144–45. According to Richard, the magistrates gave the order to demonstrate that Parlement incarnated the royal majesty to the same degree as the princes of the blood.

8. See, for example, the *harangues* of St. Martin, 1666 ("La règne de la justice"), 1669 ("Le tableau du juste"), and 1677 ("De la modération et la douceur"), in La Cuisine, *Parlement de Bourgogne*, I, 173–76, 181–83, and 206–9.

9. Bouchard, *De l'humanisme*, 186–92, 278–313, 328–43. Lantin's letters are collected at the BMD, Ms. 962.

10. La Cuisine, *Parlement de Bourgogne*, III, 112–13.

11. See below, pp. 185–91.

12. Bouchard, *De l'humanisme*, 310–11.

13. Jean Bart, "Coutume et droit romain dans la doctrine bourguignonne du XVIIIe siècle," *Mémoires de la société pour l'histoire de droit et des institutions des anciens pays bourguignons, comtois et romands* 24 (1967): 141–71.

14. Bouchard, *De l'humanisme*, 310.

15. Bouchard, *De l'humanisme*, 91–101, 186–98; 273–308.

16. Bouchard, *De l'humanisme*, 96, 289.

17. J. H. M. Salmon, "Renaissance Jurists and 'Enlightened' Magistrates: Perspectives on Feudalism in Eighteenth-Century France" *French History* 8 (1994): 387–402.

18. Church, "Decline."

19. Claude des Rubys, *Sommaire explication des articles de la coustume du pays et duché de Bourgogne* (Lyon, 1580).

20. Michel Petitjean, "Le rôle des avocats dans la formation du droit coutumier bourguignon," *Revue de la société internationale pour l'histoire de la profession d'avocat* 5 (1993): 37–40; Bouhier, "Commentateurs."

21. Petitjean, "Rôle des avocats," 43–45; Bouchard, *De l'humanisme*, chap. 10; Kingston, *Montesquieu*, 36–38.

22. Perrier, *Observations*; [Joseph Durand], *Instituts au droit coutimier du duché de Bourgogne*, nouvelle edition (Dijon, 1735); Taisand, *Coutume Générale*; Jean Bouhier, *La coutume du duché de Bourgogne, enrichie de remarques de MM. Philippe de Villers, Jean des Pringles et Jean Guillaume, anciens avocats au Parlement de Dijon* (Dijon: Antoine de Fay, 1717); François Bretagne, *Coutume Générale des pays et duché de Bourgogne, avec les observations de M. François Bretagne, Seigneur de Nan-sous-Thil, Conseiller au Parlement de Dijon, Celles de Me. Nicolas Perrier, Avocat, sur le premier titre, des Notes de Mes. De La Mare et Jehannin, Avocats au même Parlement, et plusieurs arrêts rendus en interpretation de*

quelques articles, etc. (Dijon: A.-J.-B. Augé, 1736); Guillaume Raviot, ed., *Arrêts notables du parlement de Dijon, recüeillis par M. François Perrier, Substitut de M. le Procureur Général, avec les Observations sur chaque question,* 2 vols (Dijon: Augé, 1735).

23. [Durand], *Instituts au droit coutumier, Avertissement.*

24. Bretagne, *Coutume générale,* Dedicatory epistle and *Avertissement.*

25. Taisand, *Coutume générale, avertissement.*

26. Taisand, *Coutume générale,* 373–74.

27. Perrier, *Observations,* 11; Taisand, *Coutume général,* 116; Bart, "Coutume et droit romain," 148–49.

28. Jean Melenet, "Dissertation sur le rapt" (BMD Ms. 351), 197–203.

29. Greenberger, "Lawyers," 176–78, 154.

30. See, for example, the *requêtes* by Gabriel Guillaume and Pierre Petit on behalf of the Estates of Burgundy and the "Mémoire pour faire voir que le franc-aleu roturier à été établi de tout tems au Duché de Bourgogne," by the conseiller Le Belin reprinted in Taisand, *Coutume générale,* 137, 145.

31. Taisand, *Coutume générale,* dedicatory epistle and *avertissement*; [Durand] *Instituts au droit coutumier,* 1–2.

32. Bouchard, *De l'humanisme,* 504–5.

33. Greenberger, "Lawyers Confront Centralized Government," 170. Zöe Schneider has recently emphasized how customary law served as a practical restraint on royal sovereignty; see "Village and State."

34. Taisand, *Coutume générale,* 17, 471, 529; [Durand], *Institutes au droit coutumier,* 124.

35. Bouchard, *De l'humanisme,* 505.

36. Greenberger, "Political Thought," 225–27; "Edit du roi qui confirme à perpétuité tous les possesseurs des terres et héritages en Franc-Aleu, Franc-Bourgage, et Franc-Bourgeoisie dans leur franchise et liberté," (Aug. 1692) reprinted in Taisand, *Coutûme générale,* 130–31; [Durand], *Instituts au droit coutumier,* 41–42.

37. The pieces are all reproduced in Taisand, *Coutüme générale,* 130–59.

38. Greenberger, "Political Thought," 224–25; Greenberger, "Lawyers Confront Centralized Government," 169–70.

39. Fevret, *De la sédition,* 11–12.

40. Bréchillet, "Les Nopces de Bontemps," in Valcke, "Société joyeuse," III, 643–74.

41. [Bréchillet], *Description et interpretation,* 55–60.

42. Ernst H. Kantorowicz, *The King's Two Bodies: A Study in Medieval Political Thought* (Princeton, NJ: Princeton University Press, 1957), 212–23; Richard A. Jackson, *Vive le Roi! A History of the French Coronation from Charles V to Charles X* (Chapel Hill: University of North Carolina Press, 1984), 85–90; Sarah Hanley, "The Monarchic State in Early Modern France: Marital Regime Government and Male Right," in *Politics, Ideology and the Law in Early Modern Europe,* ed. Adrianna E. Bakos (Rochester, NY: University of Rochester Press, 1994), 110–12; Robert Descimon, "Les Fonctions de la métaphore du mariage politique du roi et de la république: France, XVe–XVIIIe siècles" *Annales, E. S. C.* 47 (1992): 1127–47.

43. Hanley, "The Monarchic State," 110.

44. [Durand], *Instituts au droit coutumier,* 78–79; Taisand, *Coutûme Générale,* 192, 217–18.

45. Greenberger, "Political Thought," 224–25.

46. Taisand, *Coutume générale*, 519–29; Bretagne, *Coutume générale* (1736), 7–8, 363–66. On the *droit d'aubaine*, see Wells, *Law and Citizenship*.

47. Charles Loyseau, *Traité des siegneuries* (Paris, 1608). For a fuller explanation, see Howell A. Lloyd, "The Political Thought of Charles Loyseau (1564–1627)," *European Studies Review* 11 (1981): 65–66; Keohane, *Philosophy and the State*, 126–27; Church, *Constitutional Thought*, 328–32.

48. [Durand], *Instituts au droit coutumier*, 47–48.

49. On Taisand's life and works, see Papillon, *Bibliothèque*, II, 305–8 and Bouhier, "Commentateurs," xxxix–xl. On Taisand's time in Paris, see Bouchard, *De l'humanisme*, 85–89.

50. Taisand, *Histoire du droit romain*, 76, 105–7.

51. Taisand, *Histoire du droit romain*, Dedicatory epistle, 1–2, 8.

52. Taisand, *Coutume générale*, Dedicatory epistle.

53. Taisand, *Coutume générale*, *avertissement*; Bouhier, "Commentateurs," xl.

54. Jean Bart, "Du droit bourguignon au droit français" *Annales de Bourgogne* 49 (1977): 95.

55. Taisand, *Coutume générale*, *avertissement*, 1st unnumbered page.

56. "Huitiéme Lettre dans laquelle il est prouvé par l'histoire que La Bourgogne est pais-coutumier. (Dijon, 6 Oct. 1729)," BMD Ms. 304. The "Letters" have been attributed to Guillaume Raviot. The author of the "Letters" describes himself as a senior Dijonnais avocat, and the letters themselves appear to have been written in response to a polemic by a Parisian avocat. On the "foi de Bourgogne" in the sixteenth century, see Mack P. Holt, "Burgundians into Frenchmen: Catholic Identity in Sixteenth-Century Burgundy" in *Changing Identities in Early Modern France*, ed. Michael Wolfe (Durham, NC: Duke University Press, 1997), 345–70.

57. The avocats' ideas were thus similar to those of the magistrates described by Salmon in "Renaissance Jurists."

58. Dubost, "Absolutisme et centralisation," 394–95.

59. Mousnier, "Comment," 55; Mousnier, "Participation des gouvernés," 231; Parker, "Sovereignty," 49, 71–74. On the contested concept of privilege in the eighteenth century, see Kwass, *Politics of Taxation*, and Bossenga, *Politics of Privilege*.

60. Souvert, *Avis*, 4, 25; Fevret, *Discours* (1631), 5; Fevret, *Abus*, dedicatory epistle to king. This dedication appeared only in the first edition (Dijon, 1654). On Bréchillet, see above, chap. 3.

61. Fevret, *Abus*, I, 88–89. N. Perrier, *Observations*, 53–59, followed Jean Bacquet in requiring that more stringent requirements be met to satisfy the conditions for irrevocability. One of these was monetary payment, which the city satisfied by paying 80,000 livres to Louis XIV for confirmation of its privileges, which in 1643 were characterized as being "*à titre onéreux*." See AMD B-2bis and B-3 no. 64. On the concept of *privilèges à titre onéreux*, see Mousnier, "Comment," 55 and Parker, "Sovereignty," 53–54.

62. AMD B-317, fol. 161v (11 June 1679); N. Perrier, *Observations*, 8–10.

63. City council deliberations, 11 June 1679, AMD B-317, fols. 161v–162r.

64. City council deliberations, 11 June 1679, AMD B-317, fol. 162.

65. Keohane, *Philosophy and State*, 129–33; Church, *Richelieu*; Oestreich, *Neostoicism*.

66. Keohane, *Philosophy and State*, 133–34.

67. City council deliberations, 11 June 1679, AMD, B-317, fol. 162v.

68. City council deliberations, 11 June 1679, AMD, B-317 fol. 161v.

69. Papillon, *Bibliothèque*, I, 249–50. The paucity of details concerning Gilbert's life has also been noted by Rivière, "Introduction," viii, and Tocanne, "Aspects," 213. On Gilbert's reception as an avocat, see Bourée, "La Liste des avocats," 320.

70. Talle rolls (1697), AMD L-260, lists taillables by profession. Gilbert is listed on the second page of the section titled "Advocatz en Parlement." Unlike the other years, the 1697 roll notes that Gilbert's taille was paid "*par son pensionnaire*," though it does not suggest whom this might be. For 1699 and 1710, see AMD L-261 and L-271.

71. For the tableau of 1710, see Ptolomée de Dijon, *Almanach de Dijon* (1710). Gilbert's stroke is described by Papillon, *Bibliothèque*, I, 249. The details of his burial are recorded in Papillon's notes to the front page of the Dijon manuscript of the *Histoire de Caléjava*. For this, as well as a brief discussion of Gilbert's "Projet," see Rivière, "Introduction," viii–ix.

72. Rivière, "Introduction," xxii.

73. Papillon, *Bibliothèque*, I, 249–50. On the survival of two copies of *Caléjava*, see Bouchard, *De l'humanisme*, 153, and Marc Serge Rivière, "Introduction" to Claude Gilbert, *Histoire de Caléjava, ou l'île des hommes raisonnables: Critical Edition* (Exeter: University of Exeter Press, 1990), 6–7. Gilbert's work has been reprinted twice in the last thirty years (in a facsimile edition published by the E.D.H.I.S. in Paris in 1970 and in a critical edition by Rivière, cited above. See the bibliography in Marc Serge Rivière, "Introduction," v–xxxiv. Other analyses include Bouchard, *De l'humanisme*; J. C. Davis, "Utopianism," in *Cambridge History*, ed. Burns and Goldie. 329–44; Raymond Trousson, *Voyages aux pays de nulle part: Histoire littéraire de la pensée utopique* (Brussels: Editions de l'Université de Bruxelles, 1975); Marc Serge Rivière, *Utopia in 1700: A Study of the* Histoire de Caléjava *by Claude Gilbert* (Townsville, Australia: James Cook University, 1987); Bernard Tocanne, "Aspects de la pensée libertine à la fin du XVIIe siècle, le cas de Gilbert," *XVIIe siècle* 2 (1980): 213–24; Yardeni, *Utopie et révolte*; I. O. Wade, *The Intellectual Origins of the French Enlightenment* (Princeton, NJ: Princeton University Press, 1971).

74. Gilbert, *Caléjava*, 47, 213–15, 77–79. See also Rivière, *Utopia*, 25–26, 36–38.

75. Rivière, "Introduction," xviii; Rivière, *Utopia*, 31–33, 71–73.

76. Gilbert, *Caléjava*, 138; Tocanne, "Aspects de la pensée libertine," 223; Rivière, *Utopia*, 91. On the parallels with Grotius and Pufendorf, see Rivière, *Utopia*, 114–15.

77. Rivière, *Utopia*, 15, 38–39; Rivière, *Utopia*, "Introduction," xiii–xxvi; Tocanne, "Aspects de la pensée libertine," 215; Trousson, *Voyages*, 112–17.

78. Rivière aptly sums up this view, writing, "Gilbert shows the degree of commitment to a philosophical cause which we have come to associate with the eighteenth-century *philosophes*, and his objective seems to come as close to Diderot's famous axiom—'*changer la façon commune de penser*'—as one could expect at the end of the seventeenth century." *Utopia*, 13. See also Rivière, "Introduction," xiii; Yardeni, *Utopie*, 56; and Bouchard, *De l'humanisme*, 156–57.

79. Rivière, *Utopia*, 13.

80. Among the works Gilbert cites are Cicero, *De natura deorum* et *De officiis*; Tacitus, *Annales*; Seneca, *Liber de vita beata*; and Juvenal, *Satires*. Gilbert also remarks that "we find the complete theology of Christianity in Homer" (45–46).

81. Sandoval, *Life of Charles V*; Paul Rycaut, *L'histoire de l'état présent de l'Empire Ottoman*. Gilbert also cites a work by Dericault entitled *Etat de l'Empire*. See Rivière, "Introduction," xii.

82. Gilbert's use of scriptural references clearly follows in the footsteps of Christian humanist thinkers such as Erasmus. At the end of Book X, he counsels his readers: "It is a good idea to read the passages of Scripture which are cited in this book at the same time they are cited, and even more often that which precedes and follows them. Sometimes, to understand the vulgate, one must turn to the Greek" (250). On Saint Thomas and the Council of Trent, see pp. 208 and 259–60. In addition to his citing Cicero and Seneca and Lucretius, see 225–26 and 327.

83. Gilbert, *Caléjava*, 25; Rivière, *Utopia*, 34.

84. Rivière, "Introduction," xxix.

85. Gilbert, *Caléjava*, 168–69.

86. Gilbert, *Caléjava*, 320–21. On the idea of the "perfect magistrate," see Jonathan Dewald, "The 'Perfect Magistrate': Parlementaires and Crime in Sixteenth Century Rouen," *Archive for Reformation History* 67 (1976): 284–300.

87. Tocanne, "Aspects de la pensée libertine," 224.

88. Tocanne, "Aspects de la pensée libertine," 325–27.

89. Tocanne, "Aspects de la pensée libertine," 14–17. See also Rivière, "Introduction," xix–xx.

90. Aware of the Europeans' treatment of their colonies in the Americas, Gilbert says, the Caléjavans refuse to reveal the exact location of their island (pp. 27–28). Nevertheless, the Baltic setting of the book's early chapters was highly unusual, as most late-seventeenth- and early eighteenth-century "fantastic voyages" were set in the Southern Hemisphere, often near Tierra del Fuego. See Wade, *Intellectual Origins*, 376.

91. Gilbert, *Caléjava*, 3–13, 108.

92. Gilbert, *Caléjava*, 118–20.

93. Gilbert, *Caléjava*, 29.

94. Gilbert, *Caléjava*, 32.

95. Gilbert, *Caléjava*, 251–305.

96. Gilbert, *Caléjava*, 28.

97. Gilbert, *Caléjava*, 69.

98. Gilbert, *Caléjava*, 70.

99. Bossuet, V, 4, 1; Domat, "The Ideal Absolute State," 78.

100. On the contrast between the "philosopher-jurist" and the Platonic "philosopher-king," see Kelley, "Jurisconsultus Perfectus," 90.

101. Beik, *Absolutism and Society*, 333–34; Parker, *Class and State*, 110, 192–93.

102. Norbert Elias, *The Court Society*, trans. Edmund Jephcott (New York: Pantheon, 1983); Solnon, *La cour*; Emmanuel Le Roy Ladurie and Jean-François Fitou, *Saint-Simon and the Court of Louis XIV*, trans. Arthur Goldhammer (Chicago: University of Chicago Press, 2001); Olivier Chaline, "The Valois and Bourbon Courts, c. 1515–1750," in *The Princely Courts of Europe: Ritual, Politics and Culture Under the* Ancien Régime *1500–1750*, ed. John Adamson (London: Weidenfeld and Nicolson, 1999), 67–93.

103. Gilbert, *Caléjava*, 311–17. On the parallel with Descartes' *Discourse*, see Bouchard, *De l'humanisme*, 156–57.

104. Gilbert, *Caléjava*, 317–24.

105. Gilbert, *Caléjava*, 325–27.

106. This number is derived from combining the works listed by Wade, *Intellectual Origins*, 374 and Yardeni, *Utopie*, 17–18, and is not intended to be exhaustive. In contrast, Trousson, *Voyages*, 91, has identified only one utopian work of a similar bent for the first half of the seventeenth century in France, the anonymous *Histoire du grand et admirable royaume d'Antangil, incogneu jusques à présent à tous historiens et cosmographes* (Saumur, 1616).

107. Hazard, *Crise*, 15–36; Keohane, *Philosophy and State*, 318–19; Bouchard, *De l'humanisme*, 143–61.

108. Keohane, *Philosophy and State*, 318–21; Yardeni, *Utopie*; Trousson, *Voyages*, 103. See also Davis, "Utopianism," 332–34; Rivière, "Introduction," xi–xiv, xxvii.

109. Yardeni, *Utopie*, 11–12.

110. Yardeni, *Utopie* 33.

111. François de Fénélon, *Telemachus, Son of Ulysses*, ed. and trans. Patrick Riley (Cambridge: Cambridge University Press, 1994). My analysis is based largely on Keohane, *Philosophy and State*, 335–38. See also Wade, *Intellectual Origins*, 382–83; Yardeni, *Utopie*, 97–98.

112. Trousson, *Voyages*, 101.

113. See Introduction, n. 27.

114. Trousson, *Voyages*, 109–10; Keohane, *Philosophy and State*, 318–21; Wade, *Intellectual Origins*, 379–81. On the "Renaissance Monarchy," see Claude de Seyssel, *The Monarchy of France* (1519), trans. J. H. Hexter, ed. Donald R. Kelley (New Haven, CT: Yale University Press, 1981), and Major, *From Renaissance Monarchy*. Other utopists, such as Tyssot de Passot, held similar views. In the *Voyages et avantures de Jacques Massé*, for example, the protagonist discovers a land where the king is subject to the laws and the notion of divine right is unknown. See Trousson, *Voyages*, 113–14.

115. Trousson, *Voyages*, 105–8; Wade, *Intellectual Origins*, 376–79.

116. Trousson, *Voyages*, 111–12.

117. Tocanne, "Aspects de la pensée libertine," 214–23; Trousson, *Voyages*, 112–13, 117; Wade, *Intellectual Origins*, 383. Even Rivière, who parts company with the others by devoting considerable atttention to Gilbert's social and political views, writes, "It is astonishing to see the place that religious questions occupy in the *dijonnais* avocat's utopian novel." "Introduction," xix.

118. Others who support this view include Bouchard and Rivière. Bouchard's discussion of Gilbert, however, is rather summary, and Rivière's erroneous claim that Gilbert was a magistrate at the Parlement of Dijon leads him to underestimate the radical nature of Gilbert's utopia. See Bouchard, *De l'humanisme*, 153–57; Rivière, "Introduction," xiv, xxvii–xxviii; Rivière, *Utopia*, chap. 4. For Rivière's misidentification of Gilbert as a parlementaire, see "Introduction," xxvii, and *Utopia*, 3–4.

119. Yardeni, *Utopie*, 65–68. Rivière, "Introduction," xiv, also notes that Gilbert's interest in social and political reform was much more pronounced than in the utopias of Foigny, Veiras, and Tyssot de Patot.

120. Keohane, *Philosophy and State*, 258–59.

121. Gilbert, *Caléjava*, 41–70.

122. Gilbert, *Caléjava*, 262–63, 314–17. According to Davis, "Utopianism," 342, rejection of Divine Right theory in favor of human-centered theories of political legitimacy was common among late-seventeenth- and early eighteenth-century utopists.

123. Gilbert, *Caléjava*, 118, 69–70.

124. Gilbert, *Caléjava*, 138.

125. Gilbert, *Caléjava*, 69–71. The only distinguishing characteristic of the Glebirs' residence is that it is capable of housing eight hundred to nine hundred people. Many of the book's dialogues take place during the Avaïte's voyage to report the results of his trip to the Glebirs.

126. Farr, *Authority and Sexuality*; Hanley, "Engendering the State"; Hanley, "The Monarchic State"; Hanley, "Social Sites of Political Practice"; Maza, *Private Lives.*

127. Gilbert, *Caléjava*, 122–25; Rivière, "Introduction," xxviii; Rivière, *Utopia*, 127–30. For early modern attitudes toward divorce in France, see Farr, *Authority and Sexuality*, 23–26; Hanley, "Engendering the State," 13–14; Hanley, "Social Sites," 37–52; Maza, *Private Lives*, 263–311.

128. Gilbert, *Caléjava*, 128–29. See also Rivière, "Introduction," xxviii; Rivière, *Utopia*, 121–27.

129. Karpik, *Les Avocats*, 116–17.

130. Kingston, *Montesquieu*, 21.

131. See, in particular, Habermas, *Structural Transformation*, 10–11.

Conclusion

1. Smith, *Culture of Merit*, 263–67; Nachison, "Provincial Government," 297–98; Kwass, *Privilege and Politics*, chap. 3; Collins, *State*, 142–46; David Kammerling Smith, "Learning Politics: The Nîmes Hosiery Guild and the Statutes Controversy of 1706–12," *French Historical Studies* 22 (1999): 493–533; Smith, "Structuring Politics in Early Eighteenth-Century France: The Political Innovations of the French Council of Commerce," *Journal of Modern History* 74 (2002): 490–537.

2. See above, pp. 126–27.

3. City council deliberations, 23 June 1705, AMD B-345, fol. 7.

4. Etienne Baudinet, Jean-Pierre Bureteur, and Claude Marlot served for fourteen, nineteen, and thirteen years respectively. Philippe Baudinot, who was mayor from 1729 to 1731, died in office, as did Marlot. Bureteur was removed from office for his role in the Montmuzard affair analyzed below.

5. Bureteur's election was held on 9 April 1731; Marlot's election was held on 27 May 1750. See AMD B-366, fols. 1r–10v; B-384, fols. 72r–77r.

6. City council deliberations, 20 June 1729 and 27 May 1750, AMD B-365, fols. 1r–10r; B-384, fols. 72r–77r. Many of those present at eighteenth-century elections were members of either the municipality or the civic militia. In Marlot's election, for instance, personnel of the mairie cast 46 of the 168 votes.

7. City council deliberations, 22 June 1737, AMD B-371, fol. 78.

8. Ligou, "De Louis XIV," 169, claims that this division was established by the arrêt of 20 April 1668. I find no evidence of this in the arrêt. Many échevinages did not follow this pattern until roughly 1730, when it appears to have become common.

9. Four new échevins were named in 1724. Two were named in 1726, 1731, 1739 and 1741. Only one new échevin was named in 1734 and 1735, and the entire city council was continued in 1744. City council deliberations, 21 June 1724, 22 June 1726, 23 June 1731, 23 June 1734, 23 June 1735, 23 June 1739, 23 June 1741,

and 23 June 1744, AMD B-362, fols. 193v–194v; B-363, fols, 160r–161v; B-366, fols. 93r–94v; B-368, fol. 86v; B-369, fol. 94v; B-373, fols. 81v–82r; B-375, fols. 90v–91r; B-378, fol. 60v.

10. Circular letter, 5 Jan. 1736, BMD Ms. 2243.

11. Circular letter, 5 Jan. 1736, BMD Ms. 2243. Although Dijon was not included in the register, it seems highly unlikely that similar records were not kept for Burgundy's capital. If anything, the Condés were probably better informed about potential officeholders in Dijon than they were about those in the region's smaller and remoter towns.

12. See, for instance, Montigny to mairie, 16 June 1728, 15 June 1734, and 16 June 1737, AMD B-469.

13. City council deliberations, 14 July and 11 Aug. 1740, AMD B-374, fols. 101v–102r, 120.

14. Condé to mairie, 17 Sept. 1717, AMD B-469; Condé to mairie, 29 May 1730, AMD B-466; city council deliberations, 15 May 1737, B-371, fol. 60.

15. City council deliberations, 27 Apr. 1737, AMD B-371, fol. 51.

16. In 1731, for instance, the mairie complained that sieur Burée, the captain of St.-Michel Parish, had failed to provide the necessary musical instruments and to march at the head of his parish at the annual Sainte Hostie procession. After he insulted the city magistrates, the mairie complained to Condé, who removed him from office. Five years later, Condé removed the ensign of St.-Pierre Parish from office on the mairie's complaint after he ordered the nocturnal guet to arrest a girl "contre tout règle." See the city council deliberations of 20 Aug. 1731 and 29 Dec. 1736, AMD B-361, fols. 108r–109v and B-371, fol. 224v.

17. City council deliberations, 25 Sept. 1737 and 29 May 1743, AMD B-371, fols 121v–122v; B-377, fols. 54r–55r.

18. See chap. 1, n. 30. The avocats Hervy, Devoyo, and Fromageot, for instance, all served more than fifteen consecutive years as lieutenants. Examples of the new process for naming lieutenants can be see in the deliberations of 23 Dec. 1722 and 2 Aug. 1753, AMD B-361, fol. 287v and B-369, fol. 127r.

19. In 1722, for instance, Jacques Varenne, the son of the retiring conseil Claude Varenne, was named to the post in his father's place. When the apothecary Petit resigned as captain of St.-Jean Parish three years later, his son was named ensign of St.-Jean after the two other parish officers were promoted. City council deliberations, 8 Aug. 1722 and 14 Apr. 1725, AMD B-361, fol. 250; B-363, fol. 31v.

20. City council deliberations, 27 May, 11 July 1722, and 5 Jan. 1737, AMD B-361, fols. 226, 242v; B-371, fol. 1v. In 1731, the mairie insisted that the procureur-fiscal of the Justice of St. Bénigne remove his seals from a house at the moulin du Chêvre morte on the grounds that it fell under the city's high, medium, and low justice rights. City council deliberations, 8 Aug. 1731, AMD B-366, fols. 159r–160v.

21. City council deliberations, 21 May and 16 Sept. 1727, AMD B-364, fols. 49, 105v–107r.

22. City council deliberations, 25 June 1729 and 13 Apr. 1731, AMD B-365, fols. 17r–18r; B-366, fols. 16v–18v.

23. City council deliberations, 17 and 20 Feb. 1723, AMD B-362, fols. 18r, 20v–21r; mairie to Intendant de La Briffe, 1727, AN G^7 166–70, no. 281.

24. City council deliberations, 4 July 1734, AMD B-368, fol. 108.

25. La Briffe to Controller-General, AN G^7 166–70, no. 183, no. 187, no. 202, no. 213, 7 Aug.–14 Sept. 1721; city council deliberations, 27 Aug. 1721, AMD B-361, fols. 114v–115v.

26. City council deliberations, 2 June 1731, 17–19 Dec. 1741, 14 Aug. 1744, and 22 May 1748, AMD B-366, fols. 67r–68v; B-375, fol. 163; B-378, fol. 83v; B-382, fol. 45r.

27. City council deliberations, 26 Nov. 1722, 29 Dec. 1731, 19 July 1736, and 22 Nov. 1743, AMD B-361, fol. 278r; B-366, fol. 264r; B-370, fols. 106r–107v; B-377, fol. 121v.

28. City council deliberations, 3 Feb., 14 and 23 June, and 24 Nov. 1731, AMD B-365, fols. 414v–420v; B-366, fols. 78r–79r, 94v–95v, 234r–240v.

29. City council deliberations, 6 Feb. and 7 Aug. 1723, 5 Jan. 1724, 30 Sept. 1720, 30 Mar. 1725, 4 June 1732, and 14 July 1736, AMD B-362, fols. 14, 95r, 141r; B-359, fol. 299r; B-362, fols. 25v–27v; B-367, fol. 90r; B-370, fol. 101.

30. Collins, *State*, 144–45, 241–42.

31. City council deliberations, 12 Mar. 1740, AMD B-374, fol. 33v. According to Julian Swann, St.-Florentin also supervised the Estates of Burgundy and until his death in 1775, strengthened central supervision of that body as well. See *Provincial Power*, 234.

32. The one exception appears to have been the urban militia, whose members were named by St.-Aignan and not St.-Florentin.

33. City council deliberations, 10 May 1741, AMD B-375, fol. 66v.

34. City council deliberations, 28 Nov. 1744, AMD B-378, fol. 117. There is no evidence that St.-Florentin actually consulted with the king, and it seems unlikely that he would have done so. Nonetheless, the rhetorical shift is significant.

35. City council deliberations, 10 May 1740 and 22 June 1743, AMD B-374, fols 62r–63r; B-377, fols. 68r–69r.

36. City council deliberation, 9 May 1742, AMD B-376, fol. 56. On the cultural significance of the "sovereign's gaze," see Smith, "'Our Sovereign's Gaze.'"

37. [Jean-Baptiste Petitot], *Réponse des vicomte-mayeur et échevins de la ville et commune de Dijon au quatrième mémoire de M. Fyot de la Marche, premier président du Parlement de Dijon, sur son projet de la sous-inféodation de Montmusart, la Motte St. Médard et dependances, avec attribution de toute Justice Haute, Moyenne and Basse* (Dijon, 1749). All references are to the edition preserved in BMD Ms. 1992. As the mairie noted in the *Réponse* (fol. 82r), it had already granted three earlier requests by Fyot de la Marche concerning Montmuzard, including an exchange of lands in the area. See the deliberations of 2 Apr. 1749, AMD B-383, fol. 42r.

38. Ernest-Léon Lory, *Une page d'histoire municipale dijonnaise* (Dijon: J. Marchand, 1869), 4–5. The summary of the affair that follows relies considerably on Lory's account, as well on the *Réponse* and the municipal deliberations for 1749–50.

39. Fyot claimed that the territory in question consisted of 300 arpents. The mairie objected that *dijonnais arpents* were much larger than those of Paris and that Fyot's earlier requests had also referred to "autres heritages." The mairie also claimed that Fyot's proposal would create problems for those who pastured their animals in the lands outside the city and the inhabitants of the nearly village of St.-Apollonaire. "Troisième Mémoire" and "Quatrième Mémoire" in Lory, *Page d'histoire municipale*, 134–35, 156–57; [Jean-Baptiste Petitot], *Moyens des vicomte-mayeur et échevins de la ville et commune de Dijon contre le projet de M. Fyot de la Marche, Premier Président du Parlement*

de Dijon, tendant à la sous-inféodation de Montmusart, la Motte St Médard et dépendances; avec attribution de toute justice, haute, moyenne and basse (Dijon, 1749), fols. 96v–97r, 102. The *Moyens* is preserved in BMD Ms. 1992. All references are to this edition.

40. Lory, *Page d'histoire municipale*, 3, 6.

41. *Réponse*, fol. 83r.

42. Lory, *Page d'histoire municipale*, 10–11.

43. "Quatrième mémoire" in Lory, *Page d'histoire municipale*, 168–70.

44. Bureteur recused himself from deliberations concerning Montmuzard in January 1750 as a relative of Fyot de Marché. AMD B-384, fol. 2r (7 Jan. 1750). Fyot's "Quatrième mémoire" also observes that the mayor had remained neutral throughout the affair. Lory, *Page d'histoire municipale*, 166–69.

45. The "Quatrième Mémoire," 168–69, describes Guyton as the leader of a cabal against Fyot at the mairie. The *Réponse* describes in detail the improprieties in Guyton's and the syndics' efforts to have the plan ratified.

46. Courteille to mairie, 17 May 1749, in Lory, *Page d'histoire municipale*, 173–74.

47. Lory, *Page d'histoire municipale*, 18–19; *Réponse*, fol. 83v.

48. Cocquard was a member of the literary society of the parlementary president Richard de Ruffey, which included a number of the city's leading intellectual figures. See Works of the Society of Richard de Ruffey, BMD Ms. 1597.

49. Lory, *Page d'histoire municipale*, 23–25.

50. St.-Florentin to Bureteur, 25 May 1749, in Lory, *Page d'histoire municipale*, 178–79.

51. Lory, *Page d'histoire municipale*, 33–38; city council deliberations, 17, 23 July 1749, AMD B-383, fols. 90, 94r–95r.

52. [François-Bernard Cocquard], "Observations anonymes sur la proposition de M. le premier president du Parlement de Dijon, concernant une érection en fief avec toute justice," in Lory, *Page d'histoire municipale*, 114–30.

53. "Troisième mémoire de M. le premier président, ou, reflexions sur l'Anonyme," and "Quatrième Mémoire de M. Delamarche, premier president du Parlement de Bourgogne," in Lory, *Page d'histoire municipale*, 132–72.

54. Lory, *Page d'histoire municipale*, 64–65.

55. Bell, *Lawyers and Citizens*; Maza, *Private Lives and Public Affairs.*

56. City council deliberation, 18 Oct. 1749, AMD B-383, fols. 130r–132r.

57. *Réponse*, fols. 83r–86v.

58. *Réponse*, fols. 84r–85r, 91v.

59. *Réponse*, fols. 88r, 89v.

60. *Moyens*, fol. 96r.

61. *Moyens*, fol. 97r.

62. *Moyens*, fols. 98r–102r.

63. Lory, *Page d'histoire municipale*, 64–79. The "effacement" of the registers consisted of drawing an "X" through the offending deliberations, accompanied by a marginal note stating that it had been suppressed by an arrêt of the royal council. The actual contents of the deliberations in question remain easily legible.

64. *Réponse*, fol. 85r; St.-Florentin to mairie, 27 Oct. 1749, in Lory, *Page d'histoire municipale*, 195–96.

65. Lory, *Page d'histoire municipale*, 58–59.

66. Lory, *Page d'histoire municipale*, 87–93.

67. *Réponse*, fols. 93v–94r.

68. Christopher Brooks, "Professions, Ideology and the Middling Sort in the Late Sixteenth and Seventeenth Centuries," in *The Middling Sort of People: Culture, Society and Politics in England, 1550–1800*, ed. Jonathan Barry and Christopher Brooks (New York: St. Martin's, 1994), 130–31; Hindle, *State and Social Change*, 5–6; Braddick, *State-Formation*, esp. chap. 4.

69. See, for instance, Cynthia Herrup, *The Common Peace: Participation and the Criminal Law in Seventeenth-Century England* (Cambridge: Cambridge University Press, 1987); Keith Wrightson, *Poverty and Piety in an English Village: Terling, 1525–1700*, 2d ed. (New York: Oxford University Press, 1995); Hindle, *State and Social Change*; Braddick, *State-Formation*.

70. Guillaume Davot, "Commentary on Loisel's *Instituts Coutumiers*," BMD Ms. 291, pp. 1–2. According to a note on the inside front page of the volume, the manuscript consisted of Davot's notes for his lectures on French law at the University of Dijon.

Bibliography

I. Archival Sources

A. Archives Nationales, Paris

Series G^7 no. 156–70, Correspondence, Intendants of Burgundy and Controllers-General (1678–1740).

Series V^6 no. 368, no. 385, no. 538, no. 540, no. 546, Conseil Privé du Roi (May–June 1658) (June 1659) (Apr.–Dec. 1668).

B. Archives Condé, Chantilly

Series M and N, Henri II de Bourbon, Correspondence.

Series P and T, Louis II de Bourbon, Correspondence.

C. Archives Départementales de la Côte-d'Or

BII 356, Mayoral Court of Dijon, Inventaires après décès.

C 3415, Estates of Burgundy, Avocats et Conseils de la Province (1614–1712).

C 3474, Estates-Général of 1614, Payment Receipts for Deputies for the Third Estate of Burgundy.

C 3511, Estates of Burgundy: Municipal Offices, Mayors, Special Affairs (1679–1784).

E 100, Marriage contracts, J. Blanot and Marguerite de Frasans (1609); Charles Blanot and Françoise Manin (1634). Testament of Jean Blanot, avocat au Parlement (1651).

E 356, Marriage contract, Jacob Chesne and Anne Parize (1613). Catalogue of books belonging to Jean Casotte, avocat à la cour (17th century).

E 675, Marriage contracts, Etienne Deslandes and Bernarde Bouchard (1599); Bernard Deslandes and Suzanne Berbis (1642).

E 678, Marriage contract, Etienne Devoyo and Marguerite Delettre (1677).

E 679, Genealogy of the Devoyo family.

E 922, Constitution of 50 livres of rente by Pierre Guillaume, avocat, and others, in favor of Charles-Bénigne de Thésut, Conseiller au Parlement (1644).

E 933, Contrat de reception de Marie Jachiet, daughter of Nicolas Jachiet, into the Ursuline convent of Dijon (1621).

E 1033, Marriage contract, J.-B. Joly and Anne Le Belin (1681).

E 1346, Marriage contract, Donation mutuelle between François Malteste and Marie Arviset (1642).

E 1351, Genealogical Tables for the Manin family.

E 1435, Marriage contracts, Blaise Parise and Bénigne Monin (1675).
E 1609, Genealogy of the De Requeleyne family.
E 2036, Marriage contracts, Claude Dubois and Marie Soyrot (1626); Benigne Soyrot and Claude Delettre (1636). Testament of Gabriel Soyrot, avocat au Parlement (1634).
E 2126, Marriage contract, Pierre de Villers and Jeanne Chisseret (1603).
E 2166bis–E 2166(5), Recueil de généalogies de familles bourguignonnes provenant de la collection de M. Vailliant de Meixmoron, antiquaire à Dijon.
4E2 733, Marriage contract, Joseph Leboeuf and Jeanne Fleutelot (1642).
4E2 791, Marriage contracts, Claude Bourrelier and Anne Davignon (1662); Guillaume Magnien and Catherine Papillon (1664).
4E2 1963, Marriage contract, Abraham Caillet and Marie-Therèse Parissot (1668).
1F 239, Jean Bouhier, "Livre IV: Des Avocats."
1F 250, Excerpts of the Registers of the Company of St. Yves (1678–1763).
32F 899–79, Papers of Philibert de La Mare, avocat au Parlement de Dijon.
32F 1028–1556, Papers of the Tisserand family.
32F 1557–1743, Papers of the Morelet family.

D. Archives Municipales de Dijon

B 3, Privileges of the City of Dijon (1516–1781).
B 6–6bis, Sale of Municipal Offices.
B 11–12, Vicomtes-Mayeurs, Privileges, Ennoblements, and Rights (1432–1773).
B 16, Vicomte-Mayeurs, dispute with Bailliage (1626).
B 17, Nominations of Vicomte-Mayeurs by Henri-Jules and Louis-Henri de Bourbon (1681 and 1711).
B 18, Gardes des évangiles.
B 20–20bis, échevins.
B 30–37bis, Avocats et Conseils de la Ville (1604–1740).
B 39, Assemblies of Notables.
B 75, Deputy to Royal Court, Instructions to seek confirmation of privileges and promises made following city's surrender (1595); precedence debates among échevins; formularies for municipal officials' oaths of office.
B 80, Precedence lawsuit between avocats and échevins (1633).
B 80–80bis, Echevins deputized to Estates of Burgundy, payments (1631–1718).
B 81, Parlementary arrêt giving vicomte-mayeur status just behind the lieutenant-général au Bailliage (1643); precedence lawsuit at Parlement between conseils de la ville and other members of the municipal government (1648–49).
B 119, Charters, edicts, letters patent, and arrêts of royal council, Parlement, and other sovereign courts concerning mairie.
B 236–384, Registers of city council deliberations (1598–1750).
B 429, Summary of important city council deliberations (1594–1789).
B 460–477, Correspondence, mairie de Dijon with governors, lieutenants-généraux, and intendants of Burgundy.
C 33, Lieutenants de la Mairie de Dijon.
H 7–8, Milice bourgeoise officers (1605–1713).
H 9, Milice bourgoise officers, deliberations (1579–1730).

I 119. Seditions.
L 213–274, Taille rolls (1601–1720).
M 184–223, Maire de Dijon, accounts (1629–50).

E. Bibliothèque Municipale de Dijon

Ms. 291, Guillaume Davot, "Commentaries on Loisel's *Instituts Coutumiers.*"
Ms. 299, Jean Melenet, "Répetoire alphabétique de droit."
Ms. 304, "Lettres pour la question de sçavoir si la Bourgogne est pais coustumier."
Ms. 300, Jean Melenet, "Institutes au droit coustumier de Bourgogne."
Ms. 306, Chartes des privilèges, franchises et libertés des habitans et commune de Dijon.
Ms. 309, Recueil d'arrêts et règlements du Parlement de Dijon concernant l'élection des maires, échevins et autres officiers municipaux des villes de son ressort.
Ms. 311, Jean Melenet, "Recueil des arrêts du Parlement de Dijon."
Ms. 346, "Recueil des harangues et mercuriales prononcés par des gens du roi pour des rentrées de la Cour."
Ms. 351, Jean Melenet, "Dissertation sur le rapt" and "Traité de l'adultère."
Mss. 543–45, Pierre Taisand, Letters (1665–68).
Ms. 538, Pierre Taisand, "Recueil de pièces historiques, imprimées et manuscrits, prose et vers. Pièces divers sur les événements du regne de Louis XIV, dont plusieurs adressées à M. Moreau, avocat-général de Chambre des Comptes à Dijon."
Mss. 748, Gaudelet (auditeur en la Chambre des Comptes de Dijon), "Journal des choses arrivées à Dijon depuis l'année 1650 jusqu'en l'année 1669."
Ms. 755, Tableau des officiers de la Chambre des Comptes de Dijon, suivant l'ordre de création des officiers et l'état des finances, gages et augmentation des gages auxdits officiers.
Mss. 766–67, Recueil des arrêts du Parlement de Bourgogne.
Ms. 774, Registers of the Parlement of Burgundy, excerpts.
Ms. 911, Recueil des mémoires historiques concernant La Bourgogne, et Dijon en particulier (15th–18th centuries).
Ms. 933, Nicolas Perrier, "Recueil d'arrêts du Parlement de Dijon," 3 vols + table.
Ms. 973, Claude Gilbert, "Projet d'un réligion raisonnable."
Ms. 974, Recueil des pièces imprimées et manuscrits concernant la ville de Dijon (14th–19th centuries).
Ms. 994, Pièces historiques relatives à Dijon et à son administration (17th–18th centuries)
Ms. 1011, Pierre Genreau, "Journal et registre domestique d'un procureur au Parlement (1614–1669)."
Ms. 1139, Recueil historique, sedition of 28 Feb. 1630 (Lanturelu).
Ms. 1140, Jean Godran des Chasans, "Mémoires dur les quatre derniers ducs de Bourgogne," and "Mémoires historiques concernants l'institution de l'ordre de la Toison d'Or, et la noblesse et faictes heroiques des chevaliers dudict ordre."
Ms. 1283, "Extraits des registres de la chambre de ville concernant les charges des capitaines, lieutenants, et enseignes des paroisses."
Ms. 1597, Literary Society of Richard de Ruffey.

Ms. 1611, André Chenevet, "Annales de la ville de Dijon, ou Mémoires pour servir à l'histoire civile et ecclesiastique de la ville et banlieue de Dijon" (18th century).
Ms. 1992, Pieces Concerning the Dispute Between the Mairie de Dijon and Fyot de La Marche over the subfeudation of Montmusard (1749–50).
Mss. 2241–42, Jean Melenet, "Coutumes générales du duché de Bourgogne, comté de Charollois et terres d'outre Saône qui n'usent de droit écrit."
Mss. 2239–40, Correspondence, Princes of Condé and Rigoley family (1662–1772).
Ms. 2324, Attestations given by Parlement (1656–1700); Certificats d'usage given by avocats (1667–1739); Excerpts of the registers of the Company of St.-Yves (1655–1717); Joseph Durand, "Discours et harangues" (1680–1709).
Ms. 2941, Paul Court, Translations of Infanterie dijonnoise pieces.
Ms. 3213, Receuil des pieces sur la mairie de Dijon.

F. Bibliothèque du Centre Georges Chevrier pour l'Histoire Bourgogne du Moyen-Age à l'Époque Contemporaine

François Perrier, "Plaidoyers" (ms. late seventeenth or early eighteenth century).

II. Printed Works by Dijon's Avocats

Bannelier, Jean. "Notes." In *Traités sur diverses matières de droit françois,* edited by Gabriel Davot. Dijon, 1751.
[Bréchillet, Etienne]. *Dessein des arcz triomphaux erigez à l'honneur du roy, à son entrée en la ville de Dijon, le dernier de janvier, mil six cens vingt-neuf.* Dijon, 1629.
[——]. *Description et interpretation des portiques erigés à l'entrée de très hault et très puissant prince, Louis de Bourbon, Prince de Condé . . . en la ville de Dijon, le 6 mars 1648.* Dijon, 1650.
[——]. *Le chariot des déities à l'honneur de M. le Prince.* Dijon, 1632.
[——]. "Les nopces de bontems avec la Bourgogne (1636)." In *Théâtre de l'Infanterie dijonnoise,* edited by Joachim Durandeau, 22–49. Dijon: Darantière, 1887.
[——, & Pérard, Bénigne]. "Le retour de bontems, dédié à M. le Prince (1632)." In *Théâtre de l'Infanterie dijonnoise,* edited by Joachim Durandeau, 1–70. Dijon: Darantière, 1887.
Casotte, Jean. *Stances sur le progrez des armes de Monseigneur le Prince.* Dijon, 1648.
Chevannes, Nicolas de. *Mausolée dressé à la mémoire de M. César-Auguste Bellegarde, Baron de Termes.* Lyon, 1621.
[Cocquard, François-Bernard]. *Lettres ou dissertations où l'on fait voir que la profession d'avocat est la plus belle de toutes les professions, et où l'on examine si les juges qui président aux audiences peuvent legitement interrompre les avocats lorsqu'ils plaident.* London [Dijon], 1733.
Davot, Gabriel. *Traités sur diverses matières de droit français.* 3 vols. Dijon, 1751.
[Durand, Joseph]. *Institutes au droit coutumier du duché de Bourgogne.* Nouvelle édition. Dijon, 1697.
Fevret, Charles. *De claris fori Burgundici oratoribus dialogus.* Dijon, 1654.
——. *De la sedition arrivée en la ville de Dijon le 28 fevrier 1630, et jugement rendu par le Roy sur icelle.* Lyon, 1630.
——. *Harangue faite au parlement le 20 novembre 1631, sur la présentation et lecture du gouvernement de Bourgogne en faveur de Henri de Condé.* Dijon, 1631.

———. *Harangue faite au parlement de Dijon, le 11 mars 1647, à la présentation des lettres du gouvernement de Bourgogne en faveur de Louis de Condé.* Dijon, 1647.

———. *Harangue faite au parlement en 1660 sur la présentation et lecture des lettres du gouvernment de Bourgogne en faveur de Louis de Condé.* Dijon, 1660.

———. *Traité de l'abus, et du vray sujet des appellations qualifiés de ce nom d'abus.* 2d ed. Lyon, 1667.

Gelyot, Louvain. *La brigue defaicte. A la memoire de Jean De Frasans, escuyer, sieur d'Orain et Terrans en partie, advocat en parlement, conseiller du roy, vicomte maieur de la ville et commune de Dijon . . . és années 1603 et 1604, et mort en la mesme charge le 13 du mois de janvier 1609.* Dijon, 1609.

[Gilbert, Claude]. *L'histoire de Caléjava, ou l'isle des hommes raisonnables. Avec le paralelle de leur morale et du Christianisme.* N.p. [Dijon], n.d. [1700].

Griguette, Bénigne. *Éloges des hommes illustres peints en la galerie du palais royal.* Dijon, 1644.

———. *La mort de Germanic Caesar, Tragedie.* Dijon, 1646.

———. *Le tableau des passions humaines réduits en sonnets.* Dijon, 1657.

———. *Les armes triomphantes de son altesse Monseigneur le duc d'Espernon pour le sujet de son heureuse entrée faite dans la ville de Dijon, le huictième jour de May 1656.* Dijon, 1656.

———. *Stances sur la très-sainte et très-miraculeuse hostie de la Sainte-Chapelle de Dijon.* Dijon, 1665.

Guillaume, Pierre. *Discours fait au parlement de Dijon au mois de mai 1639 pour M. de la Motte d'Audencourt, présenté à la charge de lieutenant-général pour le roi dans les pays de Bresse, Bugey, Valromey et Gex, et comté de Charollois, sous le gouvernement de Monsieur le Prince.* Dijon, 1639.

Malpoy, Pierre. *Entrée de très haut et très puissant Prince Henry de Bourbon, Prince de Condé . . . Gouverneur et Lieutenant-Général pour Sa Majesté en Provinces de Bourgogne, Bresse et Berry, en la Ville de Dijon, le trentiesme du mois de septembre 1632.* Dijon, 1632.

[———]. "Le Chariot de Triomphe du Roy (1629)." In *Théâtre de l'Infanterie dijonnoise*, edited by Joachim Durandeau, 9–39. Dijon: Reveil Bourguignon, 1908.

[———]. *Rejouissance de l'infanterie Dijonnoise pour la naissance de M. le Prince de Conty.* Dijon, 1630.

[Perard, Bénigne]. *A la Bourgogne, pour l'entrée de Monseigneur le Prince dans la ville de Dijon.* N.p., n.d.

[———]. *Les voeux de la ville de Dijon à Monseigneur le Prince.* N.p., n.d.

Perrier, Nicholas. *Observations de droit et de coutume selon l'usage du Parlement de Dijon.* Dijon, 1688.

[Petitot, Jean-Baptiste]. *Réponse des vicomte-mayeur et échevins de la ville et commune de Dijon au quatrième mémoire de M. Fyot de la Marche, premier président du Parlement de Dijon, sur son projet de la sous-inféodation de Montmusart, la Motte St. Médard et dependances, avec attribution de toute Justice Haute, Moyenne and Basse.* Dijon, 1749.

[———]. *Moyens des vicomte-mayeur et échevins de la ville et commune de Dijon contre le projet de M. Fyot de la Marche, premier président du parlement de Dijon, tendant à la sous-infeodation de Montmusart, la Motte St. Médard and dépendances; avec attribution de toute justice, haute, moyenne and basse.* Dijon, 1749.

Souvert, Jean de. *Advis pour messieurs les gens des trois estats du päis et Duché de Bourgogne, sur le subject de leur assemblée du mois de may prochain, mil six cents cinq.* N.p., 1605.

———. *Articles presentez à Messieurs des trois estats du pays de Bourgogne pour y estre par eux deliberé en leur assemblée.* N.p., n.d. (prob. 1605).

———. *Remonstrance à Messieurs des Trois Estats du pays et duché de Bourgogne, au subject de leur assemblée du huictiesme d'Aoust prochain, mil six cens onze.* N.p., n.d. (prob. 1611).

Taisand, Pierre. *Coutume générale des pays et duché de Bourgogne avec le commentaire de Monsieur Taisand . . . dans lequel cette coutume est expliquée par le droit romain, les loix des anciens Bourgugignons, par l'usage, le commentaire de monsieur de Chasseneuz, les annotations de monsieur Bégat, président au parlement de Dijon, du sieur avocat Despringles, & autres . . .* Dijon, 1698.

———. *Histoire du droit romain, où il est traitté de son origine, de son progrès, de sa décadence, de son rétablissement, de sa perfection, et de son authorité; et par occasion des vies en abregé des jurisconsultes anciens et modernes.* Paris, 1678.

III. Other Printed Sources

Almanach de la province de Bourgogne, et particulièrement de la ville de Dijon. Dijon, 1773–88.

Edit du Roy, portant creation de maires perpetuels et d'assesseurs dans les hôtels de villes et communautés du royaume. Dijon, n.d. (prob. 1693).

Bodin, Jean. *The Six Books of a Commonweale.* Edited by Kenneth Douglas McRae. Translated by Richard Knolles. Cambridge, MA: Harvard University Press, 1962 (orig. 1576).

Bossuet, Jacques-Bénigne, *Politics Drawn From the Very Words of Holy Scripture.* Edited and translated by Patrick Riley. Cambridge: Cambridge University Press, 1990.

Bouhier, Jean. "Histoire des commentateurs de la coutume du duché de Bourgogne." In *Oeuvres de jurisprudence de Jean Bouhier,* edited by Joly de Bevy. Dijon, 1787–88.

———. *La coutume du duché de Bourgogne, enrichie de remarques de MM. Philippe de Villers, Jean des Pringles, et Jean Guillaume, anciens avocats au parlement de Dijon.* Dijon, 1717.

Bretagne, François. *Coutume Générale des pays et duché de Bourgogne, avec les observations de M. François Bretagne, seigneur de Nan-sous-Thil, conseiller au parlement de Dijon, celles de Me. Nicolas Perrier, avocat, sur le premier titre, des notes de Mes. de La Mare et Jehannin, avocats au même parlement, et plusieurs arrêts rendus en interpretation de quelques articles, etc.* Dijon, 1736.

Breunot, Gabriel. *Journal, 1575–1602.* Edited by Joseph Garnier. 3 vols. Dijon: J.-E. Rabutot, 1864.

Brulart, Nicolas. "Harangues de la rentrée de Saint-Martin." In Elisabeth-François de La Cuisine, *Le parlement de Bourgogne depuis son origine jusqu'à sa chute,* I, 133–226. Dijon: J.-E. Rabutot, 1864.

Coquille, Guy. *Les oeuvres de Maistre Guy Coquille, sieur de Romenay: contenant plusieurs traitez touchant les libertez de l'eglise gallicane, l'histoire de France et le droit françois.* Bourdeau, 1703.

Dijon, Aiba de. *Almanach Chronologique.* Dijon, 1723–68.

Dijon, Ptolomée de. *Almanach de Dijon, ou la conoissance des temps et des saisons.* Dijon, 1683–1722.

Garnier, Joseph, ed. *Correspondance de la mairie de Dijon.* 3 vols. Dijon: J.-E. Rabutot, 1870.

Isambert, F.-A., et al. *Recueil des anciennes lois françaises*. 29 vols. Paris: Belin-le-Prieur, 1821–33.

La Roche Flavin, Bernard de. *Treze livres des parlemens de France*. Bordeaux, 1617.

Le Bret, Cardin. *De la souverainété du Roi*. Paris, 1632.

Lenet, Pierre, *Mémoires de . . . procureur-général au Parlement de Dijon et conseiller d'état*. In *Nouvelle collection des mémoires relatifs à l'histoire de France depuis le XIIIe siècle jusqu'à la fin du XVIIIe siècle*. Edited by Michaud and Poujoulat, 26: 185–632. Paris: Didier, 1854.

Loisel, Antoine. *Pasquier, ou dialogue des advocats du parlement de Paris*. Translated and edited by M. Dupin. Paris: Videcoq, 1844 (orig. 1602).

Loyseau, Charles. *Traité des seigneuries*. Paris, 1608.

Malteste, Claude. *Anecdotes du parlement de Bourgogne, ou histoire secrète de cette compagnie depuis 1650*. Edited by Charles Muteau. Dijon: J.-E. Rabutot, 1864.

Millotet, Marc-Antoine. *Mémoires des choses qui se sont passées en Bourgogne depuis 1650 jusqu'à 1668*. Edited by Charles Muteau. Dijon: J.-E. Rabutot, 1864.

Palliot, Pierre. *Le Parlement de Bourgogne, son origine, son établissement et son progrès, avec les noms, arms et blasons des presidents, chevaliers, conseillers, avocats, procureurs-généraux et greffiers*. Dijon, 1649.

Papillon, Philibert. *Bibliothèque des auteurs de Bourgogne*. 2 vols. Geneva: Slatkine Reprints, 1970 (orig. 1745).

Pasquier, Etienne. *Récherches de la France*. Paris, 1621.

Petitot, François. *Continuation de l'histoire du parlement de Bourgogne depuis 1649 jusqu'en 1733*. Dijon, 1733.

Raviot, Guillaume, ed. *Arrêts notables du parlement de Dijon, recüeillis par M. François Perrier, substitut de M. le Procureur Général, avec les observations sur chaque question*. 2 vols. Dijon, 1735.

Rubys, Claude des. *Sommaire explication des articles de la coustume du pays et duché de Bourgogne*. Lyon, 1580.

Saint-Julien, Pierre de. *De l'origine des bourgongnons, et antiquité des estats de Bourgogne*. Paris, 1581.

Seyssel, Claude de. *The Monarchy of France*. Edited by Donald R. Kelley. Translated by J. H. Hexter. New Haven, CT: Yale University Press, 1981 (orig. 1519).

Sullot, Claude. *Le journal de . . . procureur au parlement de Dijon*. Edited by Joachim Durandeau. Dijon: Sirodot-Carré, 1911.

Tacitus, *The Annals of Imperial Rome*. Translated by Michael Grant. London: Penguin, 1980.

IV. Secondary Sources

Acerra, Martine. "Les avocats du Parlement de Paris (1661–1715)." *Histoire, économie et société* 1 (1982): 213–25.

Adamson, John, ed. *The Princely Courts of Europe: Ritual, Politics and Culture under the Ancien Regime, 1500–1750*. London: Weidenfeld and Nicolson, 1999.

Amelang, James S. "Barristers and Judges in Early Modern Barcelona: The Rise of a Legal Elite." *American Historical Review* 89 (1984): 1264–84.

Anderson, Perry. *Lineages of the Absolutist State*. London: NLB, 1974.

Antoine, Michel. *Le conseil du roi sous Louis XV.* Geneva: Droz, 1970.

———. *Le dur métier de roi: études sur la civilisation politique de la France d'ancien régime.* Paris: Presses Universitaires de France, 1986.

———. "La monarchie absolue." In *The Political Culture of the Old Regime,* ed. Keith Michael Baker, 3–24. London: Pergamon, 1987.

Apostolidès, Jean-Marie. *Le roi-machine: spectacle et politique au temps de Louis XIV.* Paris: Éditions de Minuit, 1981.

Arbassier, Charles. *L'absolutisme en Bourgogne: l'intendant Bouchu et son action financière d'après sa correspondance inédite (1667–71).* Paris: Picard, 1921.

Baker, Keith Michael. *The French Revolution and the Creation of Modern Political Culture.* Vol. 1 of *The Political Culture of the Old Regime,* ed. Keith Michael Baker, Colin Lucas, and François Furet. Oxford: Pergamon, 1987.

———. *Inventing the French Revolution: Essays on French Political Culture in the Eighteenth Century.* Cambridge: Cambridge University Press, 1990.

Baker, Keith Michael. "Defining the Public Sphere in Eighteenth-Century France: Variations on a Theme by Habermas." In *Habermas and the Public Sphere,* ed. Craig Calhoun, 181–211. Cambridge, MA: MIT Press, 1992.

Bakos, Adrianna E. ed. *Politics, Ideology and the Law in Early Modern Europe.* Rochester, NY: University of Rochester Press, 1994.

———. *Images of Kingship in Early Modern France: Louis XI in Political Thought (1560–1789).* London: Routledge, 1997.

Barbey, Jean. *Être roi: le roi et son gouvernement en France de Clovis à Louis XVI.* Paris: Fayard, 1992.

Barry, Jonathan, and Christopher Brooks, eds. *The Middling Sort of People: Culture, Society and Politics in England, 1550–1800.* New York: St. Martin's, 1994.

Bart, Jean. "Coutume et droit romain dans la doctrine bourguignonne du XVIIIe siècle." *Memoires de la societe pour l'histoire du droit et des institutions des anciens pays bourguignons, comtois et romands* 24 (1967): 141–71.

———. "Du droit bourguignon au droit français." *Annales de Bourgogne* 49 (1977): 93–106.

Bedos-Rezak, Brigitte. "Civic Liturgies and Urban Records in Northern France, 1100–1400." In *City and Spectacle in Medieval Europe,* ed. Barbara A. Hanawalt and Katheryn L. Ryerson, 34–55. Minneapolis: University of Minnesota Press, 1994.

Beguin, Katia. *Les Princes de Condé: rebelles, courtisans et mécènes dans la France du Grand Siècle.* Seyssel: Champ Vallon, 1999.

Beik, William H. *Absolutism and Society in Seventeenth-Century France: State Power and Provincial Authority in Languedoc.* Cambridge: Cambridge University Press, 1986.

———. "The Absolutism of Louis XIV as Social Collaboration." *Past and Present* 188 (2005): 197–224.

———. "Louis XIV and the Cities." In *Edo and Paris: Urban Life and the State in the Early Modern Period,* ed. James McClain, John Merriman, and Ugawa Kaoru, 68–85. Ithaca, NY: Cornell University Press, 1994.

———. *Urban Protest in Seventeenth-Century France: The Culture of Retribution.* Cambridge: Cambridge University Press, 1997.

Bell, David A. "The 'Public Sphere,' the State and the World of Law in Eighteenth-Century France." *French Historical Studies* 17 (1992): 912–34.

———. *Lawyers and Citizens: The Making of a Political Elite in Old Regime France*. Oxford: Oxford University Press, 1994.

Benedict, Philip. *Rouen During the Wars of Religion*. Cambridge: Cambridge University Press, 1981.

———. "French Cities from the Sixteenth Century to the Revolution: An Overview." In *Cities and Social Change in Early Modern France*, 7–68. London: Unwin Hyman, 1989.

———, ed. *Cities and Social Change in Early Modern France*. London: Unwin Hyman, 1989.

Bercé, Yves-Marie. *La naissance dramatique d'absolutisme, 1598–1661*. Paris: Seuil, 1992.

Bergin, Joseph. *The Making of the French Episcopate, 1589–1661*. New Haven, CT: Yale University Press, 1996.

———. *Crown, Church, and Episcopate under Louis XIV*. New Haven, CT: Yale University Press, 2004.

Berlanstein, Lenard. *The Barristers of Toulouse in the Eighteenth Century (1740–1793)*. Baltimore: Johns Hopkins University Press, 1975.

———. "Lawyers in Pre-Revolutionary France." In *Lawyers in Early Modern Europe and America*, ed. Wilfrid Prest, 164–80. New York: Holmes and Meyer, 1981.

Bernstein, Hilary J. *Between Crown and Community: Politics and Civic Culture in Sixteenth-Century Poitiers*. Ithaca, NY: Cornell University Press, 2004.

Bertucat, Charles. *Les finances municipales à Dijon depuis la liquidation des dettes (1662) jusqu'à 1789*. Dijon: J. Nourry, 1910.

———. *La jurisdiction municipale de Dijon: son étendue*. Dijon: J. Nourry, 1911.

Bien, David D. "Offices, Corps, and a System of State Credit: The Uses of Privilege under the Ancien Régime." In *The Political Culture of the Old Regime*, ed. Keith Michael Baker, 89–114. Oxford: Pergamon, 1987.

Bizzocchi, Roberto. "Church, Religion and State in the Early Modern Period." In *The Origins of the State in Italy, 1300–1600*, ed. Julius Kirshner, 152–65. Chicago: University of Chicago Press, 1995.

Black, Jeremy. *A Military Revolution? Military Change and European Society, 1550–1800*, Atlantic Highlands, NJ: Humanities Press, 1991.

Bonney, Richard. *Political Change in France under Richelieu and Mazarin, 1624–1661*. Oxford: Oxford University Press, 1978.

Bordes, Maurice. *L'administration provinciale et municipale en France au XVIIIe siècle*. Paris: Société d'Éditions d'Enseignment, 1972.

Bossenga, Gail. *The Politics of Privilege: Old Regime and Revolution in Lille*. Cambridge: Cambridge University Press, 1991.

Bossy, John, ed. *Disputes and Settlements: Law and Human Relations in the West*. Cambridge: Cambridge University Press, 1983.

Bouchard, Marcel. *De l'humanisme à l'encyclopédie: l'esprit public en Bourgogne sous l'ancien régime*. Paris: Hachette, 1930.

Bourcier, François. "Le régime municipal à Dijon sous Henri IV." *Revue d'histoire moderne* 17 (1935): 97–120.

Bourdieu, Pierre. "La force du droit: élements pour une sociologie du champ juridique." *Actes de la recherche en sciences sociales* 64 (1986): 3–19.

———. "Rethinking the State: Genesis and Structure of the Bureaucratic Field." In *State/Culture: State Formation after the Cultural Turn,* ed. George Steinmetz, 53–75. Ithaca, NY: Cornell University Press, 1999.

Bourée, André. "La liste des avocats au parlement de Bourgogne." *La revue de Bourgogne* 6 (1916–17): 162–65.

———. "La liste des avocats au parlement de Bourgogne (suite)." *La revue de Bourgogne* 7 (1918–19): 92–93, 265–67.

———. "La liste des avocats au parlement de Bourgogne (suite)." *La revue de Bourgogne* 12 (1924): 319–32.

———. *La chancellerie près le parlement de Bourgogne de 1476 à 1790, avec les noms généalogies et armoiries de ses officies, suivi d'un supplement sur les secrétaires du roi près le parlement de Bourgogne.* Dijon: Alfred Bellais, 1927.

———. "Les substituts du procureur-général au parlement de Bourgogne et les trésoriers-payeurs des gages de MM. du Parlement." *Mémoires de l'Acadèmie de Dijon* 116 (1960): 41–52.

Bourgeon, Philippe. *Le barreau de Dijon aux 17e et 18e siècles. Discours prononcé à l'ouverture de la conference des avocats, le 20 décembre 1884.* Dijon: Jacquot, Floret et Cie., 1885.

Bouwsma, William J. "Lawyers and Early Modern Culture." *American Historical Review* 78 (1973): 303–27.

Braddick, Michael J. *State Formation in Early Modern England, c. 1550–1700.* Cambridge: Cambridge University Press, 2000.

Breen, Michael P. "Legal Culture, Municipal Politics and Royal Absolutism in Seventeenth-Century France: The Avocats of Dijon (1595–1715)." PhD dissertation, Brown University, 2000.

———. "Addressing *La Ville des Dieux:* Entry Ceremonies and Urban Audiences in Early Modern Dijon." *Journal of Social History* 38 (2004): 341–64.

———. "Representing the City: Avocats and the Negotiation of Municipal Authority in Seventeenth-Century France." In *Entre justice et justiciables: les auxiliaires de justice du moyen-âge au XXe siecle,* ed. Claire Dolan, 347–64. Québec City: Presses de l'Universite Laval, 2005.

———. "Law, Patronage and Municipal Authority in Seventeenth-Century France: The Aftermath of the Lanturelu Revolt in Dijon." *French History* 20 (2006): 138–60.

Brockliss, L. W. B. *French Higher Education in the Seventeenth and Eighteenth Centuries: A Cultural History.* Oxford: Clarendon, 1987.

Brooks, C. W. *Pettyfoggers and Vipers of the Commonwealth: The "Lower Branch" of the Legal Profession in Early Modern England.* Cambridge: Cambridge University Press, 1986.

———. *Lawyers, Litigation and English Society Since 1450.* London: Hambledon Press, 1998.

Bryant, Lawrence M. *The King and the City in the Parisian Royal Entry Ceremony: Politics, Ritual and Art in the Renaissance.* Geneva: Droz, 1986.

———. "Politics, Ceremonies, and Embodiments of Majesty in Henry II's France." In *European Monarchy: Its Evolution and Practice from Roman Antiquity to Modern Times,* ed. H. Duchhardt, R. Jackson, and D. Sturdy, 127–54. Stuttgart: Franz Steiner Verlag, 1992.

Burke, Peter. "Tacitism, Scepticism, and Reason of State." In *The Cambridge History of Political Thought, 1450–1700,* ed. J. H. Burns and Mark Goldie, 479–98. Cambridge: Cambridge University Press, 1991.

Calhoun, Craig, ed. *Habermas and the Public Sphere.* Cambridge, MA: MIT Press, 1992.

Campbell, Peter R. *Power and Politics in Old Régime France, 1720–1745.* London: Routledge, 1996.

Cassan, Michel. *Le temps des guerres de religion: le cas du Limousin (vers 1530–vers 1630).* Paris: Publisud, 1996.

Chaline, Olivier. "The Valois and Bourbon Courts, c. 1515–1750." In *The Princely Courts of Europe: Ritual, Politics and Culture under the Ancien Regime, 1500–1750,* ed. John Adamson, 67–93. London: Weidenfeld and Nicolson, 1999.

Chapman, Sara E. *Private Ambition and Political Alliances: The Phélypeaux de Pontchartrain Family and Louis XIV's Government, 1650–1715.* Rochester, NY: University of Rochester Press, 2004.

Chartier, Roger, Marie-Madeleine Compère, and Dominique Julia. *L'education en France du XVIe au XVIIIe siècle.* Paris: SEDES, 1976.

Chartier, Roger, and Hughes Neveux. "La ville dominante et soumise." In *Histoire de la France urbaine,* vol. 3, *La ville classique de la Renaissance aux Révolutions,* ed. Emmanuel Le Roy Ladurie, 16–285. Paris: Presses Universitaires de France, 1980.

Chaume, M. "Histoire d'un banlieue: recherches sur la consistance première et les limites successives du ban territoriale de la justice municipale de Dijon." *Memoires de la societe pour l'histoire du droit et des institutions des anciens pays bourguignons, comtois et romands* 8 (1942): 36–83.

Chaunu, Pierre. "L'état de justice." In *Histoire économique et sociale de la France, 1450–1660,* vol. 1, *L'état et la ville,* ed. Pierre Chaunu and Robert Gascon, 49–192. Paris: Presses Universitaires de France, 1977.

Chevalier, Bernard. *Les bonnes villes de France du XIVème au XVIème siècles.* Paris: Aubier Montaigne, 1982.

Chittolini, Giorgio. "The 'Private,' the 'Public,' the State." In *The Origins of the State in Italy, 1300–1600,* ed. Julius Kirshner, 34–61. Chicago: University of Chicago Press, 1995.

Church, William F. *Constitutional Thought in Sixteenth-Century France.* Cambridge, MA: Harvard University Press, 1941.

———. "The Decline of the French Jurists as Political Theorists, 1660–1789." *French Historical Studies* 1 (1967): 1–41.

———, ed. *The Impact of Absolutism in France: National Experience under Richelieu, Mazarin, and Louis XIV.* New York: Wiley, 1969.

———. *Richelieu and Reason of State.* Princeton, NJ: Princeton University Press, 1972.

Collins, James B. *The Fiscal Limits of Absolutism: Direct Taxation in Early Seventeenth-Century France.* Berkeley: University of California Press, 1987.

———. *Classes, Estates and Order in Early Modern Brittany.* Cambridge: Cambridge University Press, 1994.

———. *The State in Early Modern France.* Cambridge: Cambridge University Press, 1995.

Compère, Marie-Madeleine. *Du collège au lycée (1500–1850)*. Paris: Gallimard-Julliard, 1985.

Cornette, Joel. "Fiction et réalite de l'etat baroque (1610–1652)." In *L'état baroque: regards sur la pensée politique de la France du premier XVIIe siècle,* ed. Henry Mechloulan, 9–87. Paris: J. Vrin, 1985.

———, ed. *La monarchie entre Renaissance et Revolution, 1515–1792*. Paris: Seuil, 2000.

Cosandey, Fanny, and Robert Descimon. *L'absolutisme en France: histoire et historiographie*. Paris: Seuil, 2002.

Coulet, Noël and Jean-Philippe Genet, eds. *L'état moderne: Le droit, l'éspace, et les formes de l'état*. Paris: Editions du CNRS, 1990.

Crook, J. A. *Legal Advocacy in the Roman World*. Ithaca, NY: Cornell University Press, 1995.

Dainville, François de. *La naissance de l'humanisme moderne: les jesuites et l'éducation de la société française*. Paris: Beauchesne et fils, 1940.

Davis, J. C. "Utopianism." In *The Cambridge History of Political Thought, 1450–1700,* ed. J. H. Burns and Mark Goldie, 329–44. Cambridge: Cambridge University Press, 1991.

Delbeke, Francis. *L'action politique et sociale des avocats au XVIIIe siècle: leur part dans la préparation de la Révolution Française*. Louvain: Uystpruyst, 1927.

Descimon, Robert. "L'échevinage parisien sous Henri IV (1594–1610): autonomie urbaine, conflits politiques, et exclusives sociales." In *La ville, la bourgeoisie et la genèse de l'etat moderne (XIIe–XVIIIe siècle),* ed. Neithard Bulst and Jean-Philippe Genet, 113–50. Paris: Editions du CNRS, 1988.

———. "Les fonctions de la métaphore du mariage politique du roi et de la république: France, XVe-XVIIIe siècles." *Annales, E. S. C.* 47 (1992): 1127–47.

———. "Power Elites and the Prince: The State as Enterprise." In *Power Elites and State Building,* ed. Wolfgang Reinhard, 100–121. Oxford: Clarendon, 1996.

Desmergers, Marie-Pierre. "Les fêtes à Dijon au XVIème siécle." Memoire de Maîtrise, Universite de Bourgogne, 1996.

Dessert, Daniel. *Argent, pouvoir et société au Grand Siècle*. Paris: Fayard, 1984.

Dewald, Jonathan. "The 'Perfect Magistrate': Parlementaires and Crime in Sixteenth-Century Rouen." *Archive for Reformation History* 67 (1976): 284–300.

———. *The Formation of a Provincial Nobility: The Magistrates of the Parlement of Rouen, 1499–1610*. Princeton, NJ: Princeton University Press, 1980.

Deyon, Pierre. "A propos des rapports entre la noblesse française et la monarchie absolue pendant la première moitié du XVIIe siècle." *Revue Historique* 231 (1964): 341–56.

———. *Amiens, capitale provincale: étude sur la société urbaine au XVIIe siècle*. Amiens: CRDP, 1968.

Dickinson, John A. "L'activité judiciaire d'après la procédure civile: le bailliage de Falaise, 1668–1790." *Revue d'histoire économique et sociale* 84 (1976): 145–68.

Diefendorf, Barbara B. *Paris City Councilors in the Sixteenth Century: The Politics of Patrimony*. Princeton, NJ: Princeton University Press, 1983.

Dolan, Claire. "L'identité urbaine et les histories locales publiées du XVIe au XVIIIe siècle en France." *Canadian Journal of History* 27 (1992): 277–98.

Downing, Brian M. *The Military Revolution and Political Change: Origins of Democracy and Autocracy in Early Modern Europe*. Princeton, NJ: Princeton University Press, 1992.

Drouot, Henri. "Henri IV et les officiers de la milice dijonnaise (1595)." *Annales de Bourgogne* 7 (1935): 248–61.

———. *Mayenne et la Bourgogne: étude sur la ligue.* 2 vols. Paris: Picard, 1937.

Dubost, Jean-François. "Absolutisme et centralisation en Languedoc au XVIIe siècle (1620–1690)." *Revue d'histoire moderne et contemporaine* 37 (1990): 369–97.

Edwards, Kathryn A. *Families and Frontiers: Re-Creating Communities and Boundaries in the Early Modern Burgundies.* Leiden: Brill, 2002.

Elias, Norbert. *The Court Society.* Translated by Edmund Jephcott. New York: Pantheon, 1983.

———. *The Civilizing Process.* Translated by Edmund Jephcott. 2 vols. Oxford: Blackwell, 1994.

Emmanuelli, François-Xavier. *Un mythe de l'absolutisme Bourbonien: l'intendance, du milieu du XVIIème siècle à la fin du XVIIIème siècle (France, Espagne, Amerique).* Aix-en-Provence: Université de Provence, 1981.

———. *Etat et pouvoirs dans la France des XVIème–XVIIIème siècles: La métamorphose inachevée.* Paris: Editions Nathan, 1992.

Farge, Arlette. *Subversive Words: Public Opinion in Eighteenth-Century France.* Translated by Rosemary Morris. University Park: Pennsylvania State University Press, 1994.

Farr, James R. *Hands of Honor: Artisans and Their World in Dijon, 1550–1650.* Ithaca, NY: Cornell University Press, 1988.

———. "Consumers, Commerce and the Craftsmen of Dijon: The Changing Social and Economic Structure of a Provincial Capital, 1450–1750." In *Cities and Social Change in Early Modern France,* ed. Philip Benedict, 134–73. London: Unwin Hyman, 1989.

———. *Authority and Sexuality in Early Modern Burgundy (1550–1730).* Oxford: Oxford University Press, 1995.

———. *A Tale of Two Murders: Passion and Power in Seventeenth-Century France.* Durham, NC: Duke University Press, 2005.

Fasano Guarini, Elena. "Center and Periphery." In *The Origins of the State in Italy, 1300–1600,* ed. Julius Kirshner, 74–96. Chicago: University of Chicago Press, 1995.

Finley-Croswhite, S. Annette. "Henry IV and the Towns: Royal Authority and Municipal Autonomy, 1589–1610." PhD dissertation, Emory University, 1991.

———. *Henry IV and the Towns: The Pursuit of Legitimacy in French Urban Society, 1589–1610.* Cambridge: Cambridge University Press, 1999.

Fitzsimmons, Michael P. *The Parisian Order of Barristers and the French Revolution.* Cambridge, MA: Harvard University Press, 1987.

Flamarion, Louis. *La rôle politique joué par les avocats dijonnais pendant la Réforme et la Ligue (1560–1595).* Dijon: Jacquot et Floret, 1889.

Fogel, Michèle. *Les cérémonies d'information dans la France du XVIe au milieu du XVIIIe siècle.* Paris: Fayard, 1989.

Franklin, Julian H. *Jean Bodin and the Rise of Absolutist Theory.* Cambridge: Cambridge University Press, 1973.

———. "Sovereignty and the Mixed Constitution: Bodin and His Critics." In *The Cambridge History of Political Thought, 1450–1700,* ed. J. H. Burns and Mark Goldie, 298–328. Cambridge: Cambridge University Press, 1991.

Fumaroli, Marc. *L'âge de l'éloquence: rhétorique et "res litteraria" de la Renaissance au seuil de l'époque classique.* Geneva: Droz, 1980.

Garetta, Jean-Claude. "Les archives du parlement de Dijon: étude des sources." *Mémoires de la société pour l'histoire du droit et des institutions des anciens pays bourguignons, comtois et romands* 23 (1962): 203–44.

Garin, Eugenio. *L'education de l'homme moderne*. Paris: Fayard, 1968.

Garnier, Joseph, and Ernest Champeaux. *Chartes de communes et d'affranchissements en Bourgogne*. Dijon: Darantière et Jobard, 1918.

Geertz, Clifford. "Centers, Kings, and Charisma: Reflections on the Symbolics of Power." In *Rites of Power: Symbolism, Ritual and Politics since the Middle Ages*, ed. Sean Wilentz, 13–38. Philadelphia: University of Pennsylvania Press, 1999.

Genet, Jean-Philippe, ed. *L'état moderne, genese, bilans, et perpectives*. Paris: Editions du CNRS, 1990.

Giesey, Ralph E. *The Royal Funeral Ceremony in Renaissance France*. Geneva: Droz, 1960.

———. *The Juristic Basis of Dynastic Right to the French Throne*. Philadelphia: Transactions of the American Philosophical Association, 1961.

———. "Rules of Inheritance and Strategies of Mobility in Prerevolutionary France." *American Historical Review* 82 (1977): 271–89.

Gras, Pierre, ed. *Histoire de Dijon*. Toulouse: Privat, 1987.

Greenberger, Gerald. "Political Thought under Louis XIV: The Apogee and Decline of Royal Absolutism." PhD dissertation, Brown University, 1973.

———. "Lawyers Confront Centralized Government: Political Thought of Lawyers During the Reign of Louis XIV." *American Journal of Legal History* 23 (1979): 144–81.

Gresset, Maurice. *Gens de justice à Besançon: de la conquête par Louis XIV à la Revolution Française*. 2 vols. Paris: Bibliothèque Nationale, 1978.

Gronau-Chenillet, Heide. "Le parlement de Dijon et la Fronde: un corps face à la crise." Thèse de doctorat, Université de Dijon, 1991.

———. "Le jeu des clientèles au parlement de Bourgogne sous la Fronde: la rivalité entre les familles Bouchu et Brulart." *Annales de Bourgogne* 65 (1993): 5–24.

———. "Le parlement de Bourgogne et l'intendant sous les ministères de Richelieu et Mazarin: du clientélisme condéen vers la fidélité au roi." In *Les parlements de province: pouvoirs, justice et société du XVème au XVIIIème siècle*, ed. Jacques Poumarède and Jack Thomas, 443–52. Toulouse: FRAMESPA, 1996.

Gruder, Vivian B. *The Royal Provincial Intendants*. Ithaca, NY: Cornell University Press, 1968.

Gunn, J. A. W. *Queen of the World: Opinion in the Public Life of France from the Renaissance to the Revolution*. Oxford: Voltaire Foundation, 1995.

Habermas, Jürgen. *The Structural Transformation of the Public Sphere: An Inquiry into a Category of Bourgeois Society*. Translated by Thomas Burger and Frederick Lawrence. Cambridge, MA: MIT Press, 1989.

Hamscher, Albert. *The Parlement of Paris after the Fronde*. Pittsburgh: University of Pittsburgh Press, 1976.

———. *The Conseil Privé and the Parlements in the Age of Louis XIV: A Study in French Absolutism*. Philadelphia: Transactions of the American Philosophical Society, 1987.

Hanawalt, Barbara A., and Katheryn L. Ryerson, eds. *City and Spectacle in Medieval Europe*. Minneapolis: University of Minnesota Press, 1994.

Hanley, Sarah. *The* Lit-de-Justice *of the Kings of France: Constitutional Ideology in Legend, Ritual and Discourse*. Princeton, NJ: Princeton University Press, 1983.

———. "Engendering the State: Family Formation and State Building in Early Modern France." *French Historical Studies* 16 (1989): 3–27.

———. "The Monarchic State: Marital Regime Governance and Male Rights." In *Politics, Ideology and the Law in Early Modern Europe,* ed. Adrianna E. Bakos, 107–26. Rochester, NY: University of Rochester Press, 1994.

———. "Social Sites of Political Practice in France: Lawsuits, Civil Rights, and the Separation of Powers in Domestic and State Government, 1500–1800." *American Historical Review* 102 (1997): 27–52.

———. "The Transmission of Legal Knowledge and the Genesis of Civil Society in Early Modern France." In *Historians and Ideologues,* ed. Anthony Grafton and J. H. M. Salmon, 71–86. Rochester, NY: University of Rochester Press, 2001.

———. "The 'Jurisprudence of the Arrêts': Marital Union, Civil Society, and State Formation in France, 1550–1650." *Law and History Review* 21 (2003): 1–40.

Harding, Robert R. *Anatomy of a Power Elite: The Provincial Governors of Early Modern France.* New Haven, CT: Yale University Press, 1978.

———. "Aristocrats and Lawyers in French Provincial Government, 1559–1648." In *After the Reformation: Essays in Honor of J. H. Hexter,* ed. Barbara C. Malament, 95–127. Philadelphia: University of Pennsylvania Press, 1980.

Hardwick, Julie. "Seeking Separations: Gender, Marriages, and Household Economies in Early Modern France." *French Historical Studies* 21 (1998): 157–80.

———. *The Practice of Patriarchy: Gender and the Politics of Household Authority in Early Modern France.* University Park: Pennsylvania State University Press, 1998.

Hazard, Paul. *La crise de la conscience européenne, 1680–1715.* Paris: Fayard, 1961.

Henshall, Nicolas. *The Myth of Absolutism: Change and Continuity in Early Modern European Monarchy.* London: Longman, 1992.

Herrup, Cynthia. *The Common Peace: Participation and the Criminal Law in Seventeenth-Century England.* Cambridge: Cambridge University Press, 1987.

Hickey, Daniel. *The Coming of French Absolutism: The Struggle for Tax Reform in the Province of Dauphiné, 1540–1640.* Toronto: University of Toronto Press, 1986.

Hindle, Steve. *The State and Social Change in Early Modern England, c. 1550–1640.* Houndmills: Palgrave, 2000.

Holmès, Catherine E. *L'éloquence judiciaire de 1620 à 1660: reflet des problèmes sociaux, religieux, et politiques de l'époque.* Paris: A. G. Nizet, 1967.

Holt, Mack P. "Popular Political Culture and Mayoral Elections in Sixteenth-Century Dijon." In *Society and Institutions in Early Modern France (Essays in Honor of J. Russell Major),* 98–116. Athens: University of Georgia Press, 1991.

———. *The French Wars of Religion, 1562–1629.* Cambridge: Cambridge University Press, 1995.

———. "Culture populaire et culture politique au XVIIe siècle: l'émeute de lanturelu à Dijon en février 1630." *Histoire, économie, et société* 16 (1997): 597–615.

———. "Burgundians into Frenchmen: Catholic Identity in Sixteenth-Century Burgundy," in *Changing Identities in Early Modern France,* ed. Michael Wolfe, 345–70. Durham, NC: Duke University Press, 1997.

Howell, A. Lloyd. "The Political Thought of Charles Loyseau (1564–1627)." *European Studies Review* 11 (1981): 53–82.

Huizinga, Johan. *The Autumn of the Middle Ages.* Translated by Rodney J. Payton and Ulrich Mammitzsch. Chicago: University of Chicago Press, 1996.

Huppert, George. *Les Bourgeois Gentilshommes: An Essay on the Definition of Elites in Early Modern France.* Chicago, University of Chicago Press, 1977.

———. *Public Schools in Renaissance France.* Urbana: University of Illinois Press, 1984.

Hurt, John J. *Louis XIV and the Parlements: The Assertion of Royal Authority.* Manchester: Manchester University Press, 2002.

Irvine, Frederick M. "From Renaissance City to Ancien Régime Capital: Montpellier, c. 1500–c. 1600." In *Cities and Social Change in Early Modern France,* ed. Philip Benedict, 105–33. London: Unwin Hyman, 1989.

Jackson, Richard A. *Vive Le Roi! A History of the French Coronation from Charles V to Charles X.* Chapel Hill: University of North Carolina Press, 1984.

Jacquet, Augustin. *La vie litteraire dans une ville de province sous Louis XIV.* Paris: Garnier, 1886.

Jones, Colin. *The Great Nation: France from Louis XV to Napoleon.* London: Penguin, 2002.

Jouanna, Arlette. *Le devoir de révolte: la noblesse française et la gestion de l'état moderne (1559–1660).* Paris: Fayard, 1989.

Jouhaud, Christian. "Politiques de princes: les Condé (1630–1652)." In *L'état et les aristocracies (France, Angleterre, Ecosse), XIIe–XVIIe siècle,* ed. Philippe Contamine, 335–55. Paris: Presses de l'ecole normale supérieure, 1989.

Julia, Dominique, and Jacques Revel. "Les étudiants et leurs études dans la France moderne." In *Histoire des universités,* 27–395. Paris: Editions de l'EHESS, 1989.

Kagan, Richard L. "Law Students and Legal Careers in Eighteenth-Century France." *Past and Present* 68 (1975): 38–72.

———. *Lawsuits and Litigants in Castille, 1500–1700.* Chapel Hill: University of North Carolina Press, 1980.

———. "Lawyers and Litigation in Castille, 1500–1750." In *Lawyers in Early Modern Europe and America,* ed. Wilfrid Prest, 181–204. New York: Holmes and Meyer, 1981.

Kaiser, Colin. "The Deflation in the Volume of Litigation at Paris in the Eighteenth Century and the Waning of the Old Judicial Order." *European Studies Review* 10 (1980): 309–36.

Kantorowicz, Ernst H. *The King's Two Bodies: A Study in Medieval Political Thought.* Princeton, NJ: Princeton University Press, 1957.

Karpik, Lucien. *Les avocats: entre l'état, le public, et le marché (XIIIe–XXe siècles).* Paris: Gallimard, 1995.

Kelley, Donald R. *The Foundations of Modern Historical Scholarship: Language, Law, and History in the French Renaissance.* New York: Columbia University Press, 1970.

———. "Vera Philosophia: The Philosophical Significance of Renaissance Jurisprudence." *Journal of the History of Philosophy* 14 (1976): 267–79.

———. *The Beginning of Ideology: Consciousness and Society in the French Reformation.* Cambridge: Cambridge University Press, 1981.

———. "Jurisconsultus Perfectus: The Lawyer as Renaissance Man." *Journal of the Warburg and Courtald Institutes* 51 (1988): 84–102.

Keohane, Nannerl O. *Philosophy and the State in France: The Renaissance to the Enlightenment.* Princeton, NJ: Princeton University Press, 1980.

Kettering, Sharon. *Judicial Politics and Urban Revolt in Seventeenth-Century France: The Parlement of Aix (1629–1659).* Princeton, NJ: Princeton University Press, 1978.

———. *Patrons, Brokers and Clients in Seventeenth-Century France.* Oxford: Oxford University Press, 1986.

———. "The Decline of Great Noble Clientage During the Reign of Louis XIV." *Canadian Journal of History* 24 (1989): 157–77.

———. "State Control and Municipal Authority in France." In *Edo and Paris: Urban Life and the State in the Early Modern Period,* ed. James McClain, John Merriman, and Ugawa Kaoru, 86–101. Ithaca, NY: Cornell University Press, 1994.

Kingston, Rebecca. *Montesquieu and the Parlement of Bordeaux.* Geneva: Droz, 1996.

Kirshner, Julius, ed. *The Origins of the State in Italy, 1300–1600.* Chicago: University of Chicago Press, 1995.

Klaits, Joseph. *Printed Propaganda under Louis XIV: Absolute Monarchy and Public Opinion.* Princeton, NJ: Princeton University Press, 1976.

Kleinclauz, André. *Histoire de Bourgogne.* Paris: Hachette, 1924.

Krynen, Jacques. "A propos des treze livres des parlemens de France." In *Les parlements de province: pouvoirs, justice, et société du XVe au XVIIIe siècle,* ed. Jacques Poumarède and Jack Thomas, 691–705. Toulouse: FRAMESPA, 1996.

Kuehn, Thomas. *Law, Family and Women: Toward a Legal Anthropology of Renaissance Italy.* Chicago: University of Chicago Press, 1991.

Kurczewski, Jacel. "Dispute and Its Settlement." In *Disputes and the Law,* ed. Maureen Cain and Kalman Kulcsar, 223–45. Budapest: Akademiai-Kiado, 1983.

Kwass, Michael. *Privilege and the Politics of Taxation in Eighteenth-Century France: Liberté, Egalité, Fiscalité.* Cambridge: Cambridge University Press, 2000.

La Cuisine, Elisabeth-François de. *Le parlement de Bourgogne depuis son origine jusqu'à sa chute.* 3 vols. Dijon: J.-E. Rabutot, 1864.

Le Roy Ladurie, Emmanuel. *La ville classique de la Renaissance aux Révolutions.* Paris: Seuil, 1981.

———. "Réflexions sur l'essence et le fonctionnement de la monarchie classique (XVIe–XVIIIe siècles)." In *L'état baroque: regards sur la pensée politique de la France du premier XVIIe siècle,* ed. Henry Méchoulan, ix–xxxv. Paris: J. Vrin, 1985.

———, and Jean-Francois Fitou. *Saint-Simon and the Court of Louis XIV.* Translated by Arthur Goldhammer. Chicago: University of Chicago Press, 2001.

Lefebvre, Pierre. "Aspects de la 'fidélité' en France au XVIIe siècle: le cas des agents des princes de Condé." *Revue Historique* 250 (1973): 59–106.

Legay, Marie-Laure. *Les états provinciaux dans la construction de l'état moderne.* Geneva: Droz, 2001.

Leguai, André. "Les ducs valois et les villes du duché de Bourgogne." In *Les relations entre princes et villes aux XIVe–XVIe siècles: aspects politiques, économiques, et sociaux (rencontres de Gand, 24 au 27 Septembre 1992),* ed. Jean-Marie Cauchies, 21–33. Neuchâtel: Centre européen d'études bourguignonnes (XIVe–XVIe siècles), 1993.

Lemmings, David. *Gentlemen and Barristers: The Inns of Court and the English Bar, 1680–1730.* Oxford: Oxford University Press, 1990.

———. *Professors of the Law: Barristers and English Legal Culture in the Eighteenth Century.* Oxford: Oxford University Press, 2000.

Levack, Brian P. *The Civil Lawyers in England 1603–1641: A Political Study.* Oxford: Clarendon, 1973.

Ligeron, Louis. "Les dettes des communautés du baillage de Dijon au XVIIe siècle." *Annales de Bourgogne* 53 (1981): 65–79.

Lignereux, Yann. *Lyon et le roi: de la «bonne ville» à l'absolutisme municipal (1594–1654).* Seyssel: Champs Vallon, 2003.

Lisberney, J. "La justice de Fontaine-les-Dijon au XVIIIe siècle." *Mémoires de la société pour l'historire de droit et des institutions des anciens pays bourguignons, comtois, et romands* 5 (1938): 207–10.

Livet, Georges. "Finances municipales et souveraineté royale: le cas de la ville de Strasbourg." In *Pouvoir, ville, et société en Europe, 1650–1750,* ed. Georges Livet and Bernard Vogler, 105–23. Paris: Editions Ophrys, 1983.

Livet, Georges and Bernard Vogler, eds. *Pouvoir, ville, et société en Europe 1650–1750: Colloque internationale du CNRS (octobre 1981).* Paris: Editions Ophrys, 1983.

Lloyd, Howell A. "The Political Thought of Charles Loyseau (1564–1627)." *European Studies Review* 11 (1981): 53–82.

———. "Constitutionalism." In *The Cambridge History of Political Thought, 1450–1700,* ed. J. H. Burns and Mark Goldie, 254–97. Cambridge: Cambridge University Press, 1991.

Lottin, Allain. "«Messieurs» du magistrat de Lille: pouvoir et société dans une grande ville manufacturière (1598–1667)." In *Pouvoir, ville, et société en Europe, 1650–1750,* ed. Georges Livet and Bernard Vogler, 191–201. Paris: Editions Ophrys, 1983.

Lynn, John A. *Giant of the Grand Siècle: The French Army, 1610–1715.* Cambridge: Cambridge University Press, 1997.

Maillard, Jacques. *Le pouvoir municipal à Angers de 1657 à 1789.* 2 vols. Angers: Presses de l'Université d'Angers, 1984.

Major, J. Russell. *Representative Government in Early Modern France.* New Haven, CT: Yale University Press, 1980.

———. *From Renaissance Monarchy to Absolute Monarchy: French Kings, Nobles and Estates.* Baltimore: Johns Hopkins University Press, 1994.

Mandrou, Robert. *L'europe «absolutiste»: raison et raison d'état, 1649–1775.* Paris: Fayard, 1977.

Mann, Michael. *The Sources of Social Power.* Vol. I, *A History of Power from the Beginning to A.D. 1760.* Cambridge: Cambridge University Press, 1986.

Marion, Marcel. *Dictionnaire des institutions de la France, XVIIe–XVIIIe siècles.* Paris: Picard, 1989.

Martines, Lauro. *Lawyers and Statecraft in Renaissance Florence.* Princeton, NJ: Princeton University Press, 1968.

Maza, Sarah. *Private Lives and Public Affairs: The* Causes Célèbres *of Prerevolutionary France.* Berkeley: University of California Press, 1993.

Mazzacane, Aldo. "Law and Jurists in the Formation of the Modern State in Italy." In *The Origins of the State in Italy, 1300–1600,* ed. Julius Kirshner, 62–73. Chicago: University of Chicago Press, 1995.

Mechloulan, Henry, ed. *L'état baroque: regards sur la pensée politique de la France du premier XVIIe siècle.* Paris: J. Vrin, 1985.

Mettam, Roger. *Power and Faction in Louis XIV's France.* Oxford: Blackwell, 1988.

Moore, Sally Falk. *Law as Process: An Anthropological Approach.* London: Routledge and Kegan Paul, 1978.

———. "Certainties Undone: Fifty Turbulent Years of Legal Anthropology." *Journal of the Royal Anthropological Institute* 7 (2001): 95–116.

Moote, A. Lloyd. "Law and Justice under Louis XIV." In *Louis XIV and the Craft of Kingship*. ed. John C. Rule, 224–39. Columbus: Ohio State University Press, 1969.

———. *The Revolt of the Judges: The Parlement of Paris and the Fronde*. Princeton, NJ: Princeton University Press, 1971.

———. *Louis XIII: The Just*. Berkeley: University of California Press, 1989.

Moreau, Henri. "Les subdélégues dans la généralité de Bourgogne sous l'intendant Bouchu et ses premières successeurs." *Annales de Bourgogne* 20 (1948): 165–89.

Morel, Henri. "La place de la *rex legia* dans l'histoire des idées politiques." In *Mélanges Henri Morel,* 379–90. Aix-en-Provence: Presses Universitaires d'Aix-Marseille, 1989.

Mousnier, Roland. "Comment les français voyaient la constitution au XVIIe siècle." In *La plume, la faucille et le marteau,* 231–62. Paris: Presses Universitaires de France, 1970.

———. "Notes sur les rapports entre les gouverneurs de provinces et les intendants dans la première moitié du XVIIe siècle." *Revue historique,* 227 (1962): 339–50.

———. "La participation des gouvernés à l'activité des gouvernants dans la France des XVIIe et XVIIIe siècles." In *La plume, la faucille et le marteau,* 231–62. Paris: Presses Universitaires de France, 1970.

———. *La plume, la faucille et le marteau: institutions et société en France du moyen-âge à la Révolution*. Paris: Presses Universitaires de France, 1970.

———. *La venalité des offices sous Henri IV et Louis XIII*. Paris: Presses Universitaires de France, 1971.

———. *The Institutions of France under the Absolute Monarchy*. Chicago: University of Chicago Press, 1981.

Muchembled, Robert. *Culture populaire et culture des élites dans la France moderne (XVe–XVIIIe siècle)*. Paris: Flammarion, 1978.

Muyard, Marie-Françoise. "Le rationalisme utopique dans «L'histoire de Calejava, ou de l'île des hommes raisonnables avec le parallèle de leur morale et du christianisme» de Claude Gilbert." Mémoire de Maîtrise, Université de Dijon, 1966.

Nachison, Beth. "Provincial Government in the Ancien Régime: The Princes of Condé in Burgundy, 1660–1730." PhD dissertation, University of Iowa, 1992.

———. "Absentee Government and Provincial Governors in Early Modern France: The Princes of Condé and Burgundy, 1660–1720." *French Historical Studies* 21 (1998): 265–97.

Nathans, Benjamin. "Habermas's 'Public Sphere' in the Era of the French Revolution." *French Historical Studies* 16 (1990): 620–44.

Neuschel, Kristen B. *Word of Honor: Interpreting Noble Culture in Sixteenth-Century France*. Ithaca, NY: Cornell University Press, 1989.

Ninon, Jean-Jacques. "L'avocat français au XVIe siècle." *Revue de la société internationale pour l'histoire de la profession d'avocat* 1 (1989): 35–40.

Nussdorfer, Laurie. *Civic Politics in the Rome of Urban VIII*. Princeton, NJ: Princeton University Press, 1992.

Oestreich, Gerhard. *Neostoicism and the Early Modern State*. Translated by David McLintock. Edited by Brigitta Oestreich and H. G. Koenigsberger. Cambridge: Cambridge University Press, 1982.

Ozouf, Mona. "L'opinion publique." In *The Political Culture of the Old Regime,* ed. Keith Michael Baker, 419–34. Oxford: Pergamon, 1987.

Parisot, Paul. *Les procureurs au parlement de Bourgogne.* Dijon: Jobard, 1906.

Parker, David. *La Rochelle and the French Monarchy: Conflict and Order in Seventeenth-Century France.* London: Royal Historical Society, 1980.

———. "Law, Society, and the State in the Thought of Jean Bodin." *History of Political Thought* 2 (1981): 253–85.

———. *The Making of French Absolutism.* London: St. Martin's, 1983.

———. "Sovereignty, Absolutism, and the Function of the Law in Seventeenth-Century France." *Past and Present* 122 (1989): 36–74.

———. *Class and State in* Ancien Régime *France: The Road to Modernity?* London: Routledge, 1996.

Parker, Geoffrey. *The Military Revolution: Military Innovation and the Rise of the West, 1500–1800.* Cambridge: Cambridge University Press, 1988.

Parrott, David. *Richelieu's Army: War, Government and Society in France, 1624–1642.* Cambridge: Cambridge University Press, 2001.

Patouillet, Xavière. "L'émeute ses lanturelus à Dijon en 1630." Mémoire de Maîtrise, Université de Dijon, 1971.

Pennington, Kenneth. *The Prince and the Law, 1200–1600: Sovereignty and Rights in the Western Legal Tradition.* Berkeley: University of California Press, 1993.

Petitjean, Michel. "Le rôle des avocats dans la formation du droit coutumier bourguignon." *Revue de la société internationale pour l'histoire de la profession d'avocat* 5 (1993): 35–49.

———. "Remarques sur la puissance maritale en droit bourguignon." In *A cheval entre histoire et droit: Hommage à Jean-François Poudret,* ed. Eva Maier, Antoine Rochat, and Denis Tappy, 323–33. Lausanne: Bibliothèque Historique Vaudoise, 1999.

Picot, Gabriel. *Cardin Le Bret (1558–1655) et la doctrine de la souveraineté.* Nancy: Société d'Impressions Typographiques, 1948.

Poirot, Albert. "Le milieu socio-professionnel des avocats au parlement de Paris à la veille de la Révolution (1760–1790)." Thèse de doctorat, École des chartes, 1977.

Potter, Mark. *Corps and Clienteles: Public Finance and Political Change in France, 1688–1715.* Aldershot: Ashgate, 2003.

Poumarède, Jacques, and Jack Thomas, eds. *Les parlements de province: pouvoirs, justice, et société (XVème–XVIIIème siècles).* Toulouse: FRAMESPA, 1996.

Prest, Wilfrid, ed. *Lawyers in Early Modern Europe and America.* New York: Holmes and Meyer, 1981.

———. *The Rise of the Barristers: A Social History of the Bar in Early Modern England.* Oxford: Oxford University Press, 1986.

Quarre, Pierre. *La Chartreuse de Champmol, foyer d'art au temps des ducs Valois.* Dijon: Musée des Beaux-Arts, 1960.

Ranum, Orest. *Paris in the Age of Absolutism: An Essay.* New York: Wiley and Sons, 1968.

———. "Courtesy, Absolutism, and the Rise of the French State, 1630–1660," *Journal of Modern History* 52 (1980): 426–51.

———. "Fathers and Sons: Social Values in Seventeenth-Century Robe Society," *Proceedings of the Annual Meeting of the Western Society for French History* 10 (1982): 215–26.

Reinhard, Wolfgang, ed. *Power Elites and State Building.* Oxford: Clarendon, 1996.

Reinhardt, Steven. *Justice in the Sarladais.* Baton Rouge: Louisiana State University Press, 1991.

Richard, Jean. "Autour de lantureleu." *Annales de Bourgogne* 37 (1965): 133–35.

———. "Les états de Bourgogne." *Receuil de la société Jean Bodin* 24 (1966): 299–324.

———. "Quelques aspects de l'histoire du parlement de Dijon." *Mémoires de l'Academie des sciences, arts et belles lettres de Dijon* 123 (1976): 135–46.

———. "Le parlement de Dijon et la monarchie aux deux derniers siècles de l'ancien régime." *Annales de Bourgogne* 49 (1977): 107–19.

———. "Dijon au début des temps modernes (1515–1659)." In *Histoire de Dijon,* ed. Pierre Gras, 109–42. Toulouse: Privat, 1987.

Richet, Denis. *La France moderne: l'esprit des institutions.* Paris: Flammarion, 1973.

Ricommard, Julian. "Les subdélégués des intendants jusqu'à leur érection en titre d'office." *Revue d'histoire moderne* 12 (1937): 338–407.

———. "Les subdélégués des intendants aux XVIIe et XVIIIe siècles." *L'information historique* 24 (1962): 139–48.

Rivière, Marc Serge. *Utopia in 1700: A Study of the* Histoire de Caléjava *by Claude Gilbert.* Townsville: James Cook University, 1987.

———. "Introduction." In Claude Gilbert, *Histoire de Caléjava, ou L'île des hommes raisonnables: Critical Edition,* ed. Marc Serge Rivière, v–xxxiv. Exeter: University of Exeter Press, 1990.

Robbins, Kevin C. *City on the Ocean Sea, La Rochelle 1550–1650: Urban Society, Religion and Politics on the French Atlantic Frontier.* Leiden: Brill, 1997.

Roberts, Simon. *Order and Dispute: An Introduction to Legal Anthropology.* New York: St. Martin's, 1979.

———. "The Study of Dispute: Anthropological Perspectives." In *Disputes and Settlements: Law and Human Relations in the West,* ed. John Bossy, 1–24. Cambridge: Cambridge University Press, 1983.

Roberts, Penny. *A City in Conflict: Troyes During the Wars of Religion.* Manchester: Manchester University Press, 1996.

Roland, Réné. *Charles Févret, sa vie et ses oeuvres. Discours prononcé à l'ouverture de la conférence des avocats le 13 décembre 1879.* Dijon: Eugène Jobard, 1880.

Root, Hilton L. *Peasants and King in Burgundy: Agrarian Foundations of French Absolutism.* Berkeley: University of California Press, 1987.

Rothkrug, Lionel. *Opposition to Louis XIV: The Political and Social Origins of the French Enlightenment.* Princeton, NJ: Princeton University Press, 1965.

Roupnel, Gaston. *La ville et la campagne au XVIIe siècle: étude sur les populations dijonnais.* 2d ed. Paris: Armand Colin, 1955.

Rowlands, Guy. *The Dynastic State and the Army under Louis XIV: Royal Service and Private Interest, 1661–1701.* Cambridge: Cambridge University Press, 2002.

Rule, John C. "Louis XIV, Roi-Bureaucrate." In *Louis XIV and the Craft of Kingship,* 3–101. Columbus: Ohio State University Press, 1969.

———, ed. *Louis XIV and the Craft of Kingship.* Columbus: Ohio State University Press, 1969.

Saint-Jacob, Pierre de. *Les paysans de la Bourgogne du nord au dernier siècle de l'ancien régime.* Paris: Société Les Belles Lettres, 1960.

Salmon, J. H. M. *Renaissance and Revolt: Essays in the Intellectual and Social History of Early Modern France.* Cambridge: Cambridge University Press, 1987.

———. "Cicero and Tacitus in Sixteenth-Century France." In *Renaissance and Revolt: Essays in the Intellectual and Social History of Early Modern France,* 27–53. Cambridge: Cambridge University Press, 1987.

———. "Renaissance Jurists and 'Enlightened' Magistrates: Perspectives on Feudalism in Eighteenth-Century France." *French History* 8 (1994): 387–402.

Saupin, Guy. *Nantes au XVIIe siècle: Vie politique et société urbaine.* Rennes: Presses Universitaires de Rennes, 1996.

Sawyer, Jeffrey K. *Printed Poison: Pamphlet Propaganda, Faction Politics, and the Public Sphere in Early Seventeenth-Century France.* Berkeley: University of California Press, 1990.

———. "Judicial Corruption and Legal Reform in Early Seventeenth-Century France." *Law and History Review* 6 (1988): 95–117.

Schiera, Pierangelo. "Legitimacy, Discipline, and Institutions: Three Necessary Conditions for the Birth of the Modern State." In *The Origins of the State in Italy, 1300–1600,* ed. Julius Kirshner, 11–33. Chicago: University of Chicago Press, 1995.

Schneider, Robert. *Public Life in Toulouse, 1463–1789: From Municipal Republic to Cosmopolitan City.* Ithaca, NY: Cornell University Press, 1989.

———. "Crown and Capitoulat: Municipal Government in Toulouse, 1500–1789." In *Cities and Social Change in Early Modern France,* ed. Philip Benedict, 195–220. London: Unwin Hyman, 1989.

Schneider, Zöe A. "The Village and the State: Justice and the Local Courts in Normandy, 1670–1740." PhD dissertation, Georgetown University, 1997.

Scherb, Bertrand. *L'état bourguignon, 1363–1477.* Paris: Perrin, 1999.

Segaud, M. "La Fronde en Bourgogne: le rôle du parlement et de la chambre de ville de Dijon." Mémoire de diplôme d'études supérieures, Université de Dijon, 1909.

Seigel, Jerrold E. *Rhetoric and Philosophy in Renaissance Humanism: The Union of Eloquence, Petrarch to Valla.* Princeton, NJ: Princeton University Press, 1968.

Sharpe, J. A. "'Such Disagreement betwyx Neighbours': Litigation and Human Relations in Early Modern England." In *Disputes and Settlements: Law and Human Relations in the West,* ed. John Bossy, 167–87. Cambridge: Cambridge University Press, 1983.

Simonnet, J. *Les avocats au parlement de Bourgogne (1554–1654).* Dijon: J.-E. Rabutot, 1886.

Skinner, Quentin. *The Foundations of Modern Political Thought.* Vol. 2, *The Reformation.* Cambridge: Cambridge University Press, 1978.

———. "Meaning and Understanding in the History of Ideas." In *Meaning and Context: Quentin Skinner and His Critics,* ed. James Tully, 29–67. Cambridge: Cambridge University Press, 1988.

Smedley-Weill, Anette. *Les intendants de Louis XIV.* Paris: Fayard, 1995.

Smith, Jay M. "'Our Sovereign's Gaze': Kings, Nobles and State Formation in Seventeenth-Century France." *French Historical Studies* 18 (1993): 396–415.

———. *The Culture of Merit: Nobility, Royal Service, and the Making of Absolute Monarchy in France, 1600–1789.* Ann Arbor: University of Michigan Press, 1996.

Smith, David Kammerling. "Learning Politics: The Nîmes Hosiery Guild and the Statutes Controversy of 1706–12." *French Historical Studies* 22 (1999): 493–533.

———. "Structuring Politics in Early Eighteenth-Century France: The Political Innovations of the French Council of Commerce." *Journal of Modern History* 74 (2002): 490–537.

Solnon, Jean-Francois. *La cour de France.* Paris: Fayard, 1987.

Sommerville, J. P. "Absolutism and Royalism." In *The Cambridge History of Political Thought, 1450–1700,* ed. J. H. Burns and Mark Goldie, 347–73. Cambridge: Cambridge University Press, 1991.

Steinmetz, George, ed. *State/Culture: State Formation after the Cultural Turn.* Ithaca, NY: Cornell University Press, 1999.

———. "Introduction: Culture and the State." In *State/Culture: State Formation after the Cultural Turn,* 1–49. Ithaca, NY: Cornell University Press, 1999.

Strauss, Gerald. *Law, Resistance and the State: The Opposition to Roman Law in Reformation Germany.* Princeton, NJ: Princeton University Press, 1986.

Swann, Julian. *Provincial Power and Absolute Monarchy: The Estates-General of Burgundy, 1661–1790.* Cambridge: Cambridge University Press, 2003.

Temple, Nora. "The Control and Exploitation of French Towns During the Ancien Régime." *History* 51 (1966): 16–34.

———. "Municipal Elections and Municipal Oligarchies in Eighteenth-Century France." In *French Government and Society, 1500–1850,* ed. J. F. Bosher, 70–91. London: Athlone Press, 1973.

Terrade, Christine. "Les avocats au parlement de Dijon." Mémoire de maîtrise, Université de Dijon, 1971.

Thireau, Jean-Louis. "Lumières et ombres de la profession d'avocat au tournant des XVIe et XVIIe siècles d'après le «dialogues des avocats au parlement de Paris»." *Revue de la société internationale pour l'histoire de la profession d'avocat* 5 (1993): 51–67.

———. "L'absolutisme monarchique a-t-il éxisté?" *Revue française d'histoire des idées politiques* 6 (1997): 291–309.

Thomas, Alexandre. *Une province sous Louis XIV, situation politique et administrative de la Bourgogne de 1661 à 1715, d'après les manuscrits et documents inédits du temps.* Paris and Dijon: Joubert, 1844.

Thuau, Etienne. *Raison d'état et pensée politique à l'époque de Richelieu.* Paris: Armand Colin, 1966.

Tilly, Charles. *Coercion, Capital and European States,* A.D. *990–1992.* Oxford: Blackwell, 1992.

Tocanne, Bernard. "Aspects de la pensée libertine à la fin du XVIIe siècle, le cas de Gilbert." *XVIIe siècle* 2 (1980): 213–24.

Tocqueville, Alexis de. *The Old Regime and the Revolution.* Translated by Alan S. Kahan. Edited by François Furet and Françoise Melonio. Chicago: University of Chicago Press, 1998.

Trenard, Louis. "D'une Culture régionale à une culture française: Lille de 1667 à 1715." In *Pouvoir, ville, et société en Europe, 1650–1750,* ed. Georges Livet and Bernard Vogler, 381–91. Paris: Editions Ophrys, 1983.

Trousson, Raymond. *Voyages aux pays de nulle part: histoire littéraire de la pensée utopique.* Brussels: Editions de l'Université de Bruxelles, 1975.

Valcke, Juliette. "La société joyeuse de la mère folle de Dijon. Histoire (XVe–XVIIe s.) et édition du répertoire." PhD dissertation, Université de Montréal, 1997.

Vaughn, Richard. *Valois Burgundy.* London: Penguin, 1975.

Vignier, Françoise. "La justice de Magny-sur-Tille (XVe-XVIIIe siècles)." *Mémoires de la société pour l'histoire du droit et des institutions des anciens pays bourguignons, comtois et romands* 23 (1962): 278–88.

Wade, I. O. *The Intellectual Origins of the French Enlightenment.* Princeton, NJ: Princeton University Press, 1971.

Wallace, Peter C. "Civic Politics and Civic Values in Colmar, 1648–1715." *French Historical Studies* 18 (1994): 907–37.

———. *Communities and Conflict in Early Modern Colmar, 1575–1730.* Atlantic Highlands, NJ: Humanities Press, 1994.

Weber, Max. *The Theory of Social and Economic Organization.* Translated by A. M. Henderson. Edited by Talcott Parsons. New York: Free Press, 1947.

Wells, Charlotte. *Law and Citizenship in Early Modern France.* Baltimore: Johns Hopkins University Press, 1995.

Wilentz, Sean, ed. *Rites of Power: Symbolism, Ritual and Politics Since the Middle Ages.* Philadelphia: University of Pennsylvania Press, 1999.

Wolf, Eric R. "Facing Power–Old Insights, New Questions." *American Anthropologist* 92 (1990): 586–96.

———. *Envisioning Power: Ideologies of Dominance and Crisis.* Berkeley: University of California Press, 1999.

Wrightson, Keith. *Poverty and Piety in an English Village: Terling, 1525–1700.* 2d ed. New York: Oxford University Press, 1995.

Yardeni, Myriam. "L'ordre des avocats et la grève du barreau parisien en 1602." *Revue d'histoire économique et sociale* 44 (1966): 481–507.

———. *La conscience nationale en France pendant les guerres de réligion (1559–1598).* Louvain and Paris: Éditions Nauwelaerts, 1971.

———. *Utopie et révolte sous Louis XIV.* Paris: A.-G. Nizet, 1980.

———. "Histoires de villes, histoires de provinces et naissance d'une identité française au XVIe siècle." *Journal des savants* (1993): 111–34.

Zeller, Gaston. "L'administration monarchique avant les intendants. Parlements et gouverneurs." *Revue historique* 197 (1947): 180–215.

INDEX

Page numbers in italics refer to tables or illustrations in the text.